PENGUIN BOOKS

MARCHING HOME

Kevin Coyne is the author of *A Day in the Night of America* and *Domers: A Year at Notre Dame* and has contributed to many newspapers and magazines. He was born and raised in Freehold, New Jersey, where he lives with his family.

Praise for *Marching Home*

"It may be the best book about my generation that I have read. . . . His prose is clean, direct, authoritative. He does not call attention to himself but achieves Orwell's standard that 'good writing is like a window pane' through which the reader views the subject."
　　　　　　　　　　　　　　　　　　　　　—*The Boston Sunday Globe*

"*Marching Home* is the real thing . . . It grows and ramifies and resonates until this nutshell contains the world. . . . In its modesty, its refusal to be anything other than ordinary, *Marching Home* becomes a majestic work that will endure."
　　　　　　　　　　　　　　　　　　　　　　　　—*Los Angeles Times*

"An honest counterweight to the commercial patriotic sentimentality of Tom Brokaw's *The Greatest Generation*."
　　　　　　　　　　　　　　　　　　　　　　　—*Chicago Sun-Times*

"Tough-minded and honest about matters that many sentimentalists are disinclined to confront."
　　　　　　　　　　　　　　　—Jonathan Yardley, *The Washington Post*

"Rare investigative and narrative gifts . . . Coyne's volume preserves the richest—and most unsettling—kind of history."
　　　　　　　　　　　　　　　　　　　　　　　—*Booklist* (starred)

"The masterly writing illuminates some of the major American social and economic themes of the past century . . . highly recommended."
　　　　　　　　　　　　　　　　　　　　　　—*Library Journal* (starred)

"A notable achievement in understanding as well as reporting."
　　　　　　　　　　　　　　　　　　　　　　　　　—*Kirkus Reviews*

"[*Marching Home*] is head and shoulders above much of the near competition with graceful storytelling and enough social commentary to appeal to fans of Studs Terkel."
　　　　　　　　　　　　　　　　　　　　　　　—*Publishers Weekly*

"Kevin Coyne's gift goes beyond his considerable writing skills. What he has done in *Marching Home* is understand that the stories of six men from one small town can matter to many, because their stories so closely mirror the experiences of the majority."
　　　　　　　　　　　　　　　　　　　　　　　—*Asbury Park Press*

"[A] superb account."   —*The Denver Post*

"*Marching Home* is . . . an ambitious, heartfelt homage to men who helped save our civilization."   —*The New York Times Book Review*

"Although Kevin Coyne does give a finely-rendered account of what close combat felt like in World War II, what makes his book original, I think, is something else. It's the way he follows his warriors home to a country quite different from the grateful nation of Greatest Generation cliche. They return to a community riven by labor strife, racial tensions, political corruption, and suburban sprawl that changes, almost unrecognizably, the town that sent these men off to war. There is an ancient truth here: no matter how great the military victory, its aftermath is never triumphant."

—Adam Hochschild, author of *King Leopold's Ghost*

"I cannot think of any more appropriate coincidence than the fact Kevin Coyne and Bruce Springstreen share the same hometown, Freehold, N.J. It's the place that inspires the art of both these men, one of whom is rightly revered and one of whom should be after this extraordinary book. What Kevin Coyne does in *Marching Home* is what Springsteen has done in so much of his music—bear witness to the struggle and honor of ordinary lives, capture the preciousness of community and the tragedy when community is lost. Where so many other books and World War II and the 'greatest generation' end neatly with victory, Coyne follows his characters all the way from battlefield valor through imperfect peace. This journey across the decades is an unforgettable work by a breakthrough writer."

—Sam Freedman, author of *Small Victories: The Real World of a Teacher, Her Students, and Their High School*

"Master storyteller Kevin Coyne follows six boys from his hometown who helped win a war and build a country. I so enjoyed this heartfelt book about the boys who fanned out across the globe and marched home to face a whole new series of battles."   —James Bradley, author of *Flags of Our Fathers*

"During World War II, I was a kid growing up in just the kind of town from which Kevin Coyne draws his unforgettable home-front/war-front story. He has it just right, particularly the phenomenon of ordinary Americans, who might otherwise have never left the four corners, suddenly thrust as players on the world stage in the greatest drama of the twentieth century. To anyone old enough to want to return to those days, to anyone young enough to want to experience them, *Marching Home* will take you there."

—Joseph E. Persico, author of *Roosevelt's Secret War*

MARCHING HOME

To War and Back with the Men of
One American Town

Kevin Coyne

PENGUIN BOOKS

PENGUIN BOOKS

Published by the Penguin Group

Penguin Group (USA) Inc., 375 Hudson Street, New York, New York 10014, U.S.A.
Penguin Books Ltd, 80 Strand, London WC2R 0RL, England
Penguin Books Australia Ltd, 250 Camberwell Road, Camberwell, Victoria 3124, Australia
Penguin Books Canada Ltd, 10 Alcorn Avenue, Toronto, Ontario, Canada M4V 3B2
Penguin Books India (P) Ltd, 11 Community Centre, Panchsheel Park, New Delhi – 110 017, India
Penguin Books (N.Z.) Ltd, Cnr Rosedale and Airborne Roads, Albany, Auckland, New Zealand
Penguin Books (South Africa) (Pty) Ltd, 24 Sturdee Avenue,
   Rosebank, Johannesburg 2196, South Africa

Penguin Books Ltd, Registered Offices:
80 Strand, London WC2R 0RL, England

First published in the United States of America by Viking Penguin,
a member of Penguin Putnam Inc. 2003
Published in Penguin Books 2004

10 9 8 7 6 5 4 3 2 1

THE LIBRARY OF CONGRESS HAS CATALOGED THE HARDCOVER EDITION AS FOLLOWS:
Coyne, Kevin.
Marching home : To war and back with the men of one American town / Kevin Coyne
p. cm.
ISBN 0-670-87150-8 (hc.)
ISBN 0 14 20.0386 7 (pbk.)
1. World War, 1939–1945—Veterans—New Jersey—Freehold—Biography.
2. Veterans—New Jersey—Biography.   3. Freehold (N.J.)—Biography.   I. Title.
D769.85.N3 F743 2003
940.54'1274946—dc21   2002066359

Printed in the United States of America
Set in Minion
Designed by Francesca Belanger

For my father and my mother,

Budd Coyne (1934–1999) and Anne Coyne

Without drawing too heavily on its storied past, Freehold has individuality produced by a fusion of rural, urban and residential life. In an unobtrusive way it seems to embody America's growth . . .

—WPA Guide to New Jersey (1939)

Of the sixteen million Americans who served in the armed forces during the Second World War, nine hundred or so came from a small town in the middle of New Jersey that was remarkable only for how fully it mirrored in one place the lives of so many other towns in so many other states. These men, and about a dozen women, left their homes and farms and factory jobs in Freehold, many for the first time ever, and fanned out to every corner of the conflict that swept up the world like no other in history. There were no generals among them, no Medals of Honor, just the ordinary span of tedium and heroism. One of them was on a battleship at Pearl Harbor the day the war started for America, and another was in a B-29 over Nagasaki on the day it effectively ended. For the twenty-one who didn't come back, an equal number of small, white wooden markers still stands as a remembrance on a sacred triangle of grass on Main Street.

They were part of the generation that shaped America more than any other in this century—the generation that grew up with the Depression, came of age fighting a war to save the world, and returned home to remake that world in its image. To them fell the hardest task the nation had asked of its citizens since the Civil War, the "rendezvous with destiny" that Franklin Roosevelt saw as their fate. In them dwelled a sense of certainty and purpose as yet unmatched by any succeeding generation, a will and a drive that built the richest and the mightiest nation the world had ever seen. From them came the best of all we are today.

This book tells the story of six of those men and their lives in a town that, with its rare mixture of village intimacy and city diversity, offers a remarkable microcosm of the whole sweep of American history—from

George Washington, who led troops into battle across the surrounding fields, to Bruce Springsteen, whose father was among the nine hundred who served and whose uncle was the last of the twenty-one to die. In the story of these six, and of their hometown, is the story of the sixteen million and their nation—the story that is, after all, the great epic of the American century.

CONTENTS

1: A CERTAIN WAR

Stu Bunton, radioman
USS *Santa Fe* (the Mediterranean and the Pacific)

★

Walter Denise (Da-NICE), rifleman
324th Infantry Regiment (France and Germany)

★

Warren ("Jake") Errickson, radio intercept operator
121st Signal Radio Intelligence Company
(Australia and New Guinea)

★

Jim Higgins, intelligence sergeant
391st Bombardment Group
(England, France and Belgium)

★

Bigerton ("Buddy") Lewis, private
1317th Engineer General Service Regiment (Colored)
(England, France, Belgium, Holland, and Germany)

★

Bill Lopatin (Lo-PAY-tin), waist gunner
322nd and 394th Bombardment Groups (England)

★

1.

Spring 1941

All over town, people set down their newspapers and rose from their evening chairs to close the windows against the coming storm. The humid May breeze that had floated so heavily through their homes all afternoon—teasing the gauzy, white curtains into a languorous waltz, whispering promises about easeful summer days ahead—had grown suddenly into a fierce and unexpected wind, its speed gusting toward danger. The curtains became full-bellied sails. The lace doilies flapped their wings beneath the heavy end-table lamps. On the antimacassars draped atop the sofas, the fringes bristled like the hairs on the back of a cat's neck. The newspapers blew off the ottomans where they lay waiting the return of their readers, who were even now sprinting up the steps two at a time, racing the rain to the upstairs bedrooms.

The storm had gathered somewhere out over the potato fields that sprawled across the surrounding countryside for a half day's walk in every direction, and it was bearing down on town along a path as straight and swift as any of the spokelike roads that emanated from the courthouse square toward every corner of the county. The flooding rain—three-quarters of an inch in just five minutes—left the rich, loamy earth dotted with brief ponds and rivulets, threatening to drown the young, green tentacles of the potato vines. The shroud of black clouds deepened the dusk sky into the darkness of a much later hour. Freehold was an inviting target for any invader—an abrupt, close-packed cluster of wood-frame houses, brick factories and stone storefronts, floating like a leafy, green island in the middle of a dun farmland sea—and the prospect of an audience seemed only to increase the storm's ferocity. The wind blew harder, the lightning flashed faster as the storm neared the edge of the town's dense canopy of tall street oaks and elms.

The diffuse, flailing energy of the storm collected itself into a fist, a knot of power so concentrated that some witnesses later described it as a minitornado, and it started punching right at the border where the farms gave way to houses. A large barn collapsed at the Reed farm, burying two cars and a grain drill. At the old Fisher farm next door, two corn cribs toppled over and the machine-shed door fell onto a potato planter, bending its axle. The crown of a tree was torn off and flung almost a quarter mile out into the middle of a field. An ESSO sign flew across the highway and wrapped itself around a pole.

The storm shouldered on into town, thrashing at whatever stood in its way. At the rug mill, the watchman's shanty—with the watchman, his lantern and stool all still inside—tipped over and barrel-rolled three times. Over by the racetrack, a tree limb fell on the stables, and a garage was lifted off its foundation and deposited twenty feet away, smack in the middle of Yard Avenue. The glass roof on Bastedo's greenhouse shattered, and a jagged, crystal rain fell on seedlings still too young to plant. A chimney toppled over and crashed through a roof on Haley Street. A power line snapped and fell across Broadway at Elks Point, sputtering like an electric snake. An uprooted tree on Main Street crushed a picket fence. At the town's highest, proudest point—the Battle of Monmouth monument, dedicated in memory of the epic day when Washington's soldiers chased away the entire British army in the largest single land battle of the American Revolution—the draped figure of Liberty Triumphant stood bravely atop the ninety-four-foot granite column, lightning exploding all around her head, as one of the stately, spreading copper beeches that lined the sloping green park at her feet was split and killed by a bolt from the sky.

And then—for a crackling, booming, unnerving instant—the sky went blank, obliterated by a blinding white flash. The town's stunned citizens instinctively looked up to trace its source, but the light had actually come from down among them. Lightning had struck the power-company substation, just behind the battle monument and down the street from the Colored School, and two high-tension lines—each carrying 4,600 volts of electricity and never meant to meet—had fused together in a spasm of mutual destruction.

When darkness returned to the sky, it descended also on the town.

The lights in the houses flashed blue before flickering out, and all the radios—tuned now to Horace Heidt on WEAF or *Can You Top This?* on
WOR, but waiting for the all-station broadcast of President Roosevelt's
fireside chat in less than an hour—faded to silence. Looking out their
windows, people could see nothing but darkness. In all of Freehold, the
only lights still on were in the few downtown business blocks around the
courthouse, which were served by a separate feeder line, and in the old
section of the rug mill, which had its own generator.

In the newer, five-story section of the mill, the looms clattered to a
halt—the wide tongues of rug hanging limp and unfinished, while the
separate, single strands of wool stretched taut from their hundreds of
spools, as yet unwoven into the larger, richer whole of the finished pattern. The weavers and creelers, the loom fixers and burlers, the spare
hands and foremen, all left their positions and streamed toward the tall
steel-frame windows that ran the whole length of the building. Those
who had driven rather than walked to work this evening scanned the
street checking their parked cars for damage. Tree limbs had crashed
down on two cars. A telephone pole had smashed the hood of a third, but
the wire still attached to it saved the car even further injury, holding the
pendulous bulk of a fallen tree just inches over the roof.

The storm left town as abruptly as it had entered, its strength flagging
as it headed east over the fields toward the ocean, trailing behind it a long
tail of gradually diminishing showers. The rug mill sent four hundred
workers home, and called off the midnight shift. Boy scouts and volunteer firemen were dispatched to guard live lines, set out warning lights
and detour traffic. In kitchens all over town, as the ponderous blackout silence bore heavily down, people dug candles out of their emergency
drawers and smoothed the scattered sheets of their newspapers across
their tables to resume the stories the storm had interrupted. The front-
page headline on the *Asbury Park Evening Press*, in this edgy spring of
1941, was bold enough to read even by candlelight: BRITISH FLEET DE-
STROYS *BISMARCK* it announced. Out among the deep, iron-gray swells of
the Atlantic, on the far side of the same ocean where the storm was now
hovering, British ships had been going down at the rate of fifty or more
each month, victims of merciless German U-boats, and for them to turn
around now and sink the enemy's deadly new battleship was cause for
both celebration and hope.

The headline over the next story was only slightly smaller: ENTIRE

WORLD ANXIOUSLY AWAITS PRESIDENT'S FIRESIDE CHAT TONIGHT. Germany had been blitzkrieging across Europe for almost two years—Japan had been inflicting a similar cruelty upon Asia for even longer, but to less notice on these shores—and with each new attack, each fresh atrocity, it seemed less likely that America could remain on the sidelines much longer. The first peacetime draft in the nation's history had already put almost a million young men in uniform, quickly quadrupling the size of the army. The Lend-Lease Act, signed by Roosevelt just two months earlier, was sending weapons and supplies to a besieged Britain. Americans sitting by their radios wondered what came next.

When Roosevelt began his speech, his voice was heard in Freehold only by the few souls who happened to be in the small, remaining pocket of light downtown—the shot-and-beer regulars in the Main Street bars, the traveling salesmen in the lobbies of the small hotels, the shopkeepers in the upstairs apartments. "I have tonight issued a proclamation that an unlimited national emergency exists and requires the strengthening of our defense to the extreme limit of our national power and authority," the president declared. "Your government has the right to expect of all citizens that they take part in the common work of our national defense—take loyal part from this moment forward."

Roosevelt vowed that the United States would resist any German attempts to claim control of the seas, that the armed forces would be placed in "strategic military positions," and that "articles of defense" would have "the undisputed right-of-way in every industrial plant in the country." He didn't actually declare war—that power was reserved for Congress—but his rhetoric was so forceful, his tone so imperial, that some listeners thought he had.

"The war is approaching the brink of the Western Hemisphere itself," he said, telling the nation what it already knew, but what it dreaded hearing. "It is coming very close to home."

Waking to a calmer morning, many people in town found their empty downstairs rooms alive with unexpected light and sound—the still-switched-on lamps and radios that had surged back to life as power was restored while they had slept. On the way to breakfast, they turned off the lamps, but left the radios on, listening to news of the speech the storm had preempted. The situation, they learned, was as unsettled globally as it was locally. Out on their front walks, squinting against the early sun, they waded through the storm's tidal wrack, exchanged raised eyebrows of astonishment with their neighbors and calculated the odds of resuming a normal routine today. The rug mill was still closed, and would stay closed until noon at least, but the schools—to the great dismay of all the spring-fevered students slogging through these last eternal weeks—were open.

Down on Main Street, Stu Bunton stepped around the fallen branches and gingerly made his way toward a ritual that not even the storm could delay—his regular morning rendezvous with the half dozen or so other high school juniors with whom he traveled through life. His hair was the same color brown as his eyes, and he kept it in a crew cut that no weather could disturb. Stu and his friends spent much of each day together, starting with bleary, muffled greetings in front of the diner, and ending with a final evening cigarette in front of Church's Sweet Shop, the narrow, jukebox-powered soda fountain that was always filled with local teenagers. They were barely a year away from graduation now, and they had begun talking more about what they imagined lay beyond their town, and less about what they knew lay within it. As they had grown, Freehold had begun to feel as if it were shrinking around them. It was an old and settled place that had everything they needed—places to work, girls to date, family to watch out for them—but not everything they wanted. They had seen Tommy Dorsey and the other big bands in Asbury Park, had taken the two-hour train ride north to New York City, and they were eager to know what else was still out there. Once assembled this morning, they fell into step for the short march toward the tall, white cupola of the redbrick high school, navigating through a landscape in which many things were not in their proper places.

Stu stood taller than most of his friends, with a lean, athletic frame that was well suited for basketball, but the coach had told him he needed to give up smoking to build his wind, and that was a sacrifice he wasn't ready to make. He was also quieter, with a more serious demeanor, and as they walked together under the arching oaks, he carried a burden heavier and more complex than theirs. On a family visit to the World's Fair in New York two years earlier, wandering amid utopian visions of a better tomorrow, he had been given a hint of his own family's future, though he hadn't recognized it at the time. While strolling in the shadow of the Trylon and Perisphere, his father had lost his balance and stopped short, the power to his leg somehow cut off for a moment. Back home, the doctor found a brain tumor. The elder Bunton, just fifty, died on the operating table. The diminished family—Stu, his mother and older sister—lived in a rented house on Mechanic Street, directly across from the gravestone cutter. Stu worked down at one end of the street now, soda jerking after school at the corner drugstore and making up the occasional batch of formaldehyde mixture for the undertakers; and it was expected that he would ultimately take a job at the other end of the same street, in the rug mill, the factory that loomed above all the others and ruled the town's economy.

Stu's father had arrived in Freehold from Glasgow, via Canada, soon after the mill opened in the first decade of the last century, part of a migration of skilled weavers from Great Britain that filled the pews of the Presbyterian and Episcopal churches and ensured plenty of local volunteers for the Great War. (He had enlisted, but the war ended before he got overseas.) The weavers were the working aristocracy of the town, paid according to how much carpet they could coax from their looms, some earning more than eighty dollars a week at a time when fifty dollars would keep a family going. When his father worked the evening shift, Stu would bring a lunch pail over to the mill and hand it through the window. A weaver's son had an insider's claim on one of the coveted broadlooms, but Stu's head had been turned recently. On career day at the high school, he had accompanied several other boys to the local state police barracks, where he heard a trooper describe a life that seemed to offer a thrilling blend of authority and mobility, as well as the sort of steady government paycheck that would ease his widowed mother's burden.

Bigerton Lewis's route to school this morning took him in a different direction. He left his home on Throckmorton Street, next to the railroad siding where the farmers brought their potatoes to be graded and shipped each harvest, and started walking the three blocks across the black neighborhood known as the Peach Orchard toward the small rise at the edge of town where the Freehold Colored School sat. Crossing Haley Street, he looked up at the caved-in roof of the house where the chimney had fallen, and then, a few doors down, gratefully noticed the undamaged structure of the Bethel AME church, where his family had long been mainstays of the congregation. His skin was several shades lighter than his large, brown eyes, and his hair was cropped even closer than Stu's. His cheeks still carried the roundness of a boy not yet fully grown. As he climbed the hill to school, he could see the work crews still busy at the power substation, repairing the storm damage. Down in the gully on the other side, the ragged men were stirring in the hobo jungle—the men that Mr. Read, the indomitable principal, warned all the students against becoming.

The Colored School often made do with cast-off equipment and outdated books, and its eight grades shared just four classrooms, but it was fortunate enough to be led by George Read, a proud and learned man who taught his students about Marian Anderson and Paul Robeson and helped instill in them the belief that they were as capable of building worthy lives as their counterparts in the white schools across town. Buddy Lewis, as Bigerton was known to all, was one of the six eighth graders who had passed the entrance exam black students were required to take for the integrated high school; the rest of the class would go straight to work, or to the manual training school. He was the youngest of twelve children, and he had learned that if he wanted to be heard he needed to speak up, and to keep speaking. His voice rose in pitch when his excitement grew. He was tall and lean, the fastest runner in the school, and he was already dreaming of the varsity letters he hoped to collect in football, basketball and track. Several of his older brothers had established the family's athletic reputation; his brother Guggy, a slugging center fielder, was the only black player on the semipro baseball team the rug mill sponsored.

Blacks had lived in Freehold from the earliest years of its settlement, in the 1690s, but not until the 1820s did free blacks finally outnumber slaves. Buddy's ancestors were buried at the old Bethel cemetery, where small government stones marked the graves of soldiers who had served with the United States Colored Troops in the Civil War, and his family now stood among the most prominent in the Peach Orchard. His father was a mason, his mother a stalwart of the Colored Republican Club, entrusted with the get-out-the-vote money each Election Day. His own life, though, was an often confusing array of both open and closed doors. At the upcoming graduation, a joint ceremony with the other grammar schools, he and the other black students would walk down the aisle with the white students beside whom they would soon be sitting in class, but then they would go their own separate ways again. In leaving the Colored School, Buddy was entering a world where segregation was less explicit, but no less real. No signs marked the boundary lines in town, but everyone knew where they were. In the Liberty Theater, black patrons sat in the rear of the right section. At the larger Strand, next to the courthouse, they sat in the balcony, the right, not the left. Now that the weather was warming, Buddy would be visiting the shady pond just outside town, where he and his friends would swim off the floodgates by the roadside, staying clear of the sandy beach that was reserved—not by law, but by custom, habit and every racial message he had absorbed in his life so far—for whites.

As Bill Lopatin drove to work the morning after the storm, heading west on Main Street against the stream of school-bound students, he passed the marquee announcing the new double feature *(Mr. Dynamite* and *The Pioneers)* at the Liberty, the theater he and his father had refitted when silent films gave way to sound. The Liberty renovation—replacing the tin ceiling with a curve-edged acoustic one, trading the view-blocking support columns for I-beams, all in a flurry of sixteen-hour days in the summertime, when movie traffic slackened—was one of the last big jobs for Lopatin Construction before the Depression sent the small family firm into its own much longer slump. Bill had been out of high school for more than a decade already, and for many of those years business was so scant for the half dozen or so local builders that wood had regularly sat until it rotted in the lumberyard on Broad Street. Orders for new houses slowed to a trickle. Father and son sometimes found themselves digging foundations by hand, just to have enough work to fill the day. They hammered together chicken coops down in the sandy land south of town that was no good for potatoes. They even built some houses on speculation, with their immigrant's reluctance to believe that America would stay on its knees forever.

Over the last few years, their faith and patience had finally been rewarded, as buyers did in fact emerge again, and business began a slow climb, helped in part by President Roosevelt and his new Federal Housing Administration. The Lopatins were building a new house now, a large two-story colonial overlooking the highway to Trenton, for a prominent local lawyer who had hired them after presiding over their contract signing several years earlier with another home buyer: Neither party had ever appeared in the office again with a complaint, the best testimony a lawyer could hear. Bill was just about finished framing the house, and he was anxious this morning to see how the skeleton of two-by-fours had fared in the storm. He was short and sturdy, with a round face and a fringe of dark hair, balding on top. His eyebrows were heavy above his dark eyes. His voice sometimes had a gruff edge, carrying the barest trace of an immigrant's accent, and he wasn't shy about using it to express his opinions, sometimes as bluntly and directly as he swung a hammer. His father and his three uncles spanned the whole political spectrum—Republican, Democrat, socialist and communist—and from the debates that ensued he had learned how to make himself heard. Sitting beside him in the truck was Pingo, an apolitical chow-collie mix who was in the habit of walking downtown to the butcher shop to cadge a bone, then waiting until he saw a car he recognized to catch a lift back home.

From Pingo on up to the family patriarch, Bill's grandfather, the Lopatins were familiar figures in Freehold, having risen quickly to positions of consequence in the community since emigrating from Russia at the start of the century. Bill's father had come first, joining some other Lopatins who, fleeing the pogroms, had already established themselves here. Bill, his mother and four siblings were supposed to follow soon after, but history intervened, with the World War and the Russian Revolution stranding them in Gomel for years longer than expected. They finally started for America in November 1919—an epic journey across a war-ravaged continent, traveling in trains packed with desperate, displaced refugees, in horse-drawn sleds that slowly crossed the snowy woods from one village to the next, Bill's mother bartering her embroidered linen at each stop for food, all of them weak and sick and wary of soldiers, and then finally squeezed into steerage across the Atlantic. They arrived in New York ten months later, minus Bill's eldest sister, who died along the way. Bill learned his English numbers by counting bushels of corn during the harvest on his grandfather's farm, on land bloodied by Washington's army during the Battle of Monmouth. On his first day of school he sat and watched all the other third graders file out of the room when a bell rang. His teacher motioned with her hand to her mouth: Lunch, she was telling him. By fourth grade he was winning spelling bees. After graduating from Freehold High School, he went on to college, first to New York University to study accounting, which he didn't like, and then to the University of Pennsylvania to study architecture, which he did. But the Depression dried up his tuition funds and sent him home to build houses rather than design them. From his first shaky steps on the roof, he had blossomed into a skilled carpenter, and when he reached the Barkalow house that morning, Pingo bounding out of the truck ahead of him, he wasn't surprised to find the frame standing straight and true, unshaken by the storm.

•   •   •

Out in the potato country two miles north of town, alongside the road that led to New York, Jimmy Higgins boarded a Freehold-bound bus that had just crested the hill and stopped in front of his house. It was a regular, inevitable ritual for anyone who lived in the outlying rural districts, the trip into the bustling town that loomed over the villages and crossroads in its orbit with the weight and pull of a small city. Jimmy had a shock of wavy brown hair, a small gap between his front two teeth, and the crinkly laugh lines of someone much older, inscribed there by the smile that seemed always to crease his face. On weekdays he came into Freehold to go to the high school. On Saturdays—the day the farmers came to sell what they raised, buy what they didn't and then sit on the railing by the courthouse and watch the county pass before them in a shoulder-to-shoulder sidewalk circuit—he came to work as a quarter-an-hour produce clerk at the Big Chief supermarket next to the Strand. Before long, though, he would be traveling a new road. On a Friday night barely two weeks hence, he would march into the high school auditorium with 127 of his classmates to receive his diploma. (A panel discussion had just been added to the graduation program: "What Ought the High School Teach in the National Emergency?".) The following Monday morning, he would start a three-year undertakers' apprenticeship at a funeral home in Plainfield, for fifteen dollars a week and a room upstairs. His career choice had been made long ago, and was recorded for posterity in the yearbook alongside his class nickname, "Giggles," bestowed in recognition of an affable manner that seemed perpetually on the edge of laughter, despite the gravity of both his prospective profession and his own family's history.

Death, as Jimmy had learned early and sadly in his life, was a steady business to be in. He had already lost two grandmothers, two uncles and, most tragically, his father, which had left him, at the age of nine, the eldest of four children. His family, like many of the local Irish, had come to Freehold as potato-famine immigrants before the Civil War, escaping their blighted land to work the healthy crop here, first as tenants, and then, within a generation or two, as landowners themselves. His father's farm was 203 acres of potatoes, alfalfa, corn and grain, thirty-six dairy cows, and the turkeys they sold each Thanksgiving to Zlotkin's butcher shop—all of which his widowed mother was forced to sell at Depression prices. After his father's death, the family moved to his grandmother's much smaller farm, twenty acres on the Marlboro road with just enough room for some market vegetables. Like Stu, he had assumed an adult's burden much sooner than he was meant to, and he carried it with a cheerful demeanor that seemed to acknowledge the futility of any response but laughter and goodwill in the face of life's essential tragedy.

Through the window of the bus that was bringing him to school that morning, Jimmy could see the sprawling, sprouting acres of several large farms, a vision of the kind of home that might have been his had his father lived. He wanted to reclaim for his family the stability that was lost with the farm, and he knew that undertakers were men of substance and means. Those who did not fear death—and he did not—were respected by those who did. When the bus reached town, he could see the ravages of the storm that had passed harmlessly over his own home, jarring evidence of how calm things can be in one place, and how tumultuous in another so near.

A few fields to the east and just over the horizon, Walter Denise bounced gently in his pickup along the shady, rutted lanes that crisscrossed his family's orchard, scanning the peach trees for storm-inflicted wounds. He drove through stands of Golden Jubilees and Triogems, of Summercrests and Sunhighs, the bright spring blossoms already fallen, the infant fruits just emerging for the time of growing. Everything had been made ready for these next few critical months—the pruning done, the spraying begun, the equipment repaired, the irrigation pipe laid, the migrant pickers embarked on their long, stooped, crop-to-crop journey north—and Walter was anxious that nothing interfere with the orchard's passage to maturity. Tree-toppling, limb-snapping storms were always a threat, but this one, much to his relief, had only stopped long enough to shake off a few branches as it rushed toward town. He turned into the apples and found their soldierly ranks standing similarly intact. The orchard was planted in straight and uniform rows, the orderly blueprint of a tame and miniature forest, but Walter was never in danger of losing his way as he threaded through the green maze of sameness. A few years earlier, when he was still in high school, he had, at his father's direction, mapped out the entire orchard, all twelve thousand trees and 335 acres, on sheets of graph paper. It was a useful document to consult at harvest time, but it had the even greater effect of imprinting on his mind a grid of belonging, a sense of what things, himself included, were planted where.

Walter's family had been rooted in the local land for more than two centuries, and he carried himself with the assurance that came with such deep genealogy. The Denises were among the original Dutch settlers (the name was originally spelled deNyjs), arriving in 1712, before even the courthouse that gave the town its weight and prominence, when Freehold was nothing but a few dozen widely scattered homesteads and a tiny village (blacksmith, shoemaker, store, inn) clustered at an intersection of the Burlington Path, an old Leni-Lenape road that cut diagonally across the colony. The rolling green land here then was the kind of land the Old World dreamed of when it dreamed of the New: rich, ripe, primordially fertile, where peaches, a royal luxury in Europe, were so abundant that swine feasted on the surplus. Walter's ancestors fought in the Revolution, and they fought again when the town raised a regiment for the Civil War. Most recently, his father had ridden with the cavalry in the World War.

Walter was small but strong, a varsity wrestler back in high school, his physical agility camouflaged by glasses that gave him a scholarly look, and he carried himself with a straight-backed military bearing. He graduated at sixteen, and thought about studying engineering at Rutgers, his father's old school, but he chose instead to serve his apprenticeship as the orchard's sole heir. He didn't love the orchard the way his father did, but he was an only child, and he felt a sense of duty toward it. As he turned the pickup and headed toward the barn, he well knew how much this land, this life, had cost.

When Private Jake Errickson arrived in town two days later—stepping out of the car that had carried him on the last leg of his hitchhiking journey from Fort Meade, Maryland—he wondered for a moment whether he was in fact on a three-day pass home, or if he had somehow wound up on maneuvers instead. The cleanup had been slow in the parts of town where the storm hit hardest, and because he had told no one he was coming, no one had told him what to expect. His surprise appearance was his first visit home since April, when his number (237) had come up in the lottery and he, acting on the theory that the sooner he left the sooner he would return, went down to the draft board on Court Street and asked to be sent in the next allotment. At Fort Dix, the army put him in the Signal Corps and shipped him off to Fort Meade, where he trained with the same dishpan helmets and Springfield rifles the doughboys had used in the trenches of France. He had never been so far or so long away from home before, and he was eager to stand in his blade-sharp uniform in the doorway of the house on Jackson Street his family had rented for many years. Square-jawed and lean, he set his garrison cap at a rakish angle over his wavy, light-brown hair. None of the clothes he had worn before had ever made him look as good as these did. He turned at the post office, but fallen trees blocked his path and detoured him onto the next street over. When he finally reached home, he found his parents in the basement, cleaning up the mess left by a three-foot flood. He hung his uniform in his room, careful to preserve its creases, and set to work.

The location of the Errickson house was bad in a storm—at a low place in the road where water was quick to collect—but it had been good for Jake's career. The rug mill was directly across the street, and every morning the mill superintendent parked his car right out front, unwittingly offering himself as a personal personnel office to a job-seeking Jake, who had graduated from high school into a Depression-thin market. Jake timed the superintendent's comings and goings and made it his business to appear on the sidewalk at the appropriate moment each day with a polite request for work. He was stolid and reserved and tended toward the solitary, happiest when tramping through the woods at the edge of town with a shotgun, hunting rabbits.

His persistence with the superintendent finally earned him a job as a creeler, tying yarn into the bobbin frames so the weavers could keep the looms running uninterrupted. He had to fill out a job card for each frame he finished, and in his careful, meticulous handwriting a supervisor saw the precise, diligent mind of a potential manager. Plucked off the track that might have made him a weaver, he was moved into the payroll office as a clerk. The mill was revered as a steady and benevolent employer, and Jake, young as he was, already was planning to spend his entire work life there. Awaiting him sometime soon, he hoped, was the kind of paycheck that would allow him to do what his father never could: buy a house of his own. He didn't know exactly where the job would lead, but he did know when he would be returning to it. His army hitch was for one year, as it was for all the draftees, and when he came home in April of 1942, he expected it would be for good.

As the big clock atop the courthouse swept past ten on Memorial Day morning, the thick line of spectators that stretched across all the downtown storefronts leaned forward expectantly, craning their necks toward the brass-band blare that had just begun somewhere in the leafy distance. Main Street was in a rare daylight state, empty from curb to curb, trafficked only by a few boys circling on bicycles, giddy at their fleeting freedom. The limbs and wires downed by the storm four days earlier had all been removed, and a clear path lay ahead for the marchers who had gathered at Elks Point, the shady green triangle where the road from the north flowed into the road from the east to form the town's main tributary. A color guard from Post 54 of the American Legion, uniformed veterans of the Great War, headed the column, flags held high. The 165th Field Artillery Band fell in next, a blocky wall of sound, heavy as fog, that caused the women along the route to quiet their children and the men to remove their hats.

The parade's unhindered passage this morning, along a street that was impassable so recently, was welcome reassurance to the watching crowd that their town had survived the storm intact, and that they could turn their attention to other business. The rug mill had just announced major expansion plans—building a four-story addition, buying the old cannery complex—that seemed to bode well for Jake Errickson's postarmy prospects. Buddy Lewis had a new place to meet his friends after school: The county chapter of the Urban League had opened the Colored Community Center in the Odd Fellows Hall on Haley Street, and the Joe Louis Boys Club had been organized to "turn out a class of colored youth that will be a credit to his race." Freehold's most famous resident, Frankie Hayes, in his seventh year as a catcher for the Philadelphia Athletics, had just gone seven for eight in a doubleheader against the Senators, pushing his average to .328 and moving manager Connie Mack to declare that "he is now more valuable to us than ever before." The federal government was proceeding with plans to buy three farms to use as camps for 250 "Southern Negro" migrant workers, hoping to replace the squalid shacks many of them lived in, despite the unified local opposition of ministers, merchants, politicians, editorialists and the farmers themselves. "The present arrangement works fairly well," Walter Denise's father, Tunis, who employed up to 150 pickers at the height of his season, told the Rotary Club. Housing conditions were not so grim, he argued, as to require federal intervention. "It's not *The Grapes of Wrath.*"

Marching in smart cadence behind the band came the First Battalion of the 119th Quartermaster Regiment, mostly local men from a National Guard unit that, before it was federalized and absorbed into the army, had drilled on weekends up and down Court Street. They were scheduled to leave in a few days for maneuvers in Virginia. The cheers that greeted them this morning—from a crowd larger, it appeared, than any since the grand parade back in 1933 that was decreed by Roosevelt to celebrate the new National Recovery Administration, and to help lift the nation's spirit from the depths of the Depression—were more immediate and heartfelt than the cheers of previous Memorial Days. More was at stake now, everyone knew, than at any time since 1918. The town had begun to understand that the greatest peril of that violent evening earlier in the week hadn't come from the storm itself, but from what the president had said during it.

The signs of war were unmistakable and unavoidable. Letters had been arriving from the weavers' families in England, describing the ominous drone of German bombers, the fire and rubble of the Blitz. A British War Relief Committee was formed, and raised enough money to buy a mobile kitchen for Kidderminster, the rug town that had dispatched so many emigrants to the Freehold mill. In a more symbolic gesture of moral support, local officials sent Winston Churchill a cannonball from the Battle of Monmouth. The sewing machines at Eisner's, the garment factory on Elm Street, were busy stitching together uniforms for a big new order from the army. The neighboring military installations were stirring noticeably: Fort Hancock, guarding the mouth of New York Harbor at Sandy Hook, aimed its giant new eighteen-inch coastal railway gun out at waters that might become hostile at any moment; the naval air station down at Lakehurst was sprawling deeper into the sandy pines; maneuvers from Fort Dix were ranging across some of the outlying farms; and the recreational pier the WPA was building in Raritan Bay had been commandeered by the navy. The anxious air proved too suffocating for one twenty-three-year-old farmer: After writing a note that told of his fear of the draft and where it might send him, he sat down in a kitchen chair and fired a shotgun into his chest.

The hometown soldiers were followed in the parade route by a green-clad company of tree-planting troops from the Civilian Conservation Corps camp. Fewer than a hundred of them, half the number of a few years ago, remained in the rickety barracks on Jerseyville Avenue, their ranks depleted by an economy that was already rising to a wartime pitch. Defense plants were rushing to fulfill Roosevelt's recent pledge that America would become "the arsenal of democracy," luring grateful workers who could barely remember the last decent paycheck they had seen. The small, aging platoon of Spanish-American War veterans, the senior marchers since the death of the last local Civil War veteran several years earlier, paraded behind the CCC boys, halting to salute the dignitaries on the courthouse reviewing stand. Next to pass were the veterans of the most recent war, some of whom had sons in the battalion at the head of the line. The last soldiers marching up the street were the youngest, the cadets from the Freehold Military Institute, a rich-blooded boarding school almost a century old, accompanied by their band and their distinguished, white-haired leader, Major Charles Duncan.

The uniforms that followed were of the civilian variety—Boy Scouts and Girl Scouts, the Elks Band, the Junior Minutemen fife-and-drum corps, the volunteer firemen and their trucks, the first aid squad and their ambulances—and when the last marchers had finally crossed the railroad tracks and passed the firehouse, some of the more devout spectators fell into step on the sidewalk behind them, carried by the fading melody toward the place at the edge of town where the morning's ceremonies would end. Released from the close-walled downtown corridor, the drumbeat widened, seeping through the green spaces between the large, deep-porched homes of the Main Street elite. Church steeples rose from among the houses at intervals as regular as the color-guard flags among the marchers. Conspicuously missing from this stately Protestant procession of white clapboard and stone were the denominations that had arrived later in town and been relegated to less visible locations: the Catholic church, Freehold's largest single congregation; the synagogue, which counted several Lopatins among its twenty-six founding members; and the AME and Second Baptist churches, which stood amid the Peach Orchard homes of their members.

After passing the last house on Main Street, the boxy white colonial the British commander had seized as his headquarters during the Battle of Monmouth, the parade turned into the tree-lined grove of Maplewood Cemetery and wound among headstones that wore the same old family names as the streets in town. Jake Errickson's grandfather was buried here, a small Grand Army of the Republic shield marking him as a veteran of the Civil War. Stu Bunton's father was here, too, the grass on his grave barely a season old. At the large stone marking the plot of the Conover family, descendants of the town's early Dutch settlers, the parade dissolved into a loose crowd, forming a wide and reverent circle around the grave of Captain James Conover, after whom the local GAR post had been named. While leading Company D of the Fourteenth New Jersey Infantry in the Battle of Monocacy in the summer of 1864, Conover was felled by a rifle bullet from a vastly larger Confederate force that was charging the Union line across an open Maryland field. Buried a few rows over was Major Peter Vredenburgh of the same regiment, which consisted of nearly a thousand county volunteers who had first mustered and trained on the same field where Washington once battled the British. Two months after Monocacy, at the Battle of Opequon Creek near Winchester, Virginia, Vredenburgh had sat astride his horse, Dolly, and rallied his men to charge a Confederate battery. "Do the best you can and I will do the best I can for you," he told them before springing forward over the crest of the hill and into an enemy fusillade. A three-inch shell ripped through his neck, killing him instantly. Dolly, a piece of her ear gone, careered riderless across the battlefield. She eventually was returned to Freehold, where she solemnly led the Decoration Day parade each year until 1884, when she finally died the peaceful, old-soldier's death denied her master.

Flags held high and eyes fixed forward, the color guards stood as still and silent as the gravestones that surrounded them on all sides. Milling above the dead with the impatience of the living, many in the waiting crowd instinctively scanned the grounds in search of the places where they had buried their own. The annual May procession to the cemetery had begun soon after the Civil War as a pilgrimage to decorate the graves of the newfallen soldiers, and it had continued unbroken even through the years when the dimming memory of battles, and the shrinking line of uniformed marchers, caused the acute meaning of the day's rituals to recede. This morning's service, though, like so much else in the town's recent life, had been transformed by the terrible knowledge that war was abroad again in the world. Heads bowed as a priest from the Catholic church, tapped by the local clergy rotation as the leader of this year's prayer service, offered a benediction. They were raised again as he began to speak.

"In every period of our nation's history," he said, surrounded by souls who had witnessed it all, "our boys have proven themselves worthy of their sires, and gave their lives to vindicate justice, and to secure the continuance of liberty under the law."

Like most Memorial Day orators, the priest echoed the themes of the

Gettysburg Address. "We must dedicate our lives anew, to the perpetuation of these things for which they died," he said, as he might have any other year as well. But then he took up Roosevelt's more recent message, linking the day's old rituals to the nation's new responsibilities. "In the event that this country does go to war, it is the duty of its citizens to participate in the war program, in whatever capacity each individual may be called upon to serve."

A bugler stood ready to play taps, a melody that today would carry both the loss of the past and the fear of the future, but before the notes could ache out, the priest had a final pair of questions to ask, questions to which all present—he hoped, the world hoped, God hoped—already knew the answers.

"Are we of this generation going to keep faith with those whom we are gathered here to honor? Are we going to preserve this nation which they helped to found and protect?"

2.

The Pacific and the Mediterranean, 1941–1943

Jake Errickson

The trucks rumbled slowly out of the dim, scrubby pines and across the dormant cotton fields, a single-file convoy of army six-by-sixes bouncing roughly along a narrow dirt track that was never meant to carry such a burden. Under the steady pounding, the road shuddered awake from its Sunday morning peace, nervously jarring its unexpected visitors with yawning ruts and washboard ripples. Jake Errickson shifted uncomfortably in his hard, narrow seat in the open back of one truck. He winced at each jolt, looking out to see if they hadn't run off the road and into the fields. Though it was early in December, a patch of unseasonable warmth had brought summer to North Carolina, with temperatures high enough to raise a sweat. Clouds of fine, red dust billowed up and stuck to the soldiers' skin like flour to chickens about to be fried. Somewhere up ahead of them lay the clear, paved surface of the highway that would lead back to Fort Meade, Route 301, waiting in the unseen distance like a smooth promise of home.

"It's like somebody put a mud pack on me," Jake said to his seatmate when they were finally cruising up the highway and the wind was drying their sweat, tautening their faces with masks of encrusted dust that left them craving even more the showers that were still at least a day away.

Ten of them sat facing each other in the flatbed rear of the truck. Squatting on the floor between them were the cumbersome machines they had spent the last months mastering—the 206-C radio direction finders. With radar still a new and immobile technology, the Signal Corps used direction finders to pinpoint an enemy's position by homing in on the location of their radio transmissions. So far, though, the only enemies the equipment had been tested on were other American soldiers, in maneuvers. To shape its unwieldy legions of reluctant draftees into a capable fighting force, the army—which grew in just a year from 250,000, the small standing defense of a democracy with no belligerent neighbors, to almost a million and a half—had staged vast war games in recent weeks: 500,000 men in Louisiana, 300,000 in North and South Carolina. The new soldiers wore old doughboy helmets and wrapped puttees around their calves as if marching on Château-Thierry, manned antitank guns that consisted of empty pipes attached to pairs of bicycle wheels, tossed one-pound sacks of flour as grenades, gazed up occasionally at the drone from one of the sparse corps of planes, and were ever grateful that an ocean separated them from the steel behemoth of Nazi Germany, whose eight-million-strong army now bestrode Europe all the way from the English Channel to the outskirts of Moscow.

Jake's outfit, the 121st Signal Radio Intelligence Company, was among the better-equipped at the maneuvers, and it served at various times with each of the two armies that were engaged in mock battles, the Red and the Blue. They set up their direction finders on what concealed heights they could find in the rolling farmland, four teams spaced at five-mile intervals to take fixes on the enemy from separate angles, their combined trajectories zeroing in precisely on the target. The bulky metal boxes bristled with knobs and dials and were each crowned by a loop antenna that rotated like an owl's head, scanning the night for predators. Hour after hour, Jake and his companions slowly cranked the antennae around, catching the messages that sped invisibly through the air around them, the signals fading in and out of their headphones, hearing as language, translating into words, the Morse code pulses that until recently had sounded to them like nothing more than random noise.

"That's a dit," the sergeant had said back at Fort Meade, hooking a telegraph key up to an amplifier, and taking the tone of a kindergarten teacher as he commenced their first lesson, "and that's a dot. Put the dit and the dot together to get the letter 'A.'"

Jake had quickly mastered the new alphabet, and adapted well to direction-finder duty. The work was orderly and precise, and required many of the same habits of mind—the attention to detail, the capacity to maintain focus through long stretches of tedium and repetition—that had earned him his promotion at the rug mill. He would be glad to leave it behind soon, though. He had four months left before he was due to be mustered out. His job, his girlfriend and his future were all waiting for him back home.

Jake was riding in the middle of the convoy, a dozen and a half trucks carrying the entire 150-man company, unattached to any larger division, traveling alone as it lumbered into Virginia and passed through Petersburg, the last great battleground of the Civil War. He was eager to get back to the base in Maryland, which was near enough to Freehold that he often could—if he didn't pull guard duty or get knocked down for something at the regular Saturday morning inspection—race home for a quick weekend. His barracks buddy from Elizabeth, who kept a car at camp, would drop him off in Trenton, and pick him up again at the same corner on Sunday night.

Late in the afternoon, nearing suppertime, the convoy pulled over just outside the gates of Fort A.P. Hill, and started making a bivouac for the night. Almost eighty years earlier, Jake's grandfather had been in this same piece of Virginia, as a Union private assaulting the impregnable Confederate positions on the heights of Fredericksburg. Now, in the command car at the head of the line, somebody set up an intercept radio and tuned it in the direction of some friendly transmissions, hoping to pick up Glenn Miller on a Washington station. Jake was unloading his gear when he heard a sudden commotion ahead. He looked up to see a cluster of men collecting around the radio. The news they were hearing reached him faster than he could reach them, passing back from truck to truck with a speed rivaling the messages they had been trained to eavesdrop on.

"The Japs bombed Pearl Harbor," somebody said.

Most of the nation had heard of the attack an hour or two earlier, sometime after the convoy had left the calm, unsuspecting streets of Richmond and was rolling through the voiceless countryside, sealed away in that curious cocoon of military life, in which a soldier can be simultaneously at the center of the action and on its periphery. Back in Freehold, Bill Lopatin had been sitting with a customer, finalizing the details of a contract for a house he was going to build, when the bulletin came over the radio. Buddy Lewis was still in his Sunday church suit, strolling up Throckmorton Street with a girl on his arm—"sporting," he called it— when somebody he passed told him about the attack.

The news stunned the soldiers into an anxious silence that was filled with both respect for the dead and concern for their own future. This meant war, they knew. This was why they had been drafted. Their one-year hitches, they suspected, had just been extended indefinitely.

"Jesus, we'll never get out of this thing," one of Jake's truck mates said when conversation resumed.

The identity of today's attackers surprised them almost as much as the attack itself. All through boot camp and training, through barracks strategizing and barroom philosophizing, through the maneuvers in which they had squinted hard and pretended to see Europe in North Carolina, their presumptive foe had been Germany, not Japan. The news from Pearl Harbor was sketchy, but lurid, and in the absence of information, they turned to the kind of speculation that often grows into rumor, and sometimes into fact. Where would they be sent, and when? To join the troops already in the Philippines? To Hawaii? Australia? How would the Japanese fight? What kind of ships and planes did they have? Jake and his friends paged through the old geography lessons in their heads to form a picture of where their battlefields might lie.

The night air was cold, far more like December than the day had been, and the men rubbed their arms for warmth as they stood around the radio, listening to news bulletins that answered none of their most pressing questions. As the night deepened, and the news thinned, they drifted off to the blankets they had spread on the ground. Jake put on his heavy overcoat and wrapped himself up tightly, but the cold and the uncertainty kept him from finding any comfort in sleep. Sometime around 2 A.M. he saw that somebody was starting a bonfire. He rose and joined a slow, ghostly parade of his blanket-caped companions, all drawn through the shadows toward the flame as they had earlier been drawn toward the radio.

"Where did all the heat go?" Jake wondered aloud. "It's like someone pulled the cork out."

"Make some coffee," the company commander ordered the cook, as they all gathered closely around the fire, seeking the heat more than the light.

They wanted the night to be over, so they decided it was. They stood around the fire until dawn, sipping from canteen cups and imagining the war that, by the time they returned to Fort Meade in the middle of the next afternoon, had already been formally declared. They barely resumed their camp routine before they were ordered back to North Carolina for another round of maneuvers. The days were colder now, and stretched ahead of them toward an end no one could see. Jake's term of service, like everyone else's, had been officially fixed at a length that sounded like eternity: "for the duration." The company was still at Fort Bragg, finding targets for the artillery to practice bombarding, when they heard the news they had been expecting for more than a month.

"Errickson, I'm not supposed to do this," the captain said when he called Jake in. Jake noticed the damp eyes, the quavery voice, and felt an extra stab of devotion to his commander, whose tough but generous compassion for the men bespoke a West Point breeding. "I'm gonna give you three days to go home because you're going overseas."

Jake took a train to Baltimore, then to Trenton, then hitchhiked to Freehold, which had just buried its first casualty: Corporal Lloyd Simmons of the 76th Coast Artillery, and the Second Baptist Church, killed in an army truck crash. The war felt even nearer to Jake at home than it had at the base. German U-boats were stalking American ships along the shore, and fears ran high about the possibility—the certainty, some officials were saying—of an East Coast equivalent of Pearl Harbor. The Strand was letting servicemen in for just a dime, so he took his girlfriend to the movies, trying to pretend for a few hours that it was just another date, not the last they would have for a duration no one could guess at. His mother cried when he left; his father looked as if he wanted to, but didn't.

Back in Maryland, Jake didn't have to wait long before the final orders came, and his company was loaded onto a troop train bound for the Brooklyn Port of Embarkation, and the Pacific theater. The train stopped at Fort Dix late on a Saturday afternoon, the last day of February 1942, and when Jake stepped off he found waiting for him a surprise that moved him to an uncharacteristic impulsiveness. His girlfriend was standing there alone, in the fading winter light. She knew his train would be passing through, and she had caught a ride south from Freehold with a friend, on the small chance that she might be able to see him one more time. She had been waiting for hours, with no car, and no plan about what to do next.

"Go ahead, Jake," his friend Johnny Reinert said. "You've got time. We won't be leaving until morning."

Jake and his girlfriend hopped the next bus to Freehold, less than an hour north, and walked through the Saturday night crowd downtown, exchanging greetings with friends who had already said their goodbyes, and who looked at him as if he were an apparition. At his parents' house, the conversation ran long past midnight, his presence a gift everyone was eager to savor, and reluctant to let go of. The latest local war news was particularly alarming, and made his imminent parting even harder. Two nights earlier, a U-boat had torpedoed an oil tanker, the *R.P. Resor,* within sight of Manasquan, the beach town where people from Freehold flocked on sunny summer weekends. Only three from the crew survived. Several bodies among the forty who died washed up in the Manasquan inlet.

It was three-thirty in the morning before Jake was finally able to pull himself away. His sister and her husband gave him a ride back to Fort Dix, driving slowly through the sleeping town, following the same Main Street route as the Memorial Day parade but continuing on past the cemetery and out through the dark potato fields, rolling alone toward the point where the good soil gave up and the farms yielded to the black and empty pine forests. They took their time, believing they had enough to spare: The train, Jake thought, wouldn't be leaving until daylight at the earliest.

"C'mon, Jake! Hurry up!" his friend Johnny was calling as Jake arrived in the predawn gloom to find the train loaded and ready to pull out.

"Wait, I gotta get my stuff," Jake said, turning to retrieve his gear: two large barracks bags to carry and one small musette bag to sling over his shoulder.

"It's already on the train," Johnny said. "C'mon, get on."

Jake was barely on board, and just a few steps ahead of an AWOL charge that would have landed him in jail, when the train shoved off toward Brooklyn. Waiting at the dock for them was the *Uruguay,* a converted cargo ship more accustomed to ferrying bananas from South America, its holds strung with hammocks three levels high to accommodate several thousand Pacific-bound soldiers. The radio intelligence company that boarded the ship that Sunday had shrunk considerably from its maneuvers size. A few of the best code listeners, ham radio hobbyists in civilian life, had been plucked out to serve on merchant marine ships making the murderous North Atlantic passage to Great Britain. Another contingent was on its way to Iceland. Jake was traveling to the exact opposite point on the globe, Australia, with forty-four other enlisted men, one lieutenant, four 206-C direction finders, and many other crates filled with intercept receivers, spools of wire, plotting equipment and assorted electronic gear.

The ship left as soon as they were aboard, slipping away with no fanfare, only worry about the prowling U-boats. At dawn the day before, the *Jacob Jones*, a destroyer that had just left the same port to patrol for subs in the wake of the *Resor*'s sinking, had itself been torpedoed off Cape May, the first navy victim of Germany's new assault on American coastal waters. Only eleven crewmen survived. Steaming out of New York harbor now, the Statue of Liberty fading in the distance, the *Uruguay* joined a large convoy that began zigzagging down the East Coast toward the Panama Canal, the ships abruptly shifting directions in a pattern meant to elude anything unseen that might be stalking them. Navy blimps hovered overhead, watching for periscopes and telltale wakes. In the middle of the convoy, protected by rings of transports and warships, was its most valuable member, the new aircraft carrier *Hornet*.

The sub alert sounded several times on the *Uruguay* as it lumbered south, but the convoy reached Panama unscathed. As Jake's ship crept through the canal, the soldiers at the rail tossing pennies down to the children who ran alongside, he was approaching a war that America was losing badly.

"The Pacific situation is very grave," Roosevelt wrote to Churchill at just about the time Jake was entering it.

With that first wave of planes at Pearl Harbor—183 dive-bombers, torpedo bombers and Zero fighters dropping suddenly from the clear Sunday-morning sky three months earlier—Japan had launched a massive campaign that swept across the western Pacific with a speed and ferocity rivaling Germany's conquest of Europe, provoking a war not just with the United States, but the world. In one hundred days of lightning victories since then, days when Jake's company was still practicing in maneuvers, the Japanese expanded their empire until it covered a tenth of the globe. They took Hong Kong, Wake, Guam and a long string of the islands that spill off Southeast Asia. They marched through the jungles of the Malay Peninsula and, though outnumbered two to one, forced the British to surrender Singapore, the heretofore impregnable Gibraltar of the east. They raced through Burma and stood at the gates of India, raising fears that they would continue west and link up with Germany. In the Philippines, they were advancing on the mountainous, malarial Bataan peninsula, where the besieged American troops were shooting pack mules and iguanas to supplement one-thousand-calorie-a-day rations while waiting vainly for reinforcements who were not on the way. The Japanese, the world soon learned, had more aircraft carriers, better planes, bigger battleships—the Americans had none at all in the Pacific after the attack on Pearl Harbor—and hardened soldiers willing to die in droves for the emperor. They were not, they had quickly shown, the weak, inept and cowardly race of caricature. They would not lie down meekly before the onslaught of mighty Americans.

While the American navy worked to restore its fleet, and replace the eighteenth-century charts it had been forced to rely on in some unfamiliar waters, the army moved into Australia, the last major Allied outpost in the western Pacific. The army's mission was both to help defend Australia from a feared invasion—the Japanese had already bombed the north coast city of Darwin and occupied most of Papua and New Guinea, the nearest northern neighbor, and much of the Australian Army was off fighting with the British in North Africa—and to prepare a counterattack. As the *Uruguay* was steaming toward Australia from the east, a much smaller vessel, a mahogany-hulled PT boat carrying General Douglas MacArthur, was approaching from the infested waters of the west, stealing by night through the enemy blockade of the Philippines. MacArthur had been ordered by Roosevelt out of the deep-rock, last-stand tunnels of Corregidor Island, and charged with plotting a strategy that would pierce the imperial wall now encircling half the Pacific and drive the Japanese back to Tokyo.

The *Uruguay* tensed up for a few alerts as it crossed the Pacific, but the more constant enemy was tedium. The ship was too small for anything but eating, sleeping and waiting. The showers were saltwater, and the soap the men were issued proved about as useful as wax in cleansing anyone of the rank odor that accumulated week after tropical week. Each dawn was welcomed for the chance to escape the ripe, poorly ventilated sleeping holds, and to gulp the fresh air topside. Craps games erupted occasionally, but Jake, with just twelve dollars in his pocket, stayed clear. Two-thirds of the way across, though, a boiler in the engine room broke down.

Jake stood at the rail on the deck of his motionless ship, anchored off the coast of Bora Bora, and watched the rest of the convoy—all those planes and guns meant to protect slow and vulnerable freighters like the *Uruguay*—vanish over the western horizon. Before he was inducted, he had never been farther from home than Philadelphia, had barely even heard of places like Bora Bora, and now he was stranded here on a crippled ship. Repairs went on for a day and a night, another day and another night. Jake and the other soldiers could do little but feel even more isolated, and watch the natives paddle outriggers out toward them.

"Bananas, one dollar!" the islanders shouted, and Jake watched as some of his more flush compatriots lowered the money in baskets and hauled the bunches up.

On the third day, the ship was fixed. With no destroyers riding shotgun, no neighbors to share the danger, the men on board were wary and vulnerable as they resumed their way west, and grateful when they reached Auckland unscathed on the Saturday before Easter. A dockside band serenaded them before they sailed again the next morning, at an hour when Jake should have been singing "Jesus Christ Is Risen Today" with the rest of his family back home at the Presbyterian church on Main Street. The men of the 121st were forty days out of New York as they crossed the Tasman Sea, and their world had been nothing but ocean for so long that they wondered if they had been transferred to the navy. On the forty-first day, just about the time Jake was originally supposed to return to Freehold at the end of his one-year hitch, they reached Melbourne, where, to their great relief, they disembarked into a city that looked, and a language that sounded, something like home. But the news that greeted them was even grimmer than the news that had sent them off: The Americans had just surrendered to the Japanese on Bataan, and all that remained of the United States Army in the Philippines were some guerrillas who had withdrawn to the hills, the long, hungry line of prisoners marching at gunpoint on the deathly route to internment, and the bunkered remnant in Corregidor, enduring an unrelenting artillery barrage that was reducing the island to rubble. Jake and his company unloaded their listening gear onto a continent that had no operational radar stations.

"Australia, Australia," some of the soldiers sang as they left the ship, "we've come to help you fight, fight, fight!"

Stu Bunton

The planes pretending to be the enemy appeared over Freehold in the postchurch quiet of a Sunday afternoon in May of 1942, just a week before Memorial Day—four planes that were too big, too fast and too low to be anything but trouble. The air raid wardens who had studied the silhouette charts immediately recognized the intruders as bombers that could have no good intentions in flying so close to unarmed civilians.

When the planes swooped down over the two-block stretch of the rug mill, the fattest target in town, they dropped their payload. Thousands of white leaflets came fluttering through the spring sky like snow, falling lightly across all the surrounding blocks—settling onto the Hudson Street grammar school, the Sinclair oil tanks on Ford Avenue, the end-of-the-line railroad siding where the steam engines idled each night and on the roof of the house where one of the wardens, Stu Bunton, lived with his mother and sister. Each sheet was meant to represent a German paratrooper whose mission it was to kill Americans, and before they had all come to rest the wardens had summoned the troops whose job it was to defend against them. More than one hundred soldiers sped to the scene in trucks and jeeps from the army camp that had taken over the old CCC barracks, spilling out with bayonets fixed, machine guns emplaced, to meet the invaders.

The mock attack continued all through the afternoon and all across the county, part of an elaborate readiness exercise meant to avert any East Coast reprise of Pearl Harbor. Planes were buzzing the coastline, and soldiers were vaulting over the boardwalk rail in Asbury Park, rushing to turn back the invasion boats attempting a beach landing. In Freehold, the bombers had ravaged all the main streets, leaving phantom craters whose edges were outlined by lime. The municipal building was an exploded ruin, and the local defense council had relocated to the sheriff's office. A mock German plane sat parked in the grassy center of the Route 9 traffic circle, as firefighters doused the imaginary flames. A gang of saboteurs, working from clandestine headquarters in the Freehold Paint Store, was foiled before they could carry out their plot to bomb the rug mill, the Liberty Theater and the central telephone exchange; the leader, a woman, was the last to be captured, chased down on foot on Court Street by the police chief himself. Ambulances raced jaggedly through the pockmarked streets, picking up the casualties, whose white armbands distinguished them from the uninjured. Three hours after it started, the invasion was over—the enemy vanquished, the town unconquered.

Because it was near New York and the Atlantic, Freehold felt particularly vulnerable to enemy attack, and had started preparing for war when war was still on the other side of the ocean: The defense council held its inaugural public meeting three weeks before Pearl Harbor; and volunteer aircraft observers had been taking shifts up on the roof of the mill for almost a year already, scanning the sky night and day for unfamiliar planes.

"We are not only in danger of an attack, but we know it is coming, and we must be ready for it when it comes," a major from Fort Hancock on Sandy Hook told more than a thousand defense council members who crowded into the high school auditorium for a recent mass meeting. No real bombers had yet appeared over town, but German U-boats were still lurking off the local beaches, taking control of America's coastal waters as no other foreign invader had since the War of 1812.

In Church's Sweet Shop, the question for Stu Bunton and his friends wasn't whether they'd join the war, but when. Although they were graduating soon, just a few weeks after the invasion maneuvers, nobody was making any big plans for the future. Even if the draft age wasn't lowered from twenty to eighteen, as they expected, nobody believed the fighting would end before their call came. The war was theirs now, they understood, not their fathers', and it was being fought by people they knew. Herb Spitzner, the older brother of one of the sweet-shop regulars, had just stopped home on leave, and with him came an eyewitness account of Pearl Harbor. He was a fireman first class on the *Nevada*, which had raised its colors and played "The Star-Spangled Banner" even as Japanese planes were strafing the deck, and he was caught down below in the battery room when the old battleship was hit—by a torpedo that ripped a hole in its side, and at least five bombs that mangled its superstructure. The smoke and fumes left him unconscious; he would have drowned when the ship flooded and beached had not someone pulled him to safety. Fifty of his shipmates were killed. Another local sailor was also at Pearl Harbor that morning, but he wasn't as lucky: Edward Ryan, a 1940 graduate of Freehold High School, was among the 415 men who died on the battleship *Oklahoma* when it took five quick torpedo hits and sank in just fifteen minutes.

After graduation, Stu found waiting for him the job he had hoped to avoid, at the rug mill where his late father had been a weaver. He worked from Monday to Friday as a creeler, filling the bobbin frames with yarn, then came in on Saturday mornings to clean the oil from under the looms and bring his pay up to fourteen dollars a week. The mill, like most American factories, had quickly been enlisted in the war effort, taking a small part in the massive industrial mobilization that was necessary before the Allies could launch any offensives. Restricted by government order to 25 percent of its previous wool supply, the mill converted many of its looms from rugs to duck, weaving rolls of the light canvas the army needed for tents, gun covers, tarpaulins, bomber linings and the like. The machine shop went on a three-shift schedule, turning brass and iron castings into diffusers for the steam condensers in battleship power plants. The union even voted to forgo Sunday overtime pay. "No effort is being spared to produce whatever is possible for defense purposes in our plant," the mill superintendent said.

It was the summer of his eighteenth birthday, and Stu was restless and frustrated, wishing he were somewhere else—exactly where, he wasn't sure, just as long as it wasn't where he already was. At night sometimes he would return to the mill as an air spotter, climbing out onto the roof to peer through the high-powered binoculars the navy had donated to the local observation post; and whenever the town staged an air-raid drill or a blackout test, it was his duty as a warden to make sure all the lights were doused at his end of Mechanic Street. He left the mill, quickly and gladly, after a neighbor tipped him to a job at nearby Camp Evans, a new satellite facility of the Army Signal Corps installation at Fort Monmouth. For twenty-five dollars a week, he hauled supplies around the hilly waterfront grounds where Marconi had built the first commercial transatlantic radio towers, and where the army was now conducting radar research and training operations. He was soon promoted to the mailroom, and assigned the job of riding with an armed guard and a driver to the Belmar post office to pick up the pouches of secret mail.

By autumn 1942, Freehold had sent enough people into the service—more than four hundred already, more per capita than any other town in the county—that an Honor Roll was erected in front of the courthouse, listing all their names. One Saturday morning each month, the latest allotment of draftees gathered outside the draft board headquarters on Court Street and, in a flurry of tearful goodbyes, boarded a bus to Fort Dix. October was the month for Jimmy Higgins, whose undertakers' apprenticeship had been interrupted indefinitely. On his last night home he went to a roadside spaghetti house with his mother and three siblings, the first time they had ever dined out as a family, and the final occasion they would all share together for nobody knew how long. For the first few farewell Saturdays, the American Legion had mustered up band music and speeches, a patriotic attempt to send the new soldiers off with the kind of flag-waving flourish that had dispatched the doughboys to the last world war. The brassy trappings only made the leave-taking more emotional, though, and the ceremony was quietly dropped; at Jimmy's departure the legionnaires confined themselves to passing out free cigarettes. Jimmy declined his. Unlike Stu, he hadn't yet acquired the habit; only later did he learn that the war was a place of long pauses aching to be filled, and that smoking was the best form of waiting.

Proud photos of the new servicemen in their dashing uniforms beamed from the front page of the newspaper each week. One face had appeared more often than any other lately—Private Johnny Bartek of Bannard Street, who had worked as a creeler in the rug mill before becoming a mechanic in the Army Air Corps, and whose sister had unveiled the Honor Roll at its official dedication. A plane carrying Bartek was missing in the Pacific, a loss that would have gone unremarked anywhere but locally if not for the identity of one of the other men on board: Captain Eddie Rickenbacker, the storied World War I flying ace who was on a round-the-world inspection tour of American air bases. Their B-17 Flying Fortress was headed from Hickam Field in Hawaii to MacArthur's new headquarters in Port Moresby, New Guinea, flying alone across a remote stretch of ocean where the smallest navigational error could leave a plane sputtering toward limbo, when it failed to reach the island where it was due to refuel. Bartek was carrying in the pocket of his jumpsuit a copy of the small New Testament the Baptist minister in Freehold had given all the congregants who were leaving home for war. The search, so far, had found only water.

With the town draining of able young men, the Honor Roll at the courthouse lengthening with names, the draft age dropping officially to eighteen and the story of Johnny Bartek hovering over all the local news, Stu and his sweet-shop buddies were finally moved to act on the decision they had been weighing for months: Should they wait to be drafted into the army, where they would only see as much of the world as they could march across? Or should they enlist now and join the navy, where they might sail to places beyond their landlocked yearnings? The army offered mud and snow and K rations, but you could cling to the earth when the guns started. The navy offered clean sheets and hot meals, but a torpedo might leave you burned and broken and adrift in the middle of the swallowing sea. The dying in the navy might be harder, Stu and his friends concluded, but the living was better, and so, being eighteen and not completely stripped yet of their own sense of immortality, they opted for the living. One morning in the first week after Bartek's disappearance, while search planes with fading hopes still circled the central Pacific, eight of them went to the New York Central train station next to Stu's home and rode to Manhattan for their navy induction physicals.

Back at Camp Evans for a few weeks, finishing out his job as he awaited orders to report, Stu was called in by his boss and offered a reprieve. "You can stay here," she told him. His mother was a widow and he was her only son, a status that could have kept him in a civilian job at home. "I can get you an exemption."

But all Stu could see when she said that was a town empty of all young men but him, and a ship leaving port on a journey he didn't think he should miss. "I'd rather go," he told her.

Jake Errickson: Australia

Jake Errickson sat on his cot in one of the pyramidal tents his company had pitched in a park just north of Brisbane, mopping his brow and missing his first winter in twenty-three years. The calendar said he should be wrapped in wool, like everyone back home in Freehold, but the latitude disagreed: Here below the equator, sweating through a Southern Hemisphere summer along a coast where palm trees grew on the beaches, the most fitting attire was the T-shirt he had worn on duty all day at his radio listening post. His tent rose high and shadowy above him, the olive drab canvas cascading down from the tall central pole to the four wall flaps, rolled up this afternoon to air out the sleeping quarters. Most of the other tents were open, too, except for the two large ones set off to the side, which sheltered the company's electronic heart—racks of intercept radios, Teletypes, a locked safe filled with cryptographic materials, recording machines, wax cylinders, frequency meters, maps and all the other equipment needed for eavesdropping on Japanese transmissions. Wires snaked out from the radio tents to fifteen antennas strategically spaced among trees shielding them from any enemy planes that might risk a visit. Cooled by the canvas shade, Jake flipped through the latest issue of *Yank* magazine, the military weekly that—with its football scores and Betty Grable pinups and muscular tales of men and machines in battle— tried to help American soldiers bridge the almost unfathomable gap between their homes and their war.

RICKENBACKER FOUND ALIVE, one headline announced, and in the list of other survivors from the missing plane Jake saw the name of Johnny Bartek, the skinny redhead he had known in the rug mill.

The story of the missing plane offered the kind of inspirational uplift that was becoming more familiar, and more necessary, as the war unfolded, outlining in miniature the idea on which the whole American effort depended—the resilience, even heroism, of ordinary people in extraordinary times. Pushed too fast by a tailwind much stronger than measured, Rickenbacker's plane had overshot its island and, out of gas, set down roughly instead in the deep swells of the Pacific. In the frantic effort to untangle the three tiny life rafts, Johnny Bartek cut his hand to the bone. The blood attracted sharks that bumped their noses menacingly against the skin-thin raft bottoms. The eight men were equipped with four oranges, no water, two fishing lines with hooks but no bait, a pair of bailing buckets, a rope to lash the rafts together, a compass, pliers, some battered aluminum paddles, a first aid kit and a gun that fired eighteen flares no one ever saw. For a week they drifted toward death through hot, dry days and cold, dry nights, dreaming of what there was no sign of—rain to drink, islands to land on, the engines of rescue planes. When Rickenbacker noticed Bartek quietly reading the pocket Bible, he suggested twice-daily prayer services, complete with hymn singing; "Onward, Christian Soldiers" was a favorite. On the eighth day, after prayers had ended, a seagull landed on Rickenbacker's head. He reached up slowly, grabbed it, and within minutes the providential bird was plucked, divided eight ways and devoured. Its intestines baited hooks that caught a mackerel and a sea bass. Rain finally came that night, and the men laid out their clothes to soak it up, wringing the sopping garments straight into their mouths. They continued the prayer services faithfully after their raw feast, but the sustenance they received through the next two weeks was mainly spiritual. One of the men died. Rare squalls brought a few swallows of water; sharks chased a couple of leaping mackerels into the raft; a school of small fingerlings ventured near enough for a handful to be grabbed; but no more miraculous birds descended, and the seven men who were left on the twenty-fourth day adrift, Friday November 13, were nearing their own ends when a skeletal Bartek reached up to tug on the shirt of a dozing Rickenbacker.

"Listen, Captain—planes," he said.

A small pontoon plane landed near their raft and the sickest of the three men was loaded into the cockpit. Bartek was lifted up onto the right wing and tied into a sitting position, his bony legs dangling over the edge; Rickenbacker rode on the left wing. The plane taxied to a PT boat, which then took the men to a navy base at Funafuti in the Ellice Islands. Bartek had lost more than 40 pounds—from 136 down to 90—but he still had his Bible.

As Jake read of his onetime coworker's rescue, he gave thanks that his own war so far had been uneventful by comparison. Since their April arrival in Australia, his unit had been trundling up and down the eastern coast in search of a proper perch from which to hear the enemy. They started on top of a small mountain outside Melbourne in the south, where they were first instructed in the Japanese telegraph code—the Romaji and Kana codes were based on five-character groupings, rather than the three characters their ears had grown accustomed to—and where a six-inch snowfall on the Fourth of July kept them from joining a parade honoring American troops in the city below. A slow truck convoy then carried them all the way up to Townsville in the north, nearer the action in both Guadalcanal and New Guinea. While the Townsville station monitored Guadalcanal, the small tropical island that was the target of the first American land offensive of the war, Jake was dispatched with a five-man direction-finder team to listen in on New Guinea from Cloncurry, a dusty town in the empty middle of the kind of flat, arid cattle country he had seen before only in the B Westerns back at the Liberty Theater. Cloncurry had a drug store, a general store, a movie theater, a few small hotels to choose from for bunking, an Allied airstrip where they set up the direction finder and air so dry that an unoiled gun left on the ground overnight would have not a speck of rust on it in the morning. While the Japanese were trying to reach Port Moresby, the main Allied base in New Guinea—clambering single-file along the only trail that crossed the island's steep and jagged interior mountains—Jake's team in the Australian outback was trying, with little success, to pinpoint their plane movements. The aircraft transmissions were too swift for the direction finders, short bursts that were gone before the bearing could be secured.

Transferred to Brisbane, the Allied headquarters city in the middle of the coast, Jake's company suffered its first casualty on the train ride south. All the trucks were loaded onto flatbed railcars, the seats facing backward—giving a view of where the men had been, rather than where they were going—and as the train started over the bridge that crossed the Mary River, two of the cooks on the kitchen truck stood up on their seats for a better look at what was ahead. Their heads slammed into one of the bridge's overhanging girders, and they fell unconscious into the water below. The train stopped and the company went after them. One cook was rescued. The body of the other, a husky and affable tent mate of Jake's, didn't turn up until the next day. The men of the 121st buried their dead comrade in a treeless military cemetery in the Brisbane suburb of Ipswich that was fast filling with American graves. Jake was a pallbearer—he had never been one before—and he was surprised at the weight. After taps was sounded they returned to duty, leaving their friend half a world away from anyone beside themselves who might visit his grave.

Hunched over his direction finder each day, spinning through the frequencies on the dial, trying to discern patterns in the crackly static that filled his headphones, Jake was adding tiny brushstrokes to a portrait of the enemy only a few commanders ever saw as a whole. He dutifully recorded the information he collected but didn't understand, and sent it back to base camp, where it was then fed into an intelligence network that stretched all the way back to Washington. By analyzing the location, volume and timing of Japanese radio traffic, and adding these reports to the information gleaned from other sources (army and navy, Allied and civilian, human and technical), intelligence officers were able to see the enemy more clearly: the deployment of troops, the movement of ships and planes, the flow of supplies and even in some cases, since many Japanese codes were broken, the actual plans for operations. Earlier in the year, just a few weeks after Jake's unit landed, the Allies had read enough coded messages to determine that a Japanese invasion force in the Coral Sea was headed for Port Moresby, an ideal site from which to launch the long-feared attack on Australia; the navy was able to turn them back, in the first sea battle in history where ships never fired upon, or even saw, other ships, and all the attacking was left to carrier planes.

Barely a month after that, more intercepted Japanese messages had helped the Americans win the most important battle yet in the Pacific war. A monstrous enemy fleet was steaming toward the westernmost American base at Midway Island—four carriers, eleven battleships, twenty-two cruisers, sixty-five destroyers, twenty-one subs and eighty troop transports, an armada so large that Roosevelt feared at first that it might try to continue all the way to California—but the mightily outnumbered navy learned exactly what the plan was, and repelled it. American dive-bombers screaming down at a seventy-degree angle from the sky over Midway, grimly following a first wave of attack from which only six of forty-one planes returned, sank three Japanese carriers in just five minutes, and drew a line beyond which the enemy would be hard-pressed to venture again; a fourth carrier was sunk the next day. The victory was so decisive that the Japanese were forced to abandon their strategy of offensive conquest and retreat into the unaccustomed role of defenders for the first time in the war.

At the new camp in the Brisbane suburb of Northgate, Jake's direction finder found the enemy more often than it had in Cloncurry, homing in on the lengthier, easier-to-track transmissions of the Japanese fleet. The traffic was especially heavy in the neighborhood of Guadalcanal, where the marines were fighting back nighttime banzai charges and slashing their hands on the scalpel edges of the man-high kunai grass, and where the navy had lost so many ships, and sunk so many others, that the deadly, wreck-thick coastal waters came to be christened Ironbottom Sound. Among the ships sunk in the long string of sea battles off Guadalcanal were the *Hornet,* the aircraft carrier from Jake's convoy (and the launching pad for the brash and inspiring bombing raid over Tokyo by Jimmy Doolittle's B-25s), and the *Juneau,* a cruiser whose seven hundred victims included the five Sullivans, brothers from Iowa who had asked to serve together, and whose deaths came to symbolize the devotion of Americans to duty and to each other. Also killed on the *Juneau* was one of the Borden brothers from Freehold, less known to the world but better known to Jake.

At the end of 1942, the one hundred thousand Americans in Australia were still walking a golden path through a country that regarded them as saviors. An American in uniform couldn't turn around in public without making a friend. In one bar Jake fell in with some Australian soldiers who had just returned from fighting Rommel at Tobruk, and who made it hard for him to buy a drink. He kept clear of the native rum that had the kick of an anesthetic, but he was partial to the Castlemaine's Four X, a stiff beer with a strong malt flavor that came packaged for serious consumption in bottles twice as big as the ones back home. The Australian women were appreciative of the Americans, too, and Jake had recently been freed to return their attentions.

He had been exchanging letters with the girl who had surprised him at Fort Dix, but something seemed to be missing from them lately. A soldier depended more than a civilian knew on messages from home—mundane, inspiring, passionate, any kind of word at all, it didn't matter. Letters were savored for the taste they gave of life beyond the war, read

and reread until they came apart at the folds. But then a letter came from
one of his friends in Freehold: Jake's girlfriend, the friend wrote, had been
seen keeping company with another young man. Jake wrote to her to ask
if what he had heard was true. She was honest with him in her letter back,
and told him it was. No one knew how long the war might last, or how
short life might be, and relationships unsecured by diamonds or wedding
bands had a high mortality rate.

Some of his friends in the company had been singed by similar letters, and their sympathy—along with some bottles of Four X—helped
ease his disappointment. What also helped was his newfound sense of
freedom. He was young, single and handsome, his wavy brown hair and
his sharp uniform making him look a bit like Robert Taylor in *Waterloo
Bridge*, and when a pair of pretty sisters came flirting by his guard post at
camp one afternoon, he was quick to ask the elder one for a date.

The camp sat in a shady park that was popular for afternoon strolls,
and on the Sunday of his first date Jake was on guard duty there again,
shooing away the locals who hadn't yet learned that the grounds had been
enlisted in the war effort. "I'm sorry, you can't go through here," he told a
middle-aged couple coming too near the tents.

"Why not?" the woman protested. "We've been going through here
for years."

"It's a military installation," Jake explained, and they turned to leave.

The house where his date lived was barely half a mile from camp, and
when he knocked, the door was opened by a woman whose face he remembered but who he hoped had forgotten his.

"Aren't you the lad who chased us out of the park today?" she asked,
and he started to shrink, afraid that now it was his turn to be chased away.
But whatever momentary annoyance she might have felt had since passed,
replaced by the grateful warmth he had come to regard as the defining
Australian character trait. "Oh, don't worry, dear. That wasn't your fault."

Jake took Dot to the movies that night and enjoyed her company so
much that he kept coming back regularly, even after a flood in the park—
the water in the tents as deep as the water in his parents' basement on the
night of Roosevelt's speech—forced his unit to relocate a few suburbs
west to Stafford. Dot had thick brown hair that was parted on the side and
fell in waves to her shoulders, and small brown eyes that crinkled when
she smiled. She rode the train into Brisbane each morning to her job, decorating cakes in a bakery. She had a boyfriend of sorts, but he was off

serving somewhere with the Royal Australian Navy, and she didn't seem to regard him as an obstacle. Jake worked a schedule about as regular as the war could offer, and he and Dot were usually able to meet twice or more each week. They danced at church socials where three-piece bands wheezed through "I Don't Want to Set the World on Fire," returned to the movies often enough that he grew used to the curious local custom of ducking out at intermission to the soda fountain or fish-and-chips shop and soon forgot the girl back home, the boy at sea. They were sitting in a park on a summery Christmas Eve, listening to "White Christmas" drift out of the nearby ice-cream shop, when they began to realize they were caught in something deeper than a soldier's wartime crush.

Jake was quickly absorbed into Dot's family, adopted as a son by her parents, and a sibling by her sister and her brother, whose legs, like Roosevelt's, had been withered by polio. An extra place was set at the table when Dot's mother made a roast beef dinner, or her father laid on one of his Sunday-morning breakfast spreads. When Jake broke out with a high temperature and chills at a Saturday-night party at their house, it was Dot's mother who recognized the first signs of dengue fever and put him to bed, nursing him until a truck came from the base hospital the next day. Dot's parents had come to Australia after the First World War—her father from England, her mother from Scotland—and they were deeply curious about America, that other great magnet for immigrants seeking a new homeland; Jake, though, was equally curious about Australia.

In another place, at another moment, their courtship could have proceeded at a more deliberate pace, but the war that brought them together was also rushing them along, forcing them always to remember what the young often forget—that the hours are measured, and time is passing. The unseen chaperones on all of their dates were the officers who were deciding where and when Jake would go next. The Pacific war slowed to a lull in the first half of 1943, after half a year of brutal fighting that pushed the Japanese off Guadalcanal, drove them back on New Guinea and foretold a hard road ahead to Tokyo. America was girding for a massive, sustained offensive, stockpiling arms that poured from homefront factories in astonishing, exponential feats of production: Airplane manufacturing multiplied more than twenty-fold in just two years, and was set to double yet again this year. Stateside boot camps were adding new men to the service at a similar rate. More than six hundred names were on the Honor Roll now at the courthouse in Freehold.

In April, Jake's company more than doubled in size and acquired a new name—the 126th—when reinforcements arrived. With the new soldiers came word of a new assignment: New Guinea, where the army was battling north along the coast. Movement orders were imminent, and Jake was locked in a pensive limbo, wondering how much longer his romance could last, how much more distant his home could seem.

He was sitting in his tent after duty one afternoon when he heard his name called at a volume that often signaled trouble. "Errickson, report to the orderly room," the PA loudspeaker blared.

He found himself face to face with an officer, a female second lieutenant, but he was too shocked to salute, and she was too excited to remind him. "I thought you were in Tempe, Arizona," he said to his sister, Georgianna.

"I was, but I enlisted," she said.

Since training at a Trenton hospital, Jake's older sister had nursed her way across the country, spending a year or two working in a place that caught her interest—a nurse could always earn her keep—and then moving on when her new home started to feel as small and familiar as her old one in Freehold. She saw Alaska, Montana and Texas this way, and now, as an army nurse, she was headed places that would otherwise never have been on her itinerary. Her one request was that she serve in the same theater as her brother. She was due back at camp that night, but on his next day off, Jake took Dot to meet her, finding in their joint company a brief but comforting measure of familial stability rare for a soldier of his station.

The first detachment from Jake's unit left for New Guinea in early May, lugging their radio equipment first to Port Moresby and then to Dobodura, where they tried to sniff out the enemy spotters who were thought to be lurking in the jungle, spying on Allied plane movements. Reinforcements followed in July, assigned the additional mission of monitoring air traffic from Japanese bases farther up the coast and at Rabaul, the vast enemy fortress on nearby New Britain. Their information helped fighters from the Fifth Air Force find and shoot down several Japanese planes. By August, two other detachments were also operating, in the Australian outback, and in another part of New Guinea.

Jake remained at the base camp in Stafford, which was intercepting enemy messages at the rate of more than twenty thousand a month, but when each new batch of men departed he felt his own turn drawing nearer, and his time with Dot running out. With the future so hazy, he decided his best course was to clarify the present, so he wrote to his brother back home, granting him power of attorney and asking him to cash in the rug mill insurance policy. As soon as the $150 arrived, he bought a diamond ring, and slipped it into his pocket on an off-duty afternoon when he had a date with Dot. He was, as always, wearing his uniform; dungarees were acceptable in camp, but in public soldiers were supposed to look like gentlemen. They rode the train down to Brisbane for an early movie. After dinner, they were walking toward the Central Station when he steered her across the street into Anzac Square, a spare, green, block-sized park dedicated to the memory of the soldiers from the Australia and New Zealand Army Corps in the First World War, sixteen thousand of whom landed on the beach at Gallipoli and dug into the steep mountains for a gallant but futile battle from which only four thousand returned alive. At the head of the park rose an imposing stone memorial—a tall Doric colonnade set in a closed circle, roofless, open to the sky above. An eternal flame burned alone at its unadorned center. They sat on a bench, and Jake reached for the ring.

"You know what you're in for?" he asked, reminding her that they had not only a war to endure, but continents to bridge. Not many more places on the globe were farther from Brisbane than Freehold was, and once they got there—if they got there—they might not ever get back.

"I'll be willing to go," she said, and through her answer, for a moment, the future became more than the war.

Stu Bunton: Sicily

In the last, dead hours of a starlit summer night, the *Brooklyn* rocked silently in the dark and choppy Mediterranean, its engines stilled, its long guns bristling like spikes. The target—the island of Sicily, the southern tip of the Axis empire that had consumed the European continent—glowed several miles off in the northern distance, its craggy silhouette illuminated by the fires of a fight that had already begun. Panicky searchlights chased after the Allied planes that were dropping bombs and paratroopers onto the island. Tracer bullets from the antiaircraft guns scratched bright, lethal lines across the black sky. The ship's crew, warned against talking, smoking or wearing white caps, stood tense and quiet at the battle stations they had first rushed to when general quarters sounded two hours before midnight. Up in the cramped, sealed radio room where Stu

Bunton sat wearing headphones at a typewriter, the door to the outside was rigged to extinguish the lights inside whenever it was opened. The enemy knew by now that the invasion ships had arrived, but the Allies wanted the fleet to remain cloaked until the vast extent of it could be seen at dawn. Stretched invisibly and noiselessly in all directions around the *Brooklyn* was the greatest armada yet assembled in history—more than three thousand ships of every description.

Even through his headphones, Stu could hear when the enemy opened its defense. As the Allied landing craft streamed through the shallows, and the soldiers spilled onto the dark beach, the German Stukas and Messerschmitts ventured out over the sea, dive-bombing the fleet. A bomb from one exploded just one hundred feet off the *Brooklyn*'s port beam, shaking Stu's seat in the radio room, and soaking the gunners on deck with a geyser of spray that reached as high as the mainmast. The ship shuddered again when its own five-inch guns began shooting back at the buzzing planes. Several minutes later, at 4:41 A.M., came the command that Stu knew was coming, but that made him instinctively brace himself anyway.

"Commence firing when ready," the captain ordered, and the shells from the ship's biggest guns, the six-inchers, boomed out toward pre-arranged target number 43, an antiaircraft gun position near Castel Sant'-Angelo in the small seaport city of Licata.

With a great rumbling blast, the *Brooklyn* joined a fleetwide naval bombardment that erupted with an explosive fury to rival Mount Etna, the volcano looming beyond the horizon on the north side of the island. A noon light flashed across the dark sky—arcs, bursts, streaks, bolts, beams, blazes, pulses and the occasional steady lamp of an enemy parachute flare that floated through the maelstrom like a lone scout on patrol.

"How did I get into this?" Stu asked himself as the battle escalated around him.

Back in the sweet shop on Main Street he hadn't imagined the navy quite like this. He and his friends had been split up after induction, and he had hoped to be assigned to the navy's blimp division in Lakehurst, near enough to Freehold for frequent trips home. The navy sent him instead to radio school at Auburn University in Alabama. His expertise in radios consisted of knowing how to tune in WNEW on his nightstand Philco to catch his favorite big bands on the *Make-Believe Ballroom,* but he did know how to type, courtesy of Freehold High School. Like Jake

Errickson, he mastered Morse code, but his job was to receive messages from his own side. He sat at a typewriter, turning the pulses in his headphones into letters on paper. The messages arrived in five-letter groupings—ALRKJ, for instance—which were then given to an officer for decoding. The work seemed clean and safe, until now.

The sky began to gray by 5 A.M., and the ship's spotters could just barely discern the outline of a plane that was dropping bombs eight hundred yards off the port beam. The guns were trained on it, and on every other German plane that ventured within range.

"Enemy aircraft shot down," came a report at ten minutes past five. The *Brooklyn* had been firing at it, but several landing crafts had, too, and no one could say for sure who should claim the kill.

The planes kept coming, and by the time the sun rose behind the haze a few minutes before six, a destroyer and a minesweeper from the Allied fleet had already been sunk. The *Brooklyn* methodically pounded the targets it was assigned—more antiaircraft guns, coastal batteries, machine-gun positions, low planes stalking landing craft near the beaches, even some enemy troops marching toward Licata from the west—as it steamed back and forth along the coast with its team of destroyers. In the radio room, Stu's chair shuddered with each shot, while his headphones filled with messages as impenetrable to him as the Japanese transmissions were to Jake in Australia. Of more immediate interest were the TBS broadcasts, the talk-between-ships messages playing on the loudspeakers as the commanders relayed orders. From the crackly, clipped voices Stu could piece together a picture of what was happening outside.

"Cease firing on friendly aircraft."

"Are you in communication with fire control party on the beach?"

"Go in close and fire on twenty-seven, twenty-eight, and twenty-nine."

"From shore fire control, one spot short one thousand yards. Your fire very effective. Keep it up."

"Cover the advance of these LSTs with smoke. Close into the beach."

"Take under fire enemy coastal battery 063354. Rapid fire for two minutes."

"Do you have a plane up that can spot for me?"

Scanning the room as he stretched his neck, Stu caught a glimpse of his buddy Buford Osmond plugged in at one of the other radio positions, and wondered why he had ever listened to him. They had met at radio school in Alabama and become fast friends—the tall and quiet Northerner to whom the South was a mystery, and the slow-talking Georgian who knew just what to do with the grits they were served at breakfast each morning. Stu finished high enough in his class to earn a radioman third class rating, and a posting, along with Buford, on a communications ship docked in Norfolk. But a ship that didn't move wasn't going fast enough for Buford, who volunteered them for a warship. The next day they were on their way to the *Brooklyn,* a light cruiser, smaller and faster than a battleship, larger and stronger than a destroyer, that was headed for the Mediterranean.

Another explosion rattled Stu in his seat. He had never been this close to danger before, and it was peeling away his shield of youthful invulnerability. One of his sweet-shop buddies had already been wounded in the Atlantic, machine-gunned on a life raft by the U-boat that had torpedoed his ship, and Stu wondered if his own turn was coming. The more bombs and shells that fell out there, he knew, the more chances there were of him dying a teenager.

"With all these planes," he asked himself, trying to calculate the odds, and make them come up in his favor, "are they gonna get us?"

The *Brooklyn* was a stalwart of the prewar navy—a veteran of many Atlantic convoy crossings, as well as the 1939 opening of the World's Fair where Stu's father had first noticed the symptoms of the brain tumor that would soon kill him—and to an eighteen-year-old's eyes, its crew had looked forbiddingly old and salty. Stu and some of the other newcomers to the overcrowded ship were forced to sleep in hammocks on the mess deck. They had to wait for the movies to end at night before they could turn in, and they had to be up early in the morning to make way for breakfast. He knew he had reached the war when the ship passed Gibraltar, and he watched a destroyer board, evacuate and then sink a small fishing boat that had been spying on Allied traffic entering the Mediterranean. Docked in Oran, Algeria, he bought a banana soda, saw a USO show and waited to be told his role in the first major Allied assault on Hitler's Europe.

Had the Americans been fighting the war alone, Stu might never have seen the Mediterranean, a region regarded in Washington as strategically irrelevant. Roosevelt and his commanders believed the straightest road to Berlin started in northern France, and it was their preference to pour men and matériel into England in preparation for a massive cross-Channel invasion. But Stalin—whose nation was the only one among the Allies actually fighting the Germans on the ground—had wearied of waiting for action, and demanded a second front be opened, somewhere, anywhere, to relieve the pressure on his army, which was feeding bodies by the millions into the slaughter along the vast, insatiable eastern front. Without the Russians, the other Allies knew, the war might well be lost. So in November of 1942, as the navy was losing more ships to Japan off Guadalcanal, American and British troops landed in Morocco and Algiers. With Patton pushing from the west, and his British counterpart Montgomery driving from Alamein in the east, the Allies squeezed Rommel right off the African continent. The retreat in the south was echoed in the east, where the Russians had finally stopped the German advance in an epic battle at Stalingrad that was almost medieval in its cruelty and totality— house-to-house fighting through the broken streets, cavalrymen sweeping across the frozen steppes on Siberian ponies, starving Germans scavenging rubbled basements for rats. "The hinge of fate had turned," Churchill said later, and the Allies were now poised to attack what he liked to call "the soft underbelly of Europe."

When the *Brooklyn* had left port to join the armada assembling off the north coast of Africa, Stu and his crewmates were still wondering exactly where they were going. The Germans didn't know either, and had been further confused by an adroit bit of Allied spy craft: A corpse dressed as a British officer was set afloat off the Spanish coast carrying false papers that pointed toward Greece and Sardinia as the invasion targets, with Sicily as a diversionary feint. Steaming broadly toward the real target, passing just north of Malta, the invasion fleet met an enemy against which it had no weapons—a fierce Mediterranean mistral, a forty-mile-an-hour wind that whipped up the waves and left the troops down below vomiting from seasickness. One by one, the barrage balloons tethered to the ships, their wire cables a defense against low-flying planes, broke loose and sailed slowly away, as if from a child's careless grasp. But by midnight, as the ships parked off the south coast of Sicily, the wind had providentially died, and the sea calmed enough for a landing operation that went almost as smoothly as planned. Many of the Italian garrison troops—their loyalty to Hitler wilting in the face of an overwhelming opponent—surrendered without firing a shot.

Several hours into the invasion, the radio room speakers were crackling with instructions from the officers on the beach, calling in targets for the *Brooklyn*'s guns, when Stu heard a message that pushed him out into the booming din.

"American flag is flying on Castel Sant'Angelo."

Leaning on the railing outside the door, he looked across the water and through the smoke to see what seemed a huge flag rising over Licata, flying as bravely as it does in "The Star-Spangled Banner." The flag's message was stirring: Civilization had regained a small foothold in Europe. The battle, though, was not yet won. Stu returned to work, and to the foul sandwiches—filled with some kind of meat a few notches below bologna, "horse cock," they called it—that were substituted for real meals when the crew was called to general quarters. Scorched wadding from the guns littered the deck as the ship pounded the shore all through the day, 1,152 six-inch shells in all by the time Stu retired to his hammock.

Stu felt older when he awoke the next morning, and he resumed his post as the ship settled into the deadly routine of battle. The beaches were filling fast with soldiers, tanks, trucks, jeeps, artillery pieces and all the other things the Allies would need to push the Germans off Sicily, and Italy out of the war. When Stu stuck his head out the radio room door, his gaze was drawn beyond the flag toward sights that induced more fear than euphoria. German Panzers rumbled over the road above the beach, emblazoned with ominous black crosses he had previously seen only in newsreels, close enough to engage in a duel with the navy cruisers and destroyers.

The enemy was losing, but not yet surrendering. Late in the afternoon, Stu felt the deepest boom yet, a dense thud followed by a cascade of sharper, smaller echoes. Outside, he saw clouds and plumes and ribbons of smoke and fire as if from a city aflame. A flight of Heinkels and Focke-Wulfs had hit a nearby Liberty ship packed with ammunition, all of it now feeding on itself in an implosive chain reaction.

"Are we gonna go like that?" he wondered to himself.

The ammo ship's wreckage burned all through the evening, an inadvertent beacon endangering all the ships around it. Just past ten, Stu heard the buzzing drone of an approaching attack, a storm of enemy planes drawn by the fiery light. He braced for a hit as the bombs tattooed the water all around the *Brooklyn*. Three 500 pounders exploded just fifty yards away, spewing shrapnel that bit into the paint on the ship's side. Less than an hour later, some jittery Allied gunners, both on shore and on the ships, began shooting at some low-flying planes approaching the coast, thinking they were another wave of enemy torpedo bombers. The planes were, in fact, Allied transports carrying paratroopers, but the message hadn't gotten through clearly enough. Twenty-three American planes went down, and almost one hundred Americans died, some of them, chutes aflame, plummeting horribly, disbelievingly, into the sea.

By the fourth morning after the invasion, the danger seemed largely past, and the Brooklyn was groping blindly through a world that was murky and gray in every way—the predawn light, the thick bank of fog, the knowledge of what lurked in the waters ahead. But shortly after 5 A.M. came an explosion that revived and clarified everyone's fears—a mine, somewhere up ahead. Four minutes later came another, much nearer, explosion, a heavy thud back around the fantail. The ship had stumbled into a minefield, and been hit. The Brooklyn swung slowly left and tried to inch its way out, but soon hit a second mine, this time up between the bow and gun turret number two. Stu felt the ship lurch and heard some commotion outside. Some men had jumped overboard in panic.

The engines were stopped, and the ship sat dead in the water, safe from mines, Stu hoped, but a tempting target for any enemy planes that might dare venture out. He didn't feel the ship listing, and initial reports were that the damage wasn't critical, but the stillness made him nervous. The Brooklyn waited and watched until the fog finally lifted, and the minesweepers arrived to clear the field. By ten the ship was moving, to Stu's relief, creeping into a safe patch of sea, where it stopped again and sent divers down to inspect the damage; by three it was steaming toward Algiers to get patched up enough to make the long trip back to America for more lasting repairs. It was there in port, as the ship prepared to cross the ocean where U-boats still prowled with lethal efficiency, that Stu Bunton's first birthday away from home passed without any celebration, without much notice at all from him, in fact, because it already seemed so disconnected, so out of time, with what his life had become. He had finally turned nineteen years old.

3.

The Air Corps in Europe, 1943–1944

Bill Lopatin

The plane was nearing the Channel when Bill Lopatin stood up from his small radio desk behind the cockpit, glanced once more out his porthole window at the peaceful summer fields of an English afternoon twelve thousand feet below, and started the short walk back to his machine guns. The five other crew members were already at their stations—the pilot and copilot at the helm, the bombardier, the turret gunner and the tail gunner all squeezed into their Plexiglas cocoons as naked as display windows. Around them in every direction were thirty-three other B-26 Marauders, arrayed in a tight box formation. At this altitude the light was sharp and frozen, carrying all of the sun's glare but none of its warmth. Bill maneuvered along the narrow catwalk through the bomb bay with the same agility that had kept him aloft on the roof beams of the houses he built with his father. Shouldering close on either side of him, hanging expectantly in their racks, were the eight 300-pound bombs scheduled for delivery on a Nazi airdrome in occupied France. He crouched low, trying to work delicately with hands made clumsy by three layers of gloves—silk, chamois and finally a fur-lined gunner's mitten—that imprisoned all but the thumb and trigger finger. He armed the bombs by easing out a small cotter pin from the fuse in each of their noses, then slipped the pins into the pocket of his lucky brown leather flight jacket, hoping to pass them out later to his crewmates as souvenirs of their first mission together over enemy territory. Reaching the waist of the plane, almost breathless from the exertion at this oxygen-starved height, he knelt and slid open the twin Plexiglas windows, pointing the barrels of his two .50-caliber guns out into an empty sky that soon would fill with war.

"Test your guns," Bill heard the pilot say when he plugged in his headset, and he fired several rounds over the Channel, which even in August looked like a cold place to ditch.

Bill scanned for danger in the distance, looking down on the world from an unfamiliar height. The twin-engine B-26 was the army's first three-hundred-mile-per-hour bomber, meant to fly low and hit hard, and Bill was accustomed to training flights where the ground rushed by close below, and the wings tipped up to clear the occasional tree. Combat, however, had forced the medium bombers into a quick retreat. Bill's outfit, the 322nd Bombardment Group, was the first B-26 unit deployed in the European theater of operations, and on only its second mission—in May of 1943, while Bill was on his way across the Atlantic—it lost every plane it sent out to the target. Eleven Marauders were dispatched to attack power stations at Ijmuiden and Haarlem in Holland; one turned back with electrical problems; the other ten, skimming low over the waiting Nazis, were shredded by flak and fighters. Two survivors paddled five days and seventy miles across the North Sea in a tiny life raft before a British destroyer noticed a white T-shirt waving from the end of an oar. The fifty-eight other airmen were either dead or prisoners in German camps.

Bill had arrived at a base that was enveloped in what was, even for wartime, an uncommonly dense pall of gloom and uncertainty. He knew his assignment was dangerous—the colonel who had sent the crews off from the States had choked up when he told them how few might return—but this was suicide. Every plane shot down, not a single one returned: The blunt force of that fact stuck in his head like a hammer blow. Did the same fate await his first mission? But the Marauders were grounded from combat after his arrival, confined to training flights for two months, until a new strategy emerged: Fly them at medium altitudes, between ten thousand and twelve thousand feet, the upper limit for flying without oxygen and about half as high as the heavy B-17s and B-24s that were bombing Germany; and send them out to cripple the Nazi airfields that dotted Northern Europe, like the Beaumont-le-Roger fighter base in Normandy where Bill's plane was headed today, his first time in enemy skies.

The life of an airman in England in 1943 was, as he was quickly learning, the most schizophrenic the war had to offer. The country was filling quickly with tank drivers and truck mechanics, riflemen and cooks, stevedores and file clerks, closing in on half a million already and set to more than triple again before the arrival of the big day they were all preparing for, the impending invasion of France; but the airmen were the only ones among them who were regularly exchanging fire with the enemy, flying out on missions that might end with a plunge toward death or imprisonment on foreign soil. The Red Army was fighting toward Berlin from the east—at the recent Battle of Kursk in Russia, 4 million men and thirteen thousand armored vehicles had faced each other in the largest tank battle of the war—and the Americans and British were fighting across Sicily toward the Italian mainland. From the west, though, the only attacks came from the air—squadrons of planes dropping bombs on cities, factories, dams and other strategic targets, trying to weaken the enemy before the invasion. Just two weeks earlier, Allied bombing raids had sparked a firestorm in Hamburg that killed more than forty thousand civilians and reduced half the city to rubble.

Bill watched from his cold, bright perch as the green meadows of France came into view across the horizon. The European continent was just rising from war the last time he saw it—as a young boy traveling a hard road from Russia to America with his family—and now it was preparing to greet his return with a barrage of live fire. He knelt on the thin skin of aluminum that was his only shield against harm, weighed down by the thought of impending battle. The mission had been called on such short notice that he had no chance to distinguish it in his mind from all the training flights of the last year. The target orders arrived at base headquarters just after lunch, which meant a frantic rush to get the planes up and back before dark, when the Americans, who bombed by day, yielded to the night-flying British. The crews were immediately summoned to a briefing so hastily prepared that no good target map was available to show them, and no time was left to dispatch a plane to a nearby base to retrieve one. They were told the route, the weather, the number of antiaircraft guns and fighters they might meet and what little else was known about a target no Marauder had bombed before. Before they could worry too much about what they were about to do, they were in their planes, sprinting down the runway thirty seconds apart. Each plane climbed steeply up to the assembly point where they gathered into a wing-to-wing gang that sped toward France.

The mission route lay arrow straight across the briefing map, but the planes traveled a crooked path through the sky, banking up and down, veering right and left, moving together with the darting symmetry of a school of fish, never flying straight for more than the twenty seconds the Germans needed to fix them in sight. The speed and maneuverability that allowed a Marauder to take such effective evasive action had also earned it a pair of less flattering nicknames: "The Flying Prostitute," because it had a beautiful body, but a short wingspan that provided, in the crews' well-worn phrase, "no visible means of support"; and "The Widow Maker," because of an accident rate high enough to attract the attention of a Senate investigating committee led by Harry Truman. It was, the pilots knew, the kind of hot plane that demanded takeoffs and landings of nerve-jarring speed, and that quickly punished any hesitation or error in handling. Modifications in design and training had eventually made the Marauder more lethal to the enemy than to its own crews, but its reputation endured, and it still occasionally claimed the unlucky and the unwary: Just two days earlier Bill had watched four squadron mates die when their plane swayed and dived just after takeoff, crashing into a tree.

As the small French town of Montfort-sur-Risle passed below them, the planes approached the mission's most dangerous moment—the initial point, where they would level off and, for thirty endless seconds or more, fly to the target along a course as fixed and unswerving as a railroad track, a tactic that provided their bombs a steady platform to fall from, and the German guns an easier target to shoot at.

"Bandit climbing at five o'clock low," the turret gunner announced from his rotating bubble just above Bill's head, warning of the enemy fighter approaching. All the crew tensed their fingers on their triggers.

Bill's plane was near the rear of the formation, the third plane in the second flight of the second box, and it was the first to glimpse the enemy, a yellow-nosed Focke-Wulf 190 with black crosses on its wings, rising to nip at the tail of the attackers. Bill squinted anxiously out his window, but the enemy fighter was almost directly behind now, at an angle that blocked his view. What he did see, though, rocketing toward him from below, were what the veteran airmen had warned him were an even greater peril—the shells from the antiaircraft gunners on the ground. Evil black clouds appeared suddenly in the clear, blue sky when a shell exploded, flinging hot shards of metal in random, deadly patterns against which he had no defense. When an enemy plane attacked, the veterans had said, you at least had a chance to fight back with your own guns; but when you flew through a field of flak all you could do was sit tight and hope none of it hit you.

"There go the Spits," said the turret gunner, the only crew member who could see the dogfight unfolding half a mile behind. Six British Spitfires, the fighter escorts that had met the Marauders over Beachy Head on the southern coast of England, sped toward the German fighter, guns flashing, driving it away from the bombers. Trapped and wounded, the Nazi plane was engulfed with smoke from its own fire, then sank at an angle that was no longer flight.

"They blew him clean out of the sky," the turret man reported.

"There's another coming in at five o'clock low," interrupted the tail gunner.

Bill swung his gun in the direction of the warning and faced there, for the first time in his life, someone who was trying to kill him. The Focke-Wulf climbed out of the pastoral landscape at a menacing pace, attacking at an angle Bill's gun couldn't reach. Pinpricks of flame appeared as the German squeezed off two or three gun bursts and closed within four hundred yards. The cramped rear of the Marauder echoed with the sputtering racket of the fifty rounds the tail gunner fired in return. Both shooters missed, and the Focke-Wulf slid to seven o'clock, rolled onto its back and, using its armor-toughened belly as a shield, sailed back down out of sight.

As he searched for traces of the last attacker, or hints of the next, Bill felt his own plane settle into its bomb run, a steady, deliberate motion that clashed with his instinctive urge to speed up in the presence of danger. He never knew before how slow 220 miles per hour could seem. More Focke-Wulfs, joined by some Messerschmitt 109s—a dozen or so in all it seemed—had swarmed up to defend the airdrome, striking mostly at the other side of the formation, out of Bill's sight. His attention was drawn instead to the columns of smoke rising from the fields and roads and woods ahead, from almost everywhere, in fact, except the base itself. The first box of Marauders had missed the target, several of them overshooting it so far that they were now carrying their bombs to what they thought—what they hoped—was another airfield a few miles distant.

"Bombardier, ready to drop bombs," the pilot said.

The bombs dropped from the plane's belly with what seemed to Bill a lightness that belied their weight, floating down through the sunny, cloudless sky. He counted only four bombs from his plane; the other four, he surmised, must have gotten hung up on the bomb rack. The second box of Marauders, like the first, also wasted too many bombs on fields and woods, but it did manage to place some on the airdrome, even scoring a direct hit on a small château that looked as if it might have been commandeered by the Germans as an officers' billet. Wherever a bomb hit, whatever had been there the instant before was transformed into a column of smoke and ash and dust. If all the bombs had hit their intended targets, the airdrome would be invisible now, shrouded by a single, billowing canopy, but as the Marauders made a hard right turn back toward England, their payloads delivered, Bill saw too much earth. The isolated charcoal-gray pillars marked the kind of bomb dispersal pattern that would earn only a "fair" rating back at base.

Ten miles and several villages past the target, four more German fighters came up to challenge the bombers, firing a few farewell shots before the Spits ran them down. Bill's parting vision of combat came thirteen minutes after his first—two flak bursts just one hundred feet below the left side of the plane, and nine thousand feet above the town of Lisieux. The Channel beckoned the Marauders to safety ahead, and once it was under their wings again they counted their ranks to find that their brief visit to France had cost them no planes and no men. They added up everybody's claimed hits, too, and speculated that the Germans had lost nine fighters, a total that reflected bravado and hope more than reality. Bill clambered back through the bomb bay, stopping to fish four firing pins from his jacket pocket and return them to the stranded bombs that hadn't dropped. At his radio desk again, he watched gratefully as England filled his window—the southern coast and Portsmouth first, then brave, battered London, and finally the rolling green farmland of East Anglia, where the potato fields that bloomed beside the airfield they descended upon made his new home feel something like the old.

The harsh geometry of Andrews Field—the concrete runway slashes where the bombers of the 322nd landed, the hardstand loops where they parked—was part of a pattern freshly stamped on the lush English countryside by the army engineers who were opening new bases almost weekly to accommodate the onslaught of American planes. It welcomed Bill back with an austere comfort that, to eyes altered by combat, now looked like luxury. He debriefed with the interrogators, accepted coffee and a doughnut from the Red Cross girls, lined up for dinner in the mess hall—he was going to have to get used to mutton, because there wasn't much beef—and retired to the Nissen hut he shared with thirteen other airmen. The oblong, cylindrical arc of corrugated steel looked like a half-buried drainage pipe, and sheltered, however draftily, a narrow cot where he could sleep with little fear of anyone shooting at him.

Bonded by battle, the airmen tended to keep the same company on the ground as they did in the sky, traveling together to the village pub, to the local Red Cross dances, and to London on the forty-eight-hour passes they had every other weekend. They removed the stiffening bands from their caps, to let the crowns flop rakishly down, and their wings shone on their chests. They already knew what the rest of their comrades would soon learn—how wide and terrible a gulf had opened between what the world once was and what it had become; and how costly, and necessary, it would be to close it.

The war had sharpened in many Americans an appreciation of their nation's blessings that had been dulled by the Depression, and Bill felt it with a special acuity. He had an immigrant's abiding patriotism, the kind that never forgot how different the new country was from the old, how much was permitted here that had been denied there. His family had not only survived but had prospered in America, and he was grateful for both the haven it provided and the opportunity it offered. A debt was owed, and his service was a step toward repaying it. The other five members of his flight crew were serving the country of their birth; he was serving the country of his choice. They all knew equally well what they were fighting for, but he had a better idea of what they were fighting against.

"One has to be far from home to be able to appreciate the true meaning of the terms 'home' and 'my hometown' and to realize how much one misses them and how worthwhile they are to defend," he had written recently in a letter to the *Freehold Transcript*. "Multiply our little Freehold by the thousands of cities, towns and farm communities and it results in the United States—'home' to all of us."

Bill had left Freehold for boot camp in the spring of 1942, the same week his father built some storage closets for the office the Red Cross was setting up in the American Legion post on Main Street. "Please consider this bill paid," Sam Lopatin wrote on the invoice, "and enter this amount to our credit as a contribution."

Bill had expected that someone with building skills like his own would be assigned to the Corps of Engineers, but the army put him in the Air Corps instead and sent him to radio school. His knowledge of aviation was limited to a single half-hour ride in a barnstormer over Freehold, a trip of sufficient interest that he then volunteered for flight

duty—the only way to get on a plane at the time—and went off to gun-
nery school. If he was going to be in the Air Corps, he reasoned, he might
as well be in the air. His older brother, Sol, was in the Air Corps, too, on
the ground overseas somewhere, but Bill didn't know at what base, or
even what hemisphere, until he got overseas himself. Because the B-26s
couldn't hold enough fuel to fly directly from America to Europe, they
took a circuitous route, from the Caribbean to South America to North
Africa, crossing the Atlantic at its narrowest point. When Bill's plane
landed in Morocco, he climbed down through the nose wheel well and
straightened up to find an old friend from Freehold standing in front of
him. Frank Gibson was a navy lieutenant now, and he had a stack of
hometown newspapers in his tent, one of which revealed that Sol was a
headquarters clerk with a B-17 heavy bomber group in England. On his
first weekend pass after reaching England, Bill tracked his brother to a
base about eighty miles away from his own.

"I walked in on him (surprise) early this morning as he was coming
off duty," Bill wrote home about their first meeting in fourteen months.
Sol was asleep after a long overnight shift, still in his uniform—the first
time Bill had seen him wearing one. "He was up all night and had dozed
off in a chair in the Red Cross lounge. Gosh, it looked good to see him
snoozing in a chair on a Sunday. Just like old times . . ."

Through the Teletype reports that crossed his desk, an anxious Sol
monitored Bill's missions, and worried—as he watched the airmen from
his own outfit disappear at an alarming rate—about his brother's fate.
Despite the lack of long-range fighter escorts, and the cautionary lesson
of the British, whose heavy losses had prompted a switch to nighttime
saturation bombing of German cities, the Americans were sticking res-
olutely to a plan for which they were already paying a high price: daylight
precision bombing of factories, oil depots, airfields and other strategic
targets in Germany. Too many of the bombers that flew into the dense
clouds of flak and fighters over Germany didn't fly out again. In a single
week in October, the Americans lost 148 heavy bombers and crews, a casualty rate that would, if unchecked, soon leave the Air Corps with nothing but ground forces; of the 291 planes sent out on the Thursday of
Black Week, as it came to be known, only 30 came back undamaged. The
bombing campaign that some strategists believed might preclude the
need for a land invasion seemed now as if it might itself become another
victim of the war it was supposed to end.

On the front where Bill fought, though, the victories outnumbered the losses. "The Marauder has found its place in the sun," General Hap Arnold, the four-star chief of the Air Corps, told the airmen from Bill's group at a September gathering at Wing Headquarters. Lifted from the low level of that fatal early raid over Holland, the B-26s were soaring high and deadly over their targets—shipyards, power plants, chemical works, railroad marshaling yards and, most importantly, the scores of Nazi airbases that webbed the occupied triangle from Cherbourg to Paris to Amsterdam.

Bill's crewmates and their plane—christened *We Dood It* by the pilot, after Red Skelton's signature phrase—returned intact from their next ten missions, each one of which deepened a bond already deeper than anything they had ever known outside their own families. Theirs was an improbable marriage—a logger from Oregon, a shoe salesman from Detroit, high school boys from Arkansas, Louisiana and Kentucky, and a builder from Freehold, a mixture fashioned by chance and fate, and mirrored in other planes and ships and rifle companies all over the war. At thirty-one, Bill was the oldest by more than half a decade, and the only Jew—the first Jew, in fact, that a couple of the men had ever met. Religion was no barrier in the plane, though; the only faith that mattered was the faith each man placed in his crewmates. What united them was the same force that had united Bill's family on its journey to America—the understanding that each one's life depended entirely on the others. When a mission was called on Yom Kippur, Bill didn't hesitate. He chose to observe the holiest day of the Jewish year by fulfilling what he believed was his supreme obligation at the moment: his duty to his crew. He knew that if anything happened to them up in the air while he was down on the ground praying, a lifetime of atonement in all the Yom Kippurs ahead would not erase his guilt.

In England, Bill's life constantly reminded him of something it had shielded him from in America: the fearful knowledge of just how quickly it could end. Before each mission, he was issued, like all the other airmen, a .45-caliber pistol, a small stash of escape money and a few lessons on how best to pass through occupied territory: Clench your cigarette in your teeth like a peasant, don't shave every day, and leave your gun with the Resistance if they manage to get you out. A copilot from the 322nd who had made that shadowy journey—bailing out of a flak-damaged Marauder on a mission to Rouen in August, then slipping slowly and secretly back to safety through the Underground—returned to the base two months later and offered the assembled crewmen a ground-level account of a world they hoped to see only from above. Whenever a wing mate went down in combat, Bill tried not to notice the orderly who came into the hut to remove the lost man's belongings; and he then tried not to get too close to the replacement flier who soon appeared in the empty cot. It was enough, he knew, to worry about his own crewmates; he couldn't afford to worry about everyone. His own stores of sympathy and grief were limited, and had to be husbanded against a future of uncertain sorrows. Returning from the occasional milk run, an easy mission with little opposition, Bill would see the gentle cloudscape whispering toward him from England, the pink edges backlit by the setting sun, and be filled for a moment with a peace like home; but any lingering tranquillity would quickly be obliterated the next time out, when he saw instead a shell from a Nazi .88 clip the wing of a nearby plane, sending it into a fatal spin. On a bleak day in November, when the Teletypes clattered with news of several lost or damaged Marauders, Bill received a telegram from his brother.

"Am worried," Sol wired. "Reply immediately."

Just back from a flak-heavy visit to an Amsterdam airdrome, Bill confirmed one more safe return—news he was happy to celebrate, but loathe to analyze. As their missions mounted, he and his crewmates often asked themselves the central question of the war—why did he die, while I live?—but rarely outside the private silence of their own minds: To ask it aloud, they feared, might cause it to be answered by a Nazi gun. Some men credited God for their survival, but the God of Bill's beliefs didn't have time to sort through the mass of humanity, assigning individual fates. Good men died and bad men lived, Bill knew, and there was no discernible logic to it. Life was, as far as he could see, without design or reason. Some combination of chance and skill would determine whether he lived or died. To urge luck to his side, though, he did indulge in some pet superstitions. Whenever he climbed into the plane for a mission, he made sure the "worry bird" was there, a fuzzy stuffed animal that someone in the crew had brought back from a London weekend. He didn't dare fly without his lucky leather jacket. And when they were called for their thirteenth mission, he joined the rest of the crew in euphemistically dubbing it mission 12A.

"The target is a construction site approximately two miles southwest of Martinvast and five and a half miles southwest of Cherbourg," the

briefing officer told the assembled crews that November morning, pointing toward an enlarged aerial photograph that depicted a scene of no obvious interest or logic—some excavated gashes in the earth, surrounded
by concrete buildings and railroad tracks. "Activity at the site started
toward the end of July, and in general appearance it's similar to last week's
target near Calais."

Reconnaissance flights and Resistance spies first began noticing this
unusual construction activity back in the summer, alerting the Allies to a
new Nazi tactic whose full and awful dimensions were only now becoming clear. The long pits were apparently being dug as launch sites for some
new kind of pilotless flying bomb—the "rocket guns" that German scientists were developing on the Baltic island of Peenemünde, an August target of the heavy bombers. The sites were clustered in Pas-de-Calais, where
the trenches pointed like stilettos toward London, and on the Cherbourg
Peninsula, where they were aimed toward Bristol, and they threatened a
return to the dark time of the Blitz, when terror rained randomly on the
civilians of Britain before the Germans finally withdrew most of their
bombers to the Russian front. The Marauder crews were told little about
the new targets, but they sensed much from the urgent secrecy of the
briefings.

"Practically from the time you cross the coast on the way in, until you
cross the coast on your way out," the briefing officer continued, tracing
the route across the map with his pointer, bisecting the Cherbourg Peninsula as if he were slicing off a wart, "there will be considerable concentration of flak to your right. It is reasonable to assume that the enemy has
anticipated further attacks on targets of this kind and has strengthened
his defenses, possibly by moving in railway flak."

Even without any new rail-mounted artillery, the Nazis had a fear-
some welcome awaiting the Marauders—thirty heavy guns near the target, forty-four at Cherbourg, twenty on the Cap de la Hague peninsula,
twenty-four on Alderney island, plus whatever was on the ships off the
coast and at the land positions not charted yet. Sixty Focke-Wulfs and
Messerschmitts were reported lurking in the neighborhood, too, but they
worried Bill less than the ground guns did. He had seen the holes that flak
cut in planes, and in men; he preferred an enemy he could shoot back at.
Sitting at his radio desk awaiting takeoff, Bill looked at the day's codes,
printed on thin paper it was his duty to swallow if he were forced to ditch,
and then at his watch. It was eleven in the morning of November 11 ex-

actly twenty-five years to the minute since the guns of the Great War fell silent, and the Armistice was signed in a railroad car in a forest clearing barely two hundred miles from today's target.

"Here come the Spits," Bill heard the pilot announce at noon, as they rendezvoused with their fighter escorts over the Channel just off Portsmouth.

The weather that had seemed so accommodating at the base—revealing fully half the sky, more blue than they had seen in several soupy, grounded weeks—was worsening the farther they flew from home. A tattered blanket of clouds spread wide below them all the way to the horizon, concealing all but some scattered patches of choppy water, and perhaps, they feared, their landfalls and target, too. As they reached France, though, the clouds began to open. Through the breaks came views of a cluster of barrage balloons floating up like plump black sausages, and the tiny isles of St. Marcouf sprinkled across the bay, their signpost for a hard right turn toward Martinvast. At his waist gun position, Bill scooped up a handful of the thin aluminum strips that filled a box beside him and tossed them from his window, a sparkling tinsel rain meant to confuse the German radars with false readings. The Spits spied some fighters loitering in the distance, but none rose to challenge the bombers.

"There it is," the pilot announced soon after they crossed the French coastline. "Hold on now."

A thick field of flak was blooming in the sky ahead, sooty smoke puffs that looked as if the clouds themselves had been blackened and shredded by the shells screaming up from below. The first two boxes of Marauders, eighteen strong apiece and six minutes ahead, had already passed over the gunners of Cherbourg, giving the enemy a chance to sharpen their aim, and to fix the trailing formation in their sights. As Bill's plane straightened course at the initial point, he tightened his grip on his machine gun and wished for an enemy he could see. Flak bursts speckled the view out both his windows. One shell exploded near enough to show him the red flame in its heart. He heard the hot shards of metal rattle like stones against a fuselage he knew a screwdriver could pierce if pressed hard enough. He tried to will the target to appear in the patchy landscape below, and tried not to feel like the bull's-eye on the dartboard in the pub he favored back in England. The launch site they were seeking was smaller than their usual targets, just a few hundred yards square, but through the drifting clouds they finally spotted a distinctive pattern of earthworks that matched the briefing photos. Bill was watching the fat pair of two thousand pounders plummet earthward when he felt an unexpected nudge on his shoulder. He turned and found there the tapping foot of the turret gunner who was stationed in the bubble above, and he quickly scrambled around to see what had happened. Peering up into the sunny blue hole, he saw a face covered with red.

"I'm hit, Pat," Clyde Duke told him. Bill's crewmates had turned his last name into a nickname that no one else in the world knew him by.

He left his guns and squeezed up beside Duke. Some flak had shattered the Plexiglas, whipping sharp fragments and sprung wires around the small, trapped space, lashing Duke's face and eyes. Bill eased Duke down from the turret dome, leaned him gently against the bulkhead and called the news up front. When he swabbed the blood away, he saw that the damage was less than it seemed—a rare and blessed discovery in war.

The plane had reached the French coast now, and the flak was thudding again after a brief lull, a fierce farewell from the gunners of Cap de la Hague and Alderney island below. Bill knew that the loss of Duke's guns, free to spin and shoot at an enemy attacking from anywhere above, left a larger chink in the plane's armor than the loss of his own, so he climbed back up into the turret and surveyed the war from a new angle—a wide-lens cirrus panorama, spidered in spots by the cracked glass, and blotted by the persistent storm of flak. He could no longer see how much earth was below them, only how much sky was above. But when he tried to rotate the turret, it wouldn't move; the flak had cut the wires.

"It's not working," Bill told Duke as he slipped back down. "I'm going back to the waist."

Looking down through the clouds again at the fading French coast, Bill saw that the Marauders had finally outrun the ground gunners. He breathed his relief out deeply, then noticed something he must have missed in his rush back to position—to his left, just a hair below eye level, a small slice of daylight in a place that should have been dark. It was a flak hole, he saw, the mark left by a speeding shell fragment that had ripped through the aluminum skin while he was gone. Turning quickly from the entrance wound, projecting the flak's whizzing, burning route through the cabin, he found the exit wound in the same spot on the opposite side. He looked back and forth a few times, imagining what would have happened had he been sitting there when it hit.

"Look at this," he called to Duke, tracing the trajectory with one hand as the other instinctively, protectively, clasped his neck. "It would have taken my head right off."

By what margin—by how many minutes, how many seconds even—had the flak missed him, he wondered? What would his fate have been had Duke not tapped him on the shoulder? He had never been in the company of his own death before, and he felt the nearness of eternity crowding the present out, untethering him from the moment and setting him briefly adrift outside time and space. He looked out his window and saw a picture of the afterlife—a floor of clouds concealing all evidence of the continued existence of the earth below. To anchor himself back in his own body, he inventoried the scene around him—the round vents polka-dotting the steel barrel of his machine gun, the dark blood clotting on Duke's face, the fur peeking from the edge of his mitten, the hatch leading to the bomb bay, the cathedral light spilling down through the turret opening, and then, creeping patchily toward him through the breaking clouds, England, beautiful England, England in all its sodden, gray glory, proof that the world was still there, and that he was still part of it.

A voice came through his headset. "Pat, stay back there and send Duke forward for landing," the pilot told him.

Duke groped through the bomb bay to Bill's seat at the radio desk. Bill slid his window shut and noticed the other flak holes in the fuselage now, flecks of light pricking the shadows, scores of them, it seemed. The plane descended, but barely slowed as it neared the base. Bill longed for his usual seat in the front as he braced to meet the ground in an uncomfortable, unsecured, unfamiliar position.

"Hang on, we've only got one wheel," the pilot warned. The flak had damaged the hydraulic lines to the landing gear, too.

Skimming low over the fields and past the control tower, the plane was still doing 105 mph when it touched crookedly down, and Bill, bouncing roughly in the rear, felt the runway lodge in his spine. The pilot tried to wrestle it straight, but it veered off the tarmac and bumped to a stop in the bordering field.

"Oh, my aching back," Bill said, using a phrase the American GIs repeated so often, on so many different occasions, that the British initially wondered if lumbar weakness was some kind of national affliction. This time, though, Bill meant it literally, as a genuine expression of pain, not as a figurative expression of exasperation. Gingerly, he eased himself down through the nose wheel well to join the rest of the crew in counting flak holes. They got to 120 before they gave up. Their plane had been shot up the most on a day when no planes had been shot down.

"Looks like we've got our first Purple Heart," said Malcolm Enlow, the engineer and Bill's best friend in the crew, gesturing toward Clyde, who was being helped into the ambulance that had raced to meet them. The rest of the crew climbed into the jeeps that would take them to interrogation. They all had Air Medals already, and they were halfway toward the Distinguished Flying Crosses they would get if they completed twenty-five missions, but no one had been wounded yet.

"He's welcome to it," Bill said, knowing well that survival was its own reward.

Jimmy Higgins

The sergeant bumped across the base in a jeep stenciled with the legend PILOTED BY HIGGINS and came to a landing outside the Nissen hut where he reported promptly at eight each morning to man his battle station. The early light pierced the accumulated shadows inside, slanting through the window flaps that were cut into the hut's curving side like a row of hooded, beady eyes. Shucking his topcoat, Jimmy Higgins switched on his lamp and sat down at the desk that provided him a clear but distant view of the war. Maps, charts and sheaves of papers surrounded him on all sides, the raw material from which he and his colleagues—the five other enlisted men and three officers of the intelligence section of the 391st Bomb Group, another B-26 outfit stationed just a few miles from Bill Lopatin's 322nd—fashioned their daily portrait of the battlefield. Germany lurked in one file cabinet, France in another, and Holland and Belgium and all the other captive nations where the enemy was now, and the Allies planned to go soon.

The major strode sharply into the hut—S-2, they called it—carrying the field order that had earlier been Teletyped to the 391st's commanding officer from Ninth Bomber Command. "Here's where we're going today—Ijmuiden," he said. "What do you have on it?"

Jimmy and the other S-2 men set to work. They unfolded small site maps, and consulted the large theater maps that lined the walls, bristling with pins and pennants that marked the enemy's flak positions and airdromes with a deceptively placid rationality. They traced the route from

England to Ijmuiden, and added up all the guns and planes they knew about along the way capable of hitting a B-26. They collected all the most recent reconnaissance photos of the target, and studied the rows of squat, blocky structures rising from the Dutch coastline—the concrete-roofed, steel-doored sheds the Germans were building to shelter E-boats and R-boats, the small, swift enemy torpedo craft that darted through the North Sea shielding their own ships and attacking the Allies. Once the pens were finished, the harbor at Ijmuiden would be able to service and protect almost twice as many E-boats as before, strengthening the German defenses against the invasion everyone on both sides of the Channel knew was coming.

All eight B-26 groups were sending planes on today's raid, 344 in all, to avenge a loss many of the newly arrived crews knew only as a barracks scare tale—the two inaugural low-level Marauder attacks the previous May on the power plant at Ijmuiden, the first unsuccessful, the second disastrous. "Aside from the purely tactical nature of the target, there is another consideration that makes this target an important one," the field order for the day, March 26, 1944, reminded those who knew, and instructed those who didn't. "Ten aircraft crossed the enemy coast. None came back. German radio propaganda made much of these two unsuccessful attacks. There is an old score to settle."

Old score though it was to the veterans, Ijmuiden was virgin ground to Jimmy, another new page for the mental atlas he had been compiling so quickly and voluminously in the year and a half since the war sprung him from the narrow borders of his former life. After he had left Freehold for Fort Dix, the army put him in the Air Corps and shipped him a little farther south—to Atlantic City, where the summer hotels were standing duty as barracks, and raw boot-camp recruits had taken the place of promenading vacationers. It was his first visit to the grand seaside resort, and he spent it doing jumping jacks on the beach, shooting targets set in the surf, crawling through sand that worked its way into his itchy woolen underwear, and drilling up and down the boardwalk chanting, "These GI boots will march through Germany." He bunked on the sixteenth floor of the Ritz-Carlton with Bill Lopatin's older brother, Sol, who roused him at reveille each dawn. At night they tacked blankets over the window, under orders of a shoreline blackout meant to hinder the U-boats still prowling the coastal waters. He finally left New Jersey on Thanksgiving Day in 1942, swept up in the vast tide of servicemen that was washing back and forth across the continent, packed onto one of the troop trains that moved from base to base, port to port, city to city, in a surge of mobility unprecedented in American history. He was riding—for the first time ever, like most of his traveling companions—as far as the whistle went.

Jimmy's train stopped in Colorado, where he saw his first mountains, and the thin air caught him short of breath. After finishing clerks' school there—it would have been too logical for the army to assign an apprentice undertaker to graves registration—he joined the newly formed 391st and spent the next year touring a string of the scrubby, windblown air bases that had been freshly bulldozed all across the South. He went from Florida to South Carolina to Kentucky and then finally to New York, where, on January 17, 1944, just about the time that Bill Lopatin was earning his Distinguished Flying Cross, he boarded the *Ile de France,* an ocean liner turned troop ship, for a rough, frigid dash across the North Atlantic. The ship docked in Scotland, at what appeared to him the bleakest end of the earth. But when a train finally deposited the group near their new base in Matching Green, amid the dormant winter potato fields of the pastoral Essex countryside, it looked more like home than anything Jimmy had seen since leaving.

As near to the war as he was now, Jimmy saw fewer dead bodies and worked more regular hours than he had in his civilian job. His duties were clean and predictable, well-suited to his orderly cast of mind, and the allotment the government sent home from his pay each month was more help to his mother than he could have provided from his apprentice's salary. Most mornings, as the mission clock began ticking, he took a bird's-eye tour of the continent, poring over maps and photos of Cambrai, Creil, Le Grismont, Malines and other places rendered bombworthy by the presence of Nazis. Most afternoons, as the clock ran down, he drifted outside to join the basewide ritual of counting the planes as they appeared in the distance, and praying that the number returning matched the number that left. Twice so far, he had come up one plane short, and six times he had seen the red flare that signaled wounded men on board. In the evenings, he caught the latest movie at the base's makeshift theater, or pedaled his army-issue bicycle to the village pub (the jeep was restricted to official duty), or danced with the English girls at the local dance hall, or, if the mess hall was particularly unappetizing, waited hungrily for the arrival of the fish-and-chips truck, where a late snack came wrapped in a greasy newspaper cone. Every second Saturday morning, freed by a weekend pass, he rode a GI truck twenty-six miles southwest to London, checked into the Regents Palace Hotel, and squeezed through the throngs of American soldiers—one million and counting in Great Britain already—in nearby Piccadilly Square. He visited the tombs of kings past at Westminster Abbey, the home of the king present at Buckingham Palace, and wandered wide-eyed through a city whose millennial history made Freehold's colonial roots look shallow, and whose blocks of blackened rubble constantly reminded him that he was a soldier, not a tourist.

The skies above the base at Matching Green thrummed day and night with the insect drone of Allied planes. The Marauders of Jimmy's group had flown their first mission barely three weeks after arriving, with the Union Jack of the former tenants still flapping over the field—attacking the same target Bill Lopatin had on his first mission six months earlier, the Beaumont le Roger airdrome in France. Less than a week later, they were assigned a part in the largest air operation the Americans had yet mounted—"Big Week," which dispatched the heavy bombers of the Eighth Air Force to pummel aircraft factories in Germany, and sent the medium bombers of the Ninth Air Force to strike airfields in Holland and rocket-launching sites in France. After one more week a commendation came over the Teletype.

"Your bombing of Amiens Marshalling Yard on afternoon 2 March was the best done by any group of IX Bomber Command," the commanding general wrote. "In view of your short experience in this theater this is particularly commendable. Congratulations."

Just after ten on the March morning of the Ijmuiden mission, the Marauders stood fueled and ready on the hardstands, waiting to take off just after noon, while the crews sat tensely in the briefing room, eager to learn what the next few hours of their lives would bring. The major who would tell them tucked a sheaf of papers under his arm and left the S-2 hut. At his desk, Jimmy cleared away Ijmuiden for the moment and turned to another of his duties—compiling information for the 391st's monthly report. The group had flown seventeen missions so far, dropped almost seven hundred tons of bombs, and avenged the loss of two of its own planes by shooting down two of the enemy's. As he worked, he wondered how the numbers would change today—whether he would be adding or, he feared, subtracting later this afternoon, when the planes were back and the debriefing reports were streaming into S-2—but he knew that divining the final score was beyond his, beyond anyone's, power.

Bill Lopatin

As Bill Lopatin watched from his waist window, the Dutch coastline crept toward him over the horizon, five miles and closing, its sharp edge blurred by ground smoke from the first wave of bombs. The sky, for once, was a clear, peaceful blue, the clouds sparse and white. Rising unscathed beside the E-boat pens ahead were the tall stacks of the Ijmuiden power plant, not a target itself today, but a reminder of the first Marauders who had come here to destroy it and were instead destroyed themselves. There had been only ten planes then, but there were hundreds now, the largest assemblage of B-26s ever dispatched from England on a single combat mission. Bill looked down to track the black puffs of flak from an enemy ship directly below, and then looked back up and around to find himself surrounded in every direction by friendly company. The same German guns that had downed those first invaders last year had already begun blasting again, but this time the numbers were on the Americans' side.

"Bombardier, ready for bombs away," Bill heard the pilot announce through the headphones.

The E-boat pens were being built to withstand Allied air raids, sheltered by eight-foot-thick roofs of reinforced concrete; to disable them would require as much finesse as strength. The plan was not to try to smash the pens by battering the roofs with bombs, but to place the bombs instead like deadly gifts at their doors, sealing the entrances. The other target was the cofferdam that was keeping the harbor dry during construction; the bombs would batter it until it breached, flooding the pens out.

Bill was near the tail of the attack, flying with a crew of strangers on his first mission since being transferred out of the 322nd and into the newly arrived 394th. At the head of the line was his old group—led by three Purple Heart veterans of the first Ijmuiden mission who were eager to fire the opening shots of this return visit. So many planes had already dropped their bombs by the time Bill was over the target that he could see nothing below him but a pall of smoke and flames. He watched his plane's bombs fall and then disappear—four 1,000-pound semi-armor-piercing bombs that he could only hope were on their way to where they were supposed to go. The last planes banked and started home.

Some of the Marauders were limping as they left Ijmuiden, riddled with flak holes and searching for a place, anyplace, to land, but 343 of them made it back to England. The only one that didn't was from the 394th. Home in Boreham, Bill climbed down from his unblemished plane and made his way across a base where bulldozers were still carving hardstands into the fresh earth. After debriefing, he sought out his five old crewmates from the 322nd, who had been parceled out among the green crews like so many grizzled good-luck charms. The men of the new Marauder groups had trained longer, and on better equipment, than the earlier crews—they flew with oxygen, for instance, which kept their senses sharper aloft—but because they had never faced a swooping, shooting Messerschmitt over enemy ground, their ranks were leavened with a generous allotment of transferred veterans.

"The whole place was on fire," one of the rookies said excitedly in the mess hall, still high from Ijmuiden.

"That doesn't mean we got it," explained Bill, who wasn't surprised when he learned later that the mission had been less successful than it looked. Not everyone had gotten the message about where to aim, and most of the bombs had fallen loudly but uselessly on the concrete roofs. A number of boats and buildings, including a mess hall apparently filled with lunching Nazis, were destroyed, but the pens remained operational, despite more than six hundred tons of bombs.

Ijmuiden left Bill just a dozen missions shy of the fifty his crew had been told would be enough to send them home. (The standard tour of duty for heavy bomber crews, with their longer missions and lower survival rate, was twenty-five; for German airmen it was until the end of the war, or death.) Upon arriving at his new station, he had included a cryptic message in a letter to his brother, Sol, which was meant to tell how long he had left. "I hear that Aunt Rose moved to Freehold, to 37 Tsumsoff Street," he wrote. What Bill knew that Sol would know, and the army censor wouldn't, was that Aunt Rose hadn't moved anywhere, that Tsumsoff was not the name of a street in Freehold but a Yiddish word meaning "near the end," and that thirty-seven was the number of his completed missions. After his unlucky thirteenth mission on Armistice Day, and a night in the infirmary with pulled back muscles, he had quickly rejoined the winter air campaign. He faced the brutal flak at the Amsterdam-Schipol airdrome. He scoured the enemy coast for the distinctive ski-shaped buildings that marked the Nazi rocket-gun sites. On a mission to

Cormette, France, he watched two neighboring planes shot from the sky, and all he could do was count the number of open parachutes escaping from the flaming, spinning wreckage, hoping it added up to all the crewmen on board; but it didn't. *We Dood It* gave way to another plane, *Lights Out,* which featured a nose cartoon of a fist uppercutting Hitler into oblivion, but the crew remained intact, bound by ties that even the army knew enough not to break. The six of them left together for the 394th in early March; 188 other men from the 322nd were already gone by then, dead or missing.

Reassembled after Ijmuiden in their new plane, *Dina-Might,* Bill's crew was soon flying a busier mission schedule than ever before, preparing the ground for the long-awaited invasion meant finally—in answer to the pleas of a captive Continent, and an impatient America—to break the stalemate in Europe. The Russians were pushing the Germans back all along the murderous eastern front—and food was now reaching Leningrad, where a million people had died during the nine-hundred-day siege, and the starving survivors had resorted to making soup from the dried glue in furniture joints—but the Americans, with the notable exception of the airmen, were mostly standing still. The troops that had landed at Sicily, and later and more bloodily at Salerno and Anzio, were stalled halfway up Italy. England was bursting with Americans, but for most of them the biggest battle was getting safely past the prostitutes who clustered at the top of the Underground steps in Piccadilly Circus hailing each passing uniform with a flirtatious "Hello, dearie."

Bill, though, was seeing less of London than he had before. For the Marauders, the war's next stage had already begun: The air plan for Operation Overlord, the code name for the cross-Channel invasion, took effect in late April, assigning them more, and different, targets. It became their job to disrupt the enemy's capacity to fight the coming Allied wave. Sometimes flying two missions in a single day, they hit bridges, rail yards, gun positions and the few airdromes where German planes were still based. Most of the enemy fighters were gone from occupied skies now, withdrawn recently to defend Germany itself, but the flak remained heavy. When Bill's crew attacked a railroad gun position at Dunkirk, where the Allies had been chased off the continent four years earlier, the Nazi gunners found the Marauders before they were halfway across the Channel, and fired on them steadily all the way to and from the target. "Hot Spot," Bill wrote on the fuse tag he saved as a souvenir.

As the invasion neared—exactly when, few lower than Eisenhower knew, but that it would be soon, everyone could feel—seasoned combat crews like Bill's became too valuable to send home, and the fifty-mission limit was lifted. Bill's mood darkened, and his fuse shortened, at the news. The crews were given no new mission number, finite and consoling, to aim for, only told they would stay as long as they were needed. Just how long could that be, he wondered? He had been prepared to die in combat, but the impending end of his tour had made him begin preparing to live again instead. To have survived as long as he had, to have gotten so close to what seemed the end and then to find it receding before him like a mirage, only hardened his fatalism. He had to erase Freehold from his mind, the visions of peace and home that had penetrated his protective shell, and begin focusing again only on the moment immediately ahead. His strategy for enduring the war was to inhabit only the present; the future was too distant, too precious, too disturbing, to contemplate.

To ease the grumbling, the veteran crews, Bill's among them, were offered furloughs. Bill and his crewmates voted to give the one thirty-day stateside leave they received to the copilot, the only man who had a wife awaiting him back home; the rest were set free in Great Britain for two weeks. After they finished their forty-eighth mission, Bill and the two other sergeants from the back of the plane, Malcolm Enlow the tail gunner and Clyde Duke the turret gunner, took the bottle of whiskey they were issued and rode together into London. Bill planned to visit Scotland, a place his brother, Sol, had become smitten with, but first he stopped with them at a pub.

"Hey, look who that is over there," Bill said, pointing down the bar toward a familiar but wholly unexpected face—a fellow flier from their group who had been shot down over France and listed as missing.

To celebrate their comrade's resurrection, they stood a round of drinks, and then, of course, another, and another, and another, until the barman, bound by the staggered-hours rule that puzzled the Americans as much as the warm beer did, finally called "Gentlemen, time, please," and sent them floating down the street to the next open pub. The story of their friend's crash, and his subsequent escape with the help of the Resistance, repeated like a tape loop, punctuated by a string of toasts—to him, to them, to the dead, to the living, to anyone and anything worth drinking to, a list that grew longer as the evening went on. Bill hadn't been much of a drinker in Freehold, but the war had taught him about alcohol's value as an anesthetic: The airmen who didn't drink, he had noticed, were usually the ones who wound up in the flight surgeon's office with the nervous jitters of combat fatigue.

Two weeks later, Bill slid back into base with a head that felt two sizes too large for his cap. "So how was Scotland?" one of his hut mates asked.

"I don't know, I never got there," he said, as much to himself as to his questioner. "That was the longest binge of my life."

Bill flew six missions in his first six days back, as the Marauders raced to finish their work before the invasion. Twenty-two railroad and highway bridges crossed the Seine river between Paris and the sea, and all twenty-two were marked for destruction before D-Day, the date of which the tides and the generals had already secretly fixed. The Germans were clustered at Pas-de-Calais, where they expected the Allies to invade; if the bridges were down, they would have a harder time funneling reinforcements south to the actual invasion site in Normandy. When his plane attacked a bridge, Bill rooted for the bombs to hit the ends, where the damage to the anchoring piers was more lasting, rather than the middle, where a gap could easily be spanned. By May 28, just sixty-seven days after entering combat, the 394th had flown fifty missions, reaching that milestone faster than any other Marauder group in England, and causing enough damage to the enemy transportation system to earn the nickname "Bridge Busters." By June 4, when the invasion window opened, all the targeted Seine bridges were down, and any German troops ordered south to Normandy would have to walk.

In the first dark hour of June 5, the light snapped on in Bill's hut, and the crew was roused for a mission. Briefing, they were told, was at two-fifteen. Outside, the wind was high, the clouds low and the rain steady, and as the men walked across the base they wondered what kind of fool would order them to fly in such weather. Because the planes were hidden from them by distance and darkness, they couldn't see the broad black and white bands that the ground crews had just painted around all the bodies and wings—the invasion stripes, meant to identify Allied aircraft in the crowded skies over the Channel and Normandy. Nobody wanted a repeat of what Stu Bunton had seen at the invasion of Sicily, when confused Americans had shot down their own planes. The crews gathered in the hall outside the closed doors of the briefing room, behind which huddled the only officers around who knew that today was the day scheduled to become D-Day. Bill sat down on the floor, leaned his head back against the wall and dozed off, only to be awakened again when an officer appeared at the door.

"Okay, listen up," the officer called. "The mission's scrubbed, on account of the weather."

Bill gathered his things, eager to crawl back into his cot to finish his night's sleep, and grateful that whatever the target was, it could wait for more hospitable conditions. The officer turned to leave, too, his duty of reading the war's most momentous order of the day, one that included a special message from Eisenhower himself, postponed for at least twenty-four more hours.

"You are about to embark upon the Great Crusade, toward which we have striven these many months," the supreme commander had written in his exhortation to the Allied soldiers, sailors and airmen he was sending into battle, the largest invasion force in all of history. "The eyes of the world are upon you."

4.

The Home Front, 1942–1944

Buddy Lewis

The turnout was sparse for a game the Freehold Colonials seemed likely to lose, again, and the few loyalists in the stands wrapped their jackets tightly around themselves, trying to squeeze some warmth from a bitter November Saturday. On the field, the players felt the cold nibble at their bare calves, and they blew into their hands between plays. Canvas sheeting was draped over the fence, a shield against any spectators unwilling to buy tickets, but it was blocking the view better than it was the wind, which swept raw and unchallenged across the shorn, gray farmland that stretched into the distance. The high school stood on the northern edge of town, bordering fields where farmers still occasionally turned up stray pieces of lead from a battle fought more than a century and a half earlier. One hot June day in 1778, the entire British army, twenty thousand strong, was encamped on these very grounds, in the middle of an evacuation march from Philadelphia to New York, when the charging Americans finally caught up with them and, eager to fight after the long Valley Forge winter, fired the first shots of the Battle of Monmouth.

Freehold hadn't won a game yet this season, and Manasquan, cruising toward a title, hadn't lost, but the Colonials' coach, watching closely from the sidelines, had spotted a weakness—a softness around the ends of the defensive line—that he thought he might exploit. Before he sent his offense out again, he issued a strategic order.

"Knock down the ends, and Lewis will have a field day," he told them.

The secret weapon was sophomore halfback Buddy Lewis, who was already the team's fastest runner, but who lately had become even more elusive: After studying the action at a recent Rutgers-Lehigh game, he came home to perfect his cutback move. Bent over in the huddle, Buddy listened as the quarterback called the play.

"Twenty-eight sweep on two."

He lined up as the number two back in the single wing formation, and on the second "Hut," took the ball on a handoff and sprinted around the end, which proved just as vulnerable as the coach had detected, and into the clear ground ahead. He did it again and again all afternoon, dashing from the backfield and returning punts as if at a track meet, and leaving the defense to chase his breeze. When the game ended, he had led his team to an improbable 19–0 victory.

"The Colonials had more to say than expected, and they said it with a flurry of touchdowns that saw a new individual star," the *Asbury Park Press* gushed in its account of the game. "Bigerton Lewis, a slim-built 135-pound colored boy, swept through the Manasquan team for every touchdown and brought the greatest joy of an otherwise dismal season to Coach Frank Mozelski and his scrappy, lightweight gridders."

Because he could move so freely on the football field, Buddy was able to move more freely off of it, too, his athletic prowess earning him a limited immunity against some common racial slights. If he took a booth in the diner with some white friends after school, and the waitress, reluctant to serve a black customer, brusquely set his Coke down on the other side of the table, someone would quickly slide it across to him before the snub was noted. He negotiated his sophomore year with a grace and confidence that had eluded him as a freshman, when a mild heart condition sidelined him from sports and closed an avenue that would have eased his passage into the integrated high school. He had made a few trips back to the Colored School for the kind of encouragement only Mr. Read could offer, and for some remedial lessons in diagramming sentences, a subject for which, as the overburdened teacher apologized, there had just never been time in a classroom that held all the sixth, seventh and eighth graders at once.

But Buddy was emerging as a football hero in a world that was minting real heroes daily, and whenever he let himself imagine where his speed might take him—to a scholarship at a black college in the South perhaps—something would quickly remind him of a different, more likely future. His three-touchdown romp against Manasquan was eclipsed by news of Johnny Bartek's miraculous rescue in the Pacific, and Buddy's chance to earn more varsity letters—in basketball, track and baseball—

was briefly threatened by the war effort, the seasons nearly canceled by some earnest officials who believed high school sports were a frivolous distraction in a serious time. When basketball finally did start, all the games were played in the afternoon: The gym had no blackout curtains to block the lights in its tall windows at night. In art class he made defense posters, in shop he built aircraft recognition models and in gym he did calisthenics meant to ready him for boot camp.

Outside school, too, the war stared at him constantly—from the booth in Woolworth's that sold war bonds; the tags stuck in the meat at the butcher shop that told how many ration points each cut would cost; the shuttered offices of the town doctors who had entered the service, five out of twelve so far. Gas rationing kept people close to home—except for those who had coupons designating them as essential workers, so they could drive to the shipyards at Perth Amboy and Kearny, or the aircraft plants in Ewing and Linden—and the Saturday night crowds thinned on Main Street. Claire's Furs was advertising mink-dyed muskrat, "a fine fur for these times." The navy had bought up a scrubby, unfarmed expanse of land outside town to use as a weapons depot, and the contract workers preparing it filled the empty bedrooms of sons gone to war. The soldiers billeted at the old CCC camp danced with the local girls at the servicemen's canteen at St. Peter's Parish House. At the synagogue, the rabbi spoke of his time in a German concentration camp, and at the Lions Club a marine veteran of Guadalcanal brandished the jawbone of a dead Japanese soldier. "If you don't believe the American fighting man is better than the Jap, I'll prove it to you," he said as he displayed it, teeth and all. The lighthouse up on Sandy Hook was dark for the first time in 160 years, and the familiar German cannon on Main Street was missing from its prominent spot at Elks Point, donated to the perpetual scrap-metal drive, a trophy from the last war melted down and recycled into weaponry for the current one.

Almost every young man in America, it seemed, was in uniform, and more than half of them were still stateside—at the hundreds of camps and bases and other military facilities that had, like the nearby navy depot, sprouted all over the country, especially in the South. Not even fathers were exempt from the draft any longer: President Roosevelt himself carried his own draft card in his wallet. And many of the men who were still civilians were working in defense industries. Working beside them were women—more than had ever before joined the labor force, six million in all, in shipyards and aircraft plants and every other grimy corner of the war effort. (An additional two hundred thousand of them were in uniform themselves.) Children as young as twelve were enlisted in the cause, too, as some states suspended child labor laws to help fill essential jobs. America alone was producing twice as much war matériel as Germany, Italy and Japan combined; at the Teheran Conference, Joseph Stalin offered a toast "to American production, without which this war would have been lost." General Motors made fighter planes, Chrysler made tanks, and Ford made B-24 bombers at the rate of one per hour. The Depression seemed a distant memory: The unemployment rate was less than 2 percent.

By the spring of 1943, two of his brothers had already been drafted, a third had just received notice, and Buddy, the youngest, was starting to worry that history would strand him in Freehold. His track-and-field season was over, and the next football season seemed ages away, both in relevance and time. When Payton, the brother closest to him in age and everything else, reported to the draft board on Court Street, Buddy went with him, and they asked to be sent together in the next allotment of inductees. He didn't understand the weight of what he'd done until he told his mother, and, expecting her face to light with pride, saw it sag with worry instead. On the bus down to Fort Dix, soon after the school year closed, Buddy accepted a pack of cigarettes from his brother, a token of his passage into manhood.

"Here, now you can smoke legitimately," Payton told him.

Stepping out of the bus and into the army, Buddy entered a world in which the first thing that mattered about him was the color of his skin. The receiving sergeant classified him with a glance, and with a terse "over there," pointed him in the direction exactly opposite the preceding white recruit. Buddy joined the group of men who had been placed together solely because they were black, and looked warily over at the group who had been placed together solely because they were white. Nudges and whispers of amusement passed among his group as they noticed who had been mistaken for white.

"Hey, George, tell 'em you're colored!" someone shouted across to a Freehold friend whose light skin had fooled the sergeant. The error noted, he was quickly repatriated.

The army, Buddy soon learned, operated under the same separate-but-equal rules he thought he had left behind at the Colored School—

segregated right on down to the blood given wounded soldiers on the battlefield. "We must not place too much responsibility on a race which is not showing initiative," War Secretary Henry Stimson wrote in 1940, a sentiment voiced all along the chain of command, and echoed in the civilian world. "We cannot afford to mix Negroes with white soldiers at this time," the *Freehold Transcript* agreed on its editorial page. The military persisted in believing that blacks neither could nor would fight as well as whites, despite the heroism of the black sailor who proved otherwise on the first day of the war: When bombs began falling at Pearl Harbor, Messman Dorie Miller moved a wounded captain's body off the bridge of the battleship *West Virginia*, took over a vacant machine-gun post, shot two Japanese planes from the sky, and was awarded a Navy Cross; but when he died two years later, his ship torpedoed by an enemy sub near Tarawa, he was still a messman. The navy, which had an all-white officer corps in 1940, rarely let blacks out of the kitchen; the army, which had all of two black officers that year, shunted blacks away from combat units and the Air Corps (with the exception of the Tuskegee Airmen's unit, the 99th Pursuit Squadron), and placed them mostly in service units—unloading ships, driving trucks, handling supplies, building roads and camps. Blacks and whites clashed often in the service, especially around the big southern bases—brawls, riots, murders, even lynchings— and the racial violence peaked in the summer of Buddy's enlistment. Two earlier incidents at Fort Dix itself—a fight at a USO dance and an argument over a busy phone booth—had escalated into gunfire, and left several black soldiers and white MPs dead.

Another of the Lewis brothers, Lester, was already stationed at Dix, and he managed to get all the black recruits from Freehold assigned to the same barracks. For his first five days in the army, Buddy was surrounded by family and friends, congratulating himself on the wisdom of his enlistment strategy. But then he and Payton were classified and dispatched in opposite directions—Payton to Virginia and the quartermasters, Buddy to Missouri and the engineers. First at Fort Leonard Wood, and then at Camp Ellis, Illinois, Buddy—a member now of the 1317th Engineer General Service Regiment (Colored)—learned about building bridges, blowing mines, disarming booby traps, stringing concertina wire and the myriad other tasks necessary for maintaining a war. Because the general service regiments were intended to serve as the army's skilled handymen, trained for many small jobs rather than a single big one, the chief of engineers asked that only men of what he described as "average or better" ability be assigned to them. Buddy got one more chance to see his brother when Payton's unit passed through Illinois on its way west. At intermission at the base movie theater one evening he heard a familiar voice calling his name, and he bowled over several soldiers like so many linemen to reach the chair Payton was standing on. They shared a few drinks—on Buddy's money, since Payton hadn't been paid—and made a date for the next night. But in the morning Buddy was sent out on a three-day exercise, and by the time he got back Payton was gone, and he was alone again.

It was at Camp Ellis that Buddy began to see even more clearly how the army's hierarchy was based not only on rank, but on race. The food was worse than at Dix or Wood, the supplies stretched thinner—when holes opened in his shoes, he couldn't get a new pair, and his uniform often went unlaundered—and the discipline seemed more arbitrary. His unit was out on a winter field exercise once, building pontoon bridges over the frigid Illinois River, when some sweet-hearted, apple-cheeked white girls appeared from the local service committee, bearing coffee, doughnuts, hand-knit mittens and, most surprisingly, invitations to a dance. A weary and dirty Buddy declined, and spent the evening in his tent with a bottle of Virginia Dare wine, but some of the other men accepted, only to find themselves arrested by the MPs upon their return, charged with going AWOL by a white southern officer who disapproved of such race mixing. Morale sagged and complaints rose, until the camp was scheduled for an inspection visit by General Benjamin O. Davis, the army's first, and still only, black general. The day before the inspection Buddy was helping the supply sergeant, working in the same building as the orderly room, when he overheard plans laid to dispatch the loudest plaintiffs on a long hike. "No complaints were received from the personnel of this regiment," the general wrote after his visit.

On his one furlough home, Buddy rode a coal-burning train that left his uniform even dirtier than it already was. "You're not really looking after yourself, are you?" his mother asked when she saw him.

"I'm trying, but they don't make it easy for you," he explained to her. His brother took the uniform to the cleaner, and Buddy took some precious ration stamps from his mother—rubber had been scarce since the Japanese took over the plantations of Asia—to have new half soles put on his army shoes.

On March 20, 1944, Buddy and his companions from the 1317th

climbed down to F deck on the *Queen Mary*, well below the water line, squeezed onboard with fourteen thousand other soldiers for the trip to a country where, as the House of Commons had politely informed the American army, "the colour bar is not the custom." The British had no segregation laws—with only eight thousand blacks in a population of forty-seven million, they had little to segregate against—and they prohibited the Americans from instituting any outside the bases. When black soldiers arrived—more than one hundred thousand already by the time Buddy's ship docked—they found a warmer welcome and more open doors than they ever had in America. "I don't mind the Yanks," went one oft-heard quip, "but I can't say I care much for those white chaps they've brought along." Blacks mingled freely with whites in pubs, on buses, at theaters and at dance halls, where the local girls were happy to jitterbug with them. The unaccustomed freedom heartened the black soldiers, and threatened some of the white ones, who were aggrieved by behavior that defied the codes of home. The mere sight of a black sailor kissing a white girl at a train station in Manchester was enough to spark a series of riots.

Buddy landed in England at a moment when tension had reached such a pitch that an army censorship report, after surveying the hateful language blacks and whites used against each other in the letters they wrote home, declared that "if the invasion doesn't occur soon, trouble will." While he and his regiment awaited assignment, they made a temporary camp in a game preserve that apparently didn't appear on the quartermaster's map. For the first week or more, in the absence of any food deliveries, they subsisted on the same meager rations, twice a day—peas, a slice of bread and a glut of canned chocolate pudding. Some of the men started snaring rabbits, until the preserve's overseer informed them that the animals were meant for sport, not sustenance. They soon realized that if the army wouldn't feed them, they would have to feed themselves. The truck that traveled to the nearby village each day, picking up coke for the stoves that heated the tents, began stopping at the baker's shop, too, buying bread for the hungry soldiers. One day the truck returned to camp with a more disturbing cargo—several bloodied and beaten men.

"Some paratroopers said, 'Niggers, what are you doing here?' and we started fighting," one of the wounded men explained to the crowd that gathered.

A few dozen men, Buddy among them, climbed onto the trucks and sped back to the village, hunger fueling their anger as they plotted a counterattack. They found some remorseless white paratroopers there, and shouted angrily at them through the dusky shadows. Shouts quickly hardened into fists, and the fists into a tangle of flailing punches. Some weapons were drawn. The paratroopers had knives. The engineers had bayonets. Within the mass of grappling bodies, Buddy couldn't see from his end of the brawl to the other, but he felt it reach a volume that seemed likely to consume someone.

"Two of them went down," somebody said on the ride back to camp, in a voice unable to decide whether that meant victory or defeat.

"I think they're dead," somebody else added.

The next morning, word passed through the regiment that a witness had stepped forward, a young woman from the village—exactly what crime she had seen, though, they didn't know, since nobody had officially told them that anyone had died, or even been seriously wounded—and was coming to camp to face a lineup. It sounded more like a bad night at a police station than it did a proper military investigation, the men agreed, and they sent a protest delegation to one of the officers. Soldiers, they argued, should stand for judgment before other soldiers, not a civilian guided by motives no one could tell.

"They're just looking for a scapegoat," one of the men said. "They say we all look alike anyway, how's she gonna tell who did what?"

"We'll line up," another warned, "but if she IDs anyone, she won't leave alive."

The witness walked warily through the glaring ranks of men, never raising her hand in accusation, unable or unwilling to put a face on what she said she had seen. Her departure from the camp ended the incident for the regiment: No further news or charges were heard, and no court-martial was ever convened. The officer who had permitted the lineup was transferred out, his command authority eroded by a decision the men regarded as betrayal. The quartermaster finally found them, and started delivering some proper food.

The brawl had bruised Buddy's spirit more than his body. The longer he served, it seemed, the more his race mattered. The army was constantly reminding him that he was black in ways that Freehold never had. Here he was in England, poised to fight the Germans, and he was fighting Americans instead. Weren't they all on the same side? he wondered. Didn't nationality transcend race? And those questions only led to more sweeping ones: How was it that many of his fellow soldiers from the Deep South were barely literate, that the primitive homes they described sounded no better than the most squalid quarters of the migrants who came to Freehold each summer? Was his own life at home before the war the best a black man could hope for in America?

Buddy's regiment soon moved to a more fixed address, attached to a camp in southwestern England with the 29th Infantry Division, where he discovered, to his relief, that not all white soldiers wanted to fight blacks, and that some would even cross the color line with card games and conversation. While the 29th drilled and waited—they were among the first divisions to arrive in England, and they expected to be among the first in France, too—the 1317th drove trucks, swung hammers, bulldozed roads and collected trash. One day in May, the engineers were ordered to stand for a general inspection, a signal, they surmised, that the invasion was near, and that it might include them. As the brass passed in review, Buddy stood sharp and straight, the picture of a good soldier ready for anything they might ask of him. He was surprised, though, at the demeanor of some of his older comrades, men he knew were smarter and better trained than they were acting now.

"Where's the butt end of your rifle, soldier?" an officer asked one soldier.

"I don't know, sir," he answered, though Buddy knew he did.

They were feigning ignorance, hoping that a poor showing would keep them from invasion duty. They had seen more of the army, more of life, than the teenaged Buddy had, and they carried a hard bitterness that made them skeptical of any white officer who planned to place them in harm's way. Buddy himself didn't share their cynicism yet, but he was beginning to understand where it came from.

The troops soon began spilling out of all the camps and onto the roads that led to the ports of southern England, where ships were waiting to carry them to France. Buddy was stationed with a dozen men from his regiment at a roadside field kitchen, assigned to pick up the daily food supplies from the main camp a mile away. Every morning he awoke to the thunder of Allied planes soaring eastward, and the steady rumble of arms and men parading in the same direction, at a more deliberate pace. One gray morning in early June, the thunder overhead was heavier, and the rumble on the ground hollower, and he watched the parade dwindle to its sparse end.

"It's the invasion," someone finally informed him, and he knew then what the inspectors had decided: The 1317th wasn't going yet.

The 29th Infantry was already in Normandy, splashing out of the landing crafts and storming Omaha Beach in the face of the deadliest fire barrage of the whole invasion front. So many bodies rolled in the surf and sprawled on the sand that the German commander on the bluffs above was convinced the battle was his. The Americans sprinted across the beach to the base of the bluffs, and steeled themselves for the climb up.

"They're murdering us here!" a colonel called, pointing in a direction that was equally perilous, but nearer to victory. "Let's move inland and get murdered!"

Walter Denise

The train was barreling west from New Jersey toward a destination its passengers could only guess at, and every time it slowed for a station— Philadelphia, Pittsburgh, Indianapolis and a string of other railroad towns, great and small—the fresh soldiers packed aboard leaned forward in anticipation, wondering if they had finally reached their stop. The farther they went, the more Walter Denise found himself hoping they would go farther still, all the way to the other side of the country, where he might compare the Edenic groves of California to the orchards of home. Cutting south across Texas, in the middle of autumn, he felt the heat rise toward summer, and the dust collect in the folds of his uniform. The land unreeled outside the open windows like a farmer's nightmare—seared into submission by the constant sun, so parched and barren it could barely support some stunted brush and patchy grass, a hard world away from the apple harvest back in Freehold. Walter had never seen so much land and so few trees. In El Paso, the soldiers were ordered off the train and onto trucks that took them to the army hospital at Fort Bliss. The ward buildings sat on emerald islands of manicured, well-fed lawns. The stark white walls, raked by the midday sun, glared like headlights, and caused him to raise his hand to shield his eyes.

"I hope we don't stay here long," he said, disappointed at where he had landed.

Walter could have easily, and honorably, sat the war out with a deferment—some young men around town had developed a sudden interest in agriculture when the draft started, and stayed home to tend farms barely a fraction the size of the Denise orchard—but he heard a call to serve that proved too loud to ignore. When he helped load a big rail shipment to the army at the Throckmorton Street siding, packing each car tightly with exactly 798 boxes, he knew he wanted to be where the apples were going, not where they were coming from. In answering his conscience, he was also upholding a family tradition: Dennis Denise was a major in the Third Regiment of the Monmouth militia in the Revolutionary War; and Daniel Denise, a private in the Fourth Regiment, was among the local signers of a pledge to retaliate against the "incursions and depredations" of the Loyalists who were staging raids on the early and fervent Patriot stronghold of Freehold. Walter tried the marines first, but was rejected for poor eyesight. When the army said they didn't mind his glasses, he put his red 1941 Plymouth convertible up on jacks in the barn for the duration. He had been scheduled to leave on the same bus as Jimmy Higgins, but he passed up the two-week, wind-up-your-affairs grace period the army offered before induction; applying a farmer's practical planning to an institution that, as he soon learned, operated according to an alternate system of logic, he reasoned that the two weeks more he served now would be two weeks less he would serve later.

The army operated according to an alternate view of theology, too, as he also learned. Most of the Denise ancestors belonged to the Dutch Reformed Church, but Walter's father—after attending a lecture at the urging of his fiancée that cured him of both his skepticism and his smoking—had helped establish a Freehold outpost of the Christian Science Church, a denomination that believes healing is a matter for prayer, not medicine. Walter had grown up attending services and Sunday school in temporary meeting rooms until the year before his enlistment, when a proper home on Main Street was finally dedicated. When he told the army his religion, though, it didn't seem to make much difference: His dog tag was stamped with a "P" for Protestant, his arm was stuck with the usual round of inoculation needles, and he was assigned to a medical battalion. At Fort Bliss he was sent to the pharmacy section, surrounded by pills he didn't believe in.

The raw Texas landscape held perils Walter hadn't known at home: cacti that could pierce an army shoe, and that he would try to dodge when the sergeant suddenly called "Fall!" in the middle of a desert march; boulders that crashed down the dry mountains when the rain came; dust storms that seemed to blow through the barracks just before white-glove inspections. At night the vista widened toward infinity, a skeleton of light—the stars strewn across the sky, the city and the airfield glittering across the treeless distance—outlining a grander, vaster space than any he had ever inhabited before. But as he watched the universe expand above him, he felt his duties constrict around him. He hated everything about pharmacy school—the bottles he washed, the tincture of green soap he made, the gelatin capsules that stuck to his fingers as he tried to fill them, but most of all the daily, pointless tedium of a job that seemed such a paltry contribution to the war he had enlisted to fight.

Walter attended an occasional Christian Science service in El Paso, but his main religious sustenance came from his Bible, his copy of Mary Baker Eddy's *Science and Health,* and the Sunday lessons of his youth. He didn't smoke or drink or swear, behavior that put him in rare company in the army, and he wore his faith quietly, like armor. He was returning to base from a movie in town one night, after a bus ride on which he had tried to stop a drunken argument from becoming a fight, when his shield was first tested. Walking toward the barracks, he was jumped by his brawling bus mates, and a knife pricked the back of his neck. He felt his mind clear of all thoughts but one: God is love, he declared to himself, and no harm can come to me. Their hostile grip relaxed, and he sprinted to his bunk. As his breath returned, he began to understand that what had just happened hadn't really happened at all, at least not in a spiritual sense. It had been an illusion—as all sickness and sin was, according to the principles of his religion—and he had overcome it as he had been taught to, by the power of his mind. There had been a healing, he believed, and there was nothing more to fear. In the morning, the behavior of his attackers only confirmed for him his interpretation of the night before: Every trace of knifepoint malice had vanished as they cordially beckoned him to join them in the chow line.

After six months of Texas, he was transferred to Colorado, but it was just farther down a road he didn't want to travel—stranding him in a hospital dispensary at Camp Carson, where he was tempted to sweep the bottles off the shelves in a crashing gesture of protest. That would have been a surrender, though, he realized—a rash and destructive act in defiance of all his Sunday-school lessons—so he searched instead for another way out. His classification score on the army's intelligence test was high enough to offer him two possible routes: He passed up Officer Candidate School because he didn't feel ready yet to lead troops, and chose instead the Army Specialized Training Program, which would send him to college. ASTP was the army's foresighted attempt to identify its brightest lights and start them toward becoming the kinds of professionals whose skills the war craved—engineers, doctors, language specialists, psychologists. More than two hundred thousand soldiers, wearing shoulder patches that depicted a lamp of knowledge crossed by a sword of valor, were dispatched to more than two hundred colleges and universities. In the summer of 1943, Walter began lugging physics and math textbooks back to his barracks from the lecture halls of St. Regis College in Denver. In February of 1944, he was transferred to the University of Iowa, where he slept on his first inner-spring mattress since home and drank fresh milk from the agriculture school's cows.

As the invasion of Europe approached, the army decided it needed bodies more than minds, and began shipping ASTP soldiers back to line duty. By March Walter was a medic again, on maneuvers with the Forty-fourth Division, carrying stretchers through the swamps of Louisiana and plotting another escape. He knew the risks of combat: Screening movies for the wounded Pacific veterans at the Fort Bliss hospital, he had seen the missing arms and legs, and heard the profane bitterness of men who no longer feared the authority of the army, which could hurt them no worse, they believed, than the enemy already had. He still wanted so badly to leave the medics, though, that he asked for a transfer to the branch of the army most other soldiers tried to avoid: the infantry. His sergeant threatened a court-martial, but Walter and a platoon buddy began asking around the 324th Infantry Regiment for a new home. They took their request directly to the battalion commander.

"Why did you choose Company K?" the colonel asked them. "Do you have friends in that outfit?"

"No, sir," Walter answered. "But we hear they have the best mess sergeant around."

The sergeant in the medics unit was livid when the transfer was approved, but Walter was elated, and he memorized his new M-1 rifle down to its serial number. He gratefully endured the trials meant to prepare him for combat—rising in the dark for twenty-five-mile forced marches, with a full pack on his back; crawling on his belly over a field and under barbed wire, as machine gun bullets zinged above his head. He eagerly learned about gas masks, Thompson submachine guns, sniper scopes and all the other hand tools of war. He demonstrated an aptitude for foot soldiering—with his compact wrestlers' body, his farm-boy's sense of terrain, his natural inclination to take charge—that convinced his captain to name him the company's first scout, the one among them who would lead patrols to probe enemy lines.

As the Normandy beaches filled with Allied soldiers, Walter's regiment fought practice battles at Camp Phillips, Kansas, and wondered how much stateside time they had left. Walter expected a direct trip to the front for his outfit, as replacements for the dead, the wounded and the weary, so he trained just as devoutly as he planned to fight. On a field exercise one day, he was put in charge of a scouting unit and ordered to climb a hill to capture an enemy camp on the other side. He scanned the landscape, and immediately changed the orders.

"They'll see us if we do that," he said. "We'll be silhouetted on the hilltop. Let's go around the base of it instead."

They hiked around the hill in a wide arc, using it as a shield rather than a trail. They centered the camp in their sights and were poised to pounce, but Walter held them back, ordering them to sit quietly and wait. When he finally signaled the attack, his men crept unchallenged into the camp, and seized the weapons of their sleeping opponents.

"That's not fair," protested one of the captives. "We thought you were lost."

"We knew exactly where we were all the time," Walter explained.

He had always known that—where he was, and what was expected of him—but it was harder here than it had been in Freehold. And it would only get harder, he knew, as he traveled deeper into the war ahead of him.

5.

The Pacific, 1943–1944

Stu Bunton: Tarawa to the Philippine Sea

On a narrow walkway high up the ship's bridge, Stu Bunton leaned over the railing into the night and stopped himself as he reached for his cigarettes. The *Santa Fe* was in enemy waters now, the crew had been warned, and smoking after dark was strictly prohibited. A pale half-moon appeared in a gap in the broken clouds that drifted overhead. The Pacific breeze dried the sweat that the sealed, stifling radio room had raised on Stu: November on the equator, he had learned, felt like July had in Sicily. He strained to see Tarawa in the distance, a low coral atoll that barely breached the surface, far too small a target, it seemed, to justify an invasion force of the size that now bobbed heavily in the silent darkness all around it. A powerful searchlight flashed out from the island and swept over the horizon, stopping when it found one of the transport ships where the Marines had already finished their steak-and-egg breakfasts and were waiting—just as the Japanese troops packed into the concrete bunkers ashore were waiting, too—for the battle to begin. The light flicked off, but no enemy guns followed the trail it had traced.

"You're not supposed to be out here, sailor," a passing lieutenant told Stu.

Stu fished out an ID card stamped with the magic red letters, FLAG AL-LOWANCE, which marked him as a member of the admiral's personal staff, thereby excusing him from drudge details, gaining him extra liberty in port and generally setting him apart from the twelve hundred other men on board. "The admiral said it's okay," he replied, and held his ground.

Stu knew that the admiral, sitting pensively in his bridge chair above, had said nothing of the kind, but he also knew that a junior lieutenant wasn't going up to check. With the minutes ticking toward H-Hour, the moment when the invasion would begin, the admiral had more pressing matters on his mind, like the order he had received earlier from the task force commander: "Your task is to prevent by gunfire use of airfield in event of positive indicators of air operations," it had read. "Avoid engagement shore batteries unless required in accomplishment of task."

The island had launched no planes so far, and the *Santa Fe,* the flagship of Cruiser Division Thirteen, had launched no shells. Stu peered out over the long barrels of the ship's guns, scanning the sky for a hint of the dawn that would signal the start of the bombardment, and the opening of a new theater of war. Japan had occupied and fortified a long string of small islands that stretched taut across the Central Pacific, and Tarawa marked the first stop on Admiral Chester Nimitz's campaign to reclaim them. Nimitz sent the mighty Fifth Fleet steaming westward, with orders to shell and invade, shell and invade, to shrink the enemy empire atoll by atoll, island by island, and then link up in the Philippines with the southern Pacific forces of MacArthur and Admiral William Halsey, which were now storming up the Solomon Islands chain and the coast of New Guinea.

The newly commissioned *Santa Fe* had spent a cold, foggy summer helping to expel the Japanese invaders from the Aleutian Islands, returning to Pearl Harbor in September 1943 for a dry-dock tune-up and a crew replenishment, which included two transfers from the *Brooklyn,* Rear Admiral Laurence DuBose and Radioman Second Class Stuart Bunton, whose quiet efficiency had earned him a spot on the admiral's staff. Just a year earlier, when Stu was still hanging around the sweet shop in Freehold, DuBose had guided another cruiser, the *Portland,* through the early battles of the war, from Midway to Guadalcanal; now he directed the *Santa Fe* and several other cruisers from his seat beside the captain up on the bridge, and Stu tried to watch as much of the action as he could from his own privileged perch outside the radio room just below, enjoying a higher and wider view than almost every other enlisted man aboard. One night a month earlier, a flight of Japanese Bettys had appeared in the humid sky over the Solomon Islands, where Cruiser Division Thirteen and its attendant destroyers were shepherding transports into Bougainville with invasion reinforcements. More than a dozen of the two-engine enemy bombers crashed, flaming, into the sea. As one Betty fell, the rack that held its torpedo bombs dropped onto the main deck of the *Santa Fe,* whose hull was painted the next day with three trophy flags, one for each downed plane the gunners claimed.

Still craving a smoke, Stu returned to his battle station in the radio room to wait. Just after five A.M., an urgent rush of messages pulsed in his ears, and his chest filled with the heavy thud of the ship's guns, which were finally firing on the target they had aimed at all night. Cranking the barrels up and down incrementally, the gunners methodically walked the shells along the airfield on Betio, the tiny island in the Tarawa atoll that held the main enemy base. Within five minutes, they hit a fuel dump on the strip's northern edge, and the shooting flames reddened the roiling clouds of smoke and dust. The Japanese coastal batteries answered with a barrage of shells that whistled overhead and splashed within one hundred yards of the *Santa Fe,* near enough to make Stu recall a piece of information he now wished he hadn't heard. One of the other flagstaffers had stolen a glance at the operations plan for Tarawa: The cost of the invasion, it dryly speculated, might include the loss of one of the four cruisers engaged.

Joined by three battleships and nine destroyers, the cruisers pounded Betio steadily and unforgivingly for more than three hours, pausing only long enough to open a brief window for an attack by the planes from the carriers. When the guns stopped, the smoldering island, less than half the size of New York's Central Park, looked as if it might sink under the weight of all the explosives it had absorbed, more than ten tons for each of its 291 precious, barren acres. "Gentlemen, we will not neutralize Betio, we will not destroy it," the admiral in charge of the fire-support group had told his officers, in a prediction that now seemed fulfilled. "We will obliterate it." Exactly 1,573 spent brass shell casings lay strewn across the *Santa Fe's* deck like logs in a cleared forest. The crew gathered along the railings to cheer on the marines who were streaming slowly across the shallow lagoon toward the landing beach, and then watched in horror as the island they thought they had killed roared angrily back to life.

Guns flashed from behind the shroud of the besieged island, as the bunkered Japanese rose to repel the invaders. A small fleet—too small, it seemed now—of amphibious tractors managed to deliver some marines safely onto the beach, but the landing boats that carried the rest snagged on the coral reef, betrayed by a tide much lower than expected. The men clambered out and walked into a startling barrage of shells and machine-gun bullets, wading as far as one thousand yards through chest-deep water that held them to a leaden pace and fixed them as easy targets. They fell by the hundreds, their blood darkening the turquoise lagoon. On the *Santa Fe* and the other ships, the navy gunners waited for radio messages from Betio relaying new target coordinates, but most of the men who had made it to the beach were pinned against a coconut-log seawall, too busy just trying to stay alive.

"The issue ashore is still in doubt," the ship's loudspeaker announced, and the sailors shook their heads in both astonishment and dismay, as they began to understand the determination of the enemy they were fighting.

The Japanese believed a battle must end in either victory or death—surrender, in their warrior code, was the ultimate disgrace—and they had dug themselves into the island so deeply that their commander promised it would take a million men a hundred years to dislodge them. The marines had only six thousand men, who began climbing over the seawall one by one. The shelling had destroyed the island's communications system, preventing the Japanese from coordinating a counterattack. They stayed hidden, five thousand of them, in their fortresslike network of bunkers, blockhouses and pillboxes, shooting through the narrow slits, forcing the marines to come after them with grenades and flamethrowers.

By nine the next morning, the *Santa Fe* had orders to start shelling targets on Betio again—areas 209, 208, 204, then ten minutes of rapid fire to clear a path for the marines in area 228. Stu braced as the ship shuddered under the blasting guns.

"Good shooting," the officer on the beach radioed back to the *Santa Fe*. "No enemy counterattacks. Troops now advancing."

From the reports passing through the radio room, Stu heard the battle turning toward the marines. Early that afternoon, after another battle-station lunch of horse cock sandwiches, the *Santa Fe* was ordered to watch the narrow passage between Betio and the next island in the atoll, and to destroy any enemy troops trying to escape across it. The ship edged toward the coral reef, and Stu slipped out to the railing, near enough to see eight or nine figures scrambling across the beach. He looked up when he heard a plane approach, aiming at the men.

"Get that plane out of there—that's the marines!" a voice on the radio urgently commanded. "Don't shoot, it's the marines!"

The plane pulled away, and the marines advanced unharmed up the beach, out of the sights of their own guns and into range of the Japanese.

Two days later—after a final series of desperate banzai charges, and several hundred more rounds from the *Santa Fe*—the American flag rose over Betio, and the first planes took off from the airstrip there. Of the enemy, only 17 Japanese combatants and 129 Korean laborers remained alive. All the others who had survived the American guns chose suicide over surrender—exploding grenades against their bellies, or wedging rifle muzzles under their chins and then pulling the triggers with their big toes, or simply refusing to come out when the bulldozers began burying their bunkers.

Stu had long heard of the enemy's fanatic tenacity, but to actually see it up close—to watch them sacrifice almost every living soul for what looked to him like such a worthless piece of earth—made him wonder just how long this war would go on, and whether his chances of survival were really as good in the navy as he had speculated when he enlisted. Would the Japanese hold on to every island as dearly as they had Tarawa? And how many more of these islands lay between here and Tokyo?

Its big guns cooling, the *Santa Fe* cruised protectively around the blasted coral of America's newest possession, and Stu returned gratefully to the narrow bunk that had widened and softened in his imagination during the hard hours of fitful sleep on the radio-room floor. Asleep in the bunk above was Buford Osmond, the radio-school buddy who had first volunteered them for warship duty and who had also been transferred off the *Brooklyn* and onto the admiral's staff. An enemy sub had sunk an escort carrier nearby, and the topside lookouts were keeping an anxious watch, seeing periscopes in every empty powder case that bobbed on the surface. The rest of the ship, though, quickly resumed its village routines. Decks were swept, guns cleaned, the newspaper printed. In the morning, starved for some hot food after the run of cold battle-station rations, Stu hungrily eyed even the green-tinged mountain of scrambled powdered eggs on the mess-hall grill; but after tasting them, he quickly began calculating how many meals remained before the fixed, seven-day menu rolled around again to his favorite breakfast of the week, Saturday's cornbread and baked beans. Before his radio watch resumed, he took off his shirt and took some sun back on the fantail, then stopped for ice cream at the "gedunk" stand, the onboard soda fountain that, for a brief, transporting moment at least, resembled the Main Street sweet shop where he and his friends had first pictured themselves sailors.

In the broad, blue Pacific, Stu had finally found an ocean that equaled his enlistment ambitions—far from both the Atlantic that washed the beach towns back home, and the Mediterranean that bordered the old-world nations of his geography lessons. The places out here—Espiritu Santo, Majuro, Kwajalein, where they were headed now from Tarawa—had names that sounded lifted from adventure stories, not atlases. The sea was calm and warm, and seemed large enough to hide a whole navy in. But the farther west the fleet steamed, the greater the danger grew, darkening the edges of Stu's postcard view. For several days running, a garbage-scavenging shark sliced steadily through the ship's wake, a constant enough shadow that some of the men began to regard its defiant presence as a challenge. Stu watched one afternoon as the hook on the fantail crane was baited with a slab of rotten meat and cast overboard like an ungainly fishing line. The shark bit, and as it was hoisted up the men fired enough bullets into its thrashing bulk to make sure it was dead by the time it hit the deck. When the ship's doctor sliced open its stomach, out spilled a lunch of whole fish and a large, rusty, unlabeled tin can that no one volunteered to open.

Kwajalein was the capital of the Marshalls, the next enemy island chain the Americans planned to capture; for now the *Santa Fe* ventured only near enough for a bombing raid by the accompanying carrier planes before turning around and heading back toward America. The news of a trip home was an unexpected reprieve. The visit would be brief, the crew was told, but any time at all away from the war was welcome. As the ship sailed east into safer waters, Stu felt himself uncoiling. Lone enemy subs were always a possibility, but when he took his cigarette breaks outside the radio room now, he didn't scan the horizon quite as anxiously as he had before.

The *Santa Fe* stopped at Pearl Harbor to be fitted with new radar equipment, then continued all the way to California to practice amphibious landings at San Clemente. When it docked in Long Beach, the crew was liberated for five precious days, the first time in months that Stu stepped on land that was part of a continent. Some young women were hawking magazines at the dock, and he bought a subscription to *Field & Stream,* a hopeful harbinger of a peaceful, leisurely postwar future when he again would be only the predator, not the prey.

Stu and his ship were back in the Marshalls a few weeks later, in January of 1944, just in time for the invasion. The fleet that converged on this next set of islands, though, had absorbed the cruel lessons of Tarawa, and had hardened its strategy. Stu had hardened, too, after his first Pacific battle: The Japanese had to be killed, not just defeated, and he had little room for mercy or sympathy. The guns on his ship, and on all the others, now fired longer, more accurately, and in closer rhythm with the carrier planes, blasting as clear a path as possible for the ground troops. Stu watched the landing boats parade across the lagoon toward the beach, and heard the radioed congratulations when his own ship's shells knocked out a persistent pair of the enemy's five-inch shore guns. Within a few days, and with a fraction of Tarawa's casualties, the Americans had won the islands, and leaped almost a thousand miles closer to Japan.

The unmarked front line now lay somewhere in the waters beyond the Marshalls—its precise longitude shifting daily, depending on where the fleets were and which planes were stationed on whose islands—and the *Santa Fe* raced toward it at thirty knots. The ship's temperature rose with its speed, steam heat soaking into the hull and seeping up from the furnace depths of the fire room, where the soot-covered "black gang" tended engines that gulped fuel at the rate of 125 gallons per mile. Climbing from his bunk to the bridge, Stu took care where he laid his hands: He knew that what looked like cold, gray steel was in fact hot enough in spots to ignite a match. In the radio room, the headphones throbbed with messages, nearly a thousand a day—from Washington, from Hawaii, from the captains of the other ships in Task Force 58, the fast-carrier armada that had its sights fixed on Truk in the Caroline Islands, a base as important to the Japanese as Pearl Harbor was to the Americans. Every time he stepped out for a break, letting the sea breeze clear the beeping tangle of Morse patterns from his head, he saw more American carrier planes taking off for, or returning from, Truk—each attack wave, thirty over the course of two days, carrying more firepower than either of the two Japanese raids that had started the war on a Sunday morning in Hawaii in 1941. The bombs from the planes, aided later by the shells from the ships, proved far more effective than they had on Tarawa. The critical air and naval bases on Truk were leveled without a single soldier ever landing on its beach.

The task force pressed north toward the Mariana Islands, the nearest to Japan that Stu had yet been, and then dashed back through the Carolines again, launching air strikes and dodging enemy planes all the way. One Betty crashed in flames eight hundred yards off the *Santa Fe*'s starboard quarter, the fourth the ship's gunners had shot down, and its silhouette was painted beside the others on the cruiser's hull. The speakers in the radio room broadcast the constant chatter of carrier pilots warning each other against encroaching invaders.

"Watch your rear, watch your rear," Stu heard a frantic, disembodied voice call while the ship was somewhere in the Carolines. "Bogey at ten o'clock high."

Stu still wasn't twenty yet, but the tense and jagged rhythms of the war had worked their way deep enough inside him that he was sometimes surprised to find himself rising to the kind of defiant insouciance of the old navy regulars who had seemed so intimidating back on the *Brooklyn,* not even a year ago. "Bogeys on the radar," one of his friends announced mischievously in the mess hall one day, holding up a piece of bread marred by a spray of dark flea-sized spots. The ship had returned for provisioning to Majuro, and a new supply of flour had come on board, riddled with weevils that added an unwelcome, crunchy texture to meals.

". . . Three, four, five, six in that one," Stu counted before resuming work on the main course, a large cut of fresh steak that, though the cooks hadn't advertised its origins, he could tell from the sweet, distinctive flavor was horsemeat.

Heavy with shells again, the *Santa Fe* steamed south across the equator toward New Guinea, where MacArthur's army was planning a long leap up the island's northern coast, bypassing the Japanese strongholds and invading instead the unsuspecting garrison at Hollandia. The carrier pilots cleared the sky of enemy planes, and the ships shelled the nearby airfields there. The *Santa Fe* fired blindly on a target obscured by distance, darkness and rain squalls, relying solely on radar and three aerial photographs for guidance. The invasion so surprised the Japanese that the landing American troops found tea still brewing and bowls of breakfast rice sitting half-finished. When the *Santa Fe* heard reports of a downed American torpedo bomber off Wakde Island, its two seaplanes were catapulted off the fantail deck and sent to rescue the soggy fliers.

"Hoist 'Tare Victor George,'" Stu heard Admiral DuBose order when the bomber's crew was safely aboard. The flags went up, and every ship within signal distance could read the message: Job well done.

Returning to the central Pacific, the *Santa Fe* anchored off the base it had helped win on Kwajalein. Landfalls were scarce enough that even this sparse and remote atoll beckoned like a dim memory of home to Stu and his shipmates, whose shore leave consisted of an afternoon visit to a narrow spit of palm-shaded sand that offered no bars and no women, just the hot, dense company of hundreds of other sea-weary sailors, each closely clutching his three-can beer ration. He swam in the lagoon, but it wasn't nearly as welcoming as the beach back home in Manasquan; he had to keep his shoes on as protection against the sharp coral bottom. New movies arrived on the ship, screened in the evenings back on the fantail, and a fresh batch of mail was delivered. The magazine he had subscribed to in San Diego finally came—not the *Field & Stream* he was expecting, but *Russia Today,* a propaganda organ; the young woman he bought it from on the dock had apparently been a Soviet sympathizer who believed the alliance between Roosevelt and Stalin should be more than just a temporary matter of strategic expedience.

The stopover quickly bored Stu. When he had sat in Freehold feeling stranded after high school, dreaming of the wide world he hoped the navy would show him, he had pictured richer, more alluring destinations that this desolate island. The farther he got from home, he found, the better it looked, and the more he wanted to get back to it. At least when the ship was moving, he felt that he was getting somewhere; every battle he survived, he reasoned, meant he was that much closer to the end of the war, and to home. When he was sitting still like now, though, the war seemed as if it would go on forever. While still at Kwajalein, he felt his skin beginning to itch, as if his body were telling him just how eager it was to leave. He found himself speckled with half-dollar sized sores he tried not to scratch.

"Impetigo," the doctor said when he saw the red blisters that had begun to burst and ooze and crust over. He painted them with gentian violet, as a deckhand might daub yellow chromate on the ship's rust patches, and told Stu not to touch the purple-dyed spots. "There were a lot of dead Japs in that lagoon you were swimming in. It's probably from that."

Itchy and restless as he was, though, he at least had the consolation of his position. "All hands turn to," the loudspeaker announced one morning while the ship was at anchor, and a long line of men streamed past Stu's bunk and through the hatch at his feet that led down into the ammo locker below.

"Admiral's staff," he said to someone who tried to rouse him, and then rolled back over to sleep, grateful that his status spared him from loading details.

On the same day the European war vaulted into a new stage, with the

June 6 invasion of Normandy, the *Santa Fe* weighed anchor and joined the most ambitious effort yet to push ahead the Pacific front, steaming north toward the Marianas with the Fifth Fleet. The planes from the fifteen carriers led the invasion armada, trailed by landing ships crammed with the ground troops who would storm the beaches of Saipan, Guam and Tinian, islands near enough to Japan to permit direct bombing raids by the giant new B-29 Superfortresses, which dwarfed Bill Lopatin's Marauders. Even from his perch on the bridge, Stu could count only a fraction of the force, which stretched several horizons beyond his sight— almost a quarter million men in all, more than were crossing the Channel into France today, on more than five hundred ships.

The Americans had planned to fight mainly on land when they reached the Marianas, but the Japanese made them fight at sea, too. The *Santa Fe* was standing off Saipan with Task Force 58, shielding the island where the marine invaders were battling back the banzai charges and tank attacks of the deeply entrenched defenders, when a message arrived from a submarine that had spotted a long, dark line of enemy carriers and battleships silhouetted against the central Philippines coast. "The Japanese fleet is headed for the Marianas," it reported. The American fleet turned and tensed for the attack, which came at midmorning on June 19— sixty-nine enemy planes winging in from unseen carriers farther west in the Philippine Sea.

"Unidentified planes have been picked up, bearing 333 (degrees) forty-five miles away," reported a message that arrived in Stu's radio room at 10:07.

The Hellcats had already been launched to meet the Japanese torpedo planes and dive bombers, and within forty minutes the tone of the messages had shifted from wary to exultant. "We have two more bogies at 190 [degrees]—forty [miles away] and 225—thirty-six," the message said, but the bogies were fast becoming casualties. ". . . Ten to fifteen Zekes splashed so far."

For the rest of the day—listening to the pilots' excited play-by-play on the radio room speakers, watching the swooping, spinning, smoking dogfights from his perch just outside—Stu had a ringside angle on the greatest carrier battle of the war, the Battle of the Philippine Sea, four times the size of Midway. The sky was a wide, warm and flawless blue, flecked by puffy blossoms of black smoke from the ships' antiaircraft guns, and etched by the white scrawls of the planes' vapor trails, a complex, crisscrossing diagram that described the action as sharply as the chalk lines of a coach's blackboard. The *Santa Fe* shot at two enemy dive-bombers that threatened two of the carriers in its group, the *Wasp* and the *Bunker Hill*, but most of the other attackers were stopped by the deadly screen of Hellcats. Victory was so complete that by the end of the day the battle had already been dubbed "The Great Marianas Turkey Shoot." It cost Japan two carriers and more than three hundred planes to shoot down just thirty American planes and drop a single bomb on the battleship *South Dakota*.

The next day's search planes didn't find the fleeing enemy fleet until late in the afternoon. The distance and the hour meant a risky mission—the carrier planes would have barely enough fuel for the long round-trip, and would have to return in the darkness—but the target was too tempting, and a strike was ordered. At four P.M. Stu slipped out of the radio room to glimpse a stirring spectacle—216 planes taking off from the carriers in less than twenty minutes, soaring defiantly out into the fading day. He, like the pilots themselves, wondered how many would make it back. In the scant evening light almost three hundred miles away, the Americans finally caught up with the wounded Japanese, sank one carrier and two oilers, shot down sixty-five enemy planes and lost twenty of their own before turning around. Their tanks were running low, and the home carriers were still hidden somewhere in the uncertain distance, pitching invisibly in a featureless, midsea night broken only by the barest crescent of new moonlight and the occasional flashes of lightning from a rising squall. The pilots spoke little on the way back, and Stu could measure their fear by the weight of the silence on the radio room speakers.

"Turn on the lights!" ordered Vice Admiral Marc Mitscher, the task force commander, and the American fleet came alive like a downtown Saturday night, beckoning not only the straying pilots, but also, and far more hazardously, any lurking enemy subs.

Slender columns of blinding white light rose from the *Santa Fe*'s thirty-six-inch search beams, climbing straight and high until they merged into the wide, pale nimbus that crowned the fleet. The five-inch guns joined the other ships in firing a fusillade of star shells fit for Independence Day. For the next two hours, the planes staggered down from the sky, landing on whatever carrier deck was nearest, the wrong one mostly, or crashing into the sea. The radio-room speakers broadcast the raw, urgent soundtrack of men facing their own deaths—the pilots' voices

swelling with fear and sadness, despair and disbelief, as they came to realize that their planes couldn't bring them home this time.

"I'm going down!" one pilot screamed, in a tone that pierced what
was left of Stu's shell of youthful immortality. "I can't make it!"

Some of the pilots made their final plummet with their gun switches
on, the tracer bullets marking the spot where they hoped to be found.
Eighty planes in all went down, the last casualties of a battle that had dec-
imated the enemy: Half the Japanese carriers were no longer operational,
and only 35 of the 430 enemy planes that had taken off yesterday could
still fly tonight. Destroyers dashed after survivors in the sea around the
American fleet, scanning the dark swells for life jackets and rubber rafts.
The men in the water, dozens of them, trilled their boatswain's whistles
with as much breath as they could spare, and blinked their small, waterproof flashlights, praying that their signals would last long enough to save
their lives.

Jake Errickson: New Guinea

As he groped slowly up from his damp, tropical sleep, reluctantly roused
by the reveille that was sounding somewhere outside his tent, Jake Errickson opened his eyes to find Dot's face floating beside his cot, as if veiled
by the gauzy, white cloud of a dream. Turning his head he saw the tent's
dim, dawn interior, the sleeping forms of his comrades, enveloped in the
same pale haze—the effect of the mosquito netting draped from a T-bar
overhead. His view sharpened when he sat up and pushed aside the net.
He gazed at the photograph of his fiancée that was propped up on the
empty packing crate he had converted into a nightstand, and he felt the
dead, sinking weight of every one of the thirteen hundred miles that separated them.

"C'mon, Johnny, time to go," he called toward one of his tent mates.

Jake shook out his boots, green as grass from the steady wetness, to
dislodge any scorpions that might have bunked inside overnight, and he
pulled on a khaki workshirt so infected with mold that it seemed flecked
with black paint. His thin blanket had soaked up the night's moisture like
a sponge, and he carried it outside to hang in the sun. New Guinea was
so waterlogged that Jake often thought he would have been drier in the
navy. The rain arrived dependably toward the end of each day—so heavy
and quick one recent night that a killing torrent rushed down from the

mountains and swept away some neighboring New Zealanders who had camped too near a riverbed.

Hungry for anything but the breakfast he was expecting, Jake walked to the mess tent through what looked like a grove of blackened telephone poles—the beheaded trunks of coconut palms, shorn of their lush crowns in the fiery battle that had won this coast back from the Japanese invaders. The charred shell of a landing craft sat grimly on the beach, the thick timbers of its hull exposed like bones. The battle of Buna—here in Australia's Papua territory, on the eastern tail of New Guinea island—had cost the Allies more casualties than Guadalcanal, and many of the dead were buried nearby, under the long, straight ranks of fresh, white markers in Eichelberger Square cemetery. A stark, sad photo of three dead soldiers on the beach at Buna, sprawled in the sand and crawling with maggots, was blocked for months by censors, until Roosevelt himself permitted its publication. "The American people ought to be able to see their own boys as they fall in battle," *Life* magazine explained, "to come directly and without words into the presence of their own dead."

The fighting had since moved farther up the jungle coast, where the Japanese were garrisoned in places that Jake's unit helped pinpoint. Looking up toward the hills where his direction finder was planted, Jake saw that the high peaks beyond were still shrouded by morning clouds. In those hidden mountains, along the jagged spine that bisected New Guinea's wild interior, lurked the island's greatest dangers—cannibals, headhunters, straggling Japanese snipers and raiders. In the distance ahead of him, the blasted trees marched into a tangled green thicket beyond the battle's reach, a fringe of flat land squeezed between the mountains and the ocean, thick with mangrove and nipa swamps, crossed by crocodile-infested rivers and broken occasionally by a rubber plantation or a thatched-hut village with a field cleared for taro. "Few areas in the world present so formidable an obstacle to military operation," MacArthur had said of New Guinea. The dark-skinned natives wore grass skirts and loincloths, and their tightly curled hair led the soldiers to call them "fuzzy-wuzzies." They were loyal to the Allied cause, fond of army trinkets—a spoon or a toothbrush might be reincarnated as an earring—and seemed to absorb more of the Americans' ways than the Americans did theirs. Walking along the beach one day, Jake had heard the melancholy strains of "Red River Valley" floating down through the humid air, and he traced the song to its source—a native boy, no more than seven or eight, who had climbed to the top of a palm tree, singing as he hacked off coconuts with a machete.

Lining up for powdered eggs, Jake ran a hand along his side and felt a corrugated ridge of ribs. Sapped and wilted by the climate, cut off from the hearty roast beef Sunday dinners Dot's mother had stuffed him with back in Brisbane, he had lost 35 of his original 175 pounds since arriving in New Guinea six months ago, in early September of 1943. He had flown to Port Moresby with a cadre of replacements from his unit, and then ridden slowly to Dobodura along a crushed-coral coastal road that, when wet, sucked the trucks down like mud. "There are many roads to Tokyo," a billboard there declared, quoting Roosevelt. "We will neglect none of them." He saw corpses waiting for burial, and cleanup crews hosing blood from the insides of wounded bombers.

As Jake's body had shrunk, so too had his morale. He had been in uniform for three years already, and his general longing for home had only been magnified by his engagement. Where his colleagues had vague notions and hopes about what they would do when they got out, he had specific plans, and that made the waiting all the more difficult. He was going to marry Dot, take her halfway across the world to Freehold, go back to his job in the rug mill, start a family and rent an apartment until he was promoted into a job that would pay him enough to buy a house of his own. But here he was, stuck in what felt like the remotest backwater of the war. At least Stu Bunton had the comfort of movement, which made the days pass swiftly. Jake's days dragged, as stagnant and heavy as the tropical air. His duties took him on the same short, unchanging route—from camp to the direction finder and back, over and over again—and gave him nothing but time to think about all that he was missing. The isolation was broken only by letters from Dot, and, on one happy day, another surprise visit from his sister Georgie. She was on her way to a bush hospital at Gusap when she stopped at his camp, and they attended a church service together in a chapel made of woven palm fronds. She brought him some of the new melt-resistant tropical Hershey bars. They were hard and dry, more like nougat than the creamy candy at Heckman's on Main Street back home, but they tasted better than anything else he had eaten lately, and he stored them in a coffee can to keep them from the rats.

To arm himself against malaria, Jake puckered his face at breakfast's end this morning and swallowed his daily dose of Atabrine, two yellow aspirin-sized pills washed down with warm grapefruit juice, a bitter taste that would linger at the back of his mouth all morning. He and Dot had hoped to marry before he left for New Guinea, but his marching orders arrived before he had gotten the official permission from his commanding officers that he needed before he could wed. "I have your application, but it is not approved," an officious municipal clerk named Porter—a name he wouldn't soon forget—had told him, placing bureaucracy ahead of romance. Jake left Dot without a date for their wedding, or even a year. In New Guinea he asked his captain as often as he dared about his matrimonial prospects, but he never heard the answer he wanted.

At the motor pool, Jake hefted onto the back of a three-quarter-ton truck two freshly charged six-volt car batteries for his direction finder. Bumping up the rough track to his station, one of four fanned widely through the hills around camp, he saw the two overnight men waiting wearily under the crude tin-roof shelter, the night's messages stacked neatly in a thick sheaf of five-by-seven papers. The enemy was nearer here on New Guinea, and the radio traffic was heavier than anything they had heard in Australia—a steady pulse of messages from Rabaul, across the Solomon Sea in New Britain, from Wewak, beyond MacArthur's front line up-island, and from many other smaller positions in between.

"They got the wire," one of the night listeners told Jake.

Unheard and unseen under cover of darkness, a Japanese soldier had crept out of the jungle and sabotaged the telephone cable that connected the station with the base, driving a nail through it somewhere, causing a short that Jake knew would be hard to find. Jake pushed through a curtain of vines and followed the wire out into the bush, worrying all the way that it would lead him straight to the point of an enemy knife. He found the short before he found its author, and spliced the wire whole again. His shirt was already soaked through, and when he had peeled it off, he slipped on the headphones and tapped into the stream of radio messages. By tracking the location and size of enemy units, Jake's intelligence company helped the army's commanders decide where to attack and, just as importantly, where to ignore. Rather than plowing headlong to the west, bulling toward the Philippines with a full frontal assault, MacArthur had opted for a deft series of nimble hops, bypassing and isolating key Japanese strongholds—a strategy he described as "hit 'em where they ain't, let 'em die on the vine." At Rabaul, one hundred thousand Japanese infantrymen waited for a fight that never came. As Admiral Nimitz vaulted from island to island across the Central Pacific, with Stu Bunton and the

Santa Fe in tow, MacArthur leapfrogged along the northern coast of New Guinea, with Jake Errickson and the126th trailing several steps behind.

The rain arrived on schedule, late in the afternoon of Jake's listening shift, and he heard the lightning long before the thunder arrived on his hillside, the instantaneous crackle of static electricity filling his headphones and making him wince. He turned the volume down on his receiver, and resumed trolling through the frequencies where the Japanese usually lurked, between 1100 and 1700 kilocycles. When his replacements rumbled into view, he donned a poncho and safari hat for the wet ride down to camp. To the cryptanalysts back at Central Bureau, the messages traced and collected by the field teams each day opened a wide window onto the war, but to Jake they were—except for the SOS that broke through one afternoon from a bomber about to ditch off the Admiralty Islands—just strings of meaningless gibberish, granting him no special insight into the one question that occupied every soldier's hopes and fears: Where do we go from here?

An order to move finally came in the spring of 1944, but it was only a couple of hundred miles up the coast to Finschhafen, another beachfront jungle base like Buna and Dobodura. Off duty, Jake played baseball, swam in the ocean—feet protected from the coral by sneakers, eyes alert for shark fins—and waited for the Catalina flying boat to appear with the mail. He avoided the local food, and drank water so heavily chlorinated it tasted like a swimming pool. A river ran between the 126th's camp and the supply depot that served the many army units clustered at Finschhafen, and when Jake reached it one day in his jeep—on a mission to get some new wire for the direction finders—he found that a thunderstorm had washed it away. He waded across, looped the wire around his shoulder, and was wading back when he saw slogging toward him a familiar figure that made him stop in midriver.

"If it isn't Vete Urbelis," Jake said.

"Warren Errickson," said Vytold Urbelis, a star of the football team when both of them were in high school back in Freehold.

They stopped and shook hands. They hadn't been friends at home, but it was enough for a moment that there was somebody else in this unlikely spot who knew what that home looked like. Each saw in the other proof that, even though he was standing knee-deep in the middle of a river in Finschhafen, New Guinea, he wasn't totally unmoored in the world. Each was confirmation to the other that Freehold, which had seemed to recede ever further into the past, hadn't been just a dream.

By June, almost a year after giving Dot a diamond, Jake was still in Finschhafen, and frustrated enough to buck the chain of command, appealing over the head of an unsympathetic company commander who just didn't seem to understand how important it was for him to get back to Australia.

"I'm getting nowhere with the captain, sir," he told Major Brown, whose ear he thought might be more receptive to his plea for a leave. Brown had used Jake as his driver in Brisbane, had given him afternoons off to spend with Dot, and had even been a guest at her parents' dinner table.

"Well, let me talk to him," Brown said.

Within ten days, Jake finally had his furlough, and was packing his dress uniform for the wedding. After supper on the night before he left Finschhafen, strolling back to camp from the central mess hall that served a cluster of neighboring companies, he heard a muffled clamor of jabbers and shouts leaking out of an oversized hospital tent. He pushed aside the flap to find a swarm of soldiers pressed three-deep around a plywood table across which an army blanket had been thrown. Dice were flying, and unruly stacks of cash were drifting like dunes. Craps can make losers more quickly than almost any other game, but Jake felt his luck rising. He set down his money, the Dutch guilders he was paid in, and watched it multiply. When the dice came around to him, they did whatever he asked of them. After forty-five minutes cash was spilling from all his pockets— $1,100 in all, a honeymoon nest egg to dazzle his bride with.

"Man, you've got a golden arm," said the black soldier who had been Jake's dragger during the game, tending to the bets and corralling the dice. Jake gave him twenty dollars and started out the door. The other players, heartbroken at watching so much money walk away from the table, tried to flatter and cajole him into staying.

"So long, boys," he said, escaping their grasp and leaving a winner. "See you in church."

Stu Bunton: Leyte Gulf

As Stu Bunton hauled himself up the steep steps, rushing topside toward the news he had just heard the loudspeakers broadcast, the ship beneath his feet felt as still and steady as land. Climbing through the last hatch, out of the cramped shadows and into a lurid sun that narrowed his eyes to a squint, he saw that almost the whole of the Third Fleet, riding at anchor in every direction around the *Santa Fe,* had converged into a city in Ulithi lagoon. Carriers and freighters, landing crafts and oilers, dappled the flat water like a child's bathtub navy. The habit of months at sea kept Stu's knees loose as he hurried across the quarterdeck, but there was no roll beneath his legs. A gun crew was drilling at the five-inch mount, feeding the loading machine with shells no one expected to fire today. The view to starboard, the side Stu hurried for, was blocked by the towering gray wall of the battleship *New Jersey,* looming as large over the *Santa Fe* as the *Santa Fe* would over a destroyer. He crossed the gangway that bridged the narrow canyon between the two ships, which had been yoked together temporarily.

"Requesting permission to come aboard, sir," he said, saluting the *New Jersey*'s officer of the day. "I'd like to see Seaman Joe DuBois."

Stu craned to spot the bridge where Admiral Halsey himself presided, paused to admire the mighty sixteen-inch guns—the whole ship jumped back in the water when they were fired, as he knew from watching at island bombardments—and then looked out over the deck for a face he hadn't seen in two years. Joe DuBois was a fellow sweet-shop sailor, and ever since their joint enlistment, Stu had followed his progress in the pages of the newsletter from the Presbyterian church they both belonged to. Stu found him manning a mop, half the world away from Main Street.

"I thought you'd be coming over," said Joe, who had been following Stu the same way.

All eight of the high-school friends who had joined the navy together, before the draft could put them in the infantry, were still alive and in uniform. Joe and Stu had each fought in several headline battles—the *New Jersey* and the *Santa Fe* had been cruising the same swath of the Pacific lately—but in the half hour or so they had today before their ships parted again, they dwelled instead on the news from home. A midnight card game at Murphy's on South Street had ended with a knife in someone's back. A black man had sued the town, unsuccessfully, after claiming he was beaten by two police officers. The local girls were hosting—and, to the dismay of the local boys who were overseas, sometimes dating—the soldiers posted to the old CCC camp at a weekly canteen in the Episcopal church. Farm labor was scarce, and persistent but false rumors predicted that German POWs from Fort Dix would soon be picking Freehold potatoes. Paul Fitch had killed two Japanese soldiers in New Guinea, Stacy Matthews had killed eight on Saipan, and Robert Kanze's carrier-based fighter was shot from the sky over Truk Lagoon, where he floated in hostile waters for eighteen hours before being plucked up to safety. Hardest of all for Stu to digest, though, was the story his mother had told in a recent letter: Walking to a friend's house behind the mill one evening, crossing the Central Railroad freight yards, his sister was grabbed from behind by a black man and raped. Another man heard her screams, but did nothing to help.

"They didn't get him," Stu said, his voice tight with frustration at the distance between him and the crisis. If the war hadn't taken him away from Freehold he might be a cop already, as he had planned; and if he were a cop, he might be able to do something about it, to investigate the crime, to track down suspects, anything at all that made him feel that he was helping his sister. But instead he was stuck here in the middle of the Pacific, angry and powerless.

"They will," Joe said, trying to reassure him.

On his own ship again, Stu turned his anger back on the enemy that was drawing him ever farther from home. After the Marianas, the *Santa Fe* had spent the summer jabbing north and west into the inner rings of the Japanese empire, chasing an outgunned navy that refused to contemplate its own defeat. On the Fourth of July, Stu watched the six-inch guns bombard the airdromes of a barren volcanic island few Americans had yet heard of, Iwo Jima; and listened over the radio as the pilot of one of the ship's two ungainly little Kingfisher float planes, catapulted off the fantail to spot target positions, got tangled in an unlikely dogfight. The Kingfisher's pilot was set upon by three Japanese Zeroes, and managed to shoot one down before he was forced to ditch. The *Santa Fe* later shelled the sister island of Chichi Jima Rettō, and pounced on a Japanese convoy that was trying to slip away, sinking several destroyers, oilers and cargo ships. They attacked another convoy off the Philippines, where one of the Kingfishers swooped into enemy territory to rescue two downed American flyers who were being sheltered by Filipino guerrillas. They shielded the carriers on strikes against Guam and Rota, Yap and Palau, and then anchored in Ulithi in the western Carolines—in Japanese hands just two weeks earlier, now overrun with restless sailors on beer-can afternoon liberties—to prepare for their biggest operation yet, the Pacific theater's equivalent of Normandy: the invasion of the Philippines, which would finally link Stu's war with Jake's, the Central Pacific drive with the South, and fulfill MacArthur's grand vow to return.

Stu and Joe shared no other visits through a week at Ulithi, and when their ships steamed out of the lagoon, joining a protective ring around a seventeen-carrier armada, they headed west toward Formosa. The Pacific war was moving faster now than its strategists had predicted, the carrier-plane strikes inflicting enough damage to bump several occupied islands off the invasion list and accelerate the schedule for the Philippine campaign. But before the landing crafts could disgorge MacArthur's troops onto the beaches of the central island of Leyte, the carriers were dispatched on a final preparatory mission—to sweep the sky clear of enemy planes. For three days, flying from the seas off Formosa, waves of carrier pilots attacked Japanese airfields, destroying more than five hundred planes, while losing seventy-nine of their own. In the twilight of the second day, in one of the frantic Japanese defense raids, a night-strike plane from the Typhoon attack force managed to hit the American cruiser *Canberra*.

"*Canberra* has been torpedoed in the after engine room," announced the monitor in the radio room where Stu sat at his battle station. "Engine room flooded."

Just six minutes later, the wounded cruiser's plight was clear. "Both engine rooms flooded. Two after fire rooms flooded. Request tow."

When a ship is stopped at sea in war, it becomes a target so fat and appetizing that enemies are drawn to it like sharks to blood. To shield it from the next, and perhaps last, torpedo, Admiral DuBose on the *Santa Fe* raced to surround the listing *Canberra* with a shield of circling cruisers and destroyers. By midnight the cruiser *Wichita* had the *Canberra* in tow, creeping at three knots along the thousand-mile path back to Ulithi. On the screening ships—three cruisers and six destroyers, steaming clockwise in close protective rings at faster, less vulnerable speeds—the crews stayed at heightened alert, listening for subs and looking for planes. As dawn lifted the natural cover of darkness, the ships tried to replace it with a night of their own making—puffing clouds of oily black smoke through their stacks, hoping to drape a concealing shroud over their slow parade.

"What the hell are they thinking?" Stu wondered aloud, but privately, to one of his radio-room companions after a trip outside to see the acrid haze. "You can't cloud up the whole damn atmosphere for one little cruiser."

Fighters from the supporting carriers swatted away the enemy planes for most of the day, but toward evening a few broke through. The *Santa Fe* shot down one, and deflected another that disappeared into a ball of flame before it could cross the horizon. When the attacks finally stopped at midnight, the *Canberra* was still afloat, but the cruiser that had taken its place back in the main carrier group, the *Houston*, had a hole near its keel amidships, opened by a torpedo from a Japanese bomber. By ten the next morning, the *Santa Fe* had taken on 197 new passengers, crewmen from the *Houston*, and was shepherding not one, but two limping cruisers, a target so tempting now that the Americans decided to set a trap with it.

"Don't worry," Admiral Halsey blithely signaled to Admiral DuBose after informing him that the *Santa Fe's* convoy had just become bait for the Japanese.

Blinded by smoke and inexperience, the young, barely trained remnants of the Japanese pilot corps had mistakenly seen a victory in the battle off Formosa—their wildly inflated claims of sinking eleven carriers, two battleships and three cruisers set off giddy celebrations in Tokyo—and it was Halsey's plan to prey on this hubris. The ships in the *Santa Fe's* convoy were ordered to send out radio messages in English, not code, practically inviting an attack. The enemy fleet gave chase, racing to kill what they thought they had wounded, but one of their scout planes spotted an American carrier group waiting to pounce. The Japanese ships turned back, narrowly avoiding the trap.

"All Third Fleet Ships Recently Reported Sunk by Radio Tokyo Have Been Salvaged and Are Retiring At High Speed Toward the Japanese Fleet," Halsey announced with a heavy dose of sarcasm.

The Japanese planes kept coming, though, sniffing along the oil-slick trail laid by the leaking cruisers. Under the low clouds of a gray midday, the remaining crew on the *Houston* was burying twenty-three of their dead—each flag-draped body wrapped tightly in canvas and weighted by a heavy, sinking shell—when general quarters was sounded on all the convoy's ships.

"Large group of bogies, Raid One, 075, eighty-two miles, ten to twelve planes," came the message from the carrier *Cabot*. "Fighters commencing interception."

White water sprayed the decks of the cruisers and destroyers as they spun frantically into defense positions. The Hellcats were dueling the invaders somewhere beyond sight, but three Japanese planes slipped past, dropping suddenly into view from the clouds and buzzing over the convoy like bees caught in a kitchen. The *Santa Fe*'s guns erupted as a twin-engine Frances, the fast new Japanese torpedo bomber, swooped directly toward it before turning and, passing across the bow, locked onto the *Houston.* A torpedo dropped from its wing and swam up behind the crippled cruiser. The explosion blew the *Houston*'s hangar hatch half a football field high, swept twenty men off their gun mounts and into the sea, and sparked a gas fire on the stern.

"Send destroyers to pick up crew from *Houston*," Admiral DuBose ordered as the flames jumped and the smoke billowed.

Drawn by the noise and news of the attack, Stu bolted out the radioroom door, scrambled to his bridge-rail perch, and assumed his accustomed position on what he thought was the edge of the battle. He had barely tallied the damage to the *Houston* when the guns on his own ship swiveled around and cranked down to direct their fire toward a dark, stubby line hovering just over the water. The initial barrage of exploding shells hung a black curtain across the horizon for a moment, but when the intruder emerged again, closer now and gaining, Stu recognized it as a Jill, a single-engine torpedo bomber. Two, maybe two and a half, miles out, it wasn't even two hundred feet high and it was still dropping, as if it planned a landing. It started jinking now, darting right and left through the dusky smoke blossoms bursting open all around it, showing its predatory tail fin like a shark.

The ship kept firing, even hitting, and the plane kept coming—a mile out now, one hundred feet up, flames licking from its punctured belly, wings wobbling with the effort of keeping it straight. Stu waited for the Jill to turn around, to run and save itself, but it wouldn't—the pilot apparently gripped by the same banzai frenzy that drove the suicidal defenders of Tarawa, or the Saipan civilians who tossed themselves and their children from the island's high rock cliffs rather than surrender, a sacrificial imperial fanaticism that the *Santa Fe*'s crew had as yet seen only from afar. The closer the plane came, the smaller Stu's world shrank. It wasn't rational, he knew, but it seemed that the pilot was aiming not just at his ship, not just at his section of the ship even, but at him personally, an unarmed radioman, barely past his twentieth birthday, whose only real weapon in the war was his facility with Morse code.

Stu's hands were bonded to the rail as his brain tried to absorb what was happening. Barely half a minute had passed since he had stepped out, but it felt to him like a day. He had never seen anything like this before, and he was frozen by the strange and alarming spectacle of it. The most frightened he had yet been in the war was at Sicily—the exploding ships, the diving bombers, the dying paratroopers—but that was a broad, heavy blade of fear, more like a dull, persistent ache. As much fire as had been in the air there, none of it was aimed directly at him. This Japanese plane was, though, and the fear was sharper, like the point of a knife.

"Holy Christ," he said to himself. "This is for keeps."

The plane was less than half a mile away, no farther than Stu had once walked to high school each morning, when it dropped its torpedo. The ship turned hard to the left, swinging its stern out of the torpedo's path. From the angle of the torpedo's approach, and the angle of the ship's evasion, Stu calculated that it would miss, but when he looked up again he saw that the Jill itself would not. It hadn't pulled up and away after launching, but continued plowing straight ahead, smoke and flames rising from its wounds, as if it had decided to become a bomb itself. The ship's guns were flailing at it like a cornered boxer. How much life was left in the burning plane? Stu wondered. How much chance did the guns have of stopping it? He didn't stay to find out. The plane was so close and low now that Stu, before he turned to sprint back to the radio-room hatch on the other side of the bridge, saw for the first time the face of his enemy. The Jill's mustachioed pilot, freeze-framed for one terrible, unforgettable instant, stared through the cockpit window, wearing the otherworldly mask of a man absorbed by the contemplation of his own death.

Still swerving hard to the left, the torpedo sputtering futilely in its wake, the *Santa Fe* gently turned its cheek away from the onrushing bomber's final, lunging blow. Just twenty-five feet off the starboard bow, seconds away from a grievous collision and wholesale casualties, the Jill exploded and crashed into the sea. A storm of flaming gasoline and sizzling plane fragments fell on the marines who were manning the 20 mm guns at mounts one and two on the fo'c'sle. Eight wounded men were carried to the officers' wardroom, where one of them died. A pall of black smoke rose so high and thick around the cruiser that neighboring ships mistakenly thought it had been destroyed.

"We almost got hit," Stu breathlessly told his colleagues as he shut the hatch behind him.

Sealed in the radio room again, he found everything intact but his own sense of immortality. The cruiser never broke stride, its damage not structural but human, and quickly resumed its flagship role in the rescue of the torpedoed *Houston,* which was listing even more noticeably to starboard. The destroyers approached gingerly, watching for rafts and men, living or dead, in the water. Stu heard sporadic reports of more enemy planes approaching, but none slipped through the carriers' taut screen.

"Come up alongside port quarter of *Houston,*" Admiral DuBose ordered the commander of the destroyers division. "Recommend men jump in water."

The sea calmed the next day, the sky cleared of intruders, and the *Santa Fe,* expecting a summons back to the main carrier force, moved from ship to ship through the convoy, lightening its load—transferring fuel to two destroyers, water to the *Canberra,* portable pumps to the *Houston,* and *Houston* survivors to a tanker. Stu knew that a more solemn duty was looming, too, and he unpacked his dress whites, awaiting the call to his first funeral since his own father's.

"All hands bury the dead," the loudspeakers announced, and the colors were lowered to half-mast.

Stu stood at parade rest on the fantail deck, his head bowed as the chaplain prayed. The marine killed when the plane exploded rested on a plank under a flag, feet extended out over the ship's edge, attended by eight body bearers. Stu stiffened to attention, holding a sharp salute, when the chaplain read the committal and the plank was tilted up. The flag deflated, as if a dying wind had emptied it of life, and the body slipped out, a grayish mummy-shaped phantom falling heavily toward the deep. It hit with a hollow splash that Stu felt in his belly, like a door slamming with an awful finality. He saluted again as the rifle squad fired three volleys—aiming, for once, at no enemy, but only into the saddened hearts of the crew—and he held his hand high until the last note of taps had faded.

As Stu changed back into his denims, the ship steamed west toward the Philippines, where more sailors were gathered offshore than had served in the whole navy a few years earlier. Slipping back into formation, the *Santa Fe* began patrolling the waters north and east of Leyte with the carriers of Halsey's Third Fleet. Closer in, the guns of the Seventh Fleet covered the invasion troops who were spilling onto the beach. As the first wave of Americans landed, a radio transmitter broadcast a familiar voice to the world.

"People of the Philippines," General MacArthur announced after wading ashore on the afternoon of October 20, his naturally royal tone swelling to match the gravity of a moment for which he had waited two and a half years, "I have returned."

America had returned to the Philippines with such force—the bristling armada sprawling as wide as its own island nation, the supply line stretching fat and steady all the way back to New Guinea, the ground troops moving determinedly inland—that Stu assumed, as the admirals did, too, that the only reasonable enemy strategy was a patient bunker defense. To the enemy, though, all those ships in one place looked like the biggest, and perhaps the last, target of the war, and the only reasonable strategy seemed a massive attack, relying on an abundance of daring to compensate for a shortage of strength. The Japanese divided what ships they had left, light on carriers but still heavy with battleships, into four groups—three to challenge the smaller Seventh Fleet at the vulnerable Leyte beachhead; the fourth to swoop down from the north as a diversion and lure Halsey's Third Fleet away from the action.

"The fate of the empire depends on this operation," Vice Admiral Takijiro Onishi told his air group commanders before the battle, in an address that formally inaugurated the kamikaze strategy Stu had witnessed a week earlier. The Americans didn't know it yet, but the plane that had swooped so unexpectedly on the *Santa Fe* was among the first in a wave of suicidal attacks. "In my opinion, there is only one way of assuring that our meager strength will be effective to a maximum degree, and that is for our bomb-laden fighter planes to crash-dive into the decks of enemy carriers."

In the radio room of the *Santa Fe,* on the tense and busy evening of October 23, Stu listened warily as the enemy crept ever nearer. "Major enemy force including BBs sighted by *Cabot* search," advised a message just before midnight, relaying news from a carrier plane. "BBs," Stu knew, were battleships, and Japan still had the world's largest, with eighteen-inch guns that dwarfed his own ship's. Within twenty minutes, the crew had been called to battle stations.

"Much enemy activity suggests heavy air attack this morning," warned a message from the task force commander just before dawn, as four separate groups of bogies appeared on the radar screen.

The Hellcats scrambled off the carriers at the news, winging out to shield the fleet and deflect the approaching enemy—the planes they called Bettys and Zekes, Judys and Jills—with a counterattack. Stu, listening intermittently to the pilots' channel playing in the background, followed the fight's progress through a series of terse, triumphant exclamations. "Splash one Betty!" the pilots cried as they watched their victims crash flaming into the sea. "Splash two Zekes!" The planes returned at nine-thirty, elated and almost whole, but they brought with them a furtive, unwelcome guest—a Japanese Judy that had somehow trailed unseen in their wake, and that dove through the low clouds to find a feast spread out below it. Before anything could stop it, the Judy dropped a 550-pound bomb that found its mark as easily as at target practice—hitting dead-center on the broad skillet top of the carrier *Princeton*, boring through the flight deck and hangar deck, finally detonating in the bakery, killing the men at work there and igniting the fuel, and then the torpedoes, of six planes parked just overhead. Stu watched as the smoke billowed up, the plume rising a thousand feet, and dark specks trickled down, as the men abandoned ship. Bright flames bloomed at the base of the tall superstructure. Explosions boomed as the fire reached fresh stashes of ammo and fuel.

More enemy planes arrived just past noon, and the *Santa Fe* zigzagged swiftly, trying to avoid the *Princeton*'s fate. The ship shivered under the steady thunder of its own guns, firing at four planes at once—three diving on the formation from the port quarter, one making a run on the starboard beam. When the sky had cleared again, and no new casualties were counted, the nearby cruiser *Birmingham* eased alongside the *Princeton* to take it in tow. The fire on the carrier was still burning dangerously near the aft bomb magazine, but the men had to be taken off. Line handlers, firefighters and rescue squads collected on the *Birmingham*'s open deck, separated from the *Princeton*'s persistent flames by just fifty feet of open water.

Stu was a couple of miles away in the *Santa Fe*'s radio room at half past two in the afternoon when he felt as much as heard the *Princeton* suddenly blow. A volcanic explosion ripped off the stern and aft sections of the carrier's flight deck, hurling house-sized steel plates onto the *Birmingham*. Hundreds of men were obliterated or mangled in a horrifying, convulsive instant. The *Birmingham* bore the worst of the blast, losing more than twice as many men, 229 dead, than the ship it had come to help. "The decks ran red with blood," the official report later declared, "not figuratively but literally." On the *Princeton*, the captain who had been understudying to take command left his new ship without one of his feet: The explosion had all but torn it off, and the medical officer, wielding a sheath knife and some sulfa powder, sliced through the ribbon of tendon and skin it dangled by.

What was left of the *Princeton* was still asking for a tow when a report passed through the radio room that killed any hopes of salvage: The elusive enemy carriers had finally been spotted, three hundred miles to the north. "In view of our new Jap contact to north," the task force commander radioed Halsey, "having *Princeton* sunk." After the last survivors were evacuated, a destroyer put a pair of torpedoes into the burning hulk, and the carrier, the first the navy had lost in two years, vanished in less than a minute, leaving nothing but a patch of fire on the water.

"Am proceeding north with 3 groups to attack enemy carrier force at dawn," Halsey radioed soon after, doing exactly what the Japanese hoped he would—snatching at the bait of their diversionary force and embarking on a chase that left Leyte Gulf lightly defended against the ships now threading quietly eastward through the Philippine straits.

While Stu was sleeping on the *Santa Fe* as it sprinted north, a column of towering Japanese warships slipped through the silent darkness south of Leyte. Fighting through the night—led first by some scrappy little PT boats, then backed by six lumbering old battleships, five of them raised from the mud at Pearl Harbor—the Americans managed to blast the enemy into retreat. But in the early light of dawn, the tall pagoda masts of another Japanese attack force slipped through the San Bernardino Strait to the north of Leyte, where the line of defense was much thinner—some light carriers and an outnumbered force of destroyers whose five-inch guns were no match for the Japanese eighteen-inchers.

As Stu was watching Halsey's planes take off in the morning after the fleeing bait, a fight began in San Bernardino that the Americans feared they might lose. Urgent pleas were sent asking Halsey's fleet to turn back, but they sat undelivered for hours, backed up in a communications pipeline too narrow to handle the hectic message stream of a naval battle that was quickly assuming dimensions as yet unseen in the war. The ships that were there now, it appeared, would have to fight alone, and they did. The pilots from the carriers dove boldly low, and the destroyers rushed rashly at the giant battleships, blowing a dense screen of smoke and fighting so fiercely that the enemy believed it had engaged a much larger force.

The Japanese might have won, but after several chaotic hours they turned and retreated. An American admiral's report on the action later awarded official credit to "the definite partiality of Almighty God."

Halsey finally heard the pleas from San Bernardino in midmorning, when he was just forty miles shy of the ships he had mistakenly believed were the day's main prize, and his planes had already sunk several enemy carriers. His battleships and some of his carriers turned south—forsaking a decisive surface attack for a defense they arrived too late to aid—but twelve destroyers and four cruisers, including the *Santa Fe,* continued north, under the command of Stu's boss, Admiral DuBose, chasing the wounded enemy stragglers.

Late in the afternoon DuBose's strike group found a Japanese light carrier, the *Chiyoda,* sitting dead in the water, mortally wounded earlier by the American dive-bombers. In the radio room, Stu felt the deep thud of the *Santa Fe*'s guns—281 rounds in less than eight minutes of shooting. The *Chiyoda* soon slid under, leaving just a patch of white water and flame to mark its fresh grave, the fourth Japanese carrier to die since morning.

Seven or eight other Japanese ships were still within reach—some limping, leaking trails of oil, others "going like hell," according to the search pilot—and the Americans raced into the fading light after them. A few minutes after the sun went down on the port side, faint lines of anti-aircraft fire scratched the dim, distant sky ahead. Three enemy ships, twenty-five miles out and shooting at a search plane, floated onto the *Santa Fe*'s radar screen, still fleeing north, but not swiftly enough yet to shake their pursuers.

"As soon as you are in range and have a good setup, commence firing, light cruisers on near targets, heavy cruisers on far targets," DuBose ordered from the bridge of the *Santa Fe.*

The far targets, a pair of destroyers accelerating to escape speed, were sixteen miles ahead and not getting any closer when the heavy cruisers finally opened up, the shells arcing light through the night sky as they strained across the long distance. The *Santa Fe*'s shells had a shorter trip, nine miles to a lone Japanese cruiser that, as the American heavies let the destroyers go and joined the bombardment, began to realize it was trapped. When a fire erupted on the enemy ship, silhouetting it in orange against the black sky, it turned toward its pursuers like a cornered, snarling animal.

"They're shooting back," somebody in the radio room said, and Stu slipped out to glimpse a scene unlike any he had yet witnessed—a running gun battle between ships.

Stu heard splashes in the dark ocean all around the *Santa Fe*—Japanese shells missing their target, the ship he was standing on. The enemy cruiser couldn't get away now, and was fighting with a last-stand desperation. Stu knew the Japanese guns had enough distance to reach him—some of the splashes were in front of the ship, but others were behind—but he didn't know if they had enough accuracy to hit him.

The American ships had more guns—and, as the attackers, better positions—and shot more accurately, each hit marked by a burst of flame on the enemy cruiser. Blowing stack smoke, smoldering from shell wounds, staggering from north to south, east to west—a course so jagged and unpredictable that DuBose assumed the captain was either battling a steering problem or attempting some kind of unorthodox evasive maneuver—the Japanese ship stumbled toward a stop several times, but then lurched ahead again at nearly thirty knots, returning fire as it ran and managing to elude the destroyers dispatched to kill it for more than an hour.

"We have target very, very slow, almost dead in water," DuBose finally announced at 8:03, and he sent the destroyers in again.

"Stand by—Fire torpedoes," the destroyers' commander ordered his ships, and then reported back to DuBose. "We have torpedoes in water, about five and a half minutes to run."

Trying vainly to hobble out of range, the doomed cruiser refused to accept death quietly. "Enemy opened fire on us," the destroyers' commander radioed. "I saw flashes about the time torpedoes were due to get there, and there appeared to be large explosion later. Target still seems to be swathed in smoke."

In the radio room, Stu felt both exasperation and respect as he heard the report. As wounded and overwhelmed as the Japanese were here, as hopeless as their cause seemed, they were fighting to their death, like the soldiers on Tarawa, and the pilot in the kamikaze attack. The *Santa Fe* and the other cruisers marched closer now, firing a slow, steady barrage of shells, like a carpenter hammering at a nail until it sinks compliantly into the wood. The enemy spat back a few gasping rounds.

"When you get in to ten thousand yards open up and please sink this ship," DuBose ordered the *Wichita*. "*Santa Fe* will illuminate."

The star shells whooshed up like comets and burst in a ghostly blaze of pure light, polarizing the view into stark tones of black and white, washing away the murky grays in between. The main battery's guns, lowered to a flat, point-blank trajectory, continued blasting until the enemy cruiser—just two and a half miles ahead now, burning all over and settling by the bow—was finally stunned into silence.

"Request you finish him off with a torpedo," DuBose ordered the destroyers' commander, but two minutes later there was nothing left to finish: The target had vanished, exploding as it sank, spewing up geysers of sea foam.

"Has he gone down?" DuBose asked.

"He has gone down," reported a disappointed captain whose torpedoes had never left his destroyer. "We were cheated."

"It breaks our hearts," DuBose replied, taking the same ironic tone.

The sea was clear and peaceful for as far as Stu could see now, and as far as the *Santa Fe* could reach tonight. With the next nearest targets fifty miles ahead, and the destroyers too low on fuel for a full-speed chase, DuBose turned his ships around, steaming back to the main fleet from the northern edge of a sprawling battle that, as the reports streamed in from the other admirals and the numbers were tallied, was adding up to the largest naval clash not just in the war, but in all of history: the Battle of Leyte Gulf, as it came to be called, from which twelve thousand men, three dozen warships and hundreds of planes never returned. The losses were overwhelmingly Japanese, the victory incontestably American, but Stu held no illusions about a quick surrender. After a week of close encounters with a determined enemy—from the plane's suicide plunge, to the lone cruiser that had just held out for two hours against the full force of DuBose's strike group—he envisioned the war that remained dragging on much as tonight had, a long chase through the darkness after a outnumbered quarry unwilling to stop before death. The mustachioed face of the diving pilot, forever staring into the last moment of life, hung frozen in Stu's mind as a warning of the grim resolve on the other side of the guns. How many more times would the Japanese have to lose, he wondered, before the Americans finally won?

Jake Errickson: New Guinea

The luckiest soldiers of the day stood sweating in a long line that snaked up into the paunchy belly of the workhorse C-47 that was waiting to ferry them out of Finschhafen and back to Australia, where the Japanese appeared only in the newspapers, the women's skirts weren't woven of grass, and beer wasn't limited to a six-can monthly ration. Jake Errickson, barracks bag at his feet, plucked his damp shirt away from his chest, vainly flapping at the spongy heat. Down in Brisbane, Dot was busy at her bakery job, decorating cakes for other people's weddings, unaware that her own was imminent. Climbing into the fuselage of the lumbering freighter plane—dim and bare as a boxcar, built to carry anything from cases of K rations to invasions of paratroopers—Jake folded his field jacket into a makeshift seat cushion. As the plane bumped higher and higher, gaining enough sky to clear the sawtooth jungle ridges of the Owen Stanley mountains, the lofty cold leaked inside. He stood up to shrug on his jacket and sat back down on the hard floor, shivering against the kind of winter chill he had rarely felt in the Pacific theater.

When the plane landed in Sydney, Jake was still five hundred miles away from Dot, and the train carrying him the rest of the way chugged north up the coast for an endless day and a half. Late on Saturday afternoon in Brisbane, in the quiet fading downtown light, he stepped blinking from Central Station's shadows toward the taxi stand, and glanced across the street at the solemn colonnade of the Anzac memorial, where, nine months earlier, his engagement had begun. Finally the dinner lights in Dot's house, glowing against the dusk through the cab window, shone as sweetly to him as his own home back on Jackson Street. Her mother answered the door, and managed, barely, not to faint. Jake shushed her with his index finger until Dot came around the corner and spotted him, rushing into his arms.

"Oh, you're so skinny," she said through her tears when they broke from their embrace and stepped back for a longer look at each other.

He usually trusted actions more than words, so he got right to the point. "I've got two weeks' leave," he told her. "How soon do you think we could get married?"

"You're not giving me much time," she said, but she wasn't complaining.

"I haven't got much time," he said.

At seven o'clock on Thursday evening, June 22, 1944—two nights after Stu Bunton had heard the returning pilots crashing as they fell short of the brightly illuminated carriers at the Battle of the Philippine Sea—Doris Ada Gilbert walked through a picket gate and up into the sanctuary of the Nudgee Methodist Church, a simple shingled rectangle with half-timbered eaves, just one hundred yards up the street from her parents' house, but the first step on a journey she expected would carry her halfway across the world. She had a pretty good idea of what awaited her there, and she was sure she wanted to go. Jake was not a wealthy man, she knew, and his job at the rug mill was not likely to make him one. The town he came from, the town he planned to take her to, was not one of the grand American cities she had seen in the movies, just a small county seat surrounded by farmland. But unlike some war brides, she didn't see her soldier fiancé as a ticket to a better life in a better place. She had a good life in a good place already. She wasn't a starry eyed teenager—she was twenty-four, and he was twenty-five—and she knew what she was doing. It wasn't America she wanted. It was Jake.

On the bride's side of the aisle stood the family and friends she was resigned to leaving behind. On the groom's side stood twenty-five of the American soldiers—members of Jake's unit still stationed in Brisbane—whose presence had so drastically altered the serene village rhythms of local life. Johnny Reinert, Jake's friend since signal school and his best man now, held the ring. Sentiment in some quarters ran high against wartime romances ("Australian girls seem to have lost their heads over American servicemen," the alarmed archbishop of Brisbane had written the year before in proposing, unsuccessfully, a ban on intermarriages, which eventually totaled seven thousand) but Jake and Dot had impressed those around them with the maturity and sincerity of their commitment. When the minister asked for objections, none was raised.

They honeymooned in Toowoomba, a mountain resort two hours west of Brisbane, on the edge of the Great Dividing Range. They strolled through the overlook parks that opened onto an idyllic world from which the war seemed banished—where hills rolled down from the sharp mountains into the spreading plains, eucalyptus trees rose lush and green from dark volcanic soil, the Crows Nest Falls tumbled through the Valley of Diamonds, and no enemies lurked. In the chill mountain evenings, Dot wore the fur coat Jake had bought for her with part of his craps winnings. When their two weeks were up, Jake reported back to Brisbane, expecting a quick ride back to New Guinea.

"It's not urgent," a commander with a keen sense of proportion and romance told him. "Wait until the next cadre leaves."

Jake moved into the welcome place Dot's parents made for him in their home, and reported to camp each morning as regularly as he once had to the rug mill. The embrace of his new family was so warm, the relaxed and amiable lifestyle so appealing, that, were it not for the obligation he felt toward the parents he hadn't seen in three years, he would have gladly considered transplanting himself forever. One week passed with no orders to move, then two, and as the third drifted blissfully by he began to wonder if the war had simply forgotten him.

"I think you'd better go back up now," his commander finally told him one morning, and he was soon sailing on a Liberty ship back to Finschhafen.

The fighting was all but finished on New Guinea by the time Jake returned, and his unit had earned official praise for its role in the last major battle, which he had missed—the desperate thrust at Aitape by malarial Japanese remnant battalions on half rations, led by a malnourished general whose teeth had, like many of his men's, fallen out, leaving him able to eat only the starch from the crushed trunks of sago palms. "The lull in radio traffic just prior to the enemy's attack gave us a positive indication of what the enemy intended to do," read the commendation, citing the "highly valuable" information provided by the 126th. "When this was tied in with other information the situation became very clear." Jake had barely unpacked his wedding picture before his unit struck its tents, loaded its receivers and direction finders onto trucks, and rumbled farther up the coast to Hollandia, where forces were assembling for the Philippines invasion.

"I wish I had a camera," Jake said, whistling in awe as he surveyed the immense flotilla anchored in Humboldt Bay. "It looks like you could pretty near walk all the way across. I didn't know there were that many ships in the whole navy."

They raised their camp again inland from the bay, at the end of the narrow winding tracks through the Cyclops Mountains. It sat on the flat plain surrounding the fifteen-mile-long crescent of Lake Sentani, where the Japanese had built, and then abandoned, airstrips, supply dumps, roads and barracks that 140,000 men had since transformed into an instant Allied city. After spacing their direction finders up through yet another set of hills, Jake and his unit built themselves a pair of volleyball courts and a punching-bag stand. They organized a baseball team, too, but their impatience and frustration had acquired an edge that recreation couldn't dull. "The variety of rations has declined considerably," Captain Wilson noted in his report, but more troubling was the "noticeable decline" in morale, particularly among the unit veterans like Jake whose service predated Pearl Harbor, and whose oft-promised stateside transfers had never materialized. The harbor soon drained of ships—sailing off to the battles that brought Stu Bunton face-to-face with a Japanese Jill—and Jake was left among the rear troops to puzzle over what use the war had for him now. Scrubbing his laundry in an old washtub one afternoon, he looked up when he heard the wheezing, sputtering coughs of a troubled American plane. A B-25 bomber, barely clearing the treeline, was struggling to reach the airstrip before crashing, and from its belly came tumbling a dark, heavy object—a frequency meter, as Jake found when he ran to inspect it, ditched as excess weight, exactly the kind of worn castoff that, after almost three and a half years' service, he feared becoming himself.

The routine at Hollandia was the same as at Buna and Dobodura and Finschhafen, the same even as at Townsville and Stafford—daily eight-hour shifts up at the listening post, eavesdropping on enemy transmissions. The headphones still buzzed with signals, but the war was moving so fast now, so far off New Guinea, that Jake began to wonder if what he heard still held any meaning. Through the long, leaden off-hours in camp, the waiting grew harder for him. His vague longing for home had been replaced by something more substantial—a wife and the whole bright, wide future she implied, the foundation of the rest of his life. Spinning the radio dial up in the jungle one night, wishing he were hearing big-band trumpets instead of Japanese dots and dashes, he was startled by the barking of a dog, the scrawny, old black mutt that had attached itself to the camp, and ridden along with him in the jeep. By the time he disentangled himself from the direction finder and scrambled out of the shack, the intruder was gone, and the dog was trotting triumphantly back from the brush. The top was off the dinner pail that sat outside the shack, and some of the beef stew was gone—probably sloshing around inside the constricted belly of a hungry Japanese soldier by now, Jake guessed.

"He must be starving, sneaking right up here like that," he said to his partner. More than seven thousand Japanese soldiers had fled into the jungle when the Americans invaded Hollandia. Only five hundred ever made it to the nearest enemy base, 145 miles to the west. "I wonder how many of them are out there."

Down in Humboldt Bay, where searchlights chased across the sky each night after enemy planes that were becoming as rare and elusive as the scavengers in the hills, some ships had trickled back from Leyte Gulf, and with their victory came rumors of another move for Jake's unit. It would be the longest leap yet for the 126th, all the way to the Philippines. The news excited Jake, because in it he heard what he calculated was his best chance yet at going home. The newer men in his unit would, he reasoned, be sent ahead, while the veterans would be sent back.

Each new rumor seemed only to confirm Jake's hunch, and Freehold began to feel nearer than it had since he first reached the Pacific. He began to imagine what he would do when he got home, how he would stroll into the rug mill with his uniform on. He would request a posting as near to Freehold as possible, so he could get home for weekends. Dot would be there soon, too, he hoped, and their life together would begin. With Freehold so firmly in his mind, then, it seemed almost a premonition when he encountered an unlikely piece of it here in Hollandia. Driving a three-quarter-ton supply truck back from the dock one day, he picked up a rider, a soldier standing with a barracks bag full of wet laundry slung over his shoulder. The soldier's face looked familiar, reminding him somehow of home, but he wasn't certain until it poked through the canvas with a question a couple miles up the road.

"Aren't you Warren Errickson?" the rider asked.

"And you're Bill Bryan, aren't you?" Jake replied to the soldier who, back in those hard-to-remember years when they were both civilians, had lived around the corner from him, on Bennett Street.

He dropped Bryan off at a crossroads, and when he got back to camp, he wrote to Dot, urging her to press for an early berth on one of the scarce war-brides' ships to America. The tropical sun burned hot as ever, but he was already feeling the sharp and bracing autumnal breezes of home.

"Buy some shotgun shells," he wrote in another letter, to his father, anticipating a time when he could shoot at something that he knew wouldn't shoot back. "I want to do some rabbit hunting."

In November the orders finally did arrive, just as he had hoped. He packed up two big, blue barracks bags for the trip home—a ship to California, a train to New Jersey, a furlough in Freehold, an R-and-R spell in Atlantic City, and then finally a transfer to a home-front posting. At five P.M. on the day that was to be his last in New Guinea, he lined up in the mess tent for a final meal. A Liberty ship, the *Fairchild*, waited in the harbor, and he was expected aboard by six. But after finishing his supper, he felt a stabbing pain in his abdomen more severe than the usual indigestion.

"Harry, see if there are any medics in the orderly room," he asked his friend, Harry Drake, who was also scheduled to leave. "I can't take this anymore."

Drake found a sergeant with a jeep, and they drove to the nearest medical tent with Jake bent double in the back. They laid him out on an aluminum folding table, and a lieutenant felt gently around the pain.

"You've got appendicitis," the lieutenant told him, and then turned to the men who had brought him in. "He has to go straight to the base hospital."

Before Jake was wheeled into surgery, several of his outbound buddies managed to slip out to see him one last time, mumbling awkwardly through a farewell they weren't prepared for, a rushed and abrupt ending to their long, slow years together. He woke up alone, his poisonous appendix gone, his ship sailing home without him.

The quarantine ward where he was sent to recuperate was a long tent packed close with mostly scrub typhus cases—feverish, and sometimes delirious, soldiers who had been bitten by the infectious mites that breed in rat-ridden, crowded encampments. Wooden walls rose only halfway to the roof, and the tent flaps were rolled up to let in any rare breeze that might stir the sweaty air. Jake's body was reluctant to heal in the heat, and the days dripped slowly by. At the Thanksgiving table on Jackson Street, his place sat empty. The shotgun shells his father had bought stayed sealed in a box in the basement. Five weeks passed, then six and seven, dragging him toward 1945, a year he had hoped to welcome at home.

"Merry Christmas," said someone standing at the foot of his bed one day, and he looked up to see his sister, Georgie.

The Dutch hospital ship she was assigned to, nursing the wounded as they were ferried from the Philippines to Australia, had anchored in the harbor for an unexpected holiday port call, and she spent her shore leave on a surprise visit to her brother, her third so far, and her most welcome. She told Jake some of what she'd seen—her ship had, like Stu Bunton's, been caught in a typhoon off Luzon that swallowed three destroyers whole—but their conversation soon drifted away from the war and toward the family they were missing back home. Her company briefly put Jake on familiar ground, but by evening he was stranded again. When Georgie returned to her ship, she at least could lose herself in the consuming routines of duty. Jake could only brood and long and wait. In his head he heard the song he and Dot had courted to, "White Christmas," the holiday it promised so different from how his had turned out. Alone again as Christmas dissolved into another steamy night, he dropped into the dream whose details kept shifting but whose contours had grown so familiar in recent weeks. He was trying to get away, trying to get home, and he had almost made it, but someone, something, kept getting in his way, and when he awoke in his bed the next morning, he hadn't budged from the place where he was stuck in his dream, the place he wanted to leave.

6.

The Air Corps in Europe, 1944

Bill Lopatin: Normandy

All through the day, the clouds had been lifting—over the airfield Bill Lopatin had just departed, over the Channel he could just now glimpse ahead through his waist gunner's window, over the Continent that was his destination. He scanned the distance for enemy fighters, but the briefing officer had told the crews not to expect many. The sky, for today at least, belonged to the Allies. The heavy bombers lumbered above his own flight of B-26s, and the fighters zipped below, their wings zebra-striped with the same black-and-white identification markings that had been painted on his plane the day before, and that caught his eye every time he looked out over his machine guns. The group commander himself was leading the mission, and hanging beside the five-hundred-pounders in the bomb bay of one of the thirty-seven planes were two leaflet tubes stuffed with invasion advisories for the occupiers and the occupied on the new battleground below. Bill had made this trip fifty-eight times already, but never with so much company.

"Would you look at that," he murmured to himself as they neared the French coast.

Like everyone else in England in the teeming spring of 1944, Bill knew the Normandy invasion would be monumental, but as he watched it unfold beneath him now, he realized that not even the grandest heights of his imagination could have anticipated its true scale. The choppy surface of the Channel was covered with so many ships, sprawling beyond the squinting range of every other flier in the air with him, that it might as well have been land—6,500 in all, from battleships to landing craft, more than anyone anywhere could have ever seen in one place at one time in all of history. Allied destroyers, broadside guns blazing, stood so close to shore they seemed to have run aground. Red muzzle flashes marked the positions of the big German coastal guns, one of which was the B-26s' target, and shell splashes pocked the water. A landing craft shuttling troops to the beach exploded under a direct hit, and Bill watched the small, dark forms—the bodies of men—flung cruelly through the air.

Because they had been awakened early for the scrubbed mission the night before, Bill and his crew were assigned the afternoon mission on D-Day, and left to sleep undisturbed through the opening hours of the invasion. Not long before dawn, fifty-four Marauders from his squadron had taken off into thick clouds and rain that would have grounded them on any other day, headed for the German gun positions at Varreville, near the beach code-named Utah at the western edge of the invasion front. They dropped their bombs—smaller 250 pounders that left foxhole-sized craters to shelter the men crossing the beach—several hours after the Allied paratroopers had floated down into enemy-held fields and forests, and several minutes before the soldiers splashed out of the landing crafts. Every crew but one was back at the base by the time Bill walked to the mess tent for breakfast. The lost plane had iced up and collided with another in the clouds on the way out, going down with five of its six men, including Bill's friend George Williams, who had returned miraculously in a life raft from the Marauders' disastrous inaugural mission at Ijmuiden the previous spring.

"This is it," one of the crewmen had told Bill upon returning from the early mission—the same words the colonel later used at the briefing.

Flying under the cloud bottoms at six thousand feet, higher than his squadron mates had in the grayer morning, Bill counted the tethered barrage balloons that had been lofted as a protective screen over Sword Beach, one of the British invasion beaches, and spotted a boat burning in the mouth of the river that led into the stronghold city of Caen, at the eastern edge of the front. A flight of P-47 dive-bombers accompanied the Marauders, awaiting the signal to attack the gun batteries that were weakly peppering the sky with flak.

"Calais," the formation leader said over the radio, a code word that was almost a taunt: Calais, at the Channel's narrowest point, was where the Germans had expected the invasion, and had massed their best troops and tanks.

"Ankle," came the countersign.

Sighting along the perforated barrel of his machine gun, the ammunition belt looping down to his feet, Bill found nothing to shoot at, and he watched the dive-bombers swoop low like raptors, unchallenged by enemy fighters. On the ground, though, the battle was not as one-sided as in the air. As many as one hundred thousand men had waded or parachuted ashore already, and they were moving inland, pushing ahead in a jagged, gap-toothed front line. The German defenders were a dense and fierce obstacle in some spots, thin and faltering in others. The Americans who landed at Utah Beach were five miles into France and taking prisoners already, but on Omaha Beach, where a fresh German infantry division raked fire down from the bluffs, the carnage rivaled Tarawa. A mile beneath Bill, the British had nearly reached the outskirts of Caen before German tanks drove them back toward the beach.

Between 6:22 and 6:24, the squadron dropped sixty-two tons of bombs on the coastal guns at Benerville, leaving a cloud of smoke and dust rising in its wake as it turned in a wide arc over Caen, thirty-seven planes moving as one, and flew north again toward home. The sky ahead was spotted with stray clouds, and out of one of them suddenly flew something so unexpected and unnerving that it at first seemed an apparition.

"Unmarked Marauder, eleven o'clock high," came the voice through the radio. "Open fire."

It was a B-26, just like their own, except that it lacked the invasion stripes every Allied plane was wearing today. Any plane in the air without the proper markings was presumed to be an enemy, so the gunners swung their barrels around and began shooting with the same fury and purpose they would have aimed at a Messerschmitt. Whether it was a captured bomber piloted by the enemy, or an Allied orphan that had somehow blundered aloft unpainted, no one knew, and no one found out, because it darted back into the clouds, and vanished as quickly and mysteriously as it had appeared.

The squadron returned intact to a base suffused with both the pale lingering light of a long English evening and the refracted glow of a successful mission. The loudspeakers had broadcast no general announcement, but everyone who had seen even a small piece of the day—from the night mechanics on the hardstands, searching for flak holes that weren't there, to the pilots in the officers' club, grasping for words large enough to encompass the spectacle—knew what had happened: The Allies had gained a foothold in France, finally and decisively opening the western front. By day's end 150,000 troops were ashore in Normandy, at a cost of 2,500 dead and 10,000 wounded, a fraction of the casualties that had been feared. The enemy found a fight in every direction it turned now—in the south, the Allied forces who had marched into Rome just two days earlier; in the east, the seemingly infinite waves of sacrificial Russians sprinting toward Poland; and in the west, the steady tide of soldiers and supplies rolling onto the beaches. For most of the 3 million edgy troops packed into England, the men who would actually have to push the Germans back into Berlin at gunpoint, the battle was just beginning, but for Bill and his crewmates it was on the verge of ending. When he sat down in the closing hours of D-Day to write a letter home, he fully expected he would soon be following.

Back in Freehold, Bill's family already knew more about the war than the censors would let his letter tell them. Casualties had been accumulating with a grim regularity, the gold stars of the dead replacing the blue stars of the living in the parlor-window banners—Douglas Schiverea, Anthony Pikulik, Adam Albrecht, John Adamko, Ted Throckmorton. The solemn Memorial Day services the week before had honored twenty-two of the local dead, both from Freehold itself and from all the surrounding farms and crossroads. The parade, led by a lone Spanish-American War veteran and the signal company billeted at the old CCC camp, marched out to the Civil War grave of Captain Conover, where a chorus of military school boys sang "Onward, Christian Soldiers" and a tiny cadet, just seven years old, closed with a solo of "God Bless America."

"We did not seek this war, we did all we could to avoid it, but it was thrust upon us," declared the main speaker, the Baptist minister who had given Johnny Bartek the Bible that sustained the lost Rickenbacker crew in the Pacific. "We were attacked, and now the world is witnessing the vigor with which America can press home the fight when she is convinced of the necessity of defending her ideals."

Church bells tolled on Main Street to mark the invasion, and the rug mill blew its whistle, the mingled notes carrying a complex sound of relief and foreboding through the town. On Henry Street, the Lopatins gathered around their evening radio to hear President Roosevelt's D-Day prayer. "Almighty God," the president beseeched, as the nation fell silent. "Our sons, pride of our Nation, this day have set out upon a mighty endeavor, a struggle to preserve our Republic, our religion, and our civilization and to set free a suffering humanity."

Bill crossed the Channel again the next day, and the next—to bomb a highway junction in Laval, a marshaling yard at Saint-Lô—while the ground forces beneath him drained out of England and into France through the funnels of the southern ports. The squadron flew low and often in the weeks after D-Day, buzzing down to blast obstacles from the army's advancing path. After proving their tactical value in the months before the invasion, destroying fifteen hundred locomotives and cutting all twenty-two rail and road bridges over the Seine between Paris and the sea, the Marauders had become a prime strike weapon for the ground commanders, who used them like artillery, calling in bomb drops to poke holes in the front line and block the flow of enemy reinforcements and supplies.

"Railway transportation is impossible because the trains are observed and attacked in short order," despaired one German war diary.

On the afternoon of June 13, D plus 7, Bill's plane took off into fair-weather clouds that dissipated in time for him to glimpse the Thames. The maps in the briefing room had shown that the five invasion beaches were finally linked now, consolidated into an unbroken front that stretched sixty miles wide, but stalled twenty miles inland. "Maximum enemy opposition may be expected," the field order warned about the day's target, a fuel dump in Saint Martin. The number that stuck in Bill's mind from the briefing was 108, which was how many German .88s the intelligence reports said he could expect to find shooting at him.

The sky above was clear as the thirty-eight Marauders neared France, but ahead it was black with the smoke of battle. Trucks jammed all the roads leading in from the coast, backed up until the infantry, fighting field by vicious field, could dislodge the entrenched defenders. A maze of hedgerows, centuries-dense tangles of roots and earth and brambles, blocked the way, as impenetrable as brick walls. Through the drifting, sooty haze, Bill saw the red gash where the two armies met. A village was burning and crumbling, flames licking up around the church steeple.

As the plane passed into the part of France that still belonged to Germany, bursts of shell fragments rained against it like fistfuls of flung gravel. The flak was the worst they had faced since those grim early missions, "intense and accurate" in the official rating. At what the mission's lead navigator thought was the initial point, over the town of Caumont, the first box of planes leveled off and straightened their course for the bomb run, but the fuel dump wasn't where it was supposed to be.

"We missed the IP and came in at the wrong angle," came a dismaying message over the radio. "We have to go back out and try again."

Banking hard under fire, the Marauders turned north and swerved back through the same barrage they had just endured. One plane failed to follow, shot down near the target area. Parachutes were spotted bailing out, maybe just one, maybe as many as four, no one could say for sure. Out over the Channel, the seventeen remaining planes formed up again and, like a bull pirouetting for another run at a matador, sped inland along a trajectory the abashed navigator anxiously checked and rechecked for accuracy. The second box, following the correct route, had already found the target and started home. Bill sat nearer an escape window than anyone else on board, and as he steeled himself against the danger he knew was waiting, he glanced at his parachute and briefly wondered whether it offered better odds for survival than his waist-gunner's slot.

The Marauders shouldered roughly through the heavy curtain of flak that marked the start of hostile territory, and straightened course over what they hoped was the correct initial point at Caumont. Shells were coming from everywhere, from .88s and from Panzers, from all along the main road between Villers-Bocage and Caen, from patches of forest known to the mapmakers and briefers only as Woods T-7670 and Woods T-9464. Bill hunched over the guns that were no defense against the onslaught, willing the target into view.

"There it is," the pilot finally said.

The bombs were five hundred-pounders, no heavier than usual, but as Bill watched them fall toward the fuel dump, he felt a great burden lifted from the plane, and he instinctively leaned forward, anticipating and coaxing the thrust toward home. Flak chased the planes as they zigzagged away, catching one that managed to limp past Caen before going down. Over the Channel again, where the sky ahead was clear and the only guns below were friendly, Bill began to uncoil. When the plane finally landed in Boreham, and the ground crew was approaching to count the flak holes, Bill slipped down through the wheel well. Feeling England beneath his feet once more, he was moved without thinking to a gesture that had always struck him as vaguely melodramatic in other fliers: He knelt and planted his lips on the sun-baked, oil-soaked tarmac, kissing the ground.

He was on the ground again that night, and the next, startled from his cot by the air-raid blast and scrambling into the slit trench outside the

Quonset hut. The flying bombs had finally arrived—the dreaded German V-1 rockets, whistling blindly across the Channel and scattering terror randomly on soldiers and civilians alike, launched from the sites that had been the Marauders' chief winter targets, but that had either survived the attacks or been rebuilt. As long as Bill heard the signature washing-machine rattle of a rocket overhead he knew he was safe; an abrupt silence meant it was ready to fall. Air raids were sounding at least twice a day now at the base, but only one ended with an explosion—the rocket that hit one hundred yards from the main gate, leaving a crater where an orchard had been.

Almost every week lately, Bill's Air Medal had sprouted a fresh oak leaf cluster—one awarded for each five missions completed—but he was beginning to wonder how many more it could hold. In some ways, the danger had eased for airmen since the invasion. The sky was largely clear of German fighters, which had been withdrawn to defend the homeland, and the ground below, falling gradually to the advancing Allies, was more likely to offer sanctuary, not capture, to anyone forced to bail out. (Three crewmen from the plane that went down near Caen had parachuted to safety, and then stumbled into a sublime historical moment. Sputtering out toward a British destroyer in an amphibious Duck they had commandeered on a Normandy beach, they were hailed by a landing craft that sat dead in the water. They ferried the stranded party to shore, where General Charles de Gaulle personally thanked them for returning him to French soil for the first time in four years.)

Bill had no interest in meeting de Gaulle, as his squadron mates had—or Churchill or Eisenhower, or any other generals or leaders, for that matter. The only person he wanted to meet now was the one who could send him home. He had measured enough lumber and estimated enough construction work back in Freehold to know his way around numbers, and he knew the numbers were adding up against him. Every time an airman went up was another time he might get shot down, and Bill had already been up sixty-seven times. How many more times could he fly, he wondered, and count on the Germans missing? He believed in God, but he didn't believe God was protecting him on his missions. The reason he was still alive, he believed, had more to do with math than faith. Each time his plane returned without getting hit he felt he was getting closer to the mission when it would. He felt he was drawing down a finite store of luck, and he didn't think much more could be left after the mission to Saint Martin.

On his sixty-eighth time out, Bill flew to Cherbourg, where the stalled divisions of the American VII Corps hoped an air strike could blast a hole for them in the stubborn enemy line. The Germans were dug deeply into the old French fortifications at Fort d'Octeville, raining down shells on any attempt to approach the peninsular city from the west. The Marauders hit their targets hard, destroying all the enemy guns, from the .88s down to the three-inchers, as well as the living quarters and the fire control center. Twenty minutes after the bombers left, the ground troops were able to march into the smoldering wreckage and finally capture the fort. "There were no guns untouched by fragments or hits," the commanding general of the Ninth Air Force said in a congratulatory message a few days later. "The liberation of Cherbourg was undoubtedly accomplished with less difficulty because of the efficient manner in which this strong point was completely overcome from the air."

July arrived, and the orders home Bill was expecting still hadn't materialized; he had to settle instead for a pass to London, the first since D-Day. The city was besieged by buzz-bomb attacks—sixteen hundred dead and two hundred thousand homes damaged in the first two weeks alone, a casualty rate not seen since the darkest days of the Blitz—but it remained to him and his crewmates a cherished refuge from the war, a place apart where no piercing loudspeaker could summon them to a mission, no sober officer could admonish them for having drunk too much. They headed straight to the pubs near Piccadilly that had been colonized by Americans in uniform. Alcohol, as every soldier knew, was the war's most reliable anesthetic, smoothing the harsh edges of exhilaration and sadness, tension and tedium. The beer, warm and flat, went down like water; the kick came later, sudden as a hammer blow. Within just a round or two, the crew found some benefactors.

"Put your money away, it's no good here," announced one of the paratroopers who were staking them, in gratitude for the ground and sky the Marauders had cleared of enemies.

"To the bombers," the paratrooper toasted loudly, and everyone raised a glass in celebration of being here, now, alive.

Bill had never drunk much before the war, back in Freehold, but he had never tried to kill anyone there either. As the airmen and the paratroopers exchanged their versions of battle, Bill told of the recent mission when the plane was flying low over an enemy road, and the voice of a crewmate came through his headset: "Somebody on a motorcycle at seven o'clock low." He swung around one of his twin machine guns, which had a wider range than any other on the plane's underside, and shot at the small, speeding, uniformed figure. The motorcycle went up a slope on the shoulder. The rider remained in the middle of the road, and the plane was gone before Bill could see if he got up.

"I don't know if I hit him, or if he just let go of the motorcycle," he said.

The motorcycle was a more personal, more naked, target than the fighter planes he had shot at before, but Bill, who before the war had never shot at so much as a rabbit, didn't hesitate when he had it in his sights, and was glad to have stopped it. He had come to regard his enemy with a kind of professional detachment. He had been told that, as a Jew, he might be singled out by the Germans if he were captured, but he didn't know the full dimensions of the Nazi's hatred, and there was no extra dimension to his hatred of them. What he saw them do daily was bad enough—watching a direct hit on a nearby plane, the fuselage splitting in half, the crew spilling out like apples from a bushel basket. He didn't need to know any more. When he tracked the bombs dropping from his plane, he thought only of the targets they were meant to destroy—the bridges, the railyards, the rocket sites—not any lives they might end. It had all become a simple equation, with its own internal logic and morality: The Germans were trying to kill him, so he tried to kill them. He did so without guilt, and without sympathy.

The target of Bill's first mission after London was a railroad bridge near Vitre, where the only plane hit by flak was his. The damage was minor, just a few holes the ground crew quickly patched, but he felt what luck he had left draining through them. The next day brought another railroad bridge, at Caen, but thick clouds kept the Marauders from attacking the target, and the Germans from attacking them. The sky remained gray the rest of the day, and the gloom only deepened when news drifted over from the base where Bill had been stationed until March. Thirty-five planes from his old group, the 322nd, had flown out the night before to bomb the V-1 rocket headquarters at Château de Ribeaucourt when they were spotted by a flight of twenty German night fighters. Glaring ground searchlights locked onto the bombers, and the swift Junkers and Focke-

Wulfs swooped up from behind. Nine Marauders went down, the worst toll since the inaugural disaster over Ijmuiden more than a year earlier. Had he not been transferred earlier, Bill might have joined the fatal mission, and as he wondered which of his friends were lost, he felt his insides turn with the queasiness that comes from treading too near the edge of fortune.

Fifty missions had been the original deal—dangle yourself out over Nazi fire fifty times and you'd get a ticket home—but Bill's fiftieth had come two weeks before D-Day, when the traffic across the Atlantic was a one-way, eastbound express, and nobody who was already in England was going anywhere except further into the war. He just kept flying, with little notion of what the new ceiling was, or if in fact there was any ceiling at all anymore. He had now flown on seventy-one missions, and when he awoke the next morning, a full month and three days after D-Day, he was staring at number seventy-two. The sky was overcast again, the target another railroad bridge in France. Bill looked down through his waist window over what the navigator said should be Chandai, but all he saw was a solid floor of cumulus. Clambering back to his radio desk in the front of the plane on the way home, he felt for the cotter pins in the pocket of his lucky leather jacket and reinserted them in the noses of the bombs they hadn't dropped.

Bill slept undisturbed the next several mornings, waking each time to find some of the other cots in the hut already empty, vacated by colleagues who had been called to briefings that he, to his surprise and gratitude, was spared. The missions went on—more fuel dumps and railroad bridges mostly—but he and his crewmates remained earthbound, wandering out to the airstrip each afternoon to count the returning planes. Evenings in the village pub, they inevitably indulged in some beery speculation, trying to divine from their sidelined status a sign of their future. Would their next orders, they wondered, send them to America, finally, or to France, again?

On July 14, 1944—after seventy-two missions and fourteen months in England, on what France hoped would prove the last Bastille Day under Nazi occupation—Bill and his crewmates were summoned by their commander. It was an unusual request, and as they walked toward headquarters, anticipation quickened their steps. They expected, they hoped, it was the news they'd been waiting for, but this was the army, after all, and you never knew what the army would ask you to do next.

"You're going home, all of you together," the commander said. "Do you want to go by ship or plane?"

"By ship," Bill answered, without hesitation, as all of his crewmates did, too. "I think I've flown enough."

The celebration ran late at the pub, and Bill bicycled unsteadily back to base along the dark lanes. At a corner, the bicycle went one way, he the other, like the motorcyclist he had shot at a few weeks earlier. His shoulder was wrenched badly enough that he had to hide it from anyone who might try to examine it, and then want to put him into the infirmary instead of onto the train to the Liverpool docks. His crewmates took turns carrying his barracks bag right up on board the *West Point*, which had been the luxury liner *America* before enlisting in the war as a troop ship swift enough to zigzag across the Atlantic without an escort.

The cabins were cramped, stacked four-high with bunks, so Bill spent much of the week-long passage lingering in the summer breezes on deck. The hold was filled with German soldiers, captured in the first weeks of the Normandy campaign and packed off to stateside prison camps. Bill ventured below to see them, and between their English and his Yiddish, he was able to pick up pieces of their conversations. The prisoners seemed convinced that their bombers had reduced the cities of America's eastern seaboard to a smoldering pile of rubble. But Boston, when they docked, was gloriously intact.

"Look," Bill said to one, sweeping his arm across a peaceful vista that warmed him as much as it chilled the German. "I thought you destroyed it all."

"Oh, the Americans are good builders," the prisoner countered, seeking solace in the next level of propaganda. "They build very fast."

On land, Bill got to a phone and called home. "I'm in Boston," he told his shocked mother, who thought he was still flying missions in England. "In America."

When she regained her composure, she had one pressing question. "What can I make for you?" she asked.

Bill was sweating in the July sun, the kind of humid heat he had rarely felt overseas, and he had a sudden craving for a dish he hadn't tasted in years. "How about some *schav?*" he asked—the chilled Russian summer soup made of boiled sour grass, onions, lemon juice, sour cream and chopped hard-boiled eggs.

His troop train reached New York at the morning rush hour, only to be shunted off to a siding so the commuter trains could pass first. He seethed as he looked through the windows into the other trains—at the men in gray suits and hats reading the headlines about a war so distant from them, a war he had just been fighting. He already had a soldier's suspicion of civilians, magnified by an airman's disdain for the earthbound, and this only made it worse. He hadn't expected brass bands to welcome him home, but he had expected a little respect. His service, he thought, should put him at the head of the line, not the back. What had they done, he wondered? How many missions had they flown? In New York finally, he boarded a train to Matawan, where his father and brother-in-law met him at the station. They were on Henry Street by lunchtime, with his dog, Pingo, barking and all of the neighbors pouring out of their houses to greet him. His mother had the *schav* waiting.

Freehold had sent so many boys into the war that it was overjoyed to get one back. (The same week Bill returned safely, the Askew family on Throckmorton Street received two messages in a single day regarding their son, Theodore, a gunner's mate on a destroyer in the South Pacific—a letter from him, saying he'd be home soon, and a telegram from the War Department, saying he'd been killed in action.) The Rotary Club asked Bill to speak at their weekly luncheon. The synagogue organized a night in his honor, and the master of ceremonies, "acting for admirers of the sergeant," presented him with a watch. The *Transcript* sent a reporter to interview him for a front-page story. "The only ones we didn't like to fly with were the guys who weren't afraid," he said. "We figured the smart fellows were all afraid and we didn't want the other kind."

He had two weeks before his furlough was up—an R-and-R stretch in Miami would follow, then, most likely, a stint as a radio instructor at the base where he was trained, Barksdale in Louisiana—and he spent it doing as little as possible. He slept late, visited friends and family. He wrote to his brother, Sol, who had been transferred to Russia as an interpreter. (The eastern front had pushed so far forward that Allied bombers, rather than returning to England after a mission to Germany, could now continue on to land at air bases in Russia.) And he finally saw Selma again.

Before the war, Bill had a friend in Trenton whose wife was always trying to fix him up with dates. He tended to be brusque with the women, though. "Do you like me because of me or because of my father's money?" one had asked.

"Definitely your father's money," Bill had said.

His wife's friend wanted to swear off her matchmaking after that, but she had one more—and this was it, she said—just one more woman she wanted Bill to meet. This last date's name was Selma, and Bill took her out for a beer in a bar across the street from their mutual friends' house. She was divorced, with a young daughter, and they found themselves getting along better than either had expected. They made another date, and another, but the war cut them off before they had gone out even half a dozen times. Their relationship grew instead through words. Selma was a devoted correspondent, her letters following Bill from air base to air base, sometimes bunching up in the mail pipeline and arriving in batches of a dozen at once. Bill wrote, too, though she was always after him to write more. What grew over their years of letters was a sense of inevitability— the comforting feeling that, in a difficult and uncertain time, when it meant so much to have someone thinking of you when you were alone and far away, she was the one thinking of him, and he the one thinking of her. When they met again now, their affection transferred easily from paper to life.

One sunny afternoon before his furlough was up, Bill was sitting drowsily on the front porch, trying to imagine what was ahead for him instead of dwelling on what was behind. The future he had been so wary of contemplating when he was overseas—the future he had been so uncertain he would ever see—had finally arrived, and he was relishing its wide and welcoming vistas. But then a piercing shriek split the summer stillness. It was the same sound he had heard so often in England, the signal for a German air raid or rocket attack, and it took him back there instantly. He instinctively jumped over the side of the porch, pushed aside the lattice and scrambled underneath, seeking shelter.

"Bill, it's just the first-aid whistle," somebody told him. "You can come back up."

A town ambulance squad had organized in his absence, and its garage, with the screaming siren that called volunteers to an emergency, was just a block away. Somebody was hurt here, but nobody was attacking. Bill crawled out and dusted himself off. He might be out of the war, it seemed, but the war wasn't yet out of him. He was on the home front now—where the daily sacrifices were measured in ration tickets and gas coupons, not lives—but it had been so long since he felt safe that it would take him a while to get used to it. Walking across the patch of yard, he looked up through the spaces between the overarching oaks, into a blue sky that, as he had to keep telling himself over and over again now, no longer held any peril for him.

Jimmy Higgins: The Bulge

Sitting in the cold, cramped belly of a B-26 emptied of bombs—one of the fleet from the 391st that was ferrying the group's ground troops along the cross-Channel route with the benign regularity of city buses—Jimmy Higgins, sergeant in the intelligence section, leaned over and looked down on, finally, the land he had seen before only on maps. The Normandy summer had ended, and northern France belonged to the Allies again. The German .88s whose positions he had plotted for mission briefings had withdrawn, and the skies were clear of flak. The army was racing toward the Rhine, and the Air Corps, decamping from England, was migrating to the bases the Luftwaffe had abandoned. Jimmy held tight as the Marauder bounced to a landing on the one good runway left at the Roye/Amy airfield, not far from where Nazi fighter planes had attacked a flight from the 391st on a mission back in March.

Jimmy climbed down from the plane into a bomb-sculpted landscape unmistakably nearer the war than the pastoral English countryside he had left just an hour earlier. Splintered hangars ringed the field. Scorched and abandoned skeletons of Messerschmitts and Junkers sat forever grounded. A Focke-Wulf lurked at the edge of the woods like a wounded animal, the swastika on its tail fin peeking through the autumn leaves. The runways and hardstands were cratered and rubbled. Retreating hastily a few weeks before, the Germans had tried to destroy what they were forced to leave behind, and what the Allied bombs hadn't already hit. A persistent but unconfirmed rumor held that the main runway, the one Jimmy and all the other new tenants were arriving on now, had been wired with explosives, which had been defused by the local Resistance.

A truck was waiting to take Jimmy and his colleagues to their new quarters, and he heaved his barracks bag and himself up onto the back. The four squadrons and their ground crews were stationed near the airfield, but the headquarters contingent—including S-2, the intelligence section—was billeted in the village of Tilloloy several miles away. The rutted road led through fields, planted in sugar beets now, that were among the most savagely contested of the First World War. In the spring of 1918, waves of German soldiers had risen up from the trenches here, out of the nearby sector of the network that snaked along the western front from the Swiss border to the North Sea, and stormed across the Allied lines, gaining new ground and pushing their own line forward. The truck carrying Jimmy rumbled past a cemetery where the casualties lay buried in neat white rows—some of the hundreds of thousands of men who died defending this ground, and then winning it back, in the Second Battle of the Somme.

Turning off the main road, the truck rolled up a long driveway toward a grand stone building that approximated, in size and gravity if not in style, the county courthouse back home. By the time Jimmy saw it, the Château de Tilloloy had been standing for almost three centuries, its majestic classical lines reflecting its origins in the era of Louis XIV, when the first settlers around Freehold were building nothing more than rough wooden houses for themselves. A moat quaintly encircled the château, an anachronistic defense against another age's invaders. Jimmy walked from the truck to the single bridge and, peering over the rail, found grass growing in the dry bed. Through the château's tall first-floor windows, some of which were flung open to the late September breeze, he saw ranks of gray desks filling the ballroom floor where bewigged and powdered nobles once minueted. Carved around the doorway were antlered deer and baying dogs, prey and predators, and the coat of arms of the great huntsman Charles-Maximilien de Belleforière.

"Don't get used to it, Sergeant—that's not where you're bunking," the truck driver told him. "Officers only. Enlisted men are over there."

A small village spilled off the château's left flank, and a long stable stood to the right. In peacetime, carriage horses and livestock had occupied the ground floor of the stable, and servants had lived above. Jimmy hauled his gear up the stairs, found his cot and reported to duty, crossing the moat bridge back to the main house. In a single week the entire bomb group had been ferried to France by planes, ships and trucks—losing eleven men along the way, when three Marauders crashed trying to land in a sudden evening storm—and missions were set to resume immediately. The Teletype spit out five-foot lengths of field orders, the urgent clatter echoing in a room that, like the rest of the chateau, had long since been stripped of the genteel furnishings of its prior life. Using colored pins and tiny flags, Jimmy stuck the war back into place on the map boards.

"Look how close we are," he said as he noticed that towns for which he had recently prepared mission briefings were now behind him, and the Germans weren't too far ahead of him.

Jimmy spent his days in Tilloloy the same as he had spent the last nine months in Matching—poring through intelligence reports, reconnaissance photos and maps, helping the bomber crews see where they were headed and what trouble they might find there. The Marauders were still hitting the same kinds of tactical targets—railroad bridges, road junctions, fortified enemy positions, supply depots, communications centers—but they were often flying over Germany itself now, pounding especially hard the territory between the Siegfried Line, three hundred miles of pillboxes and concrete barriers meant to wall out invaders from the west, and the Rhine River. On at least one occasion, the bombers dropped leaflets instead of explosives, trying to encourage the surrender everyone believed was inevitable.

In the evenings, Jimmy bicycled or walked over to the village that, after four years of Nazi occupation, embraced the Americans as saviors. The close-set houses of Tilloloy—with pigs and chickens roaming the small fenced yards, front and back—were arrayed around a church, dating to the Renaissance, and a fountain, destroyed in the last war and restored as a gift from the Daughters of the American Revolution. Bearing gifts of butter or sugar from the mess hall, he visited the family of Madame Omnes, who adopted him just as other villagers adopted other soldiers, doing his laundry and inviting him to suppers. He found that the eating was better in France—there were fresh eggs, and roast chickens on Sundays—but the drinking was worse. He gradually became accustomed to the white wine served in the estaminet, but the cognac tasted to him like fuel oil, and he missed the English beer.

With passes to Paris restricted to flight crews at first, Jimmy made weekend visits to Roye, the nearest town of any size, and Reims, where he stood in wonder before the soaring thirteenth-century cathedral. By November, the GI trucks were making regular Friday-evening runs south to the liberated capital, and he was joining hordes of other soldiers at the Folies Bergère and the Eiffel Tower, testing the limits of his one year of high-school French. One cold, gray morning, he wandered into the vaulted Gothic shadows of Notre Dame and saw a small knot of people—dressed in black, heads bowed—gathered in an island of light. A simple wooden casket was laid out before the altar.

"Requiem aeternam dona eis, Domine, et lux perpetua luceat eis," the

priest intoned, a refrain Jimmy had heard so many times during the undertaker's apprenticeship the war had interrupted: *Eternal rest give unto them, O Lord, and let perpetual light shine upon them.*

Jimmy instinctively stood to the side and behind, in the invisible but respectful position of his chosen profession. He didn't know if the deceased was young or old, a man or a woman, a casualty of war or disease, but he stayed and watched with a student's eye.

"*Dies irae, dies illa solvet saeclum in favilla,*" the priest proclaimed, reciting the Dies Irae: *This day, this day of wrath shall consume the world in ashes.*

There were no flowers to soften the hard stone edges of the cathedral, no organ chords to lift the prayers up through the gloom. The ceremony was starker than the funerals of Jimmy's experience back home, but far grander, he knew, than had attended tens of millions of other deaths in the years of war. He stood in the damp chill beneath the squared shoulders of the stolid cathedral towers, the unblinking eye of the great rose window, and watched the mourners file out and the hearse depart, carrying at least one body to the peaceful grave the war had denied so many others.

Somber skies draped Tilloloy, too, and the first mission Jimmy prepared for after his Paris weekend was, like more than half of all the group's planned missions in October and November, canceled. The 391st had floated into France on the sunny hopes of a summer campaign so swift and efficient that some soldiers spoke openly of being home for Christmas. Jimmy had packed up some souvenirs—an ashtray and a soup ladle emblazoned with swastikas, a German helmet—and sent them back to Freehold with a letter speculating that he might soon follow. But the summer sprint had since slowed to an autumn slog, the clouds grounding the planes, the mud sucking at the infantry's boots. A brittle supply line, stretched too thin across the five hundred miles from the sea to the front, held the advance back like a leash, and the Germans, backed up against their homeland, were fighting more fiercely than ever. Patton's tanks, which had once moved so fast that Jimmy didn't know where to pin their markers on his campaign map, had stalled, low on gas. Even cigarettes were growing scarce.

The fliers at least had their mission limits, however elastic, to aim for as a ticket home. Jimmy and the other support troops on the ground were in for the duration, a term that was beginning to seem as if it would never end. The two groups had vastly different experiences of the war, and they tended not to mingle. The war was certainly more dangerous for the flight crews, but it moved more quickly for them than it did for the ground troops, whose daily routines—almost as predictable as at any factory or office back home—gave more occasion for the kind of restless grumbling that is the byproduct of tedium. Jimmy's friends were mostly his colleagues in the intelligence section, and they could see more clearly than most of their peers how distant victory still was. As morale sputtered, even the commander in chief himself was not immune from criticism. During the Depression, in the lean household headed by Jimmy's widowed mother, Roosevelt was revered as a savior, but among soldiers impatient for home, he was sometimes regarded as a reluctant warrior—more concerned about placating the other Allies, especially the Russians, than with mounting a final assault, the swift death blow the Americans were itching to deliver.

In the second week of December, the weather cleared enough that, for a rare five-day stretch, every one of the missions Jimmy prepared for took off as scheduled. Some returning crews noticed enemy tanks and troops moving near the Ardennes sector of the front, but their reports, passed up through wing and division headquarters, never coalesced into a warning about the surprise attack that was gathering. Staring at a map of the long Allied line recently, Hitler himself had focused on its weakest stretch and seized upon a strategy that chilled his commanders: The outgunned and outnumbered German Army, after backpedaling since Normandy, would now turn and advance, slashing through the Forest of Ardennes, the same route they had followed so successfully twice before, in 1914 and 1940, then continuing on to the Meuse River and, ultimately, the port of Antwerp, splitting the Allies in two.

In the first gray hours of December 16, while Tilloloy lay silent under a fresh sheen of snow and ice that froze out the day's mission, spotlights suddenly bounced off the low-slung clouds over the Ardennes, artillery shells began raining from the dim sky, and dark waves of blasting Panzers and greatcoated riflemen rolled out of the mist. The enemy, it seemed, had risen from the grave to take its vengeance. The four divisions spread thinly along the ninety-mile front were largely overrun by the overwhelming mass of Germans, who captured more prisoners than the Americans had lost at one time since Bataan. In the craggy, roadless Ardennes, beneath the snow-bent firs, the battleground was so fluid and confused that soldiers often didn't know what side of the line they were on anymore. By midafternoon, the news was filtering up to Eisenhower and back down to Tilloloy, and a startling realization was growing: The Germans were actually gaining ground, driving a sharp wedge through the Allied line, the bulge that would give the battle its name.

Guards were doubled out at the 391st's airfield, and preparations were made to evacuate the entire bomb group if the Germans pressed too near. Nobody knew how far the Germans might get, and Jimmy tightened at the prospect of their advance. They had always been a distant enemy to him; he had never before felt them moving toward him on the ground. The planners hastily drew up new missions—reconnaissance flights to see just who was where under the dense forest canopy, as well as bombing runs to choke off the alarming advance—but the next morning's weather was still overcast and frozen, grounding all the planes. Rumors blossomed from kernels of news: The Germans were summarily shooting prisoners; English-speaking impostors were parachuting behind the lines. In some nervous sectors, MPs questioned all comers to ferret out their true nationality; one American general was arrested and held for several hours because he didn't know the Chicago Cubs played in the National League.

By the morning of the eighteenth, the weather had improved just enough that the crews were assembled for a mission. "The critical situation created by this breakthrough is apparent," the briefing officer told the fliers of the 391st, reading a message from General Anderson, head of the Ninth Bomber Command. "It is of prime importance these targets be bombed—if necessary, bombing will be done from minimum altitude." Takeoff was delayed three times before the bombers were finally able to get aloft, but worsening skies forced a recall before they reached the target. Only a handful of Marauders from other groups managed to drop their bombs, and the Germans drove deeper into Belgium and Luxembourg, unchallenged from the air.

For the next four eternal days, while the frozen corpses accumulated in the snowy woods and ravines of the Ardennes, the planes waited helplessly under the thick blanket of fog that had draped itself over them. Shopkeepers in Belgian villages sadly removed the pictures of Roosevelt they had so gratefully and recently placed in their windows. The Germans stabbed sixty miles into Allied territory, missing only the critical crossroads town of Bastogne, where the besieged paratroopers of the 101st Airborne Division defiantly refused a request to surrender. Low on ammunition, surrounded by advancing tanks and troops, the trapped Americans were counting on Patton to reach them in time. Patton, meanwhile, was counting on a higher ally: He asked his chaplain to compose a special meteorological plea.

"Grant us fair weather for battle," the prayer beseeched, "that armed with Thy power, we may advance from victory to victory and crush the oppression and wickedness of our enemies and establish Thy justice among men and nations."

The weather over northern Europe usually flows from west to east, but overnight a rare Russian High arose, a high-pressure area that pushed from east to west, as if chasing the enemy's tracks. Walking from his room in the stable to his desk in the chateau on the morning of December 23, Jimmy shielded his eyes against a blaze of white, the glass-sharp sun bouncing blindingly off the wide swath of snow that bordered the long driveway. Because no one could say how long this window, flung wide so suddenly, would stay open, the 391st planned to squeeze out two missions today, and Jimmy hurried to gather the target intelligence—a railroad viaduct in Ahrweiler in the morning, a communications center in Neuerberg in the afternoon. But none of his maps or files could answer the most critical question of all: Just how much fight did the Germans really have left in them? The Marauder crews were facing their most urgent and uncertain mission since D-Day, and they, like Patton, sought some heavenly intervention.

"I call upon every man, of all the Allies, to raise now to new heights of courage, of resolution and of effort," the briefing officer exhorted them, reading the rare Order of the Day that Eisenhower himself had issued the day before. "Let everyone hold before him a single thought—to destroy the enemy on the ground, in the air, everywhere—destroy him! United in this determination and with unshakable faith in the cause for which we fight, we will, with God's help, go forward to our greatest victory."

Hard blades of chill winter sun slanted through the tall windows of the château, where Jimmy worked steadily at his desk through the morning, pinpointing trouble spots along the afternoon's route to Neuerberg. Just before lunch, one of the jeep couriers who zipped constantly between headquarters and the airfield brought the first unsettling news: The bombers had found no fighter escorts waiting to meet them at the designated rendezvous point, but they had gone ahead anyway, alone and unprotected. More reports collected over the next two hours, and Jimmy watched in shock and sadness as they coldly mounted toward a disaster whose awful scope exceeded even the worst fears raised by the German advance. Of the thousands of planes at work in the clear skies over the Bulge today—the transports parachuting supplies to the embattled island of Bastogne, the bombers attacking with a cavalry flourish that cheered the weary infantrymen who had fought alone all week—about six hundred were enemy fighters, the last the Germans could muster, and the thirty Marauders of the 391st had the bad luck to stir up the largest swarm of them.

Heavy flak had greeted the two flights of Marauders on the approach to Ahrweiler, but it ended suddenly with a bright red burst like a Fourth of July finale. For a brief, hopeful moment, as they hit the initial point and straightened out for the bomb run, they thought they had outrun the enemy's best shot. The first flight missed the bridge, obscured by a local patch of clouds, and was swinging around for another pass when, at five minutes before noon, a screaming vision of gray and silver swooped out of the sun behind the second flight, whose bellies had just emptied of bombs. A wave of Messerschmitt 109s and Focke-Wulf 190s, a dozen of them, maybe fifteen, guns open, tracers piercing, charging abreast like a phalanx of Napoleonic cuirassiers, slashed through the bombers. Another wave followed, and another, and then, horrifyingly, still another, sixty or seventy planes in all. More than a tenth of all the German planes aloft were faced off against barely a hundredth of the Allies.

With no protective screen of fighters to shield them, the Marauders—less cumbersome than the four-engine heavies, but still never meant to joust Messerchmitts—turned to fight their way out alone. The enemy lunged again and again. Engines flamed, metal shredded, glass fractured and fuselages split for ten frantic minutes before some friendly planes appeared—the first flight of bombers returning. The crews didn't know if the bridge still stood, and they had to hit it, to stop the trains that were supplying the German front. Outnumbered and outmaneuvered, they flattened out to drop their thousand-pounders, knowing it could cost them their planes and their lives. The bridge fell, and so, within the next ten minutes, did nine Marauders. The gunners on some of the bombers were still firing as they plummeted earthward.

"The area above me and to my left, where my flight would normally have been, was a maelstrom of burning fighters and bombers, the fighters making individual attacks as in a dogfight, pulling up in wingovers to dive on planes attacked," one of the surviving pilots told interrogators after he had managed to guide his wounded craft back to base. "I cannot say how many planes were burning, but I saw only one plane apparently not being subject to attack."

Out at the airfield, the ground crews kept staring at the sky, searching for stragglers, stunned that so many planes still hadn't returned. Jimmy had always joined in this ritual back in England, going out to count the planes at the end of a mission, but the field here was too far from the château headquarters. He sat at his desk instead, blinking in disbelief at the long list of names to be typed into the reports. He counted them again with his finger to make sure his eyes weren't exaggerating. Sixteen planes were gone, and ninety-nine men were missing, the costliest mission by far for the 391st, and the deadliest encounter anywhere yet between Marauders and enemy fighters. (The Marauders were credited with seven kills of German planes, and six probables.) Of the fourteen planes that did return, twelve were damaged, and thirteen crewmen had been taken off bleeding and wounded. It was not a sky anyone wanted to go back into, but somebody would have to: One of the targets, the communications center at Neuerberg, hadn't been destroyed; it was still sending messages to the Bulge.

They managed to get twenty-one planes ready, everything that could fly, and the grim crews assembled in the briefing room for the afternoon mission. They were expecting the usual officer at the podium, but in strode the group commander himself, Colonel Williams, dressed for flying. The colonel's attire was both surprising and inspiring: He had flown fifty-six missions and, with his bombardier, compiled the best accuracy record in the group, but the division commander had lately asked him to lead from the ground instead. Orders from the general or not, he was going up today, he told them—with a well-placed dose of his familiar profanity—right at the head of the first flight, and they were going up with him. Four of the Marauders behind him took flak hits, but they saw no German fighters and they all returned intact. Their bombing was ranked "superior," the highest classification on the scale.

"Yesterday was a tough day for you. It was a tougher day for the enemy," the briefing officer told the crews the next morning, the day before Christmas, reading a message from General Anderson that outlined the German losses and praised the "conspicuous gallantry" of the 391st. "Such actions will not only break up the Hun's counterattack but will insure his defeat."

The group had faced death only in increments before, and the effort of absorbing so much of it at once now—a casualty list that would be more familiar to an ambushed rifle company—seemed to drain the light from what was in fact another day of bright sun. Jimmy passed the Christmas tree that stood in the château like a memory of home—decorated with the makeshift tinsel of "window," the thin metal strips the bombers dropped to trick the enemy radar—and tried not to think about the holiday telegrams that ninety-nine families would be getting. Almost five thousand Allied planes were in the air today, even more than yesterday—the heavy bombers punishing the bases of the German fighters that had wreaked such havoc, and thirty-nine Marauders from the 391st hitting another railroad bridge in Germany, at Konz-Karthaus. Jimmy pulled the maps for the two targets scheduled for the next day, Christmas. No holiday truce was planned or expected; that was the kind of courtly, sentimental battlefield gesture that had vanished since the last war. A turkey dinner was planned for tomorrow, and twenty-five French orphans had been invited, but first the Marauders would try to obliterate a communications center in Bitburg and a road bridge in Taben. The Germans were five miles from the Meuse River, slowed but not stopped, and there was no time to spare for festivities.

By dark, all the day's planes had returned safely from Konz-Karthaus, and word was spreading that the group's new chaplain, a Catholic priest, would offer a midnight mass. Jimmy had done most of his worshipping lately standing around the back of a jeep—the last chaplain was a Baptist minister, augmented by monthly visits from a circuit-riding priest—but tonight's mass promised to be a more formal and solemn occasion. Yesterday's losses still hung heavy and unmourned in the raw winter air, and as the night deepened, the men emerged from their billets and streamed toward the old barn that was the one building big enough to hold everyone who wanted to pray. Catholics, Protestants and Jews alike all seemed to sense that, in the absence of a memorial service, a mass to mark a distant birth might offer a comforting forum for the contemplation of some much nearer deaths.

The moon was four days shy of full, and its wan glow, amplified as it reflected off the spreading cloak of snow, had enough strength to tag shadows behind the men filing through the bluish dreamlight toward the barn. Breath fogging, bundled in Eisenhower jackets and wool pants, the congregation formed close ranks inside. A jagged hole had been opened in the roof by a bomb, and when Jimmy looked up, it framed the moon and its neighboring stars. He knelt as the priest raised a hand to offer a general absolution.

"*Ego te absolvo a peccatis tuis in nomine Patris et Filii, et Spiritus Sancti, Amen,*" the priest said, his arm tracing the sign of the cross. *I absolve you from your sins in the name of the Father, and of the Son, and of the Holy Ghost. Amen.*

The war had altered the sacrament of confession, replacing the small, dark booth of Jimmy's parish youth, the private enumeration of individual trespasses, with a sweeping and public rite of forgiveness for men with uncertain futures. Time was short, death was near, and sins had to be handled in wholesale lots. The priest genuflected before the makeshift altar, then stood and joined his hands in prayer.

"*Judica me, Deus, et discerne causam meam de gente non sancta: ab homine iniquo et doloso erue me,*" he said. *Judge me, O God, and discern my cause from the unholy nation, rescue me from the wicked and deceitful man.*

"*Quia tu es, Deus, fortitudo mea: quare me repulisti, et quare tristis incedo, dum affligit me inimicus?*" responded the soldier who was serving as his acolyte. *For Thou, O God, art my strength, why hast Thou forsaken me? And why do I go about in sadness, while the enemy afflicts me?*

Jimmy had no missal to tether him to the priest's words, as he would have back at St. Rose, so he let himself slip into the lulling current of the Latin Mass. The unfurling of the ancient ritual, the murmur of the nearly indecipherable language, seemed to open in the dim barn a space as grand as a cathedral. The eaves were lost in rising shadows that might have reached as high as the nave of Notre Dame. The homily was consoling— in English, like the Gospel, meditating on duty and sacrifice, the cruelty of the moment and the peace of eternity—but what helped even more was the sense the Mass gave of some larger order within the chaos of war, the evidence it presented of the existence, somewhere, of a listening God.

As the final blessing faded, and the reassuring taste of the communion wafer lingered in his mouth, Jimmy joined a gruff chorus of the closing hymn, "Silent Night." The song's slow, warm-blanket cadence was stretched out even further by the soldiers' plodding collective voice—the abashed and tuneless rumble of men unaccustomed to singing out loud and in public.

"Sleep in heavenly peace," they sang, artlessly but sincerely elongating the vowels and bending the notes, thinking as much of the airmen of Ahrheim as the infant in Bethlehem. "Sleep in heavenly peace."

7.

The Army in Europe, 1944–1945

Walter Denise: France

Sleeping fitfully in a foxhole not quite large or comfortable enough to be a grave, Walter Denise looked up occasionally into a sky that hadn't drained completely of light. A patchwork of gray filled the hollows in the tracery of black, bare tree limbs overhead, a glimpse of the same roof of clouds that, sixty miles north at the Bulge, shielded the German advance from Allied planes. Snow blanketed the woods all around him, and bent the branches of the few full evergreens that stood amid the skeletal oaks and elms. Stretching behind him, at the bottom of the ridge he had just scrambled up, were the open fields his company had trudged across, an expanse so wide and white that a frail glow seemed to be evaporating from it. Artillery bursts and mortar blasts reddened the low sky occasionally, booming and thudding and splintering trees, and making Walter wish for a deeper hole. Dug in on either side of him, barely in whispering range at forty or fifty feet, were two more soldiers from K Company, and beyond them stretched a thin line of other riflemen from the Third Battalion of the 324th Infantry Regiment, a fighting front far more flexible, permeable and transient than the trenches of the last war. His first night in Germany happened also to be the longest night of the year, and the enemy were doing their best to stretch it into eternity.

Shells fell steadily through the deepest hours of the night, sputtering out only when the morning light began seeping into the clouds. Walter poked up from his hole, taking the lay of a new land. The Germany that had erupted around him looked little different from the France he had left two miles behind the previous evening, on the other side of the single-lane steel-girder bridge that spanned the narrow Blies River, but he knew

that the soldiers he couldn't see would defend their homeland with a ferocity they might not have expended on a conquered nation. He heard
an awful whistle rising in the high distance, and he dove back into the
hole, pressing himself even deeper into Germany. The streaking shell exploded when it hit the crown of the woods, one of the dreaded "tree-
bursts," pelting everything in a wide arc beneath it with a hail of scorching
steel. Another shell crashed through the branches and slammed into the
earth somewhere off on his right flank, where L Company was strung out,
followed in quick succession by another, and another, the start of a barrage much fiercer than the night before. The foxhole wasn't his own—his
unit had been moved up to replace one sent north to help plug the leak at
the Bulge—and he was sorry now he hadn't a chance to shield it with a
cover of fallen wood. Bundled up in several layers of wool and fleece, he
was well insulated against the cold, but his main protection against
shrapnel was much lighter—a Bible and a copy of *Science and Health,*
tucked into the breast pockets of his field jacket. The Bible, the full King
James text of both the Old and the New Testaments, measured maybe an
inch thick, and as he lay prone under the shelling, he felt as if it were lifting him a foot too high off the precious ground. He didn't think of removing it, though, gladly accepting the added height as the price of God's
presence.

After ninety pounding minutes the barrage abruptly lifted, and Walter steeled himself for the attack he knew would inevitably follow. He
reached up and pressed his helmet down tighter on the wool cap he wore
beneath it. Resting his rifle on the lip of his hole, he sighted along its barrel into the trees he expected to come alive at any moment. Some bullets
pocked the air above his head, but the main thrust of the assault seemed
aimed at the positions to his right, beyond sight but not hearing. All
through the morning he heard gunshots and shouts—the men of neighboring L Company trying to fight off one hundred charging Germans.
Their line was held as thinly as his, and when he heard the clank and rumble of tanks summoned from behind, he guessed, correctly, that it had
been broken. He pivoted in his hole, sweeping his rifle in a full, searching
circle, watching for an enemy whose position had suddenly become a
mystery.

"Look out behind you, over there!" he shouted to the man in the next
hole.

A German soldier was stalking toward them from a direction no one had expected, a machine pistol in one hand, four extra magazines and two more guns hanging from his belt. The men in the nearby holes swung their rifles around and fired. Walter shot, too, and the German fell before he could shoot back. Walter kept his hot rifle trained at the same patch of woods, worried that the lone soldier might be trailing some company. No one else appeared, though. The dead man must have been wandering blind, Walter surmised, separated, permanently now, from his unit.

Walter kept checking behind him, but the main danger had shifted again to the faceless forest ahead, which was emitting bullets at erratic intervals. Reinforcements arrived to help the remnants of L Company, the few who hadn't been killed or captured, retake their ground. More tanks and tank destroyers lumbered into position, and engineers laid wire obstacles. Walter expected another headlong rush from the Germans, but the afternoon passed instead as a protracted, sporadic rifle duel with an unseen foe. Cramped after too many hours in his hole, he ventured out once during what he gambled was a safe lull in the shooting. He was stretching the muscles in his legs when a bullet slammed into the tree he was standing beside, chasing him back into the ground. Splintered bark sprayed against his face as he dove. Savoring his temporary haven, he felt a strange taste in his mouth. It was acrid and metallic—was it the bullet, he wondered? Had it actually been close enough that he had ingested some minute flecks of it? In breathing the air it disturbed had he somehow inhaled its molecular essence? The longer he sat there the more he realized that it wasn't really rational—that it was probably his own startled body secreting some bitter internal juices—but then again, there was little about the situation he was in that was rational to begin with.

Walter stuck to his hole, tense and bored at once. No attack came that night, nor the next day either—December 23, the day the clouds finally lifted and the Marauders of the 391st fell. An attack would come eventually, though, the Americans were sure of that, and this position, they decided, was too vulnerable; they had advanced too far too soon with too few men. An order to withdraw arrived at dusk. One squad was assigned to stay behind to cover the retreat, the six men led by Walter. Everybody else shouldered their packs, climbed out of their holes and marched back to France, while Walter and his men burrowed in again, the last ones left in Germany. He was given a radio that would tell him when to evacuate—a few hours at the most, he was assured, probably by eight-thirty or so.

At nine, feeling forgotten and alone, Walter called in. "Get off the radio," the battalion commander barked. "Maintain absolute radio silence until further notice."

He sank back into the darkness and listened as the woods pressing in all around him slowly grew animated with the grinding hum of an army rousing itself to action. A space had opened up before the Germans like a gift, and they moved quickly to reclaim it. Enemy columns passed on either side of him—men tramping, tanks creaking and groaning, snow crunching, branches snapping on protesting trees. He willed himself toward invisibility and prayed. The withdrawal his squad was meant to cover was long since complete, and he was beginning to feel unnecessarily abandoned in what had now become enemy territory. The night was ticking away, slipping toward the dawn that would leave them mortally exposed.

The radio finally called at four-thirty. "Denise, withdraw your troops ASAP," the battalion commander ordered.

Walter crept, whispering, from hole to hole, collecting his men. Tree by tree, they slipped down the hill to the edge of the woods and peeked out across the wide snowfield they would have to cross. German tanks were parked haphazardly in the distance, and soldiers were milling about. In the enemy's disorder, Walter saw his opportunity. He motioned for his men to follow him, and they walked straight across the sloping field as if they belonged there. The gloom was still deep enough, he reasoned, that any Germans who saw them would assume they were Germans, too. They proceeded unchallenged across the fields, and slid unnoticed past the shelled and battered stone houses of Habkirchen, the village on the German side of the river. The bridge to Frauenberg, on the French side, was unguarded, and they raced across, exhaling deeply as they entered friendly territory. By dawn they were digging fresh foxholes on a hill above the river. Their work was interrupted by a blast below. The bridge had exploded, just two hours after they were the last ones across it, an attempt by the retreating Americans to keep the Germans in Germany.

By dusk Walter had built a makeshift roof over the hole he expected to spend Christmas Eve in, but his squad was soon ordered down from the safer heights and into the village of Frauenberg. At one A.M., the hour when Jimmy Higgins was singing "Silent Night" in Tilloloy, Walter stood breathlessly in the shadows outside a building in the center of town, listening to what sounded like footsteps in the rubble on the second floor of the neighboring school. He had been warned against enemy patrols, and he thought he had stumbled upon one. As he was plotting how to flush them out he noticed that the noise died each time the wind stilled. He poked his head into the school courtyard and saw with relief the benign source of the sound that had made him tighten his grip on his gun—just the flapping of a loose blackout curtain. The squad continued down the main street and established a defensive line on a small rise near the last house in town. Too tired from the previous two days to do anything else, they dropped into an unplanned sleep. An explosion soon shocked them awake. Some Germans had crept near enough in the darkness to toss two potato-masher grenades at their new position. One man was bleeding from his neck, a flesh wound from the shrapnel. Walter sprayed bullets down the dark road and into the surrounding trees, but no one shot back. The attackers had melted back into the night as invisibly as they had approached.

The rest of the third platoon joined Walter's squad in Frauenberg on Christmas morning—just twenty-two men now, a number that included replacements for the dead and wounded, down from the fifty-six who had started when the 324th entered the war in October. After sailing directly from Boston to Cherbourg, part of the first convoy of combat troops to bypass England on the Atlantic crossing, the regiment had ridden boxcars to Alsace-Lorraine in France, in the southern sector of the western front, and was absorbed into the Seventh Army, which had landed on the Riviera beaches in August and rolled quickly north. Within a few days of arriving, Walter was volunteering for night patrols behind enemy lines. He would blacken his face with soot from a coal stove, turn the luminous dial of his watch against his wrist, slip a trench knife down the side of his boot, then steal out into the night to reconnoiter the territory, capture prisoners for interrogation, and try to prod the Germans into revealing their strength and positions by shooting at him.

The Germans had shot at him often, but they hadn't hit him yet, and Walter believed he had God to thank for that. His faith was deep, and he believed it was protecting him from harm. All the evil and sickness in the material world was an illusion that could be overcome by the power of his mind—that was what he had been taught as a Christian Scientist; that was what had helped him overcome the drunken soldiers who brandished a knife at him back in Texas; and that was what was helping him now to overcome the greatest evil he had yet faced.

The Christian Science church had made some practical accommodations to the war—encouraging members to serve, and permitting them to accept the vaccinations the military required, and to dispense and receive medical aid on the battlefield. It had also made a larger moral accommodation: The commandment against killing had been drilled into Walter in Sunday school, but he fired his gun without hesitation when confronted with an enemy. When he pulled his trigger in battle, he reasoned—and his church reasoned with him—even if he were aiming at the heart of a man whose eyes he could see, he was not trying to kill an individual, but to stop a larger onslaught that might otherwise consume him, his comrades and, ultimately, the world.

"As Christian Scientists we can keep love uppermost in our hearts," a visiting speaker had recently told a special Sunday gathering back home at Freehold High School in a lecture on "Winning the War and Peace Through Prayer" that was introduced by Walter's father, "even though compelled for the moment to defend ourselves against wrongdoing with material weapons in order that the evil may not destroy the good in human consciousness."

Walter didn't talk much about his faith, but his actions embodied it in a way that sometimes set him apart from his fellow soldiers. He didn't smoke, drink or swear. He had a taste for punning and horseplay, but he could also be severe and prickly. Though only a private, he sometimes acted like an officer, instinctively taking the lead before anyone else could. He had been accustomed to being in charge back home, overseeing the migrant workers in the orchard, and it was still his inclination to tell other people what to do. Incompetence, inattention and sloppiness offended him, and he wasn't shy about saying so.

Walter's regiment had spent November and December pushing the Germans back toward Germany, almost seventy miles in all—across the Alsace plains, through the Vosges mountains, out of Strasbourg. The carnage they endured and inflicted was so horrific that his faith could not always assuage his fear. He saw men machine-gunned as they clawed frantically out the hatches of burning tanks, medics shot at as they dashed out to tend the wounded. In the aftermath of an artillery barrage, he saw what was left of a forty-man German patrol spread gruesomely across a field, the dead scattered in bloody pieces, the few living squirming in agony. At Waldenbach, on what his Third Battalion came to call "Purple Heart Hill" because of the casualties they suffered in taking it, he saw an armor-piercing shell from a German tank slice neatly through both a tree and the neck of the soldier who was leaning wearily against it. The head rolled down the slope like a lost ball; the body remained standing, as if still collecting its strength. But he also saw tearful French villagers waving their long-furled flags, hailing his arrival as their liberation.

No tricolors were flying yet at Christmas in Frauenberg, where any civilians who hadn't already fled remained hidden, wary, like Walter, of lurking Germans. The reinforcements joined his squad, occupying four houses on the edge of town, each of which boasted a manure pile in front of its attached barn, frozen and waiting for spring. The town's size reminded Walter of Marlboro, one of the potato villages that orbited Freehold, but its design reflected an agricultural tradition unlike his own. Rather than living surrounded by their land, as he did back home on the orchard, the local farmers lived instead surrounded by their neighbors, in citylike proximity, riding out to work the outlying fields each day.

Christmas Day passed quietly in the village—another K-ration meal of the canned pork loaf Walter dreaded, followed by a tin of cheese to counter its ill effects on his bowels—but the platoon woke the next morning to find Germans scurrying on the other side of the river. Walter spotted one trying to cross the remnants of the ruined bridge, and raised his rifle to stop him. He heard his bullet clang off a steel girder. The German quickly scrambled back into Habkirchen, and Walter was doubly relieved—that he had stopped an intruder, and that he had done so without killing him. Every time he had fired his rifle in combat so far, he had been convinced that he hadn't hit anyone. If he saw an enemy fall, like the German who had surprised his squad from behind, he was certain it was someone else's bullet that was responsible. God was protecting him not only from being harmed, he believed, but also from unnecessarily harming anyone else.

The Germans were feinting and jabbing all along the river, probing for soft spots in the line they were planning to attack, while the Americans were straining to hold ground as far forward as they could—so far forward that friendly fire, the rounds of white phosphorous shells that kept falling short, was almost as much a danger to Walter as enemy fire. For three nights he sat with a pair of other soldiers beneath a tree on the west end of town, maintaining an outpost against persistent enemy patrols. They dug no holes, afraid the noise would announce their arrival, and tried to keep warm with just overcoats and blankets. The Germans gave them little chance to rest. Rifle fire would burst from the woods at them—another small patrol looking for a gap to slip through. Walter and his men would shoot back into the darkness, unleashing enough firepower to make themselves seem a larger obstacle than they really were. If the Germans didn't withdraw immediately, Walter's men would toss grenades until they did.

Intelligence reports had filtered up to the line about a new German offensive that was massing—Operation Nordwind, designed to slice through Alsace as decisively as the Bulge surprise had through the Ardennes—and as Walter sat waiting in the darkness, wondering just how big the attack would be, he fingered the lump of Bible at his chest, grateful that he still had it. He had almost lost it a few weeks earlier, at the end of a night far longer than this one, longer and more harrowing in fact than any other night in his life so far, a night when his character and faith were tested as never before. He thought back to that night often now, and it gave him a prayerful measure of comfort and confidence. If God had borne him through that trial, he reflected, what was there left that could ever harm him?

"Patrol to Remoncourt radioed in that they met resistance, eight hundred yards from town," announced the report that had reached regimental headquarters back in Embermenil at one-fifteen A.M. on November 2, barely a week after Walter had arrived at the front, and only three nights after his first soot-faced foray into enemy territory.

A silent, single-file column, thirty-eight soldiers long, had just entered the woods outside Remoncourt, the enemy-held town they had been sent to reconnoiter for an upcoming attack, when the point man shot at a lone German he spotted hiding behind a tree, triggering an ambush by a large and invisible force. Return fire blazed from every angle, chasing the American patrol back out into the clearing. Walter, sandwiched in the middle of the pack, was the last man out. He flung himself down beside the three other trained scouts attached to the mission, forming a line of defense to cover the retreat.

"Patrol is pinned down," headquarters was informed at 1:25. "Resistance is made up of rifles, pistols and grenades."

Mortars, bazookas and machine guns were firing, too, none of which the patrol could answer with. Half of the men had already left, the rest were soon on their way. Walter withdrew a few yards at a time, shooting and then scuttling back across the clearing. When he had some distance from the trees, and the enemy fire broke for a moment, he rose and ran with two other men until his eyes suddenly filled with a flash of white light, his ears with a tidal roar, and he found himself a few lost seconds later flat on the ground on the other side of a concertina wire fence he hadn't even known was there. The lieutenant who had been running ahead of him was entangled in the wire, moaning as he struggled to get free.

"You must have set off a booby trap," Walter said, crawling over to help. His own hand bleeding, he snipped away with the wire cutters that were part of a scout's standard field equipment.

The lieutenant staggered off with a broken arm and two tattered legs, and Walter was about to follow when an agonized stream of pleas and oaths, unmistakably American, floated over from another section of the fence, nearer the German line. Somebody was still out there, dying it sounded like, and Walter knew he might as well die himself if he left a cry for help unanswered. He ran back and found a private from I Company he had never seen before, Earl Vincent, lying on his back with an eight-inch splinter of shin bone pointing in one direction, its eerie paleness so unexpected and startling that it seemed almost to glow, and what remained of his lower left leg bent back in the other. The mine Vincent tripped had mangled his right leg, too, and torn off the boot and legging.

"Keep still and I'll get you out," Walter promised.

He gave Vincent wound tablets—the sulfadiazine pills soldiers carried that were meant to prevent infection—and water, tried to stop the bleeding with the compress bandages he carried, and wondered, now that he had assumed the burden of another man's life, how he would ever get either of them back intact. Machine-gun bursts kept his head low as he bent over the gap in Vincent's shin. He gingerly cut the wire snagged in the bloody flap of flesh and tendon that still held the leg together, and then straddled him in a crouch, attempting the fireman's drag he remembered from Boy Scouts. But Vincent's arm was broken, too, and he couldn't keep his hands locked around Walter's neck. Walter slipped down beside him in frustration just as the Germans shot up a flare, exposing the stranded pair in a harsh and wobbly light.

"Do you know the Lord's Prayer?" Walter asked in a whisper, trying to stay frozen in the ghostly glare.

"Our Father, who art in heaven, hallowed be thy name," they prayed quietly together, over and over, "thy kingdom come, thy will be done, on earth as it is in heaven . . ."

The machine-gun fire doubled when the flare faded, spurring Walter to an alternate escape plan. Lying on his stomach next to Vincent, who lay on his back, he maneuvered into an awkward embrace—his left arm draped across Vincent's chest, Vincent's left arm stretched under his chest—and began creeping like a caterpillar, pulling and pushing and lifting, inch by precious inch. Walter prayed as he went, to himself as much as aloud, and in the gloom ahead he soon made out the form of a single American soldier. Sergeant Stanley Benezet had seen someone dash to Vincent's aid, and had waited behind, alone, in case he was needed. Neither he nor Walter knew Vincent, nor did they know each other, but together they took his life into their hands. Benezet positioned himself on the opposite side, and they dragged Vincent into a deep tank track that offered a lip of mud as cover. Vincent raised his head to glimpse his wounds, and into his face came the awful recognition of how much he had lost, an expression as grievous and twisted as the leg itself.

"Lie back down and pray some more," Walter told him. "We'll get you back, don't worry."

Another flare went up, and a mortar shell exploded where they had just been, near the spot where Walter had cut Vincent from the wire. They started crawling again, before the next shell could find where they were now.

". . . give us this day our daily bread and forgive us our trespasses," they prayed, "as we forgive our trespassers . . ."

At least five hundred yards of open field stretched ahead between them and safety, and when moonlight leaked across it through a break in the clouds above, Walter felt as exposed in the dim glow as an actor on a spotlit stage. Machine guns opened up on either flank, threatening to box them in. They stuck to tank tracks as much as they could, but none offered a direct route home.

"Patrol on way back," headquarters was informed at two-thirty A.M., after most of the other men had trickled in. "Eleven still missing."

They dragged and prayed, dragged and prayed—for strength for themselves and for Vincent, for the mortars and bullets to miss, for the clouds to hide the moon and the flares to reveal nothing. Shell holes, puddled with cold water, offered occasional cover, and helped keep Vincent awake. Walter and Benezet stopped often to rub some warmth back into his battered body, and prodded him to keep talking and praying. If he slipped off now, they knew, he wasn't likely to come back.

". . . and lead us not into temptation, but deliver us from evil," they prayed together, "for thine is the kingdom and the power and the glory, forever and ever. Amen."

At four A.M.—three endless hours later—they reached the friendly side of a rise in front of their own lines. Walter and Benezet made a field litter from their jackets, thrusting cut saplings through the sleeves and carrying Vincent until they found a medic and a real stretcher. They rode with him in the jeep back to the aid station at Embermenil, and watched, amazed, as he leaned up to drink the coffee and smoke the cigarette he was offered. Walter found himself on the edge of tears, from relief at preserving his own life, and thanks for saving another's. He watched as the doctors gave Vincent blood, and cut off the dangling piece of leg. The rest of his left leg came off later, and the bottom of the right leg, too.

Walter was walking back to the company that still counted him as lost when, feeling something missing, he reflexively patted his chest. "My jacket," he said, and he hurried back to the aid station. It was soaked in blood after he used it to carry Vincent, and had been tossed into a pile of trash. He didn't care about the jacket itself, just the two precious books in its chest pockets. He sorted through the pile until he found what was left of his jacket. The books were still inside, undamaged. He took them back and held them close.

Walter touched his Bible again on New Year's Eve in Frauenberg, watching across the river for the opening shots of the expected attack. The Germans finally launched Operation Nordwind in the last hour of 1944—eight divisions rushing out of their Siegfried Line positions at the heart of the Seventh Army, nine hundred planes swooping in on Allied air bases in Holland, Belgium and France. (A single Junkers 88 struck Jimmy Higgins's base near Tilloloy, dropping a pair of five hundred-pounders that damaged nothing but an empty field.) Walter was at the northern edge of the front, above the main enemy thrust, which gained some ground but not nearly as much as the Bulge surprise two weeks earlier.

"Our people are resolved to fight the war to victory under any and all circumstances," Hitler shouted over the radio in Berlin at five minutes past midnight. "The world must know that this state will, therefore, never capitulate. . . . Germany will rise like a phoenix from its ruined cities and this will go down in history as the miracle of the twentieth century."

Walter's squad was ordered to the other end of Frauenberg, charged with guarding a weak flank where the blasted remains of a bridge over the Blies offered the Germans a steppingstone back into France. Early on the second evening of Nordwind, he sat on a sack of wheat inside a dark barn, watching the river through the rear window. Some snow had fallen earlier, and the night outside was bright enough that he could see a fair distance. One of his men was posted at the barn's twin front doors, which opened onto the road leading out of town toward the northeast, and Walter heard him now skittering closer through the shadows, trying to find somebody with his anxious whispers.

"I'm here," Walter answered quietly. "What's up?"

"There's twenty or thirty Jerries out there in white suits," reported the door guard, the latest in the line of fresh-faced replacements Walter tried not to get too close to, knowing how brief and sad their acquaintance would likely be.

Walter hadn't seen any white uniforms on either side's soldiers yet, despite the winter landscape they would have offered good cover against, and he suspected instead a jittery combat virgin's mirage—until he heard hobnail boots come clattering through the wide, creaking doors, and a murmur of German. He slipped down off the wheat bag into the dark pocket beneath the window. Counting boots and measuring voices, he pegged the visitors as a combat patrol prowling for prisoners, and he quickly decided not to challenge them and become one. He and the door guard shrank silently into the shadows. As the Germans poked nearer, Walter kept one hand on a grenade that hung by its pop-off handle from a ring on his field jacket, just above his Bible. He relaxed only when he heard the boot steps receding toward the street.

"I'm staying here for the next shift," he said when his was up at seven, and he sent his partner off. "I think there might be trouble before the night's over."

He pushed open one of the barn doors a few inches, and stood at the crack that revealed a narrow view toward the center of town, the street walled in by a corridor of close-set buildings, any one of which might have absorbed the Germans. At seven-thirty he heard some movement outside. Seeing nothing in one direction, he stuck his head out and checked the other. Four Germans stood a few yards in front of him, one carrying a machine gun, another a Panzer Faust, a bazooka-like antitank gun.

"Halt!" he yelled, and then the password, just to make sure they weren't Americans, "Pole!"

"*Was? Was?*" said the startled Germans, who could hear but not see him.

He pulled his grenade pin and the percussion cap popped like a firecracker, the signal for both tosser and target to start counting, one, two, three, and to brace for the explosion at five. Walter held on until three—he didn't want them to have a chance to send it back at him—and then threw. The Germans were racing up the hill that led out of town when the grenade landed between the last two men. The explosion knocked three of them down, but they managed to crawl away before Walter could get his rifle up to shoot.

He dashed out to collect the weapons the Germans had ditched as they scrambled off, and then alerted the rest of his squad, setting up three posts in doorways along the narrow street. These intruders, he believed, were just the first of many more, and he dispatched a runner back to the platoon command post with a warning. Machine-gun fire began crackling in the darkness beyond the last house.

"Here it comes," Walter said, and an enemy flare went up.

The Germans didn't know exactly where the Americans were, so they advanced in spasms—firing off a flare, spraying the area it lit with automatic weapons, and then marching forward, shooting as they came. Walter heard them nearing, but could see nothing clearly enough to shoot at. In the wavery light of one flare, he finally spotted two Germans hugging the walls along the other side of the street, creeping nearer one of the other American outposts, which they couldn't see, and which couldn't see them.

"I'll kneel down and fire, and you stand and fire over my head," he whispered to his partner, who had a BAR, a Browning Automatic Rifle more powerful than his own M-1.

The Germans had crept almost opposite him when Walter broke the silence. "Halt!" he said again. "Pole!"

"*Kamerad!*" they called back, and Walter squeezed off two rounds.

Sparks glinted as a bullet ricocheted off something metal at the waist of one of the Germans, a belt buckle maybe. Walter squeezed again, but nothing came: The two shots were the last in his chamber. Nothing came from the BAR either—his partner was frozen with fear—nor from the burp guns on the other side of the street, where the Germans were frozen, too, stunned by their luck at the bullet's caroming path. Walter knelt defenseless in the doorway, reaching for a fresh cartridge. It was a desperate race now, and he had lost his head start. He knew the Germans would soon thaw and shoot. He hoped his partner would, too, but he couldn't stake his life on it. As he scrambled to reload, he was startled by a nearby burst of fire—not from above, where the BAR man was still standing frozen, but from his right. The runner he had sent to the command post had returned like an angel, sooner than expected, and was shooting at the Germans. The BAR man was startled back to life by the runner's gun, and he started shooting, too, squeezing off fifteen quick rounds.

"They would have made some trouble," Walter said as they examined the bodies of the Germans, each of which was laden with grenades. He had helped stop two more enemy soldiers but again, he believed, he hadn't killed them himself. God had left that for somebody else's bullets.

No other Germans approached through the night, but in the morning some of the remaining villagers reported infiltrators who had leaked in. Walter and one of his men went door to door, flushing out German soldiers who were hiding in the basements, pantries and back corners of houses whose residents had fled. Several were wounded, and all surrendered without resistance—fourteen in all, ordered into a single-file line on the main street and marched out of town and up the hill toward the rear echelon area where prisoners were being collected. Halfway up the hill, Walter spotted the mouth of a cave, and a German soldier sitting by a machine gun.

"Come out with your hands up!" he shouted in the best high-school German he could muster.

To his surprise, out walked fourteen more Germans, part of the previous night's combat patrol, leaving behind a high-powered arsenal of bazookas and machine guns and finding, to their surprise, that they had just been captured by nothing more than a pair of rifle-toting Americans. He handled the twenty-eight prisoners with the soldierly respect he would expect of his own captors, delivering them to guards who had a different idea about how the enemy should be treated. Like many other front-line troops, Walter felt an odd, grudging sort of bond with the enemies who shared his hellish world. Soldiers who were farther removed from the action, though, the rear-echelon barracks commandos who never had a chance to shoot at anyone, sometimes held harsher views; the guards had heard reports of German atrocities against American prisoners in the Bulge, and they intended to make their own prisoners pay. The Germans were forced to strip and stand naked in the middle of the street, in cold so deep that canteens popped. Walter turned and walked back toward town, disappointed by the behavior of his fellow soldiers. As he came down the hill again, some Germans hidden on the other side of the river got him in their sights. A volley of rifle shots sent him sprawling to the ground, the bullets so close that he felt the ripple of disturbed air on his cheek as they passed.

One side of Frauenberg was clear now, but two platoons of Germans had barricaded themselves inside two houses on the other side, raining fire on any Americans who tried to dislodge them. Just before dusk the next afternoon, Walter's squad fell in beside a pair of American tanks rumbling toward the northern edge of town. The tanks fired thirty-five rounds at the houses before artillery shells from across the river disabled one and chased the other off. No one came out to fight, and the two platoons of American infantry withdrew to await a better shot. They would have to go back, though—the Germans had to be rousted. Frauenberg had to be French again.

"We jump off an hour after moonrise tonight," Lieutenant Joe Thompson told them the following day, January 5. Nordwind was stalling—the deepest German penetration reached about fifteen miles, shorter than the Bulge and not far enough to split the Seventh Army—and the Americans wanted their line drawn taut and secure through the critical crossroads at Frauenberg.

The tanks rolled out again, and at one minute past midnight the assault force moved toward town. Leading the foot soldiers was Sergeant Powell Compere, who had proven a good friend to Walter and urged him to use more caution in combat. The men used the tanks as a shield, walking behind as the guns blasted through the darkness. The Germans answered with bazookas and mortars, and, from the gun positions across the river, some larger artillery shells. In a break in the shooting, Compere held up a white flag to call for a momentary truce and, apparently ignoring his own advice to Walter, walked slowly toward the house that was believed to hold the enemy command post.

"Come out and surrender!" he called in German. Some civilians were still holed up in adjacent houses, and the Americans didn't want to sacrifice either them or the homes of the neighbors who had fled. He was hoping the Germans would realize they were finished, and would end their stand before anyone else had to die.

Compere called again, but no answer came from the house. As he turned to walk back, several windows brightened with muzzle flashes. "Look out behind you!" someone yelled, but he was already lying face-down in the street, dead.

The Americans shot back with a furious barrage that made clear their intention to stay right where they were until the Germans were gone. The tanks boomed, and the soldiers stole toward the house that Compere had died trying to spare. Within an hour, nine Germans were prisoners, and a dozen were corpses. Two more Americans died, too, including Lieutenant Thompson, killed by a bazooka shell as he searched for one of his men. The houses were shattered, but empty. Walter's platoon—the fourteen who remained of the original fifty-six—chased the survivors down toward the river, until they met a barrage of covering artillery fire and were chased away themselves back up through the streets of Frauenberg, sidestepping shell holes and poking at shadows, peering warily at a bat-tered town that looked little different than it had a moment ago, except that now, finally, it belonged to them.

Buddy Lewis: England and Belgium

On the night after Christmas, Buddy Lewis stood before a fireplace in a castle near the southern coast of England, his legs warm below the shins, but the rest of him—and the rest of the cavernous cot-filled hall, dim be-hind him in the flickering shadows—wrapped in a damp and stubborn chill. The stone walls were at least partly wired with electricity, but lights were so sparse that a guard was posted inside the dark front entrance hall as well as outside the main door. Furnishings, portraits and minor nobles had long since been exiled, leaving only a medieval shell to accommodate a soldiers' billet. Stretching blackly through the night all around the cas-tle was what remained of the primeval forest that William the Conqueror had claimed as his royal hunting ground nine centuries earlier. Buddy rubbed his hands once more at the fire before reporting to a special assembly of Company A, 1317th Engineer General Service Regiment (Colored).

In the drafty orderly room, the lieutenant cleared his throat and be-gan reading aloud from the same letter that was being read to black troops all over England and the Continent tonight. "The Supreme Com-mander desires to destroy the enemy forces and end hostilities in this the-ater without delay," he announced. "To this end the commanding general is happy to offer to a limited number of colored troops who have had infantry training, the privilege of joining our veteran units at the front to deliver the knockout blow."

Buddy barely managed to swallow a murmur of indignation. Segregation, he could see, was finally faltering in the face of desperation. Trying to restock gutted infantry units at the front, the army was raiding service units at the rear, a pool that now included, for the first time and with Eisenhower's assent, the black units previously restricted from combat. But what made him any more able a soldier now, he wondered, than he was a year and a half ago, when, as an eager enlistee at Camp Ellis, polishing his rifle and memorizing the Articles of War, he asked about becoming a paratrooper—the white-laced jump boots had made a powerful impression on him—and was told curtly that in all of the army there was but a single black parachute battalion that was already filled (the 555th of the 82nd Airborne, the "Triple Nickles") and that he'd better get used to where he was?

"It is planned to assign you without regard to color or race to the units where assistance is most needed, and give you the opportunity of fighting shoulder to shoulder to bring about victory," the lieutenant continued. "Your comrades at the front are anxious to share the glory of victory with you."

"Yeah, *now* you can fight shoulder to shoulder beside your white brothers," somebody muttered bitterly.

"Now you have a chance to *die* beside your white brothers, that's what it means," somebody else added.

The appeal echoed in the cold silence, sparking no enthusiasm in men resentful and suspicious of an army that had previously regarded them as laborers, not fighters. In the entire company, just one man accepted—a sergeant who, like all other noncom volunteers, had to take a reduction to private so he wouldn't outrank any white soldiers in his new unit. Buddy and the rest resumed the assignment that had brought them to the castle, a round of refresher training before disembarking for France.

In the exodus months that followed the June invasion, when troops were streaming steadily out of England toward the front, the 1317th had shuttled around the southwestern coast, in the vicinity of Dorset and Hampshire mostly, sweeping up some of the mess left behind. They patched roads damaged by convoys, and dismantled vacated staging camps, flimsy as chicken coops, where troops had stayed while awaiting the invasion. When Eisenhower moved to France, they helped take apart and pack up his headquarters near Portsmouth—where the trucks were emblazoned with the flaming sword insignia of Supreme Headquarters Allied Expeditionary Force, and all the drivers they saw were white—folding camouflage netting and stacking heavy slabs of concrete flooring, a luxury that Buddy, who counted himself lucky when he got a tent with wooden duckboards, had never encountered before. They spent several weeks delicately probing the sands at a beach resort, clearing mines that had been laid in fear of a German invasion. At the castle, though, their only duties were to drill, to review what they had first learned back at Camp Ellis, and to wait their own turn, finally, to leave. Buddy practiced disassembling machine guns and deploying gas masks, and he led sessions in his own specialty, handling chemical warfare equipment.

"Fall out!" the officers called out one night in early February.

Buddy assumed it was just another random inspection, and as he hurried out of the castle he felt around his neck for the leather scabbard that held his most prized overseas souvenir, a stiletto he had bought for five pounds from a British commando. He slipped the knife out and tucked it discreetly against the inside of his left forearm. Without breaking stride, he flicked up his hand and stuck the stiletto into the tree where it had waited for him before. He stood straight and tall as the reviewers passed, clean of any unauthorized equipment that could be confiscated.

"Right face!" an officer barked, but Buddy was already instinctively turning left, the direction they had been ordered in after every previous inspection, the direction on which his plan for retrieving his stiletto depended. "Forward march!"

He marched off to the right, away from the castle, away from the knife, and straight up into the back of a windowless truck trailer that, once filled with men, started rolling, though not a word had been said about where. When the doors opened, they were at the docks in Southampton, and an LST was waiting to carry them across the Channel to Le Havre. In France they stayed first at Camp Twenty Grand—one of the several staging areas for new arrivals, each named after a cigarette brand—before boarding a train for Belgium. Trucks finally delivered them to another old stone building, a convent near Neufchâteau.

"No cots here," the sergeant told them. "You can get some straw from the stables and stuff your mattress covers."

Young novices skittered along the hallway, giggling, as Buddy dragged his scratchy bed to the wing where the men were billeted. He awoke in the middle of the night to find a vision of white hovering over him—a nun who, seeing in his startled eyes that she had been mistaken for an angel, shyly folded her hands and gestured upward, silently assuring him that she had come only to offer her prayers, not shepherd him away from earth.

"I thought I'd died and gone to heaven," he told a friend at breakfast.

A few weeks earlier, the snowy woods around Neufchâteau had marked the southern edge of the Bulge, and each day now Buddy's company set out from the convent to patrol and patch roads that had been cratered by German shells and shredded by American tanks racing north to break the siege at nearby Bastogne. With no proper equipment yet— no graders or tar dispensers or loads of crushed rock—all they could do was shovel roadside dirt into the holes. After several weeks, the trucks came back and carried them across the reclaimed wedge of Belgium to a town on the northern front of the recent battle, Marche.

They moved into one wing of an L-shaped, three-story school building emptied of students. The graceful wrought-iron fence that squared off the block and enclosed the open courtyard was crudely augmented by rolls of concertina wire meant to contain the latest and most recalcitrant occupants of the open dormitories in the other wing—more than a thousand German prisoners of war. Guards watched over the rim of the fence from a platform only large enough to hold a machine gun and a shelter tent. The prisoners had been parceled out from the main enclosure near Namur to makeshift stockades like the Marche school, where they were pressed into service on road gangs that maintained the critical arteries funneling men and supplies to the front. Buddy was not only a guard now, he learned, but a foreman, too.

"Prisoners will be made to work efficiently and energetically at all times while on duty, and will never be allowed to loaf on the job," an officer instructed Buddy's platoon on the morning of their first work detail. "At no time will prisoners be allowed to smoke while working."

The guards rode in a trailer that bounced along behind a two-and-a-half-ton truck packed tight with standing prisoners, headed out to a washboard stretch of highway N29, the road to Barvaux. Buddy had a rifle to stop any German who tried to escape, but he was more worried about the Belgian citizens who were standing along the side of the road.

They had endured a hard occupation, and they were venting their rage—jeering the Germans, pelting them with garbage and stones. They looked to Buddy as if they would tear apart any German who dared to step off the truck.

At the work site, fourteen prisoners were assigned to each guard, and Buddy's were ordered to dig a drainage ditch. When one of his charges demonstrated an attitude that was neither efficient nor energetic, Buddy shouted him back to order.

A white sergeant guarding a nearby crew called Buddy over. "Let me tell you something," the sergeant said. "Get yourself a good stick and whack him in the head. That's what I do to keep them in line. I'm not gonna shoot them and go through all that rigmarole, I just whack them in the head."

Buddy accepted the advice with the half-swallowed thanks an unwanted gift evokes. Just because you stood above someone, he knew, didn't mean you had to step on them. Victory carried its own authority, and raising his rifle and his voice simultaneously was sufficient to cure any misunderstandings of language or intent. As February slipped into March, thaw damage kept the road gangs busy, and Buddy kept his prisoners in line without resorting to any sticks. The older prisoners had mostly surrendered, docile and grateful for a safe haven as the war crashed toward its suicidal end, but some of the younger ones were still fighting—breaking into goose step when marching around the courtyard, sharpening spoons and fashioning bits of glass into jailhouse weapons. Buddy and the other guards stormed through the dormitories once each night, always at a different hour to frustrate attempts at concealment, and while they sometimes got rough with the hard cases who were hiding contraband, they didn't inflict summary beatings. Punishment instead was a few hours standing at attention outside.

"We'd rather be guarded by American black soldiers than American whites," a prisoner who spoke some English told Buddy one day. "You treat us better."

After three weeks in Marche, the POW stockade was beginning to feel like the company's permanent home in Europe, but they had moved so often before, and the war was pushing ahead so far and so fast, that Buddy expected soon to see what lay beyond Belgium. The Allies had firebombed Dresden and were pressing toward the Rhine with such force that the Germans had begun calling up fifteen- and sixteen-year-old boys for military service. Roosevelt, Churchill and Stalin had already met at

Yalta to carve up postwar Europe. One off-duty evening at the turn of spring, the weather warm enough that the road crews had begun removing the DANGER—ICE signs, Buddy was smoking and lounging on the school's porch when a jeep bearing the insignia of the Ninth Army raced up. A courier sprinted into headquarters. Twenty minutes later, Buddy's sergeant emerged with the orders.

"Saddle up," he told the curious group that had gathered. "We've got to move out."

This time the trucks were open, unlike the ones that had carried them from the castle to the Southampton docks, but the journey was similarly blind. The convoy, long and slow behind the grader at its head, rolled northeast through the night and the next day, toward Germany, Buddy guessed, though no one had yet said where they were going or what they would do there. Some of the towns along the route had been reduced by the war to archeological sites, all rubble and husks, looking more like the crumbled remnants of past civilizations than settlements that anyone in living memory might have ever called home. As they drove one way up the road, they passed an infantry platoon marching the other way beside it.

"You'll be soooorry," the foot soldiers called up, the greeting offered everywhere by those coming out to those going in.

Walter Denise: France

In the hollow, fading light of a February dusk, Walter Denise sat beside an open window in an upstairs bedroom of a rough-plastered farmhouse, looking out across the shorn and frozen grain fields that encircled it like a lake around an island. The view was broad and empty, the nearest trees just smudges on the horizon. A barnyard murmur drifted up from below, an echo of the sounds outside his own boyhood window—the pigs grunting in the sty, the chickens cackling in the coop. Some beef cattle wandered in a pasture beyond the outbuildings. A steady muffled rhythm arose faintly in the distance, out in the vicinity of the village that lay unseen a mile ahead—the hoofbeats of draft horses, harmonizing deceptively with the rest of the pastoral soundtrack. Walter picked up his field telephone. The horses, he knew, were not pulling plows.

"They're moving some artillery near Rimling," he told battalion headquarters in Bettviller, half a mile behind. This was just the kind of information—noticing what the Germans were doing with their big guns—he had been sent up here to collect.

The farm had been abandoned by the Heidermuhl family when the fighting closed in, and it sat now dead in the center of the milewide swath of no-man's land between the two opposing lines. Walter's regiment had quietly commandeered it as a forward outpost, rotating squads of observers through on twenty-four-hour shifts to monitor enemy movements. The Americans had won this ground once already, then lost it in the Nordwind offensive, and were preparing to take it back again, to chase the Germans from the northernmost reaches of the last pocket of France they still held along the western front. Walter kept his attention trained in the direction of the enemy strong points the nightly patrols had found— in Rimling itself, around an old mill on its outskirts, and in a clump of forest a little farther east known as the Buchenbusch Woods. He and his men had sat in the dark through the night, taking turns sleeping, careful not to emit any light, smoke or noise that might reveal them. During the day, they dreamed of roast chicken—Walter was the designated executioner and plucker back at the orchard, and he planned to take a few from the coop when the squad was relieved this evening—but settled instead for K rations that required no cook fires.

As dusk gathered, Walter noticed the cattle milling dumbly around an area where booby traps had been laid—grenades and flares attached to trip wires meant to stop German infiltrators—near enough to prompt alarming visions of an explosion that would not only shower him with raw hamburger but pinpoint his position for an enemy artillery spotter. "Let's get them out of here," he ordered when the replacements arrived.

Ropes were tied to the cattle's halters, and each man led one down the road to Bettviller. Some American mines lay unburied along a stretch ahead, tippy half spheres hurriedly strewn as a shield against an enemy tank charge, and while the humans were careful to keep to the clear lanes, the animals were not. Several mines were sent skittering by heedless hooves. Walter could only cringe as he watched one steer step on the rim of a mine, narrowly missing the detonator and leaving it rocking like a flipped coin's landing. The cattle were finally delivered, intact, to the quartermaster section, where their lives would come to a neater, quieter end, transformed by butchers into a rare steak dinner at the field mess.

Between shifts at the farmhouse, Walter's home was a foxhole outside Bettviller, more comfortable than some other frontline accommodations he had endured, but sadly lacking in the clean sheets and pillows a Paris hotel had provided him on a precious recent leave. After securing Frauenberg a month ago, his platoon had moved to a nearby quarry, where 274 mm shells from a giant German railroad gun blasted grave-sized holes in the frozen ground, and the rain of falling shrapnel miraculously managed to miss Walter, who lay exposed just twenty feet from one explosion. Summoned unscathed from the fighting, he was informed of a tripartite change in his status—a promotion to sergeant (with the extra ten dollars he earned for his combat infantryman's badge, he was now making seventy-eight dollars a month), a medal for dragging Earl Vincent to safety (he was recommended for a Silver Star, but it came back instead as a Bronze Star with a "V" for valor), and, most unexpected and welcome of all, a three-day pass to Paris. His was only the second Paris pass in K Company; the first was awarded not for saving one life, but for taking many—for killing the most Germans, an achievement he was happy not to share. He rode for twelve cold hours with twenty-nine other lucky soldiers in the back of a two-and-a-half-ton truck and spent two nights in a surreally peaceful city where the meals were hot, the streetlights bright, and no one on the bustling boulevards tried to kill him. He danced clumsily in combat boots at the USO, and attended his first Christian Science church service since leaving America. He had a photograph taken of himself to send back home, and when he looked at it he could see, as he knew his parents would, too, that the war had aged his face beyond his years.

After supper the next evening, Walter and his squad trudged back up the road to Rimling to relieve the observers in the farmhouse. Returning to combat, he had learned, was harder than entering it: He knew now, as he didn't before, that a man could be reduced in an instant to a cloud of red mist, and any boyish notions of adventure and glory that might have sustained him as he faced his first battle had long since vanished. It was all a long, cold, muddy slog, and it had made him both less patient and more solitary. He had seen too many officers make too many mistakes, and he was less trusting now of anyone's judgment but his own, less dependent for protection on anything but his own competence and God's embrace. He climbed the steps to the dark bedroom, wishing he could have stayed in the oasis of Paris. Sitting again at the open window, he listened across the silent black fields. Their efforts at secrecy were apparently still working: Some German patrols had been reported skirting the house on previous nights, but none had yet challenged it.

In the morning, one of his men called up the stairs. "Sarge, there's somebody driving up the road," he said.

Walter bounded out to find a lieutenant from the quartermaster section and his driver parking their jeep as casually as Main Street shoppers. "What do you want, Lieutenant?" he asked sharply.

"I'm going to get some food for the battalion mess," the lieutenant said. The cattle and chickens had whetted appetites back in camp, and he had come to fatten the larder.

Walter tried to swallow his rage, but he tasted it boiling back up like a clogged drain. Here he was out on the edge of civilization, halfway into enemy hands, inhabiting his outpost with monastic discretion, and then along comes this reckless intruder, a particularly distasteful mixture of rear-echelon bluster and naked incompetence, drawing a bull's-eye for the Germans and stupidly risking the lives of the observers in order to satisfy a craving for fresh poultry. From his earliest days in the service, when the army either ignored or ridiculed his Christian Science beliefs by sending him to pharmacy training, Walter had been frustrated and angered by people who, whether through negligence, malice or folly, didn't do what they should have done. Mistakes in the orchard, Walter knew, might cost a crop of peaches, but mistakes in war cost lives. The acts of valor he witnessed were often countered by dangerous lapses of judgment, training and character—the scout who panicked and ran when he heard German voices on a mission behind enemy lines; the soldier who didn't report the location of a machine gun nest that later shredded several men; the replacement officer, a transfer from the Air Corps, who didn't know how to load or shoot his carbine until Walter showed him; the BAR man who failed to fire when the patrol was ambushed at Remoncourt; the cowardly lieutenant who abandoned his men during the attack at Avricourt, and was later promoted to captain and made a general's aide; and now this hungry lieutenant.

"I think you'd better go back, sir," Walter said, straining not to say more. "You're exposing our position."

The lieutenant continued strolling deafly toward the coop. "Wait a minute, sir," Walter tried again, scrambling around to block him. "I think it would be advisable for you to leave."

"Well, get out of my way, sergeant," the lieutenant said, trying to shoulder past.

Walter stepped back, not to let him by, but to give himself room to make the most radical move of his military career. Everything that had ever been drilled into him about the sanctity of rank leaked right out, and he reached for the .45 in his holster—no longer a noncom debating an officer, but a man defending his property, and his life. He drew his gun and barked an order that he had no authority, other than moral, to issue.

"All right, get back to where you came from," he said.

His hearing sharpened by the sight of the gun, the lieutenant turned around. As a supply officer largely insulated from combat himself, he didn't recognize Walter's threat for what it was—an eruption of dogface resentment, a reflexive display of a foot-soldier's heightened survival instinct—and worried instead that he was witnessing the final breakdown of a battle-fatigue victim, unhinged enough by the fighting to actually contemplate shooting a superior. He and his driver sped away to more familiar territory behind the lines, and Walter returned to the house, where the field telephone was soon ringing.

"What were you thinking, Denise?" the battalion commander shouted. "Do you have shell shock or something?"

"Sir, he was violating our security," Walter explained.

"I don't care what he was doing—you don't pull a gun on an officer. Get back here now. You're confined to company headquarters until further notice."

Walter spread his bedroll in an unoccupied corner of a basement in Bettviller and awaited a summons to the court-martial he assumed was his fate. He tried, unsuccessfully, to banish images of stockades and firing squads from his mind. He knew he had been wrong to pull his gun, but he still believed his anger was justified, and the news he heard the next day from the outpost only confirmed for him the magnitude of the lieutenant's blunder. The observers who replaced his own team had been startled to hear midnight footsteps creaking up the farmhouse stairs, and when the BAR man on the landing heard a guttural *"Was ist?"* in response to his challenge, he started shooting. A burst from a German burp gun sprayed up from the darkness as the intruder tumbled backward. When the lights came on, two Germans, members of the 17th SS Reconnaissance Battalion, and one American, shot through the head as he leaned over the banister, were dead. Two other Germans from the raiding party, which may have been alerted to the prize inside the house by the lieutenant's foraging, managed to escape.

Walter now had what he believed was tragic evidence that his vigilance was warranted, but no one had asked him yet to defend himself; he, and his transgression, seemed to have been forgotten. He moved freely through the headquarters area, tightening at the approach of MPs who then passed him without a glance. The officers buzzing around Bettviller were clearly occupied by some larger drama than his own—perhaps, he guessed, the attack that had been rumored all through the last quiet and bunkered week. He went to sleep uncertain of how much he still owed for his crime.

"Denise, hey, Denise," the company commander prodded, shaking Walter awake at two A.M. "I've got a job for you. You're going to be point man on the battalion attack."

"The whole battalion, sir?" Walter asked, thinking he might be trapped in a dream.

"The whole battalion," the captain assured him. "Be ready at 0400."

Walter sat up on his bedroll, rubbing his eyes. Staring into the darkness, he contemplated an assignment more immediately perilous than the court-martial he was dreading. He had led many patrols before, and even some small attacks, but never anything on the scale the captain was proposing. The whole appalling picture kept growing in his mind—the hundreds of men trailing in a broad wedge behind him, only him, all alone out front, a spear point advancing steadily toward the enemy—and he kept pushing it down, fighting it with images of home: the red Plymouth convertible mothballed in the barn; the ranks of apple trees due for their winter pruning in the orchard; the gracious old colonial farmhouse that had been part of Freehold almost as long as the Denises themselves. He prayed for protection for himself and his fellow soldiers, and he pictured his parents praying for him, too. He plucked his Bible from his breast pocket and opened to a psalm, the ninety-first, which had comforted him in the face of previous battles:

> Thou shalt not be afraid for the terror by night;
> nor for the arrow that flieth by day;
> Nor for the pestilence that walketh in the darkness;
> nor for the destruction that wasteth at noonday.
>
> A thousand shall fall at thy side,
> and ten thousand at the right hand;
> but it shall not come nigh thee.

Outgoing artillery boomed sporadically, the same slow, harassing drumbeat of the previous nights, not the kind of ground-clearing firestorm that would announce some larger action. The lines had been static long enough that the Germans were assumed to be expecting an attack, but the American plan, refined over the last week of probing night patrols, still hoped for the advantage of whatever small measure of surprise it could muster. At four A.M., Walter bent over a map bathed by a shallow pool of yellow light, following the captain's finger as it traced a route through the enemy territory beyond the farmhouse outpost. As many as five hundred or more German soldiers from the Thirty-seventh Panzergrenadier Regiment lurked among the trees in the Buchenbusch Woods, and it was the 324th's job to flush them out. Walter would be leading the Third Battalion, headed for the west side of the woods; the Second Battalion would head for the east side. To the left of the 324th, two other infantry regiments from the Forty-fourth Division, the 71st and the 114th, would be pushing ahead, too, aiming to overrun German strongpoints in Rimling, at several outlying farms, and along the railroad tracks through the Bliesbrucken forest.

"Line of departure will be passed at 0545 so that the initial breakthrough may be obtained prior to daylight and main effort made at daylight," the captain told them, reading from the colonel's order.

As H-Hour approached, thousands of soldiers gathered in a field in the darkness outside Bettviller. At the front of the pack with his platoon, Walter couldn't see the men he would be leading, but he could feel their swelling presence, a heavy, black weight filling all the space between him and the safety of the village. As much as it tried to melt into the night, the knotted bulk of the regiment inevitably emitted a sound a faint level above silence—nervous coughs and worried sighs, feet stamping to shake out the cold, the rustle of wool sleeves, the muted clank of canteens and ammo belts.

"I want you to bring up the rear of the point and make sure they're following me," Walter told another sergeant from his platoon. "I don't want to be left walking out there alone."

Walter stepped off as ordered at five forty-five A.M., no one ahead of him or beside him as he strode briskly up the road that led to the farmhouse. When the gap behind him widened enough, the next few men began walking, too, and as they moved ahead, the next line followed, and the next and the next, a wedge unfolding and broadening, slowly and silently expanding to its full force, trailing its leader like a flight of geese. A few hundred yards out, he veered off the road and into the open fields that unfurled for two unbroken miles, right up to the edge of the enemy woods. With no snow to silhouette them for German guns, the ranks advanced as invisibly as the tide. Walter listened for a counterattack—the gulp of a mortar, the thud of artillery, the deadly whoosh of a rocket—but for the first mile all he heard was the plodding murmur of marching boots striking hard ground.

After half an hour, Walter was halfway across, and enough black had drained from the night that when he turned to glance over his shoulder he saw gray shadows rolling behind him like ground fog. The Germans he was ready for were in the dark blot of woods in the gloom ahead, but his topographic instincts—the farm boy's sense of terrain that had made him a scout in the first place—kept him alert for unexpected enemies who might be shielded by hummocks or stream beds, swells or furrows in the subtly undulating ground.

"Down!" he hissed sternly when a machine gun opened up on his left flank, several hundred yards back, but the men behind him had already, as he had, flattened themselves against the earth.

Some Germans at a forward outpost had felt the night moving and heard it breathing, and they started shooting blindly, trying to stop whatever it was that was creeping toward them. As Walter pressed against the cold, damp ground, he heard a deeper noise—an exploding mine, it sounded like. Some of the Americans were carrying antitank mines to scatter around their position when they reached the edge of the woods, and Walter wondered if a German bullet had hit one, or if, in falling for cover, a soldier had tripped one, or set off a buried enemy mine. Whoever's mine it was, he knew, somebody was probably dead. He turned his head and found crouching beside him the sergeant who was supposed to be minding the rear of the point.

"What's going on?" the sergeant asked anxiously. "What do we do?"

"I want you to get back where you belong, right now," Walter said through clenched teeth.

Walter kept low and still as two more German machine guns started shooting, one more from the left and one from the right. The crossfire was erratic, and mostly behind him, but it was enough to make him halt the advance: To keep moving in the face of it, he realized, was to risk splitting the battalion, and to split the battalion was to risk weakening the planned assault. The Americans nearest the Germans fired their M-1s, tossed grenades, even set up their own machine gun, and after each volley, each explosion, each burst, Walter listened for the silence that would mean the path was clear again.

"Okay, let's get going," he said after the last machine gun had sputtered out.

As he stood he knew he was making himself the first target any other hidden German gunner would try to pick off, but he had his orders—dig in by daylight—and if he stopped, everyone behind him stopped, too, stranded in an open field in the rising gray light. Entrenching shovels slapped softly against the legs of men following him as they silently skirted the left flank of the woods and crossed a road. The spot Walter had been ordered to reach was farther forward than anywhere else along the whole line of the advance—a hill northwest of the woods that, if held by the Americans, would block the trapped Germans from retreating to, or receiving reinforcements from, the village behind it. The other companies were surrounding the woods like police around a thieves' hideaway. A thicket of heavy guns had moved up to what the Germans would be surprised to find wasn't the front line anymore.

By seven A.M. Walter and his men had scratched out some cover at the crest of the hill and were watching the new sun backlight the dense trees. The first muffled shots came from the other side of the woods, out of their sight. Two other assault companies, F and L, were slicing in on the Germans from the rear and the right flank, the planned "double envelopment." Then the first Germans appeared on Walter's side—a troop of several dozen rounding the bend on the road below, a morning relief detachment probably. They were marching in formation, shoulder arms, as oblivious to danger as if they were on garrison duty. The Americans waiting on the hill began to shoot; Walter's angle put him out of range. The Germans fell in rows, cut down by an ambush far deadlier than the one Walter had met on the night he saved Earl Vincent.

How could they not know we were here? Walter wondered. He knew that his company was doing exactly what it had been ordered to do, but he still felt a reflexive stab of regret at the loss. "What a waste."

No other Germans tried to get into the woods, and none came rushing out, as K Company stood sentinel, awaiting a challenge for the land it had seized. The counterattack finally came from afar—a barrage from the German .88s. When Walter heard the thud of the first big gun, he started

counting, one second one mile, two seconds two miles, to gauge its distance, and likely accuracy. But then came the rockets, their trajectory too
swift and erratic to predict; he had been warned about them, but these
were the first he had faced. He squeezed into his hole as the shells sailed
above, overshooting the hill mostly. One hit nearby, and he felt something
like a burning needle on the inside of his arm, near the elbow—shrapnel.
There was no blood that he could see, though, so he went on to worrying
about the next round; only later did the wound swell up and the shard of
steel have to be removed. By midmorning, the shelling had slackened, and
American soldiers were marching German prisoners out of the woods
and down the road to Bettviller. On the west side of Walter's hill, tanks
supporting the adjacent 71st Regiment were rolling through Rimling.

As the hours passed and the danger eased, Walter sat atop the hill and
watched the battalion exhale in relief as it realized it had been party to an
event of surpassing military rarity—a battle that went exactly as planned,
unfolding on the field precisely as it had on the briefing map. Casualties
were low for the Americans (two dead and twenty-eight wounded in the
324th) and high for the Germans (160 prisoners, hundreds more dead).
American soldiers were soon stringing triple concertina wire along the
new front line like homesteaders fencing in their claim. Two more miles
of Europe had been taken in the long, slow journey toward Berlin.

Walter was far enough ahead of Bettviller now, and elated enough at
having survived an assignment he had feared might kill him, that he all
but forgot the insubordination complaint still hanging over him, until he
was summoned by a field phone. "Denise, report to company headquarters" he was told.

He walked back alone over the ground he had led the battalion
across, worried more now about American officers than German guns. At
company headquarters they passed him up the line to battalion headquarters, who passed him to regimental headquarters, who passed him finally to division headquarters, where he stood nervously before an
officer, awaiting judgment.

"They've stopped giving out battlefield commissions, so you'll have
to go back to Fontainebleau for field training," the officer told him.

"Excuse me, sir?"

"They want to make you an officer. You don't have to accept if you
don't want to."

He had passed up a chance at officer training once before, choosing instead the ASTP program that sent him to college, because he hadn't felt ready yet to command men in battle—but that was before all the stealthy patrols behind enemy lines, before he had dragged Earl Vincent back from the dead, before the battle for Frauenberg, before he had led an entire battalion into German territory, before he had encountered officers who were superior to him only in rank, not in judgment, character or courage.

"I think I'll accept, sir," he said.

Buddy Lewis: Germany

The carcass of a blasted cow, cartoonishly bloated and stiff legged, sprawled across the shoulder of the clogged and narrow road, and as the long troop convoy churned slowly past, Buddy Lewis, seated in the rear bed of a two-and-a-half-ton truck, reflexively wrinkled his nose at the lingering odor. Other animal casualties, cows and horses both, lay in the field beyond. The earth was turned and scarred, tank tracks and shell holes in place of furrows. The terrain in this swath of the Rhineland, just inside the western border of Germany, was mostly flat, but the journey across it felt like a descent. The convoy snaked through the remains of a town that had unwisely tried to resist the recent advance of the surging American Ninth Army. The street was mottled with the corpses of German soldiers, as gray and crumbling as the rubble they were splayed across. A dead arm reached stiffly from the hatch of a charred tank.

Since their hasty evening departure from the POW enclosure in Belgium, Company A of the 1317th Engineers had been traveling ever deeper into the war, through a landscape more thoroughly and recently destroyed than any Buddy had yet seen. Stopping only for brief ration and latrine breaks, the trucks bounced steadily through a night and a day, another night and into another day. The men leaned wearily against each other, trading speculation about their destination.

"Take a look around for stragglers," a lieutenant ordered Buddy and some of the other men as they clambered out the back of the truck at a meal stop on the second morning.

Bleary from the journey—from the jolting, slumped-seat, half-slept nights, the bleak and blurry sameness of the stream of passing ruin— Buddy didn't quite know where he was. He unshouldered his M-1 and picked his way through the broken stones and fallen walls of what might have been Viersen or Krefeld or Mönchengladbach or some other German city from which the enemy had lately been routed, but to which civilization had not yet returned. The only sound in the abandoned street was the rattle of disembarking soldiers. Whoever had lived here before was hidden, fleeing or dead. Leading with his rifle, Buddy entered a building that looked as if it might have once been a store or a warehouse. With two other men, he crept down the stairs into the basement, where they split up to reconnoiter the separate chambers. He kept his eyes low, picking his way carefully through the unexploded grenades and ammunition that littered the floor. His limbs felt taut and springy, as if he were back in the sprinters' blocks on the high school track. He didn't know if he was really in any immediate danger here, but this was the first time he had been close enough to wonder.

As he passed through an arch into the next room, he heard behind him what he thought was the deep and stately breath of a church organ. He spun around and found no musician but the wind. He faced forward again and looked up finally from the floor—right at a German soldier sitting on the stairway ahead. If he had stopped for even an instant he would have seen that the soldier was a corpse, and posed no threat; but the instincts that had been bred in him since basic training left no room for any hesitation. His hand moved without any conscious orders from his brain, pulling the trigger and keeping it pulled until all nine bullets were gone.

No fire came in return, and as Buddy stood in the ringing silence, all he could hear was the swift, startled labor of his own heart and lungs. "What the hell's going on here?" asked the sergeant who came crashing in from another part of the basement.

They walked together to inspect the corpse, whose staring, wide-eyed face was glazed with a mannequin pallor that reminded Buddy of a doll tossed in a trash pile. "Hell, that man was dead already," the sergeant said.

"I didn't know—I just saw him sitting there all of a sudden," Buddy said. "I guess I'm a little jumpy."

Up on the street, breakfast passed undisturbed, and out on the road again, the only Germans he saw through the rear of the canvas-topped truck were as dead as the one he had shot. The convoy rolled all through the day and into a third night, the men nodding off between potholes, dreaming of the cots they left behind in Marche. The trucks finally stopped and didn't start again in a town that was backlit by the glare of floodlights.

"That's the Rhine river out there," an officer told them after they tumbled out. "We're here to provide security while they build a railroad bridge across it."

Artillery boomed and piledrivers throbbed, but the men of Company A were preoccupied by a more immediate question. "Where do we sleep?" one of them asked.

"Take this side of the street," the officer said, gesturing toward a block of small houses not so different from the blocks around Buddy's own home in Freehold. "Run these people out, and then you can sleep in their houses."

The Americans stomped up and down the street, banging on doors and barking orders, rousting the most reluctant Germans at gunpoint. Buddy was seeking a soft spot to stretch out his truck-cramped body when he was called to stand the first watch of guard duty. Tired and irritated, he walked his post grudgingly, bracing against the steady eruptions from the battery of big 155s a hundred yards away, and was in no mood for unexpected visitors when a soldier slipped up behind him.

"Whistle," said the soldier, whose accent and uniform were both unfamiliar.

"What the hell are you talking about?" Buddy snapped. His temper was so short that he assumed he was being taunted by a drunk—a drunk Dutchman, it seemed from the uniform. "Are you nuts or something?"

Three genuinely drunk white Americans staggered by from the other direction at the same moment, and Buddy tried to enlist them as allies. "This damn fool wants me to whistle," he said.

"Didn't anyone tell you that was the password?" one of them asked. Buddy had apparently paid more attention to his own muttered protests than to the instructions about the password and the countersign for the night. "'Softly'—you're supposed to say, 'softly.'"

Chastened, Buddy remembered what to say when his relief arrived, and in the morning, briefly revived, he listened closely to his new assignment. The banks of the Rhine were pockmarked with sandbag-ringed holes deep enough to hold several men and a .50-caliber machine gun. He climbed down into one, starting a twenty-four-hour guard shift with a front-row view of one of the great construction spectacles of the war. He watched as the operation unfolded before him with an energy, speed and size that surpassed anything he had yet seen. An entire army group was trying to haul itself across the largest remaining natural obstacle before Berlin, and the din it made approached the roar of battle. The river's

broad surface was clotted with steel and wood, rubber and men—the collapsed ruins of the bridge dynamited by the retreating Germans; a pair of
temporary pontoon bridges carrying a slow, unsteady line of Allied traffic; a constant shuttle of boats and barges and rafts and amphibious
Ducks; cranes swinging trestles, and steam-powered pile drivers planting
timber supports like thick clumps of leafless oaks. An eruption near the
water's edge spewed a cloud of billowing dust, and Buddy's hand tightened on his gun until he spotted the British sappers crouched nearby.
They were removing German S-mines, he saw, with the same crude
method he had learned at Camp Ellis, exploding them with dynamite dug
into an adjacent hole.

Buddy's arrival at the Rhine followed by just a few days the largest
river-crossing operation of the war—the leap by Montgomery's Twenty-
first Army Group here over the wide water barrier that had traditionally
shielded Germany's heartland against invaders. At the northern reaches
of a front that swept all the way south to Switzerland, the assault focused
on Wesel, the small city on the eastern bank the new bridge was aiming
for now. An important rail, road and river hub, Wesel also marked the upper boundary of the Ruhr Valley, Germany's equivalent of the industrial
Midwest. With the Russians overrunning Silesia in the east, and Walter
Denise's Seventh Army taking the Saar in the south, the Ruhr held the enemy's last intact concentration of coal mines and steel mills, a dense
strategic target the Allies planned to encircle and capture. The flotilla of
landing crafts started crossing on the night of March 23, followed in the
morning by a daylight airborne drop so rare in conception and overpowering in force, larger even than in Normandy on D-Day, that Churchill
and Eisenhower themselves joined the official audience.

"My dear General, the German is whipped," a delighted Churchill ex-
ulted as they watched the gliders and paratroopers rain down on Wesel.
"We've got him. He is all through."

Eisenhower was more restrained, but he later wrote that the day's
"operation sealed the fate of Germany."

The bombers and artillery had worked over Wesel before the troops
went in, and as Buddy looked across the river now, the city seemed reduced to a cratered moonscape whose powdery gray flatness was broken
only by a pair of church steeples and a small, persistent fire that no one
was rushing to extinguish because it had no place left to spread. The land
over there had become raw material again, awaiting a fresh imprint from

the engineers who were racing to get their bridge across. Troops were beginning to cross freely at other points along the Rhine, and trucks and tanks were easing across the temporary spans—the pontoons, the treadways, the floating Baileys—but the trains were still stuck on the western bank, along with the supplies stockpiled for the final push. The railroad bridge farther south at Remagen, the only bridge captured intact from the Germans, had collapsed after ten days of use. Only a new and sturdy fixed bridge could clear the bottleneck, and the engineers at Wesel didn't plan to stop until theirs was finished.

In the breaks between night watches, Buddy lay low in the hole, trying to burrow beneath the waves of noise rising from the busy river—clanging steel girders, random explosions, artillery crescendos and, underneath it all, the metronomic pile drivers pounding out the time like a stopwatch ticking toward the finish line. Sleep was scarce and fitful. He felt as dirty as a groundhog when he emerged for the next day's duty, standing guard at the headquarters of a colonel overseeing the bridge builders, a single tent pitched on a rare island of grass. A generator sputtered through the night, keeping a bulb lit inside.

"Sentry!" the colonel shouted as he emerged from the tent at two A.M., startling Buddy and his drowsy partner. "Aren't you going to salute me?"

Buddy offered a rifle salute, bringing a hand up across his shouldered weapon, and wondered what could be urgent enough to warrant such a late visit.

"Don't you have another pair of trousers?" the colonel asked Buddy's partner, whose pants had torn in the scramble of the last few days.

"Not with me, sir," the soldier answered.

The colonel lifted his sights toward a larger threat of disorder, and gestured disdainfully toward the cluster of trucks parked just beyond the fringe of his little green domain.

"I want you to keep those wagons off the grass," he ordered before ducking back into the tent where the bare bulb was burning.

"Wagons?" Buddy whispered, barely swallowing his snickers. "Where's he think the horses are?"

"He's still fighting the last war," the other soldier said.

New sentries arrived in the morning to defend the colonel's grass against wagons, relieving Buddy for what he expected would be another day in the machine-gun hole by the river. But as he walked back toward his company's billet, he noticed a line of dump trucks, a dozen or more, parked along the street.

"You go with these guys and find some railroad ties for the bridge," the lieutenant ordered.

With the supply thinning on this side of the river, the dump trucks, operated by another black unit, had been deputized to forage on the other side. Buddy squeezed in beside a driver, and the convoy slipped into the steady stream of traffic funneling onto the floating Bailey bridge. The gentle bobbing of the bridge under the truck's weight made the slow trip across feel like a ferry ride. On the solid ground of the opposite bank, the footing was similarly uncertain, the land thoroughly devoured by fighting that had pushed the front ahead farther and faster than the mapmakers could follow. Buddy was traveling blindly through territory he hoped no Germans were still trying to defend.

The dump-truck detail hunted all through the morning, but none of the battered towns of the upper Ruhr yielded any railroad ties. They were beginning to feel untethered, worried that they had ventured beyond the protective embrace of the Wesel bridgehead, when they spotted a squad of white paratroopers trudging toward them up the road.

"Where are you coming from?" called one of the paratroopers.

"From Wesel," answered the lead driver. "We're looking for some railroad ties."

"Did anybody shoot at you?"

"No, not so far."

The paratroopers were on their way back toward the Rhine from the fight they had dropped into a few days earlier, and they were relieved to bump into an advancing column of fellow Americans. In the cramped and tense waiting room of England before the invasion, it was a group of white paratroopers whose epithets had sparked a brawl with Buddy's unit, but here now in the cauldron of Germany, in the face of larger hostilities, nationality meant more than race. The paratroopers hopped aboard the trucks and directed them to a nearby power plant, and a stash of railroad ties.

Together they heaved ties into the trucks until the pile was gone. As Buddy caught his breath, he noticed a movement off to his side—a paratrooper raising his rifle, but at a higher angle and a slower pace than he would have were he confronting an enemy.

"Think you can hit that?" the paratrooper challenged, sighting upward and firing at one of the knobs on top of a high-tension pylon.

Rifles were raised all up and down the line, black truckers and white paratroopers standing side by side, plinking the electrical towers like shooters at a boardwalk arcade trying to win prizes for their dates.

"What about those windows?" a trucker suggested, and shot out a pane high up on the power plant.

Windows popped in a staccato rhythm, the glass shattering like a rush of big-band cymbals, and for a few giddy moments the hardened soldiers became truant boys. The longer their fusillade lasted, the more it sounded like a celebration. To shoot so freely and fearlessly so far inside Germany meant, they sensed, that the war in Europe was staggering toward an end. The paratroopers knew that the Rhine crossing was probably their last combat drop in this theater—no other barriers loomed that would require an airborne force—and the engineers knew that the Wesel railroad bridge was the project that, once finished, would open an unstoppable flow of supplies to feed the advance.

"Looks like we got them all," one of the soldiers said as the firing tailed off and the last shards of glass rained down.

Back in the sentry's hole again the next day, Buddy watched as several more thickets of timber piles were planted in the riverbed and crowned by trestle bents. Tall cranes swung the long steel stringers up into place, lengthening the bridge's grasp toward the far shore. Having crossed the river once already, officially, Buddy decided to explore again, unofficially, on his next off-duty evening. He and a friend liberated some plastic explosive and hitched a ride on the back of a truck headed across the twenty-five-ton pontoon bridge, dreaming of safes stuffed with diamonds and gold. All they found were stacks of paper money, as empty of value now as the dying regime that had printed it.

The bridge was moving so quickly that Buddy and his fellow guards began calculating when it would open. Maybe tomorrow, they guessed, surely by the day after. The ties they had found were being laid across the high and slender single span, right up to the edge of the small gap that remained. But on the morning of April 8, when the first train eased eastward across the Roosevelt Bridge—almost half a mile long, built from nothing in exactly ten days, five hours and fifteen minutes, named for the president who died four days after its hasty christening—Buddy and the rest of Company A were in their trucks, riding west toward a broken spot farther back in the rail network that required a dose of their muscle. A twelve-foot-tall sign was proudly raised at the bridge's entrance, listing the dozen units that helped in its construction, a rare instance of public recognition for the 1317th, but Buddy never saw it. With the bridge's completion, a continuous Allied rail line now reached all the way to Kassel, seventy-five miles east of the Rhine. By the end of the month, ten thousand tons of matériel was crossing the Wesel bridge daily, almost a third of the total Rhine traffic.

The trucks backtracked to Roermond, a small city just across the border in the southeastern corner of Holland. The Germans still held Amsterdam and the coastal regions to the north, and here in the south harsh memories of the late occupation had left the natives skittish around foreign soldiers, even their liberators. The French had been unavoidable when Buddy's unit was in France, materializing at every corner with something to sell; the Germans invisible, scurrying away in fear of reprisal; the Belgians warm, offering home-cooked meals in thanks; but the Dutch were cold, withdrawn still inside their hardened shells. Stern old men in long black robes buttoned to the neck stopped in the street and fixed baleful stares at the new arrivals.

A local railroad spur needed to be cleared of mines and rebuilt, and when Company A reported to work they were allotted the same brute tools as at previous railroad jobs—nine-pound hammers and the manual grappling tongs known as dogs. A white engineering unit working alongside them had pneumatic drills and a crane.

"We got the John Henry tools again," Buddy observed, without surprise.

After dynamiting out the mines, just as the Wesel sappers had, they swiftly began laying track in an unspoken challenge to their white counterparts. They were accustomed to being asked to do more with less, and they had learned, sometimes to their own amazement, just how strong they were when they worked together. One night while guarding prisoners in Belgium, Buddy's platoon had been ordered out to a rail crossing where a train had broken down, blocking a tank column on the road.

"I want you to push this train out of the way," the captain ordered.

"This guy's out of his mind," Buddy mumbled as he laid his hands on and leaned all his weight into the train, which budged exactly as far as a brick wall would have.

"Goddamn it, I said move it!" the captain shouted.

Someone worked a crowbar under a wheel, levering it as the men pushed again, grunting and straining, trying to keep their feet, until the train nudged ahead an inch, which might have been an illusion of exertion, and then another, which wasn't, startling them as it began a slow, heavy roll, an entire train, they marveled as they pushed, moving by no power other than their own.

"One . . . two . . . three . . ." Buddy huffed to himself now, lifting in unison with seven other men and carrying a thirty-foot length of rail into place, an operation the adjacent white crew used a crane for.

Whenever Buddy set down a rail, he picked up a hammer to pound the spikes in, sweating in the mild spring sun as if it were high summer. A steady blacksmith clang played beneath the whine of the crane and drills like a bass line. No one was keeping score or measuring track, but at the end of the day it seemed to Buddy that his side, with nothing but muscle, had outstripped the power-equipped whites.

"We're the workingest bunch of guys I ever saw, no contest," he said.

Shortchanged though it was in tools, the 1317th was lavishly appointed with a band all its own, unusual for a regiment its size. The band was born as a pickup combo back at Camp Ellis—its rehearsals so caterwauling that Buddy covered his ears when passing by—but had since grown so proficient that a larger division was preparing to snatch it up. Before it left, though, the band was enlisted in an attempt at musical diplomacy—a jazz concert that, the morale officers hoped, would melt some of the ice between the soldiers and the civilians. Buddy and the other engineers sat in the balcony of a Roermond theater one evening as the dour, skeptical townspeople filed to their seats on the floor below. The band on stage swung into credible, rousing versions of Duke Ellington and Count Basie and Benny Goodman.

"Look at them," Buddy said to his seatmate as heads below began bobbing in time to "Flying Home."

"Look at them now," he said as feet began tapping to "One O'Clock Jump."

In the days after the concert, some Dutch visitors finally ventured out to the camp—Buddy had his shoes fixed by one, his photo taken by another—but the rail work was soon done, and the engineers were shipped back to Germany. Crossing the Rhine at Wesel again, they shared the roads of the Ruhr with so many German POWs, marching in long columns or packed into trucks, that they knew the war couldn't last much longer. Everywhere Buddy turned, it seemed, he saw long lines and dense clusters of people who had been battered by the war, their thin, ragged frames a stark contrast to the well-fed, well-appointed Americans. Camps had sprung up to hold what were euphemistically termed "displaced persons"—concentration camp survivors, liberated slave laborers, refugees whose homes had been swept away by a cataclysm of Biblical destructiveness, and all the other stunned, hollow-eyed, half-dead souls who had been left wandering across the blasted desert that Europe had become.

In Essen the engineers found their best billet since the Belgian convent—a castlelike mansion near the vast and shattered Krupp armaments plant. The basement was fitted out with a duckpin alley, the sleeping quarters with chandeliers and innerspring mattresses that, after so many nights of hard ground and saggy cots, felt soft as clouds. Buddy assumed his unit would be assigned more railroad work, but as they sat idly awaiting orders he absorbed enough rumors about Germany's imminent collapse that he couldn't help dreaming of home. The May 6 edition of *Stars and Stripes* brought him back down.

"No man or woman, no matter how long he or she has been in the service, overseas or in combat, will be released from the Army if his or her services are required in the war against Japan," he read with dismay in the GI newspaper. "[D]on't write home and tell your mother or sweetheart that you'll be home next week or next month. For most of you, it just ain't so."

Two mornings later, on May 8, they were called out into formation and told what had finally and officially become true: At Eisenhower's headquarters in a commandeered boy's school in the French cathedral town of Reims, the Germans had signed a postmidnight surrender, ending the war in Europe.

"The route you have traveled through hundreds of miles is marked by the graves of former comrades," an officer solemnly told them, reading from Eisenhower's Victory Order of the Day. "Each of the fallen died as a member of the team to which you belong, bound together by a common love of liberty and a refusal to submit to enslavement. Our common problems of the immediate and distant future can be best solved in the same conceptions of cooperation and devotion to the cause of human freedom as have made this Expeditionary Force such a mighty engine of righteous destruction."

They paraded sharply back and forth in a brief and dutiful ceremony, their steps more certain than their emotions. They wanted to celebrate, but they knew the victory was only partial, and was not an occasion for wild outpourings of joy. The fighting had drifted to an end here on their side of the world, but on the other side it was still raging. The war against Japan, Buddy worried, might drag on for years more. He had read the harrowing accounts of the recent five-week battle for Iwo Jima, which made casualties of more than a third of the sixty thousand marine invaders, and Medal-of-Honor winners of five of them in a single day's action. If the Japanese fought that hard to hold a tiny, sulfur-stinking wasteland of volcanic ash 650 miles away from Tokyo, what would it take to make them surrender the capital itself?

The ceremonies were similarly subdued back home in Freehold. Under heavy gray skies that threatened rain, five hundred people gathered under the four great maples on the courthouse lawn and joined in prayer with the assembled clergy, representing all the town's congregations. The dignitaries who spoke from the steps repeatedly invoked the local servicemen whose names were inscribed on a large sign that hung prominently on the side of the adjacent building, which the Strand Theater shared with the Lincoln auto parts store. More than eight hundred names were listed, and fifteen gold stars for the dead, including Lieutenant David Oglensky, who before the war had run the store on which his own star now shone. The presiding councilman, a First World War veteran, gently reminded the children present that the Honor Roll was a sacred memorial, not a handball backboard. Two buglers from the grammar school band sounded taps.

"While Napoleon said 'Victory goes to the side with the greatest artillery,' this war has shown us that victory goes to the side with the highest ideals," the mayor said.

In Essen, Buddy and the other engineers drifted back to their billets, unsure what was expected of them. "Now what?" somebody asked quietly.

"There's still blood in our veins," Buddy said. "We're going to the Pacific."

Walter Denise was also expecting to go to the Pacific—down to the Mediterranean and straight through the Suez Canal to the China-Burma-India theater, that was what everybody was saying the plan was. He was a lieutenant now, commissioned just two weeks earlier, and he was on his way back to join his regiment after his officers' training at an old French military school south of Paris. He followed their trail across southern

Germany and into Austria, finally reaching them in a fragrant alpine valley ringed by snow-capped peaks. The only enemy soldiers he saw were corralled by the thousands in barbed-wire stockades. (Among the prisoners taken by the 324th was Wernher von Braun, the German rocket scientist.) With no more battles to fight here, he oversaw several guard outposts along the nearby borders with Switzerland and Italy, his jeep bouncing along precipitous mountain trails, and distributed the company payroll from a table on which he conspicuously set his pistol beside the teetering stacks of cash.

Jake Errickson and Stu Bunton had both managed to leave the Pacific by now—Jake after recovering from his bon-voyage appendectomy, Stu not long after the Battle of Leyte Gulf in the fall of 1944, when a new admiral came aboard the *Santa Fe,* and the old admiral's radio operators were reassigned. Jake's mother was startled at how skinny and yellow he was, a change in complexion triggered by all the antimalarial Atabrine pills he had gagged down. When he visited the mill in his uniform during his furlough, he starred at an impromptu bond rally in the third-floor shearing department. He was at an army personnel center in Indiantown Gap, Pennsylvania, now, processing other soldiers' discharges. Dot was still in Australia, waiting with all the other war brides for a scarce berth to open up on a ship to America. Stu had spent some furlough time in Freehold, too, but now he was in Boston, assigned to a newly commissioned destroyer that he expected would soon be taking him back to the Pacific. On shore patrol in the evenings, shooing drunken sailors out of Boston Common, he tasted the routines of the police officer he still hoped to become if he were ever a civilian again.

Just four days before the German surrender, thirty Marauders from Jimmy Higgins's group had dropped their bombs through clouds so thick nobody could say whether they hit their target, a German ammunition plant in Czechoslovakia. Their final mission ended with no casualties, just as most of the others had in the easier months that followed the somber midnight mass in the barn at Tilloloy. The 391st had been awarded a Distinguished Unit Citation for "the inexorable determination, outstanding skill and unhesitating courage" of the flight crews who "fought magnificently despite the overwhelming odds" on that day of terrible losses over the Bulge, adding five extra points to the number that every serviceman was counting—the more points you had earned, depending on how and where and how long you had served, the sooner you would get discharged.

Many of the fliers were packing for America, but Jimmy was still shy of a ticket home, and was preparing instead for the journey to the Pacific.

All of Bill Lopatin's missions and medals had earned him 165 points, far more than enough for discharge, but on V-E Day he was at Fort Belvoir, Virginia, wondering what had ever possessed him to transfer out of the Air Corps. After returning to America the previous summer, he had been assigned stateside duty as a radio instructor at a Louisiana air base, but he grew restless with the country-club pace there—the occasional training flights broken by easy days on the golf course. If the Army wouldn't let him go yet, he reasoned, then he might as well learn some skills that would prove useful when the war was over. To a builder like him—whose architecture education had been ended by the Depression, and whose father's construction business was eagerly awaiting his return—the Army Corps of Engineers seemed the most logical choice. But he soon wearied of heeding boot-camp commands from whiskerless lieutenants who hadn't even dreamed as much as he had seen. He had already decided to ask for a transfer back to the Air Corps. From there, he hoped, it would be a short trip home.

Buddy Lewis and the other engineers played duckpins for a few days in Essen before they were ordered to make up a train to carry themselves south to Marseilles, on France's Mediterranean coast. A ship there would take them out past Gibraltar, across the Atlantic, through the Panama Canal and into the Pacific for the rest of the war. They guessed they would be building staging areas for the troops massing for the climactic invasion of Japan's home islands, a dreaded and inevitable assault that some military planners, extrapolating from the losses at past Pacific landings, calculated could cost more than a million American casualties. MacArthur expected to lose fifty thousand men on the first day's beachhead alone.

Buddy packed himself inside one of the boxcars the regiment had scrounged up, and tossed packets of army soap and cigarettes to the hundreds of German women who lined the tracks as the steam engine pulled away. Marseilles, he found when he arrived, was a well-lubricated liberty port swarming with soldiers from every victorious nation, and he and his friends tried to get passes there as often as they could from Camp Victorette, the nearby holding area where they were awaiting their ship. In all their time in uniform, they had never been entertained so thoroughly: three weeks of beaches and baseball games, boxing matches and USO shows—Bob Hope, Mickey Rooney, Jerry Colonna—and, always and above all, bars and more bars. They tried to get some extra time in Marseilles by venturing in even when they had no passes, then untucking their shirts and posing as dark-skinned French Moroccan soldiers, answering with puzzled shrugs when queried by MPs—a ruse that worked only until they ran into French authorities who discovered that their language skills extended no further than *"non comprendre."* On the night before their ship left, they binged on the last of their cash, and fed their German money into a triumphant farewell bonfire.

Confined to the transport ship's lower deck, the regiment's enlisted men played cards, watched for dolphins and flying fish, and groused about the privileges accorded the officers and nurses who were promenading on the more spacious decks above. The ship was slow, and the only news was rumor. They knew nothing about the progress of the war in the theater they were headed for. Before leaving Marseilles they had heard of the victory in Okinawa, almost three months of brutal fighting that brought the Americans one island closer to the Japanese mainland. But had another battle started? Were the kamikazes still sinking ships?

"Now hear this! Now hear this!" the loudspeaker bellowed occasionally with an urgency that never fit the message that followed—mostly just orders to move from one side of the ship to the other for a sweep down, it seemed to Buddy. He had learned not to let it raise his blood pressure. But halfway across the Atlantic, he heard a tone in the announcer's voice that made him listen in a way he hadn't before.

"Attention all troops," the captain himself announced. "President Truman has announced that an American airplane dropped one bomb on the Japanese city of Hiroshima. It was an atomic bomb, and it had more power than twenty thousand tons of TNT."

The news raised more questions than it answered, and it left the ship in a state of both uncertainty and anticipation. Exactly what an atomic bomb was, Buddy didn't know, but it obviously came from a different arsenal than any explosive he had ever been trained in. No bomb in either his experience or his imagination was infused with such power, or warranted such an apocalyptic introduction from the president himself. In the absence of more information, the ship buzzed with speculation. What did this bomb look like, and how did it work? What was left of Hiroshima? Was this a prelude to an invasion, or the kind of miracle weapon that could preclude one? Was the war ending, or was it entering some new, more vicious phase?

Three days later, the captain made another announcement. "Attention all troops," he called. "A second atomic bomb has been dropped on Japan, this time on the city of Nagasaki."

How much longer would this go on, Buddy and the other men wondered? Would the bombs keep falling until Japan was reduced to a cinder? Would the Japanese surrender in the face of such destruction, or would they stiffen for an even more suicidal defense? Two days later, with the ship two days short of the Panama Canal, the captain made a terse final statement that answered none of their larger questions, just the smallest and most immediate one—where they were going next.

"Watch the shadow of the sun on the bow as the ship turns toward New York," he said, and all the soldiers cheered, not because Japan had lost—the formal surrender was still days away—but because they understood that in simply making it home, alive and at last, they had won.

II: AN UNCERTAIN PEACE

Stu Bunton
Freehold Police Department

★

Walter Denise
Denise Orchards and Denise Realty Associates

★

Jake Errickson
A & M Karagheusian Rug Mill

★

Jim Higgins
Higgins Memorial Home

★

Buddy Lewis
Monmouth County Courthouse

★

Bill Lopatin
Lopatin Construction

8.

Spring 1946

The baseball diamond at Lincoln Field was carved from the middle of a broad residential block, hemmed in tightly enough by its neighbors that, even though it was unfenced, it had the enclosed feel of a stadium. Cars parked along the first-base line, across the street from an overgrown gully thick with honeysuckle and catbriers that swallowed alike foul balls and the boys who chased them. Right field drifted unevenly out into the yards of the boxy little houses of Ramcat Alley, an old dirt-street black neighborhood. The backsides of some modest newer houses—bushes, trees, toolsheds, garages and the occasional run of pickets—bordered the third-base line and, turning a corner, half of left field, too. But in center field there were no restrictions, no barriers to hold anything in. The grass stretched as open and unfettered and full of possibility as everyone in Freehold seemed to feel at the moment, with the war finally over and the soldiers home. Center field reached all the way to the street and the military school beyond, and the fate of anything hit there, whether it became a home run or an out, was determined solely by the ability of the contestants—the strength of the batter who launched it, the speed of the fielder who pursued it.

By one-thirty on a Sunday afternoon in May of 1946—an hour fixed to accommodate the leisurely midday meal that followed church in most families—several hundred spectators had gathered at the field, filling the bleachers behind the backstop and spilling down the sidelines. Jake Errickson had walked over with his father, as he often had in the seasons before he shipped out to the Pacific. Buddy Lewis had come, too: His brother Guggy was back from the marines, a center fielder again for the local semipro team. The crowd applauded as the mayor strolled to the mound to throw out the first ball of the first home game of the first season after the war, the kind of everyday ritual that had been suspended for so long, and had consequently become so precious.

In the years before the war, Sunday afternoons in spring and summer were reserved for baseball—Freehold's teams taking on teams from the other towns in the county. Jake and Buddy had watched many games at Lincoln Field, and on warm Sundays overseas had often wished they were back here, watching again. Baseball had been a comfort to them when they were far from America—the makeshift games in the jungles of New Guinea and in the drizzle of England transporting them back home for a few innings. The field here in Freehold had been abandoned to boys' sandlot games the last few years, and the concession stand had fallen into disrepair and been removed. But the players were back from the service now, trading stiff khakis for baggy gray flannels with the name GULISTANS stitched in black across the chest. Gulistan was the best brand of rug the mill made, and the players running out to take the field now were the best the town could muster, Freehold's representatives in the Jersey Shore Baseball League.

"Play ball!" the umpire shouted, and the first batter from the visiting Belmar Braves stepped to the plate.

The Gulistans had won their season opener in an away game the previous Sunday against the persistent Red Bank Townsmen, when Guggy Lewis threw a strike from deep in center field to catch the tying runner between third and home for the last out of the ninth inning, preserving a 5–4 lead. The pitcher who made the final tag last week was starting again this week, whipping curveballs and fluttering the odd knuckler at the Braves. Before the war, Dave Cashion had worked up to the Double-A level in the minor leagues, going 12–3 with the Salisbury (MD) Indians, and some scouts were said to be in the crowd today, measuring how much the army had taken out of him.

What he had left, it turned out, was too much for Belmar. One after another, the Braves came to the plate and quickly returned to the bench— either striking out or tapping weak grounders. One after another, the Gulistans came up and then rounded the bases, scoring run after run. More than one home-team ball sailed deep enough into the center-field gap to spark a round of titters about whether Major Duncan could afford to replace any broken windows. The Freehold Military School had been sharpening and polishing the sons of the East Coast gentry at its turreted Victorian complex since before the Civil War—it claimed to be "the oldest junior military school" in the nation, and its steep fees kept out all but the rare local boy—but it was fading as it neared its centennial, just a year away. The boxwood hedges were ragged, the mansard roofs patchy. Fewer cadets were drilling by the flagpole each morning, or marching up South Street in uniform to the Strand for Saturday matinees. In the evenings, the distinguished white-haired profile of Major Charles Duncan could often be seen, bent over his desk, through the tall French windows of his book-lined, wainscoted study, like a glimpse into the last century. He had led the school for almost half its life, but he was aging now, and with him was passing a whole civic order, a belief in a providential world in which gentlemanly wars were conducted by an aristocratic officer class. "Loyalty and honor are fostered in the *esprit de corps* for which the school is noted," a recent catalog declared, a maxim that echoed hollowly in the stunned void left by the late war. Everyone had been a soldier then, and no one wanted to be one now.

A hat was making its way through the crowd, collecting voluntary admissions for the game as it passed along the sidelines and through the low bleachers, which were on loan from the YMCA, a cramped replacement for the ten-tier stands the military school had once maintained. The hat grew heavy with quarters. Not until the sixth inning, when the Gulistans were up 5–0, did the Braves manage to get a man as far as third base. The runner scored when the second baseman booted a grounder, but Cashion then squelched any thoughts of a rally with a strikeout.

When Jake and Buddy and all the other servicemen here today were overseas, this was what they were fighting for—the chance to watch baseball in peace again on a Sunday afternoon in spring. Near the end of the war, the army had surveyed combat infantrymen about what goals kept them going in battle: Only one in twenty mentioned the larger issues, like peace and democracy and freedom, or the "loyalty and honor" so dear to Major Duncan; the most common answer by far was "getting the task done." The nation may have entered the war with grand ambitions about defeating tyranny and securing a stable world, but its soldiers had gone with a more practical agenda—to win, and then come back as soon as they could. Collectively, their triumph had been sweeping and unmistakable ("America stands at this moment at the summit of the world," Churchill had said at the war's end); individually it had brought them something smaller but more immediately precious: "home," as the beloved columnist Ernie Pyle had written, "the one really profound goal that obsesses every one of the Americans marching on foreign shores."

The war had ended so abruptly last August that most of Freehold's servicemen were still away—Buddy's ship still approaching New York, Jake still stuck in Pennsylvania—and victory was celebrated in town mostly by civilians. On the sultry evening of V-J Day, the town's volunteer firemen arced streams of water at each other across the courthouse square, and then doused a Rising Sun flag until it was a sodden, muddy, trampled rag. Smiling widely and waving an American flag, Mr. Lee, the local Chinese laundryman, rode on one of the firetrucks as it barreled exultantly through town. The tail of a Pennsylvania Railroad freight train blocked South Street when its engine couldn't get through the throngs of cars and people on Main Street. Blizzards of paper wafted down from the upper stories of the downtown buildings, and the rug-mill whistle blew deep into the night. A week after the Japanese surrender, the Strand was packed for the premiere of *Captain Eddie,* a Hollywood biography that starred Fred MacMurray as Eddie Rickenbacker, flashing back over his life from the raft adrift in the Pacific and reacquainting America with the story of Johnny Bartek's Bible. Only later did Freehold learn that one of its own was present at the war's explosive final act: Corporal Sidney Bellamy, late of the rug mill and Center Street, was the radar-navigator on one of the two instrument-crammed B-29s that accompanied the bomb-carrying *Bock's Car* to Nagasaki.

"There never was a better time than this to be an American, and to be young," the columnist Walter Lippmann had written recently about the returning veterans. "The time to come is peculiarly their own because they have themselves earned it and done so much to make it possible. They are not merely the heirs of stronger and more resolute forefathers but they are, once again, a generation of explorers, discoverers, and pioneers, who can become the founders of good and enduring things."

Cashion set down the Braves again in the top of the seventh, the thump of strikes in the catcher's mitt accompanied by the whistle of a train in the distance, and the low rumble of boxcars crossing Main Street, sounds that were a subtle reminder of a new conflict that was looming. What was thought to be a temporary wartime measure—the sprawling weapons depot the navy built in the swamps and scrub woodland that separated the farms around Freehold from the coastal resort towns—had hardened into a permanent facility, and ammo trains were rolling through regularly. America's former ally, the Soviet Union, was becoming an enemy, and the nation's military was determined not to be caught unprepared again by another Pearl Harbor. A ship unloading shells at the depot's pier in Raritan Bay had exploded recently, killing seven sailors, wounding 165 and reminding the civilian populace just how much firepower lurked in its midst. "Let us hope, however, that Uncle Sam keeps all his atom bombs in the great open spaces of the West," the *Freehold Transcript* editorialized.

In the bottom of the seventh, the Gulistans piled on more runs than the Braves could ever hope to dig out from. Cashion himself doubled, and his catcher tripled, deep into the center-field corridor, stirring the fans' memories of the greatest catcher who ever played on this field, Frank Hayes, Freehold's only major-leaguer, the three-time all-star from East Main Street. Hayes had played thirteen professional seasons, mostly with the Philadelphia Athletics, but never had he enjoyed a bigger day than he had several weeks earlier, the same day the weapons ship exploded at the navy pier. It was opening day in Yankee Stadium, the beginning of the first season since all the star players had returned from the war—an occasion that meant to the nation what the Gulistans' return meant to Freehold— and Hayes was behind the plate for the Cleveland Indians, catching Bob Feller, who was even more overpowering against his opponents than Dave Cashion was against his today. In the top of the ninth, Hayes hit a solo home run in the left-field stands, the first run in the game, and what turned out to be the only run the Indians needed to win. In the bottom of the ninth he caught the last pitch of the game, and of Feller's no-hitter.

The Gulistans batted all the way through the order in the seventh, and knocked out two Belmar pitchers. None of the Freehold players but Cashion had any higher baseball ambitions, but as a team their play seemed too large to be contained by Lincoln Field on a Sunday in May. Their skill and confidence and exuberance matched the town's own—its pealing wedding bells and squalling babies, its humming factories and flourishing fields, its whole booming, cacophonous share in the nation's triumph. Four runs, five runs, six runs scored, the cheers swelling with the growing realization of the size of the nearing victory, until the last man rounded third, headed for the seventh run of the seventh inning and the final run of what would soon end as a 12–1 rout, and the crowd rose to welcome him as he raced, giddy and breathless, all the way home.

• • •

On the second floor of the old section of the rug mill, in the sun-raked office he shared with two other desk workers—a supervisor and the guy
who ordered the yarn—Jake Errickson bent over the Monday-morning
stack of time cards, calculating how much each weaver was due. Next to
the names on his master sheet he recorded in his careful hand the number of hours worked and yards woven, the downtime for breakage, and
the assorted piecework jobs for which the union contract had established
set prices. The office was separated from the rows of narrow jacquard
looms only by a half-wall and a wire-mesh screen like a rabbit cage,
through which conversations about yesterday's game drifted like smoke.

"The way they played yesterday, it didn't look like anybody could beat
them."

"That Cashion, he might get signed yet if he keeps pitching like that."

Jake worked through the time cards with the quiet satisfaction of a
man within reach of everything he wanted. He and Dot were finally together, here in his hometown, just the way he had imagined it when they
were courting back in Australia. She had finally arrived in Freehold last
summer—two years after he had given her a diamond ring in Anzac
Square, and more than a year after they were married at the Nudgee
Methodist Church. She left her family behind on a dock in Brisbane,
where a band was playing and a teary crowd was singing "Waltzing
Matilda" and the "Maori Farewell."

> *Now is the hour*
> *For me to say goodbye.*
> *Soon I'll be sailing*
> *Far across the sea.*
> *While I'm away*
> *O please remember me.*

She sailed to California on a ship whose dining hall was carpeted by
Gulistan—the *Lurline,* a passenger liner that was shuttling troops, and
the occasional complement of lucky war brides, across the Pacific—took
a five-day train all the way to Trenton, hopped a bus to Freehold and got
off unannounced in front of Patten's cigar store. Jake was still at the army
base in Pennsylvania, but two of his friends spotted Dot on Main Street,
quickly figured out who she was and took her to her new in-laws' house.

When Jake was finally discharged, after four and a half years in uniform, he and Dot lived for a few weeks with his parents before they found an apartment on the second floor of a house on East Main Street, across from Elks Point and the diner. Housing was in short supply—hundreds of servicemen returning at once, many of them newlyweds eager for a place of their own—but the landlord was partial to the Errickson family: Jake's father had rented from him for decades. Jake and Dot brought a bedroom set with them from his parents' house, bought a small dining-room set themselves, and paid fifty dollars for a new gas stove Dot spotted in the classifieds. Jake soon stopped waking each morning in a sweat, thinking he was still in the jungle. Dot was soon pregnant, joining a large troop of other hopeful, young brides. When the first snow of winter fell, she got up from bed and went to the window to watch as it drifted down through the beams of the streetlights, as it blanketed the sidewalk and the street, and the long lawn sweeping up to the Elks Club. She had never seen anything like it before in her life.

Anyone who left a job in the rug mill to enter the service found it waiting when he returned, and Jake had reclaimed his just a week after his discharge. The looms were being fed wool again, after weaving the last of the wartime orders for waterproof canvas and the workforce was nearing its prewar peak of seventeen hundred, among whom were Jake's father, brother, three sisters and two brothers-in-law. To supply the pent-up demand—to cover all the floors in all the houses and apartments that were rising nationally to accommodate the surge of veterans—Karagheusian had introduced two new carpet lines and was still looking for more help. "Learn a good trade—build your future," the want-ads promised. Jake had no car and no money for a down payment on a house, but even with a baby coming—Dot was due in less than a month—he had no great worries either. Week after week, the time cards piled up on his desk without fail. The mill was thriving, and so was he.

Across the Center Street bridge, in the Axminster department on the first floor of the newer wing of the mill, a frustrated Buddy Lewis tried to maneuver his fingers with the swift dexterity required by his new job—threading 189 different-colored strands of yarn into narrow tin guides on a twenty-seven-inch long cylinder called a tube frame. He wasn't hired for his nimble hands, he thought to himself as he reached the end of the row, but for his strong arm. At a pickup softball game at Lincoln Field a couple of weeks ago, his speed and control as pitcher had turned the head of players from the team the mill sponsored in the after-supper town league, and he was asked to join. After a couple of victories on the mound he was asked if he wanted a job, too. He was tested for color-blindness when he reported for work, and then sent to a bench outside the manager's office with the other new hires to practice tying knots.

Spouting fireboats and tooting tugs and Red Cross ladies bearing glasses of fresh milk had greeted Buddy's ship last August when it sailed past the Statue of Liberty and docked in a city still hung over from V-J Day, but the warm unity of victory—the same hard-won spirit that had allowed black engineers and white paratroopers finally to find common cause in the face of a larger enemy in Germany—soon began to splinter into patterns of disheartening familiarity. A homecoming steak dinner was awaiting Buddy's unit at Camp Kilmer, the New Jersey processing center where they were sent, but Italian POWs were serving them from behind the steam tables; the white soldiers who had gone before them had been served by other white soldiers. "Aren't we good enough to be served by Americans?" Buddy asked. Only after some tray rattling and loud grumbling were the Italians replaced. Raised voices were needed again that evening to get the black soldiers ahead of the POWs in line at the movie theater. Buddy was waiting for his furlough at Fort Dix two mornings later when a white private appeared in the barracks doorway.

"I want all you niggers to fall out in the company area," he said.

Before Buddy or any of the other half dozen black soldiers could protest, a white paratrooper jumped up from his bunk and knocked the visitor back through the door.

"The next time you come in here you'll know how to talk," the paratrooper said.

The bus that finally brought Buddy home stopped in front of the American Hotel after dark, and he whooped his way up Main Street, swinging his heavy bag in delight, stumbling over himself three times as he tried to sprint up the steps to his family's second-floor apartment. His mother made him pancakes and bacon, as many slices as he wanted, not the measly two the army had always decreed. On Saturday night he and a couple of his brothers who had also made it home dressed in their sharp Class A uniforms and promenaded arm-in-arm through the downtown crowds with the woman who had sent more sons into the service than any other in Freehold. Buddy basked in the glow of return for six weeks before the army summoned him to Camp Claiborne, Louisiana, for the month that, according to his point total, he still owed before discharge. The train took him farther south than he had ever been before, and at every town where it stopped for meals Buddy and the other black soldiers were shunted off to a back-street colored café.

"All you niggers get on that side of the road," a white sergeant ordered upon their arrival, but this time no one rose to their defense—not then, not ever, in a place where even the German POWs used the word "nigger," where black soldiers knew better than to venture off base into town, and where Buddy served out his time like a sentence, rejoicing when he finally boarded a train back north.

In the Axminster department at the mill, Buddy snapped the finished frame tube into the sprocket chain that hung in long loops above the loom and turned to start threading yarn into the next one. He brought his hand to his mouth as he cleared his throat, his breathing not accustomed yet to the nubbly texture of the air inside the mill. Motes of wool dust— "flight," they called it—danced in the churchlike shafts of sunlight that slanted through the walls of tall windows. Thread by thread, his morning passed, the work tedious but not strenuous, until the noon whistle blew. He went to lunch with the other men from his department, most of them older, all of them white. There were only three or four other black workers in the whole mill, none of them Buddy's age; he suspected that the only reason he was hired in the first place was his pitching arm. The weavers mostly ignored him as they ate, continuing a conversation among themselves that had already been in progress for decades.

"I think I'm gonna get that pig this weekend," said one weaver, who lived on a small farm outside of town. Buddy listened in silence—unable to muster much interest in their livestock, or their lives, or even the job itself—wondering if he would ever feel as if he belonged here.

"Okay, who's cooking supper tonight?" Stu Bunton said as he walked down the single, long corridor of cells that comprised the Monmouth County Jail.

The county courthouse overlooked the intersection that had marked the center of town for two and a half centuries, and the jail filled the first floor of a wing off its rear, just behind the neighboring Strand. The two lines of cells on either side of Stu mirrored each other—a dozen double cells in all, for those awaiting trial for more serious crimes, and two large bullpens stacked with enough double bunks to hold several dozen more docile short timers and repeat drunks. Black prisoners were locked up on one side of the block, whites on the other. A separate cell could hold up to eight juveniles. Stu wore no uniform, and had no training other than what the older guards had told him. He and another fresh young guard held down the day shift; the older guards preferred the nights, so they could sleep. One day each week he was in charge of the kitchen, and the prisoners who cooked there.

Stu had been in Cuba on V-J Day, his new destroyer just finished with its shakedown cruise and awaiting orders to the Pacific; the captain shut himself in his cabin when he learned of the Japanese surrender, disappointed that the war was over before he could become a hero. In his first weeks home, Stu kept waking in a panic in the night, believing that general quarters was about to sound, only to realize in a flash of relief and elation that he was in a bed in his mother's apartment on Mechanic Street, not on a bunk in a ship at war, and that he was free to turn over and sink back into sleep. He joined what veterans wryly called the 52-20 Club for a time, hanging around Mulholland's bar across from the library while collecting the twenty-dollars-a-week unemployment benefits he was entitled to for a year after discharge. He worked briefly at several jobs—for a contractor, in a cutlery factory where Buddy had also put in some time, in the mimeograph room at Fort Dix, in an isolated warehouse surrounded by woods at the naval weapons depot. After a .40 mm shell landed painfully on his ankle, he found the job in the jail.

Stu unlocked the door to the bullpen to let out the prisoners who were on kitchen duty. The jail's population had, as always, thinned with the warming spring. The vagrants who had intentionally gotten themselves locked up for the cold months were out now, taking the sun as they sat on the low railing that enclosed the small courthouse lawn, sleeping in the railroad jungles near the Colored School and at the end of Orchard Street. Stu had become a guard not for the money—it was his worst civilian paycheck yet—but because it seemed a good place to park himself while he waited for a slot to open in the small Freehold police department. He escorted the prisoners to the kitchen, keeping order at one end of the criminal justice system while imagining a more lasting job at the other.

• • •

Three blocks away on Henry Street, Bill Lopatin finished his supper and left the table to go back to work—not to the house where he had worked all day, which belonged to a customer, but to the house where he spent his evenings and his Sundays, which belonged to him. It stood alone on the last corner in town, behind the high school and beside a potato field, just barely within reach of the public water line. The high cost of real estate had startled Bill when he came back to Freehold: The war had brought the nation roaring out of the Depression, and in the housing market, a combination of high demand (from the hordes of returning veterans) and low supply (after so many strapped years when companies like Lopatin Construction had built hardly any houses at all) had pushed prices out of reach for many. After he had been outbid on one house, he was quick to grab the next, despite its condition. He had invested all his spare hours for months now trying to make it habitable—shoveling out a truckload of empty whiskey bottles left by the previous occupants, replacing the outdoor privy with indoor plumbing and two bathrooms, putting in closets and knocking down walls upstairs to make a master bedroom. Tonight he was hanging wallpaper, the kind of finish job that, as a builder, he had always left to someone else, but that as a frugal home-owner he was determined to attempt himself. Starting in an upstairs bedroom small enough to absorb his beginner's mistakes, he slapped on the paste and stepped up the ladder to press a sheet onto the ceiling. As he stepped back to admire his work, the paper peeled off and draped itself over his head.

Once his brief stint with the engineers had ended, once the war he had fought in Europe was over, once he was finally taken off flying status, Bill then, and only then, felt free to take the step that had come to seem inevitable over the last three years of correspondence with Selma. He had long wanted to ask her to get married, but he feared leaving her a widow or, perhaps worse, the caretaker of a wounded invalid. Not until the afternoon of June 6, 1945, exactly a year after Bill had flown over the invasion beaches at Normandy, was the rabbi invited to the Lopatin home on Henry Street to perform a wedding. The living-room shades were drawn against curious eyes outside; the license said they were supposed to wait another day, but they decided they had waited long enough already. The party was at his sister's farm, the honeymoon a Poconos weekend. He had to report to another Southern airbase, but Selma joined him this time. By the end of July he was back in Freehold, a civilian again, working on some interior alterations to a dentist's office on Main Street, right next door to the Legion hall. Bill's father had limped through the lean war years with the help of one loyal carpenter—higher government wages lured the others away to build barracks—but business soon picked up enough to keep them all working six-day weeks, leaving precious few hours for the house he and his bride were eager to move into. Selma often helped him in the evenings, and when he cursed the falling wallpaper, she laid it out again and coated it with more paste.

As the spring twilight faded over a street of quiet houses twenty miles north of Freehold, Walter Denise finished cutting the lawn, parked the push mower in the tool shed and climbed to the third-floor lair that was his off-campus home at Rutgers University in New Brunswick. Final exams were looming, and a night of study stretched ahead. He had enrolled at Rutgers on February 4, 1946, after a thirty-six-hour marathon drive—in the beloved red Plymouth convertible that had waited faithfully for him through the war on blocks in the barn—from the discharge center at Fort Knox, Kentucky. He had already lost enough time to the service, and he didn't want to miss the start of the spring semester. The GI Bill—which was sending millions of veterans to college who might never have otherwise gone—was paying for his tuition and books and a modest monthly stipend. His father had been a Delta Upsilon man at Rutgers decades earlier, and encouraged him to pledge, too, but Walter was appalled at the juvenile antics he witnessed there and at the other fraternities he visited—the peas flung across the dinner table, the pats of butter stuck to the ceiling and, most of all, the steady streams of alcohol. As one of just two of the original fifty-six members of his infantry platoon to emerge from combat unscathed, he felt a sharpened sense of purpose in his life, a belief that his survival carried with it a fresh set of responsibilities. He was at college to work, not play, and he found a more suitable arrangement in the home of an elderly woman, who provided room and board in exchange for yard work and chores. He opened his chemistry book at his desk, and tuned his radio to WQXR, the classical music station that was his quiet study companion.

Walter had returned to America last July, when most of the 44th Division was crammed into the *Queen Elizabeth* for the dash across the North

Atlantic. A lieutenant finally, he learned the privileges of rank—a state-room shared with six other officers—but also its aggravations: patrolling the decks to break up the inevitable craps games. Four days after leaving Scotland, the ship eased into New York harbor, its upper decks solid with hardened soldiers weeping at the sight of the Statue of Liberty. At Fort Dix he excitedly ordered two chocolate milkshakes, but his stomach had shrunk so much from the K-ration diet that he could barely finish them. He served out his time at army camps across the South until the medals that were still due him—two more Bronze Stars and a second Purple Heart, for the shrapnel in his arm from the attack at Buchenbusch Woods—came through and gave him enough points for discharge. Rutgers counted his ASTP college credits and put him in the class of 1949, despite his assurances that he wouldn't need that long. Turning a page of his chemistry book, he glanced up for a moment and thought of the young woman, a music major, he had met recently at an open house at the university chaplain's, but then he quickly looked down again, and got back to work.

Thirty miles north of Freehold, in the vestibule of the Plainfield funeral home where he was apprenticing, Jimmy Higgins opened a door into the night for the mourners departing a wake, taking note again, as he had often during the last few months, of how many of them were dressed in clothes they might have worn to work. Death, it seemed to him, had lost some of its old formality. Before the war, when his interrupted apprenticeship had begun, funerals and wakes were uniformly black, and anyone who came dressed the way mourners routinely did now would have occasioned indignant whispers. The funeral director he worked for no longer wore the traditional striped pants, and Jimmy's own black homburg hung unused in the closet of his upstairs room. Exactly what had caused the change, he didn't know—a straitened wartime supply of wool that made it hard to maintain a proper wardrobe; a society that had ungirdled and streamlined in the face of upheaval, shedding the burden of ceremony; or a sad and resigned accommodation with mortality by a nation that had lost four hundred thousand souls, a fraction of Russia's twenty million, but enough that almost every living American could name another who had died?

Like Buddy, Stu and Walter, Jimmy had been preparing to go to the Pacific theater when the war had ended last summer. He was at a training school near Paris, learning about Japanese camouflage techniques, and the announcement on Armed Forces Radio sent him racing to join the delirious throngs on the Champs Élysées. He drank wine all evening on the Eiffel Tower, looking out over Paris but dreaming of Freehold. He didn't get back for good until the end of October, so thin that his mother thought he must be sick. He returned not to his grandmother's small farm, where the young Higgins family had retreated when his father died, but to the house that his mother, helped by the faithful fifty-dollar-a-month allotment from his sergeant's pay, had bought in town. Jimmy had left an outhouse, but was welcomed home by indoor plumbing. He stayed for two weeks before resuming his apprenticeship in Plainfield, where, he was relieved to learn, he would only have to spend another year, not the two he had expected. The state mortician's board had given him a year's credit for his army service, freeing him to start mortuary school in the fall of 1946. But a crowd of other veterans apparently planned to use their GI Bill benefits to pursue the same career, because his application only got him as far as a waiting list. After the last mourners were gone and he had locked the door and switched off the lights in the viewing room, leaving the casket open and alone in the flower-heavy gloom, he climbed the steps to his bed, wondering if a spot would open for him in school. There were so many others like him, he thought—so many other young veterans who had done so much already in their lives and who wanted now to do so much more, to get married and have kids and buy houses, to learn trades and earn degrees and build careers. Would there be room for all of them?

A few weeks after the Gulistans' game, on the sunny morning of his first Memorial Day parade, Jake Errickson slipped on the uniform he hadn't worn since his discharge—already tight in the waist after nine months of Dot's recuperative cooking—and walked downstairs to join the marchers who were assembling at Elks Point, just beneath his living room window. Almost everybody was somebody he knew, but nobody looked quite the same. They were all in uniform, too, the men he remembered as weavers and mechanics and farmers now standing before him as tail gunners and riflemen and petty officers, the patches on their shoulders and the ribbons on their chests testifying to the terrible breadth of the late war—from bombers to battleships, infantry platoons to quartermaster companies, from Greenland to Burma, Australia to Germany. A few late stragglers arrived just before the ten A.M. step off, pushing the total to maybe 150, more than had gathered in one place at one time in town before, but fewer than had actually served. Buddy Lewis and Stu Bunton were there, but Bill Lopatin was working on his house; airmen weren't much for marching anyway. Jimmy Higgins was up in Plainfield, and Walter Denise, his exams finished, was out in the orchard.

Joined by a few older Legionnaires, the men formed into ranks four abreast and marched up Main Street along the same route that old soldiers had marched every Memorial Day since the Civil War, when Dolly, the battle-scarred gray mare who had charged the Confederates with Major Vredenburgh astride, began leading the annual procession to her master's grave. Their steps were rough at first—the months away from the service, the different styles of different units—but they soon fell into a proper cadence, pushed along by the three brass bands behind, from the high school, the military school and the Elks. Thick crowds pressed toward them from both sides as they approached the courthouse. As young boys, they had stood on the sidewalks, too, gazing up at the open cars carrying the last local remnants of the Union Army, and at the trailing ranks of veterans from the Spanish-American War and the First World War, many of whom were marching again today. But as they looked around at themselves now, framed so starkly by what they used to be, they were startled to realize what they had become. They might be young, they might feel closer in almost every way to the boys waving flags in front of the library than to the old doughboys marching ahead, but they were the veterans now.

When the war had ended, Freehold's veterans didn't all come home together in some jubilant throng, pouring out of a packed troop train into the embrace of a cheering, flag-waving crowd. They had instead trickled back individually, arriving alone, greeted only by family and friends. Back in November, the town had attempted a formal celebration. A WELCOME HOME banner was strung across Main Street by the firehouse—the power company had refused permission to use the poles in front of the courthouse—and a parade was planned. But Armistice Day dawned raw and rainy, and the truncated ceremony had to be squeezed into the common pleas courtroom. The black veterans staged their own parade in February, with Buddy Lewis carrying a flag in the color guard and two of his brothers marching at the head of the line. Today was warm and dry, though, and black and white veterans were marching together, and the town finally had a chance to come out and thank them all in public.

The parade passed through the steepled ranks of the West Main Street churches and out to the grave of Captain Conover, a hero of the war that had shaped the last century as deeply as the most recent war was likely to shape the present one. The songs and prayers and readings were punctuated by the firing squad's rifle salute, three volleys echoing in the reverent silence. In the past, the Memorial Day services had always ended out here among the dead, but during the war, a new ritual had been appended, to turn some attention to the living—the presentation of gold and silver certificates to the families of those who were killed and wounded during the previous year. A permanent war memorial was being planned for Elks Point, just outside Jake's apartment window, but for now all the town could offer were its prayers and tears and some words on paper. The marchers retraced their steps back up Main Street to the courthouse, spilling into the square where Patriots had hanged recalcitrant Loyalists during the Revolution, and where the names on the Honor Roll now numbered nearly a thousand. Pink balloons bobbed gaily over the crowd, but many lapels also wore the solemn poppies the Legion had been selling to raise money for wounded and needy veterans.

Five more gold stars had been added to the Honor Roll since V-E Day—for men who had either died in the Pacific, or whose deaths had been confirmed after they were previously listed as missing—and the families of several of the casualties stood near the steps. Twenty-one young men from Freehold were dead, and forty-two more from the surrounding territory—young men who had come to town for school and for worship, for movies and parades. A Silver Star was awarded first to a returning prisoner of war, army private Donald Sheehy, who, before his capture at the height of the Bulge, had held an observation outpost against the German onslaught and volunteered to drive a jeep through machine-gun fire to evacuate three wounded comrades. The wounded and their families stepped up next, followed by the survivors of the dead. The last gold certificate went to the young widow of Freehold's final casualty, Frank Bruno, a presser at Eisner's garment factory on Elm Street before he became a sergeant in the Seventy-seventh Infantry Division and was killed at Okinawa, the finale of the Pacific war. He left behind a seven-month-old son he knew only from pictures.

"We remember the bravery and heroism which our boys displayed all over the world so that we might enjoy life, liberty and the pursuit of happiness," the mayor said before yielding to a priest who offered a prayer.

A free and pleasant Friday afternoon stretched ahead for most of the crowd, the start of a three-day weekend—a lineup of exhibition races at the harness track, a game between the Gulistans and Long Branch at Lincoln Field, with Cashion, still unbeaten, on the mound. A low rustle began nibbling at the restless silence, but it was soon stilled by the high sopranos of the boys in the cadet choir. They sang the same song they had sung on Memorial Day for as long as anyone could remember, perhaps as long as the song had been alive, which was almost as long as the military school itself—"Our Country's Flag," a Union battle hymn composed in 1861 and dedicated to the new president, Abraham Lincoln.

> *Our country's flag let proudly wave.*
> *For freedom is our shield;*
> *The Union must and shall be saved,*
> *We'll never never yield.*

Their trim little uniforms, their pure and reaching voices, their call to battles long since fought, everything about the moment had an antique, reflective cast to it, linking this morning's crowd with all the other crowds that had stood here in the wake of other wars, swelled with the same dueling emotions of sadness and pride. They were singing about duty but it sounded like loss—a lament for time passed, lives ended, even the fading of their own school. Rumors were strengthening that Major Duncan would shut it down at term's end, and that today's performance would be the boys' last. Much was gone from the town—everyone listening felt it sharply as the cadets reached their closing verse. But something had been gained, too, though exactly what, no one could quite say yet.

> *We'll soon disperse our country's gloom,*
> *We are and will be free;*
> *The curse of God, the traitor's doom,*
> *Awaits our enemy.*

9.

Building

Bill Lopatin turned the corner onto Institute Street, a long, maple-shaded lane that dead-ended in the scrub woods at the edge of town, and parked his pickup halfway down the first block, in front of the new house he was adding to the close-set ranks that flanked it on either side. The lot had been empty a few weeks ago, but the structure growing on it now was beginning to assume a familiar form. The pale fir studs outlining the first floor marched all the way around the perimeter of the concrete block foundation. Some men from his crew were already hammering away, nailing in the joists for what would become the floor of the upstairs bedrooms, and Bill climbed a ladder to join them. Framing, feeling a building rising steadily under his hands, was his favorite part of the job; he left most of the inside finish work, the slow and tedious grace notes of molding and trim, to his father. He navigated along the rim of two-by-fours as deftly as the tightrope walkers at the traveling circus that had stopped in town this week, and pitched its tents on the baseball diamond at Lincoln Field. The morning sun slanted sharply through the skeleton of the house, creating a complex pattern of shadow and light that stretched beneath him like a net.

A row of studs bisected the first floor, the beginnings of the wall between the matching halves of the two-family house for Max Snider, whose Main Street movie theater, the Liberty, the Lopatins had once converted from silents to talkies. Bill set another joist into place, picturing the lives it would soon support. The side-by-side units were small, two bedrooms and barely nine hundred square feet apiece, but they loomed like mansions to the newlywed veterans all over town who were squeezed into their boyhood bedrooms with their young brides and their newborns, waiting for a spot to open in the tight housing market. An economy of chronic shortages—of cash during the Depression, of labor and material during the war years—had stalled new home construction for more than a decade, and the local builders were scrambling to supply the surging demand of 1947. Nationally, the number of new houses being built that year was more than one million, up from barely more than one hundred thousand just four years earlier. Moving to the next joist, Bill crossed from one side of the duplex to the other. He had been slow and wary the first time he ascended a job with his father, but he moved easily along the frame now, suspended between the fact of the ground and the possibility of a roof, held aloft by experience and confidence.

Around the corner on South Street, the Freehold Military School was finally shuttered, after holding on just long enough to mark its centennial, but almost everywhere else the town was thriving. Just two streets away from where Bill was working, the mayor had recently laid a half-dollar and two quarters into the wet concrete foundation block of the instant-coffee factory the Nestlé company was building. Two streets over in the other direction, the Eisner factory, uniform makers for the military since the First World War, had added its first-ever line of civilian clothing. The rug mill was spotlighted in a long story about the carpet industry in the *Saturday Evening Post*, complete with two pages of color photographs, and more than two thousand of its workers and their families gathered for sack races and waltz contests at the first company field day. A crowd of ten thousand braved a summer shower for a parade marking the seventy-fifth anniversary of the volunteer fire department, applauding the float carrying the newly crowned Potato Queen; at the foot of her throne sat what looked like a huge boulder—a plaster model of a White Giant, an offering from the sacred crop she represented. Moviegoers at the Strand now eased into Kroehler push-back reclining chairs, refreshed themselves in "more comfortable and sanitary cosmetic and powder rooms," and made curious visits to the "beautiful new Television Lounge."

"We believe your theatre is the most modern and comfortable theatre in New Jersey and we hope that we again will lead the way for the advancement and progress of Freehold," the owner boasted in announcing the improvements.

By August the borough engineer had issued $845,900 worth of construction permits, enough for him to declare a "building boom." While small local builders like the Lopatins built houses one at a time, outside developers were starting to buy up fields on the edges of town and plot out new streets of identical cottages. The Freehold Housing Authority had applied for $450,000 for two low-cost projects, the larger of which would be reserved for black families from the run-down quarters of Avenues A and C. "The colored people are going to be well taken care of, and regardless of whether you're black, white, green or yellow you are going to have decent housing," the mayor announced. Every night when Bill finished work at the duplex, which accounted for $16,000 of the year's permit total, he returned to the home of his own he had finally finished renovating on Robertsville Road, where he lived with Selma and her young daughter from her first marriage. From the start he had always regarded Selma's daughter as his daughter, too; now the law agreed, as his adoption of her became official.

The circus at Lincoln Field struck its tents and moved on after a few days, leaving the neighbors to sleep undisturbed by the odd lion roar, but work continued on the duplex all through the summer and into the fall. Ducts and wires were threaded through the walls and floors, and insulation unrolled like a blanket in the attic. Asphalt shingles—a material that, like premade window frames, Bill's skeptical father had been reluctant to embrace at first—protected the roof. Oak floors were laid in the living room and dining room, yellow pine in the bedrooms, linoleum in the kitchen and bath. Three coats of plaster covered the walls and ceilings, three coats of paint the moldings and trim. A brick veneer faced the exterior of the first floor, stucco the second. A pair of gravel driveways bracketed the small front yard and the concrete walk that led up to the steps. The tub went in only after all the doors and windows had locks; plumbing fixtures, like many other construction materials, were in short supply, and thieves had been raiding half-finished job sites.

Nails were scarce, too, and on an autumn morning when the duplex was almost done, Bill stopped into the lumber yard on the corner of Broad and Throckmorton and waited patiently as old man Statesir whistled while filling a paper cone with some that he needed for another job— a chicken coop south of town, beyond the Manasquan River, where the rich, loamy potato soil gave way to sand and scrubby pines. Since the middle of the Depression, city dwellers who dreamed of a simpler, rural life raising fresh eggs for market had been buying cheap parcels of land and putting up long, low houses for thousands of chickens. The Lopatins had built dozens of coops, some more than four hundred feet long. The profit margin was low, but the work was simple, a good place to break in apprentice carpenters.

Freshly supplied, Bill stopped on the next block, in front of the spare, white-shingled edifice of St. Peter's Episcopal Church, one of the few buildings left in town that had stood witness to the Battle of Monmouth. He looked up at the steeple he had once roped himself to, and examined the low railing around it he had shored up before the war. He had been invited to bid now on another job for the church, the refurbishing of a storefront in the building it owned next door.

"You here to take measurements, too?" asked Everett Matthews, who was walking out as Bill was walking in. About a half-dozen builders shared the business in town, and they regarded themselves more as colleagues than competitors. "Here, don't bother—you can use mine."

Continuing up to Institute Street, the measurements he needed for his estimate in hand, Bill hoped to find that the duplex had passed its final test. Because it was financed by a Federal Housing Administration mortgage, the house was subject to an inspection above and beyond the local codes, and three times already, to his mounting annoyance, it had failed. Three times he had corrected the minor faults the inspector kept finding, most recently installing a board as an extra firewall between the back-to-back medicine cabinets that shared the common central wall, and he couldn't imagine what else could be wrong. As Bill walked through the front door that should have been welcoming a young family home by now, a frowning crew member held out a piece of paper and shook his head.

"Not again," Bill said.

What the inspector was really looking for, Bill knew for certain now, was not another defect, but a bribe. In the eyes of the FHA man, he realized, there was nothing wrong with the house that a few choice bills in an envelope couldn't fix, but in his own, there was nothing wrong with it at all, and he stiffened at the prospect of buying the approval he believed was rightly his. He had never met the inspector, who only visited when Bill wasn't there, but he felt the inspection turning into a staring contest: How long would it drag out before he finally paid to stop it? What the inspector didn't realize, though, was how recently Bill had been a waist gunner, strafing enemies, not bargaining with them.

The next morning, instead of driving south to the chicken farm, Bill drove north to Newark, on a mission to the FHA office. The anger the war had put in him—the resentment at civilians who had profited safely at home while he dangled his life out over the German .88s—boiled back up again as he neared his target. He hadn't flown seventy-two bomber missions over occupied Europe to be treated this way by his own government. He had played by the rules, and he planned to make sure they did, too.

"He's in a meeting with an architect now," the secretary told him when he appeared before her unannounced, demanding to see the inspector's boss. "I don't know how long he'll be."

"I'll wait," Bill said, and sat down.

Waiting was one skill the army had helped him perfect, and his quiet persistence gained him an ally in the secretary. When two men emerged from the office two and a half hours later, building plans rolled up under their arms, she gestured silently toward the one he needed to see. Bill introduced himself, his house and his grievance.

"If your inspector can't come one time and find everything, then there's something wrong with him," he said. "If he's looking for a handout, he can just forget it. If I don't pass, the next call is to my congressman."

Rocked back on his heels by the blast, the supervisor was sputtering assurances about fairness and justice, about the new inspector that would be assigned, about the families who would soon be able to move in, as Bill turned to leave. Still fuming, Bill drove back home to Freehold, where, to him at least, the terrain of right and wrong was more clearly marked.

Dressed and ready at an hour when he would normally just be rising, Jake Errickson went to the living-room window of his second-floor apartment and, as the slow light of an autumn morning crept into Main Street outside, looked up toward the courthouse for the car that was coming to get him. The night shift at the rug mill was still weaving, and the day shift was just groping toward breakfast. Traffic was sparse enough that he easily spotted his ride approaching. He glanced across the street at Elks Point, and noticed that the leaves on the spindly new dogwoods were reddening. The town had planted the trees a few months ago, on Memorial Day, one for each Freehold man who hadn't returned from the war, and a bronze tablet inscribed with the names of the dead was attached to a boulder that sat solemnly on the narrow peninsula where the road split, staring at all the oncoming drivers. A quartet that included Buddy Lewis's brother had sung "Rest, Heroes, Rest" at the dedication.

"I won't be back until after midnight," Jake told Dot quietly, trying not to wake their sleeping toddler, Wayne.

Before the car could honk, he was down the steps, out the door and in the back seat. The other men in the car, and in the car that was following behind, were all newly appointed foremen in the mill, and Jake was the youngest among them. A sudden death up in the ranks had opened a spot for him as an assistant in the narrow-jacquard department. Of all his family in the mill, Jake was the first to reach management, and the first to get treated to an excursion like the one the company had planned for today. The car didn't turn toward Jackson Street at the next block, but continued north, away from where the work was.

To orient its newest supervisors, the company was giving them a glimpse of its other operations. They drove up to the mill's smaller sister factory in Roselle Park, where the raw wool—not from American sheep, whose coats were too soft, but from hardier breeds that grazed hillsides from New Zealand to Tibet—was spun, dyed and made ready to be woven into rugs in Freehold. The giant dye vats gave off the hot, sudsy smell of a laundry, and the taut lines of yarn spinning onto the bobbins vibrated like harp strings. The tour continued on the other side of the Holland Tunnel, in the sleek corporate offices in the Textile Building at 295 Fifth Avenue, where they were greeted by Arshag Karagheusian, one of the two aging founders, and his son, Charles, the vice president.

Some of the foremen already knew at least part of the story, but they listened respectfully as Arshag explained how a curious combination of ethnic intolerance, industrial chemistry, civic boosterism and shifting tastes in interior design had made Freehold home to the nation's fourth-largest rugmaker, and spawned the jobs where each of them expected to spend the rest of their working lives. Arshag and his brother, Miran, had grown up in Istanbul, the only children of a prosperous textile importer, but after their father died, and the sultan of Turkey opened a violent pogrom in the 1890s against the Armenian Christian minority of which they were prominent members, they left for America. From a small office on Worth Street in Manhattan, the brothers started importing, with little success, canary seed from Smyrna and mocha coffee from Al Hudaydah. An old schoolmate suggested they try Oriental rugs instead, and Arshag returned to Istanbul—where the persecution had eased—to scour the bazaars. The first shipment arrived in 1899, and the carriage trade was soon frequenting A.&M. Karagheusian's lavish showroom, decorated by

Tiffany Studios. As popular as the imported rugs proved, though, the high cost and short supply—a single nine-by-twelve rug might take two weavers six months to make, with more than 350 knots per inch—limited the market. Rugs made in America, the Karagheusians reasoned, would sell more cheaply, and to more people.

The Karagheusians went looking for a factory at the same time the Merchants Association in Freehold was trying to fill one. Of the several manufacturing businesses in town—the iron foundry, the bicycle factory, the plant that made rasps and files for blacksmiths, the cannery that packed beans from local fields—the Rothschild shirt factory was the largest, but its hulking brick home on Jackson Street had sat largely empty since the company's demise several years earlier. "The town is in every respect modern and progressive," the merchants advertised. "Every possible assistance is extended to manufacturers." Sixty Brussels and Wilton power looms, accompanied by the weavers who ran them, moved into Rothschild's in 1905 from Kidderminster, the capital of the British rug industry, and began producing imitation Persians for a market that was finally tiring of sentimental picture rugs depicting frolicking lambs, loyal dogs, doe-eyed children gathering flowers, and grand scenic landscapes like Niagara Falls. By 1911, the Freehold mill had 250 workers and was starting to turn a profit, and the home-furnishings pages of the Sears catalog were dominated by what came to be called "American Orientals."

The Karagheusian rug lines had names that evoked places far from Freehold—Mindora, Samarkand, Herati, Shah-Abbas, Karaban—and the more they sold, the more the mill grew. New looms and buildings were added, and the payroll climbed. In one Bronx apartment building in the early 1920s, 120 of the 125 living rooms were adorned with the same Herati—the "stork rug," as the salesmen incorrectly called it, a copy of a Chinese import featuring a bright blue waterfowl surrounded by smaller birds against a tangerine background. In 1928, the company concocted a chlorine-based bath that, when washed over the rugs, created a sheen similar to what genuine Orientals acquired from generations of bare, padding feet. The new line, Gulistan, which meant "garden of roses" in Persian, borrowed its name from both a thirteenth-century poem and the former palace of the shahs in Tehran. The effect on the industry was "electric," according to *Textile Age*. Production expanded to three shifts, and the workforce surged from 630 to 1,000 in a single year. Over the next three years, even as the nation slid into the Depression, three five-story additions to the mill were hurriedly completed, and GULISTAN was emblazoned on the enclosed bridge that spanned Center Street, connecting the old sections to the new. "We have beaten the Orientals at their own game," the mill's assistant manager gushed at the time.

"This new product immediately gave the company considerable prestige," Charles Karagheusian told the foremen now, taking over the story from his father.

In the year Jake started at the mill, a Gulistan rug was chosen for the American Building in the Paris Exposition of 1937, and was later displayed at the Metropolitan Museum of Art. The king and queen of England walked across one, a Gold Seal winner, at the New York World's Fair. Gulistans covered the floors of grand hotels and lofty boardrooms, ocean liners and state capitols, the New York Stock Exchange, the United States Supreme Court and President Roosevelt's private rail car. (After too many accidents by the president's beloved Scotty, Fala, a replacement was ordered, and a swatch of the old rug made it back to Freehold, where it hung on the wall as a treasured souvenir.) Jean Harlow sent a lock of her platinum hair as a color guide for her custom order. Other Hollywood figures submitted boudoir slippers, neckties, lingerie and sport shirts for designers to match.

When Jake left for the army in early 1941, the mill was making the equivalent of 325,000 nine-by-twelve rugs a year—enough that, laid in a twenty-seven-inch-wide strip, the width of the narrow-jacquard looms that did much of the weaving, it would have reached from the Atlantic Ocean all the way to the Pacific. Eight large trucks a day hauled the finished rolls away, feeding a national network of ten thousand retailers, serviced by sixteen branch sales offices. The annual payroll for the seventeen hundred workers in Freehold topped $2 million. Six thousand natives in China, and four thousand in Persia, worked for Karagheusian, too, weaving rugs on hand looms, following designs from the Fifth Avenue office. A company exhibit room on the Boardwalk in Atlantic City featured an automatic conveyor that displayed rug after rug after rug. "It might be going too far to say that the mill *is* Freehold," a town official said before the war, "but I do not like to think what Freehold would be without it."

The company still maintained an import division, and as Arshag showed the foremen a neat stack of genuine Persians that had been handwoven overseas, riffling the corners like a deck of playing cards, Jake tried to tally their worth, but the sum soon outran his imagination. Arshag was a familiar, paternal presence in the Freehold mill, driving down in his big black Oldsmobile for monthly visits. Today he treated everybody to lunch at a German restaurant, and asked graciously after the men and their families. Charles was cool and distant, clearly more at home with the Fifth Avenue end of the business. The Karagheusians returned to the office after lunch, but the foremen continued walking north through midtown, toward Rockefeller Center. When they entered the grand foyer of Radio City Music Hall, instead of gazing up, the way most other visitors instinctively did—up through its soaring cathedral heights, up to the dripping deco chandeliers, the towering mirrors, the craggy mountains and luminous clouds in the mural that graced the wide and sweeping stairs—they immediately cast their eyes downward, and inspected the floor.

"Well, there it is," one of them said.

"It's holding up pretty good," Jake added.

Jake recognized the carpet immediately as he bent to smooth his hand across it, a jazzy riff of abstract shapes in tones of gray, accented by the repeating silhouette of a guitar body. He had seen it coming out of the loom, but he had never seen it the way it was meant to be seen, stretching out broadly beneath the smoking, scuffling crowd. The Radio City job was the one the company, and its workers in Freehold, boasted about more than any other. The original foyer carpet stood up to what one company official called "the greatest punishment ever taken by a carpet in history," inflicted by the feet of forty-five million visitors, before it was finally replaced after eight years, proving almost as durable as the solid bronze tread at the main door, which wore flat just two years later. More Gulistan carpet, a subdued squiggle pattern, led the foremen to their seats in the main auditorium. The Rockettes kicked across the stage beneath the great sunrise arches, and the curtain parted on the main feature, a rerelease of *How Green Was My Valley*. The men from the mill watched in sadness and sympathy as the village of the Welsh coal miners lived and died with its mine.

When the steam whistle atop the dye plant blew the next morning, Jake was already at his desk in the narrow-jacquard department, and he glanced up reflexively at the clock—eight A.M., exactly, the unvarying start of another workday. A step up from his screened timekeeper's warren, the foremen's office had glass half-walls and a ceiling, a neat box sealed away from the clatter of the looms on the third floor of the old mill. Spread out before him was the sign-up sheet that catalogued what each loom in his care needed to keep the carpet rolling out today—more jute stuffing, more cotton chain warp, new pattern cards. The muffled throb swelled and leaked inside as a weaver pushed open the office door.

"The yarn's twisting up behind the heddles on me," he said.

Jake left his desk to help untangle the yarn. When the loom was weaving again he started one of his regular patrols through the clackety maze of steel and wool where he spent the bulk of his shift. The looms were set back-to-back throughout the second and third floors of the old shirt-factory section of the mill, their creels, taut with yarn, stretching out behind each one like a grand piano behind a keyboard. The narrow jacquards—almost miniature, at twenty-seven inches across, compared to the twelve-and fifteen-foot wide behemoths in broad jacquard across the bridge in the new section—were the mill's original looms, and so many of them were still operated by the original British weavers that the department was known as the "House of Lords." Some of the old weavers hung onto their looms so jealously that they were brusque with any young spare hand, especially one with an Irish surname, who seemed too interested in learning the trade. The dean of the Lords was Alf Draper, born in Kidderminster three days before Lee surrendered at Appomattox, apprenticed to the trade at the age of eight. At eighty-two, he was said to be the oldest jacquard weaver in all of America. He had left England in 1889 and worked at rug mills through the Northeast states before landing in Freehold in 1916. In the last thirty-one years, he had missed just four days of work, when he was injured in an accident, and he was at his loom again this morning as Jake passed by.

Halfway up the next aisle, the dense soundtrack thinned briefly, leaving a small, still hollow for Jake to pause in, watching an idle loom while a new set of pattern cards was tied in for the next order. The weaving of fine rugs—the transformation of thousands of slender threads into a fabric durable enough to walk on for decades—was a perpetual cycle of tension and release, tension and release, and it required machinery that was at once both bulky as a locomotive and delicate as a sewing machine. Blocked out in pointillist colors on graph paper first, the rug design was then translated into a long series of heavy cardboard punchcards that, dangling above the weaver's head, scrolled into the loom like a player-piano roll, dictating when and where each different colored thread rose to the surface. Line by line the pattern emerged, a torpedo-shaped shuttle slapping back and forth metronomically as the wires lifted and dropped, lifted and dropped, binding together all the wool, cotton and jute, the surface, the stuffing and the backing. Another loom in the line went silent for a moment as Jake approached, the weaver stopping to replace an empty shuttle with a full one.

"You've got some loops hanging there," Jake said, pointing to an edge of the carpet as the hypnotic rhythm resumed.

"How'd I miss that?" the weaver wondered, stopping the loom to check the long, skinny blades that, when sliding out, were supposed to slice the yarn that had looped around them, forming tufts.

"You stare at it so long, it all looks alike," Jake said. "When I come along, I can see it."

Jake took the stairs down to the second floor, stopping to help transfer a fresh roll of carpet from a loom to a forklift for the trip across the bridge to the burling department, where squads of sharp-eyed women would squint suspiciously at it, square inch by square inch, finding and fixing stray knots, loose threads, missing tufts and any other surface imperfections. He removed from the loom the order card that followed the rug throughout the mill and attached it to the end of the roll, tearing off the perforated section at the bottom that recorded its departure from his department. A rug for Jack Dempsey's Beverly Hills home had come through recently, and another for the Park Avenue offices of the Fred Astaire Dance Studios, but most were for more prosaic destinations. The latest Sears order, five thousand yards to be sold under the Homeart label, was starting up now, and would keep Jake busy for weeks.

As the weather chilled and winter arrived, the rug mill only grew warmer, heated by steam from its own power plant. A few days after Christmas, Jake's breath fogged the window of the foremen's office as he looked out over a town that—from the dormered roof of the grammar school across the street, through the uppermost reaches of the sycamores and oaks, all the way to the courthouse clock tower at Main and South— was draped with thicker blankets of white than anyone had seen since the Blizzard of '88. The snow had arrived unseen during the deep slumber after the holiday feast, and continued falling, heavy and slow, for twenty-two straight hours, a foot and a half in all, emphatically bringing to life the song he and Dot had courted to in sunny Australia, Bing Crosby's "White Christmas." In other, slacker years, the mill would have been closed for the week between Christmas and New Year's, but orders were brisk this year, and after a weekend of digging, he had donned his galoshes and trudged to work.

The narrow-jacquard department ran two shifts—with a rare overnight to accommodate a rush job—but Jake only worked days, leaving evenings free to walk occasionally with Dot down to the Liberty or the Strand, where the easel sign in the lobby always provoked in him a twinge of pride: "You are enjoying the luxury of Gulistan carpet woven especially for the Strand Theatre," it announced. Though they had no car, little they needed was out of reach. Within two or three blocks of their Main Street apartment were ample supplies of Easter dresses and work pants, chuck steak and green beans, end tables and electric frying pans, baby bottles and toy trucks, ice cream cones and evening papers. On Saturday afternoons, Jake often stopped at Murphy's Bar on South Street, sharing beer and peanuts with many of the same faces he worked with the rest of the week. On Sunday mornings, he and Dot and Wayne strolled up to the imposing stone bulk of the Presbyterian church at the other end of Main Street. When spring came again, Jake and his father spent Sunday afternoons in Lincoln Field, cheering on the Gulistans.

The baseball team still drew large crowds to Lincoln Field each week, but they struggled all through the summer without their star pitcher. Dave Cashion's performance the previous season—he compiled a 15–2 record, and struck out seventeen batters in one game—had led the Gulistans to the league title, but also earned him another stint in the minor leagues. He was back in Freehold by September, though, and in the Guls' last game of the season he pitched a two-hitter that lifted them into an unexpected, and much welcomed, playoff spot. They went on to win the first round of the playoffs, and the first game of the best-of-three finals over Red Bank.

Cashion's return, and the Gulistans' sudden surge, raised the town's spirits as high as they'd been since V-J Day. As Jake made his foreman's rounds in the first week of October—the week before the second, and perhaps deciding, Sunday game of the championship series—he was hardly bothered by the usual yarn snarls and false colors and mistied chain beams. The mill was humming toward all-time highs in production and sales, and the baseball team that carried its name was now, at the end, when the most was at stake, proving similarly invincible. And the mill's success was just a reflection of the entire nation's: America had just 7 percent of the world's population, but it produced 57 percent of the world's steel, 62 percent of its oil, 80 percent of its automobiles. It had emerged from the war with an economy whose size and vigor dwarfed any other nation's. Unemployment was less than 4 percent, and per capita annual income was $1,450, more than $500 higher than the nearest competitor.

But on Thursday morning, Jake walked into the office to find his supervisor on the phone, listening solemnly to what his long face betrayed as bad news of some kind.

"The old man died last night," he told Jake when he hung up.

"Which one? Miran?" Jake asked.

"Miran. We're shutting down tomorrow and the next day for the funeral."

The mill was such a closely held, tight-knit family operation that Jake felt the loss personally, as if one of his own relatives had died. Miran Karagheusian was a more familiar figure at the mill than his younger brother—when they divided responsibilities in the company's early years, he had taken over domestic manufacturing, leaving the imports to Arshag—but he had been sick lately, confined to his Long Island home, and unable to visit. He was seventy-four, and his death was mourned with genuine sadness in Freehold, where the recent mutual prosperity had erased harsher memories of earlier battles between the company and its workers. On the day after Christmas in 1935, after two years of threats, walkouts and escalating tension between the newly formed union and a company trying to weather a straitened economy, workers had arrived to find the mill's doors closed: "This plant will cease operations until further notice," the sign announced. The company, which wanted to cut wages as much as 23 percent, called it a strike; the union called it a lockout. The stoppage of work, and paychecks, hit the town so hard that a soup kitchen for hungry workers and their families was opened in the Dolly Madison ice cream store on Main Street. The mill stayed closed for two months, until arbitration finally led the two sides to accept more modest cuts, which reflected the average wage in the rug industry.

"A rare and outstanding personality," the *Transcript* eulogized Miran Karagheusian in an editorial. "If he had a fault at all it was that of over-modesty."

"From the earliest days of our company, Mr. 'MK' took a strong personal interest in the welfare of his employees," said the sympathetic statement from the Quarter Century Club of mill veterans.

On the day after the funeral, Jake watched in frustration as the distracted Guls made one error after another, handing Red Bank an 8–7 vic-

tory. The winning run scored when a fly ball dropped between two out-
fielders who each thought the other had called it. The season was beginning to feel as if it had overstayed its welcome, but Jake dutifully returned
to Lincoln Field for the deciding game a week later, on a Sunday afternoon deep enough into autumn that some boys along the right-field line
were tossing a football among themselves. Miran's death had left Jake low
and uncertain, and the Gulistans' loss had kept him there.

But then in the bottom of the third inning, Jake rose to cheer as Dave
Cashion doubled to deep center field; and he cheered again as the next
batter doubled, too, sending Cashion home for the first run of the game.
Returning to the mound with the lead, Cashion held Red Bank hitless
through the middle innings, and got two more hits himself as the Guls
kept scoring. He started to fade in the ninth, allowing two runs, but by
then it was already too late. The Gulistans won, 8–2, sparking a celebration that didn't stop when the early dusk finally cleared the field. Several
weeks later, just before Thanksgiving, the proud and grateful Foremen's
Club threw a banquet for the team at the American Hotel, where the President's Trophy was awarded to the repeating league champions, and
enough toasts were raised to stoke a glow of victory that would, everyone
hoped, warm the mill, players and fans alike, all through the winter.

The line for the seven o'clock show at the Strand, moving languidly
through the summer heat toward the ticket booth and the glass doors and
the cool, plush refuge beyond, was pressed up against the COMING AT-
TRACTIONS posters (Alfred Hitchcock's *Strangers on a Train*, Sunday and
Monday), forced to share the sidewalk with unaccustomed throngs of
shoppers on a Friday night in August of 1951. Most stores stayed open
only one evening a week, and until a few months ago, Freehold had always
been a Saturday-night town. Throughout the surrounding countryside,
farmhands would collect their pay by midday and make their way to
Main Street, merging into the shoulder-to-shoulder crowds that circuited
from store to store. But in the restless years since victory, in an economy
eager to make back what it had lost to the Depression and the war, the
downtown merchants had chafed under the old agricultural rhythms,
and pushed for Freehold to follow the lead of more "commercially progressive" neighbors like Red Bank and Asbury Park. The banks began offering Friday-evening hours, and the stores soon followed. The shoppers
passed under the Strand canopy tonight like a stream under a bridge,

squeezing through the channel narrowed by the movie line, branching off periodically into McMahon's haberdashery, Newberry's five-and-dime, Ballew's Jewelry, Al's Bootery, Dubois' Pharmacy, Frick and Deecke's market, Pinky's Tot and Teen shop and dozens of other tributaries, flowing around the knot of children that sat like a boulder in front of Freehold Furniture's display window, transfixed by the blue-gray glow of *Captain Video* on the new Admiral television sets.

The men whose wives were trying on dresses at the La Rae Shoppe or buying eggs at the Table Talk Store sat on the rail in front of the courthouse, smoking and talking with the other shopping-night bachelors. The Honor Roll hung unnoticed and neglected on the wall behind them, paint peeling and names dropping off like late casualties. No similar roll had been raised to mark the new war America was fighting, against the Communists in Korea, where one local marine had already been killed. The old war was six years past now, and the town had stretched and shifted to accommodate all the veterans who returned from it. The upper stories of the old Perrine Building across the street from the courthouse—once the town's largest department store, with cash trolleys whisking along on wires above the customers' heads, ferrying payments and receipts between the tellers' cage and the clerks—had been converted into veterans' apartments, and the Housing Commission had built a dozen little Capes at the end of Court Street. Private developers had built scores more out past the high school and next to the racetrack, so quickly and haphazardly in one place that Schiverea Avenue started entrapping trucks in the mud, necessitating an emergency delivery of road gravel. The ornate and sprawling Victorian next to Jake Errickson's apartment had been reduced to a hole in the ground by the telephone company, making way for a blocky brick building that would house all the equipment needed to replace the manual operators with an automated dial exchange. More than a million dollars had been invested in new construction locally in each of the two previous years, exploding all previous records and leading the *Transcript* to muse wishfully about whether Freehold might eventually become "a gleaming, sky scraping city." The town had even acquired a new scent—the sour percolator steam that, whenever moisture was in the air and a southeasterly breeze was blowing, wafted over from the Nescafé plant on Jerseyville Avenue, the same odor that filled the diner when the coffee grounds were emptied from the urns at the end of the day.

"Smell that?" Buddy Lewis asked as he spilled back onto Main Street with the crowd exiting the early show at the Strand. Walking beside him was Ruth, his wife of two years.

"I guess we're going to get some rain," Ruth said.

Ruth had cried when Buddy left for the war, but he hadn't really understood why at the time—she seemed so young, and they only knew each other from church, where her father was the minister. When he came home, though, he saw that she had been transformed into a beautiful young woman. At the church service that followed the parade of the returning black veterans, he noticed her gazing at him from the choir. He was invited to Ruth's sixteenth birthday party, and soon became a regular caller at the parsonage, up the street from his parents' apartment. When he left the rug mill and became a student again, collecting sixty-five dollars a month in GI Bill benefits and resuming the studies he had abandoned upon enlisting, he carried her books as they walked to the high school together. But after graduation, on their way toward marriage, Ruth's father opposed them: He expected college of his daughter, or of his son-in-law at least, and Buddy had no prospects beyond Freehold; even with his veterans' benefits, college seemed too far out of reach. All they wanted was to be together, and they didn't want to wait. Several wedding dates were set and broken before Ruth slipped out in the middle of one night and joined Buddy in a waiting taxi for the ride to Newark, where his brother lived. Her father, awaking to find her gone, sent the police in vain to the Lewis family apartment. The newlyweds returned to find that Ruth's clothes had been deposited on the front lawn of the parsonage.

While he was finishing school, Buddy had shined shoes in a Main Street shop until a customer impressed by his diligence with the brushes offered him a job at the lumberyard on Broad Street. Loading trucks for a year, he wondered when the better chance he thought he had earned in the war would finally appear. Black veterans and whites had marched in the same ranks in the homecoming Memorial Day parade, and drank together at the Legion afterward, but that brief moment of unity and purpose, the sense Buddy had that the war might actually have changed something, soon dissipated. Black veterans now marched under the banner of the Elks Club they had organized, while the Legion contingent remained all white. The desegregation set in motion by a new state constitution in 1948 freed blacks from the balcony at the Strand and closed the Colored School—when the beloved principal, Mr. Read, finally re-

tired, Ruth played Tchaikovsky's "Piano Concerto No. 1" at the testimo-
nial at the AME church—but didn't open many new career doors for
Buddy. The mill had felt unwelcoming, Nescafé seemed impenetrable,
and the phone company and the electric company turned aside his in-
quiries with lines he could clearly read between.

Buddy had watched his brother Guggy, the Gulistans' longtime center fielder, make a decent living in the local garment industry—a half-
dozen or so squat little factories, sprinkled mostly amid the houses of the
West End, near the old bean cannery the mill now used as a warehouse—
and he followed him into Shnek's, apprenticing to the trade of making
women's coats. He soon moved on to another factory, Main Cloak, as a
special-machine operator, basting collars, sewing buttonholes, stitching
hems, inserting linings. Ruth worked in the industry, too, bar-tacking
pockets at Eisner's. Many of his coworkers were foreign-born women
who taught him snatches of Polish, bantering easily across the stacks of
wool. The pay was good, sixty-five dollars a week in union wages, but the
work was erratic, pegged to the fashion seasons, with as many as six
months worth of layoffs in some years. August was one of the busy
months, though, filling orders for a winter too far ahead for anyone else
to contemplate, and he and Ruth walked directly home through the humid night after their movie. He earned some extra money working Saturdays, cleaning up and oiling the machines, as well as shortening coats
for the bargain-hunting shoppers who appeared at the door. He was due
in early the next morning.

Down the alley beside the Strand, in a small building adjacent to the
courthouse, Stu Bunton sat at a blinking radio console in a half-dark office, listening to the disembodied voices of distant policemen. In the
shadows across the room, the sturdy wooden desks of the county detectives, all six of them, sat empty.

"This is KEA-317," Stu said, speaking into the microphone. "We have
a report of a stolen car in Asbury Park, a 1951 Plymouth coupe, gray, license number . . ."

His words traveled by wire up Broadway, out Dutch Lane Road,
straight to the top of the 156-foot broadcast tower next to the county welfare home on Briar Hill, where the British had encamped the night before
the Battle of Monmouth, and sprayed out from there to several hundred
patrol cars, police stations, firehouses and ambulances in a swath of terri-

tory that stretched from the farm villages near Trenton to the resort towns along the coast. Most small towns couldn't afford the luxury of two-way radio systems, and relied instead on the county radio room in Freehold to relay their messages. If a horse got loose in Clarksburg, or a burglar was abroad in Long Branch, the call came through Stu's desk for someone to corral them. On another Friday night, a year earlier, Stu and the other operators had handled 290 messages in a single shift, dispatching rescue teams to a disastrous munitions-barge explosion in South Amboy. (In 1937—the year after it opened, when Stu was still in grammar school—the radio room had directed emergency workers to the flaming wreckage of the *Hindenburg* down in Lakehurst.)

Stu had been passing the radio room one day on his way to work at the jail next door when one of the operators leaned out the door with news of an opening inside. He hesitated at first, but then he learned what it paid—half again as much as he was making as a guard. The job reprised his navy role as a witness to violence and disorder, but after Sicily and Leyte Gulf, nothing that ever happened in Monmouth County could ruffle him much. He mingled daily with state troopers, local cops and the county detectives who shared the office, but was frustrated in his efforts to join their ranks. The first police opening in Freehold he had applied for was filled instead by the chief's son. When Stu tried again several years later, ranking first among the nine candidates who took a written and oral test, the borough council's police committee recommended his appointment and passed his name up to the mayor for final approval. But one of the failed applicants got a lawyer and, arguing that the hiring process was rigged against him, stirred up a nasty round of infighting and backbiting that had less to do with who the new cop would be than it did with who was really running things in Borough Hall. Although the department was down to five officers (the perennial Joe Clancy had finally retired and Paul Coyne, Stu's boyhood neighbor, was on extended sick leave with a bad heart), and the recent brazen robbery of a Main Street loan office (a gunman in dark glasses making off with one thousand dollars in broad daylight, leaving the manager bound and gagged) had shocked the town into realizing just what it needed to be protected against, the new appointment was frozen.

"The whole thing smells of politics," one councilman had huffed in disgust.

The debate dragged on through months of council meetings, keeping

Stu's name in the paper enough to upset his mother, before the old exam results were finally discarded. How the new tests would proceed, no one was quite sure.

"No, not yet," he told a caller now, an officer in another town, who asked about the status of his police ambitions. "I've got to start all over again, right from scratch."

Up the block and across the street on the sales floor at McMahon's, where the yellow glow inside was beginning to outshine the fading summer light outside, Jimmy Higgins headed toward the two-tiered wall of men's suits, stopping briefly first to admire the ties fanned out in the glass-topped counter. Suits were the uniform he had worn since the war, and McMahon's was where he bought them. After his apprenticeship ended, he had, to his great relief, been plucked from the waiting list and admitted to the Cincinnati College of Embalming, with all his tuition, plus one hundred dollars a month in living expenses, paid by the GI Bill. A year later, fully licensed, he landed a job for thirty dollars a week at a small funeral home in nearby Hightstown. When they buried a man there who died with no family and no assets besides an old Chevrolet, Jimmy paid for the funeral, $250, and acquired his first car. At a wake one night, curious about how much formality remained in his war-altered trade, he turned up in a brown suit. His boss discreetly informed him later that he had gone a shade too far: He should stick with black.

Jimmy kept a room near the funeral home for the nights he needed to stay over, and even served a term as commander of the Hightstown Legion post, but he mostly still lived at his mother's house in Freehold, and spent his few evenings off strolling downtown with the young woman he had been dating for several years, Angela Nolan. She had graduated from the New Jersey College for Women, a mathematics major, and was working for the Educational Testing Service in Princeton. Her father, like his, had also died young, and she lived with her mother across the street from the Elks Club, a few blocks down from the high school where she was thinking about applying for a teaching job. Their courtship was patient as their savings slowly accumulated. Jimmy wanted to get married, and he wanted to open his own funeral home, but, with sharp memories of his widowed mother's struggle to raise four young children, what he wanted first was to feel some solid ground beneath his feet. The dead of Freehold already had three places to go—including the venerable Freeman's, a century old and counting—and Jimmy knew, that, however warm and winning his personality, his first years were likely to be lean. Flipping through the rack of suits tonight, he heard Mr. McMahon slip up behind, asking what kind he was looking for.

"Not brown," he said, laughing easily, as he always did. "Black, definitely black."

As the night deepened past closing time, and the signs and the storefronts dimmed, the headlights of the shoppers' cars tunneled out into the dark sea of surrounding fields, dispersing back to their own farms and villages along the spokes of the roads that radiated out from the courthouse. The eastbound traffic streamed past Jake Errickson's apartment and onto the Colts Neck Road, along which, three miles and maybe a half-dozen farmsteads later, it passed the turreted white 1840s house where Walter Denise sat working quietly at a desk stacked with small piles of cash and coins. His mother had withdrawn the money from the bank that afternoon, as she did every Friday, and he was counting it into pay envelopes, marking the amounts in his ledger book. After a long day in the orchard, from the banging of the packinghouse to the rattle of the sprayers, he appreciated the silence. Loud, sharp noises had bothered him since the war—unwelcome echoes of artillery shells and mortar rounds. In church one day soon after his return, someone had pulled up a venetian blind too quickly, a clatter like machine-gun fire that sent him diving under a pew. He tried not to think about the war much, about what he had seen and who he had lost, concentrating instead on the twelve thousand trees and 150 workers whose livelihood he provided, and depended upon for his own.

Walter had finished Rutgers in two and a half years, just as he had told the skeptical dean he would, cramming four courses, including calculus and organic chemistry, into a summer session, while also wrestling varsity, making Alpha Zeta, the honorary agricultural society, and getting engaged to Marilyn, the music major he had met at the chaplain's social. She sang in, and he handled props for, a student production of *The Marriage of Figaro.* "There will be no wedding until the Stayman Winesaps are harvested," his father had decreed, and the last of the latest apple variety were off the trees when he and Marilyn were married two days after Thanksgiving in 1948. They bought furniture with the money Walter had saved from the army, and moved into the house amid the peaches at the west end of the orchard, not quite a mile from the 1760 house where his parents lived on a knoll lapped by apples. Their first child, a boy, was born in 1950, and was the chief reason why Walter—who had still been a lieutenant in the reserves when the war in Korea began—wasn't called up to serve.

The orchard had changed while he was away—most notably with the addition of a new grading conveyor system in the packinghouse—and he brought home with him even more ideas on how to improve its operation. To replace the old barn where apples had always been stored after harvest, he designed and oversaw the construction of a refrigerated warehouse tall enough to hold pallets stacked six high. The thick Styrofoam cemented all around the inside made the walls sound hollow when tapped upon, but twelve inches of concrete block was behind it all, holding everything up.

With the orchard entering its busiest season now—the clingstone peaches already in, and the freestones coming, the Pippins and Codlings starting in the apples—the payroll was swelling toward its peak of 150, keeping Walter at his desk later into the night each Friday. He added the hours and the bushels, subtracted what had already been advanced to those who had run short. The orchard kept a dozen or so people working year-round, but at harvest time it swarmed with migrants, mostly blacks from the South, families as well as single men, who had been following the crops north since spring. They lived in a camp across the road, and when trouble arose—a knife pulled in anger over a woman, a bottle or a suspicious ace—it was Walter who got the call. It was also Walter who handled the fickle, hectic peaches, dickering over five-bushel lots with fast-talking wholesalers who knew how fast rot could set in, while his father presided over the stately, patient procession of the more durable apples.

At noon the next day in the packinghouse, a line of workers moved toward the table where Walter sat handing out pay envelopes, just as he had as a lieutenant in Austria, but without the gun. "Try to save some this week," he called after one man who slipped out quickly, off to catch a ride into town.

The Clark house sprawled regally across a two-acre lot larger than any other on Main Street—three white-clapboard stories and twenty-one rooms framed by hedges and roses and garden paths, its deep porch hidden in shadows behind the ancient rhododendrons—and every time Bill Lopatin drove past in his pickup on his daily rounds among job sites in the summer of 1952, he imagined it leveled, replaced by a shopping cen-

ter. He had always admired the house, but now he was being asked to
judge it. Unable to sell, the house's frustrated owner had appeared before
the zoning board of adjustment recently and, in the toughest case Bill
had yet faced in his four years as a member, requested permission to tear
it down. The house was too big, the owner argued, the upkeep too costly,
the taxes too high, higher in fact than any other residence in town, for it
to remain a dwelling. The variance he had applied for would allow it to be
sold instead as a commercial property. The board had heard the evidence,
examined the architect's plans—a sleek brick and glass strip of five stores,
anchored by a small grocery, with parking for eighty cars in back—and
adjourned with a promise to issue a decision soon.

No votes had been cast yet, but as Bill passed the Clark house now,
headed toward home at day's end, he was certain of his own. Freehold's
downtown had remade itself many times over since its founding—old
buildings giving way to new, whether accidentally through fire or pur-
posely through demolition, as the business district crept out Main Street
in both directions from the courthouse, one lot at a time—but for the last
twenty-five years, it had been constrained by what had come to feel like
fixed borders: Elks Point to the east, and King's Auto, with its show window full of Oldsmobiles, to the west. Beyond there, Main Street remained
the gracious domain of the local grandees, lined with the large and fili-
greed homes of doctors, lawyers, bankers and wealthy farmers, retired to
town after selling their land. Postwar prosperity, though, was threatening
the old boundaries, spawning a building boom that was testing the natural limits of the town's growth. The phone company building next to
Jake Errickson's apartment had breached the eastern border, and the
Clark proposal was hammering at the west. How far could it go? Bill wondered as he drove. How far should it?

At the high school, Bill turned onto the street where he had just finished building a new house for himself, next door to the old one he had
renovated when he first returned seven years earlier. It was just big enough
for his small family—Selma, who had started a telephone answering
business, and their daughter, who had started high school. As a builder, he
had profited from the boom, the work steadier than it had ever been in
the twenty years since he joined his father, but as a citizen and a town official, he was wary of the shape it was taking. The local boosters might
have grand ambitions for Freehold, but it was still just a town, not a city,
and its past, in his view, should not be sacrificed for its future. If more

stores were needed, they should be built on the open land on the edges of town, not shoehorned onto a bulldozed lot in its center. On the block where his own small ranch stood alone now, he was clearing the tangled underbrush and planning several neighbors, including one for his brother, Sol.

Bill had built an office for himself in the basement of his new house, with a drafting table where he worked on plans, and a desk where he sat now with his zoning codebook, polishing his decision in the case. The town's business interests were allied behind the Clark proposal, and three other board members had already told Bill that they would vote to approve the variance. (A fourth had disqualified himself because he also sat on the board of education, which was, as the owner of the Broad Street School, a neighbor of the property.) "If Freehold is to increase its population and wealth, then it must expand in all phases of community life, including commercial enterprise," the *Transcript* argued in a long editorial favoring the variance. "The alternative to the expansion of the town's business district seems to be stagnation."

To Bill, though, the variance represented "a substantial detriment to the public good," a phrase he kept returning to like a refrain as he wrote his minority opposition report. He poked at the cases Clark's lawyer had cited in support of the application (*Augustas Street v. Collins, Greggs v. Paterson*), and watched them collapse under scrutiny: In *Augustas*, he noted, all the lots surrounding the residence were already zoned for business; in *Greggs*, the house was converted to a funeral home, not demolished. He wrote of the Clark proposal:

> This will cause a radical change in the appearance and use of the entire area . . . and would substantially impair the intent and purpose of the zone plan and zoning ordinance.
>
> I believe in the orderly expansion of a business area. . . . I recognize that as a community grows, the need for commercial and industrial areas grows, too, and it is necessary to change zone boundaries; but the zoning should not be done haphazardly and piecemeal. . . . If the business zone is to be extended it should be done by mayor and council.

The zoning board voted just as Bill had expected—three to approve the variance for the shopping center; one abstention; and a single vote, his own, against it. After the decision was announced, aggrieved neighbors brought their complaints to the next Borough Council meeting. Bill's fourth-grade teacher, now the principal of the Hudson Street School, praised his reasoned objection, but scolded his colleagues' quick assent. "If three men have the power to make such a decision, then it will be difficult to teach the youngsters in our schools democracy," she said. The neighbors, including the Reformed Church across the street, banded together and filed a suit asking the Superior Court to overturn the variance—the board's action, they argued, was "arbitrary and not warranted by the evidence"—and the Clark house was left to brood all through the fall, unwanted by its owner, uncertain of its future. As Bill passed the house each day now, he wondered what effect his decision in the case would have on another decision the town's voters would soon be making—about whether he should move up from the zoning board, an appointed position, to the Borough Council, an elected one. Would his dissenting vote brand him as a curmudgeonly foe of progress? Or would it mark him as a man who held fast to his principles?

Bill had run for council for the first time last fall, at the request of Clifton Barkalow, the lawyer who was the local Republican boss. Barkalow had been watching Bill for years—it was his house the Lopatins were building when the sudden storm blew up the spring before the war—and he saw in the calm and competent former waist gunner a potential civic leader. Bill had demurred at first but finally agreed. His public duty, he decided, outweighed his private reluctance. The war had only strengthened his immigrant patriotism—he had answered when called then, and he answered when called now. Democracy was a contract, and it demanded participation from its citizens, not just when there were enemies to be fought, but also when there were zoning decisions to be rendered, and municipal budgets to be balanced. His own boyhood journey to America had been so hard, and so hopeful, sustained across the snows of war-torn Europe by visions of a new life of freedom, that his devotion to democracy was to him a form of religion.

Bill's father had come to America in 1913, to join his own father and brother, who were already settled in Freehold, and he expected the rest of his family to follow soon after. He sent tickets for them to travel to America through Sweden, but the First World War closed that route. He sent tickets for them to travel through Siberia, but the Russian Revolution closed that one, too. Finally in November of 1919, after two years when no word was able to travel between her and her husband, Bill's mother decided that she and her five children would join him somehow—by wagon, by sled, by train, over the obstacles of embassy officials and border guards and Bolshevik soldiers. The oldest daughter died of tuberculosis, and Bill's legs were frostbitten. A doctor suggested amputation. Bill's mother believed that if she arrived in America with a crippled child, the whole family would be turned away.

"You either save his legs or he dies," she told the doctor.

After two months in bed in a hospital in Brest, Bill stood up one morning, his nine-year-old legs working again. They got to Warsaw, and then to Danzig, and into steerage on an old American military transport ship. When they reached America in September of 1920, they stayed at Bill's grandfather's farm. From it Bill could see the steeple of Tennent Church, where wounded Americans had been laid on pews during the Battle of Monmouth. As a boy, when he was a nickel short of a matinee at the Liberty or the Strand, he spent many afternoons in the Freehold library, reading about Abraham Lincoln, absorbing the majestic lessons of his new country. The politics of his own family were often contentious, and took full advantage of the freedoms America offered: His father, a socialist, had three brothers, a Republican, a Democrat and a Communist. Bill himself was always a registered Republican, the party of his beloved Lincoln, but he had voted for Roosevelt.

Some of the Republicans were reluctant to back a Jew when Barkalow first suggested Bill as a candidate, and on Election Day last year, their lack of support had cost him one of the two open seats. The other Republican on the ticket topped the field, but Bill finished third, seventy-three votes out of the running. The vote was close enough that, when Barkalow was weighing candidates again for 1952, Bill was granted another chance. As he campaigned now, he felt the weight of his chastened party gathering behind him more than it had last year, united and eager to topple Harry Sagotsky, the Democratic incumbent who was its loudest, hardest rival on the council. Bill was paired locally with the popular, incumbent councilman, Grover Emmons, a mason for whom Buddy Lewis's father worked. At the top of the ticket nationally was the general who had once been his ultimate commander, Dwight Eisenhower, the Republicans' best chance in twenty years for regaining the White House.

On weekends and in the evenings after work, Bill reluctantly trudged from door to door as he trolled for votes, forced to talk about a subject he usually avoided in conversation: himself. He was accustomed to building things, not discussing them. What he did, he had always believed, meant more than what he said. In politics, though, he found neither the straight lines of carpentry nor the sharp creases of the army, only a swampy, unfamiliar terrain where words weighed more than deeds. An election in a town like Freehold often turned more on personality than ideology, but Bill was reluctant to talk himself up too high, because it meant implicitly talking his opponent down too low. He stuck instead to his platform, which didn't differ much from the Democrats'. The county courthouse needed a new, larger home, and he wanted to keep it in town. He wanted more playgrounds for the hordes of postwar children who were scurrying underfoot everywhere, and more off-street parking downtown for the crowds of shoppers. He wanted the town's budget to match its income, and the tax rate to stay down. He also wanted, naturally enough, "to reexamine our zoning structure for the purpose of promoting the orderly growth of Freehold." The nearest he came to attacking his fiery rival was the proverb he quoted in his campaign ad: "Little was achieved by the cow that gave a full pail of milk and then got mad and kicked over her good work." He left a palm card with everyone he met: "For Integrity in Government," the slogan promised.

On the Monday night before the election, the banquet room of the American Hotel was stuffed with Republicans, several hundred of them, cheering and clapping and stirring up the largest, loudest campaign rally in anyone's memory, perhaps even since Theodore Roosevelt himself had stumped in town. Bill sat on the dais with Barkalow, the mayor, Congressman James Auchincloss and all the other Republicans who held or hoped to hold local and county offices.

"If the votes are not in the ballot boxes for General Eisenhower, then God help America," the assistant county prosecutor declared to a thunder of affirmation.

Summoned to the microphone by Barkalow, Bill bent it down slightly to match his height. "One of the first things I was taught in learning the carpenter trade was, 'Measure twice, but cut once,'" he said to applause and nods of assent, reprising the phrase that had become a slogan of sorts. "If elected councilman I will make this principle my guide in the conduct of the affairs of the Borough of Freehold."

Checking the firehouse, the schools and the other polling places on Election Day, Bill found long and patient lines of voters, all of whom, he hoped, had read the flattering editorial in the *Transcript*. While the newspaper hadn't explicitly endorsed any council candidate, it made clear its opinion of Bill, despite their disagreement over the Clark house: "a conscientious citizen with many good ideas for the betterment of the community," who "courageously turned in a lone dissenting opinion" on the zoning board. "Perhaps a little 'measuring twice' and 'cutting once' as regards municipal affairs would further the cause of good government in Freehold."

The turnout set a new record, more than 90 percent of the town's registered voters, and the counting dragged slowly through the evening. The clerks paged patiently through the paper ballots, tallying the Xs in the boxes. Bill tried to will his column higher as, district by district, the numbers were chalked on the blackboard in the firehouse, but he remained stuck in third again, behind Emmons and Sagotsky. He went home before the totals were final, disappointed and depressed about a defeat he believed was all but official. Leaving his house for work the next morning, he heard a sympathetic voice calling from next door.

"It can't get much closer than that," his neighbor said.

"What do you mean?" Bill asked.

"Seven votes—didn't you know?"

Bill hurried downtown to Barkalow's law office, overlooking the courthouse square from the second floor of the stolid stone bank building on the corner, and learned what had happened while he slept. Emmons remained the clear winner, with 1,940 votes, but the last two districts had come in unexpectedly heavy for Bill, leaving him just a breath behind Sagotsky, who had 1,810, for the second seat. Bill finished with 1,803 votes, almost 500 more than his 1951 total.

"I'd like a recount," he said firmly, and Barkalow agreed.

The counting started in the courthouse on a Monday morning a few weeks later, and finished on Tuesday afternoon with a new total: Sagotsky, 1,804; Lopatin 1,800. Thirteen ballots remained in dispute, and copies were sent to the county judge. On Friday, the two candidates and their lawyers stood in the courtroom as the ballots were scrutinized, and the judge tried to decipher the electoral intent of the hands that had scratched so haphazardly on them.

"Ballot number one, a 'yes' written in the Sagotsky box—I would submit that this is clearly a vote for my client," the Democrat's lawyer argued.

"On ballot three, these several lines marked in the Lopatin box were obviously meant to be a vote for him," Bill's lawyer said.

For several hours they haggled over black marks on paper—an O instead of an X, names written improperly in the personal choice columns, a military write-in ballot with the names entered but no marks made, a ballot with votes for three candidates instead of two. All through the proceeding, Bill kept wishing his cousins had waited another year to move out of town; the several lost votes they represented might have proved decisive.

The courtroom's tall windows were filled with early-winter darkness when the judge finally ruled. "I find that four of these votes go to Mr. Sagotsky, and three to Mr. Lopatin—the other six I'm voiding," he said. The total in the end was only two votes different than it was on election night: Sagotsky, 1,808; Lopatin 1,803. "Mr. Sagotsky, you are therefore declared the winner."

The judge's gavel banged an end to the hearing, the election and Bill's political ambitions. He wished his opponent well and then told Barkalow what he had told himself at the start of the campaign, that if he lost, it was his last. He decided now to follow in his civic life the credo he had learned in the army: Serve when asked, but don't ask to serve. Not long before the recount, Lopatin Construction had won the sealed-bid competition for the new $35,000 Colts Neck firehouse, a couple of miles up the road from Walter Denise's orchard, and Bill gladly turned his attention to a more concrete public project. The firehouse had a red-brick colonial facade, three garage bays, a meeting room and a kitchen, and it served a more immediate and useful public function than a council seat ever would. His crew dug the foundation before the ground hardened, and started laying courses of brick. The entrance door was framed by twin Doric columns, a pediment and a fan window that George Washington would have found familiar when he was passing through in 1778. The fire trucks had already moved in when Bill heard some news that pleased but didn't surprise him: The court had sided with the neighbors, and thrown out the Clark variance. The zoning board had acted "arbitrarily," the judge ruled, and "to the detriment of the public good."

"I knew I was right," Bill said to himself, a statement of fact, not victory. He may have lost in votes, he thought, but he won, as he always expected he would, on principle.

10.

Harvest

On the gentle hill behind the farmhouse, the peach trees were planted in rows that followed the contours of the land, and as Walter Denise walked along one of the curving lanes between them on an early summer morning, he was surrounded on all sides—ahead of him and behind, to his right and to his left—by a green wall of foliage. The sun was rising somewhere beyond the trees, but he was still in the shadows. The air was dry again, and his farmer's bones felt no moisture coming. The bleary crew of men with him was already disassembling the irrigation pipes, carrying the forty-foot lengths and the stubby sprinkler heads from one row to the next, where they would soak the ground for the next eight hours with a low, steady, sun-glistened rain. The deep roots of the apple trees could usually find enough sustenance even in a parched season, but the peaches couldn't reach quite deep enough. If water failed to fall from the sky, it had to be coaxed up from the earth instead, through the intricate network of dams, wells and pumps the Denises had built, which had turned their streams into ponds, and their land into an orchard.

When the water was flowing again, Walter left the peaches for the apples, driving his pickup past the migrant camp where several children were standing on the corner, waiting for the bus into town. Ever since the Colored School in Freehold was closed by desegregation, it had opened its classrooms again each summer for the children of the migrant workers who came from the South to pick the local crops. (A "heartening" experiment, *The New York Times* had declared in an editorial praising the "pronounced success" of the Migrant Summer School.) Walter stopped in at the office in the packinghouse where his father was working, then

followed the smoke out to the pruning crew. The dead branches were being pared from the apple trees and tossed into the brush burner, a billowing wood fire burning steadily in a contraption towed behind a tractor.
He continued on to the pump station at one of the ponds, where the tank
truck was drinking up five hundred gallons of water to ferry back out to
the sprayer. A migrant emptied a bag of fungicide chemicals into the
tank, then picked up a roll and chewed at his breakfast.

"You better go wash your hands," Walter said, in the exasperated tone
of a warning that had been given many times before.

The sprayer was a long, narrow rig that looked and sounded a bit like
a jet engine, with a Chrysler V-8 engine and a caged propeller that blew
the chemicals up through the trees, coating the bottoms of the leaves
and the fruits on the way up, and the tops of the way down. The orchard
held none of the terrors of the cold, dark, wild woods where Walter had
spent his war, but it plagued him with smaller hazards daily: red mites
and brown rot, devouring insects and corroding fungi. His main defense
was to spray, as many as twenty times in a season. Fruits, as he told anyone who asked why he sprayed so much, did not grow to table quality
unaided.

For the last several years, the Denises had raised a few acres of strawberries, and the last of them were being picked now by the first migrants.
Walter helped load the pickup with forty crates of Sparkles, sixteen quarts
apiece, which had already begun bleeding into their baskets. Strawberries
had a narrow window of value, and he was eager to sell this batch today,
before they ripened into worthlessness. Because the Denises sold only in
wholesale lots—they were farmers, not storekeepers, they reasoned, with
little patience for the distraction a roadside retail business would bring—
Walter drove west to the nearest farmers' market, in Hightstown.

"I'll give you a dollar and a half a crate," the buyer offered as he
sniffed around the back of the truck.

"Forget it," Walter said in disgust. "Even if I have to dump them I
won't sell them for that."

He drove north to the market in Newark, farther than he would usually go for a small load, but nearer the cities where a just-picked straw-
berry was more valued, and more likely, he hoped, to bring a fair price.

"How much you want?" the buyer asked him.

"Two and a half," Walter ventured.

"Unload 'em."

The crew had moved the irrigation pipe while he was gone, but before he went to sleep it had to be moved again. The sky hung clear and starry in the gaps between the trees, dark finally after the endless light of a June day. When the pipes were shifted and joined, dousing a new row of peach trees, Walter went down to check on the pump, which gulped gasoline at the rate of 125 gallons a day. A cherry-red glow like a brakeman's lantern broke through the darkness as he approached—the fiery light of the engine, not just the manifold and the exhaust, but the head and the block itself, on the verge of overheating after running so long without pause.

"See you in the morning," Walter called to the crew, who—barring the sudden, unexpected arrival of rain the night air didn't even hint at— would reassemble to repeat the process at dawn.

Apart from his years in the army, Walter had always lived on farm time, governed by the seasonal rhythms of the orchard whose moods and needs he knew as well as his own. Machinery, chemicals and fruit varieties might change, but each new June made the same demands on him as the last had. Every morning when he passed the packinghouse, though, he was reminded that the comforting certainty of what he could control only masked the unsettling chaos of what he couldn't. The long, rattly, corrugated building had once been an outpost of the Brakeley canned-food empire, where beans and peas from the surrounding fields were shelled and rinsed before they were hauled to the sprawling red-brick complex in town for packing. From the 1890s to the 1920s, the Brakeley company had dominated local agriculture, owning or leasing three thousand acres of cultivated land, and bringing as many as seventeen hundred workers from the cities each season to live in the barracks, separated by ethnicity and fed breakfast and supper by company cooks who also fortified their picking by packing them field lunches. Nearly two hundred thousand cans of Luxury and Warwick brand lima beans, and French Court and Cupid brand sugar peas, came off the line each day. But a crop blight, and an aging patriarch, finally doomed the business, and the rug mill bought its silent buildings for warehouse space.

Walter's father had grown up on a farm on the other side of town, but when his own father's death had summoned him home from a cosmopolitan career as a fertilizer salesman in Chicago—as the only son, he was expected to provide for the surviving women—he bought some land from the liquidating Brakeley's with the idea of growing something other than beans, the local market for which had all but vanished with the cannery's demise. He planted an orchard and waited for a crop, five to seven years for the peaches, seven to ten for the apples. While the rows of trees matured, he grew vegetables in the lanes between them. Walter had had enough tomatoes and melons as a boy to shun them as an adult.

The Denises' patience was rewarded with an orchard that grew into a local landmark, and that flourished now as an island of stability in a regional farm economy more confused and uncertain than at any time since the fall of Brakeley's. After the harvest in recent years, heaps of potatoes had sat moldering in neighboring fields, sprinkled with green dye so they couldn't be sold, dismal evidence of a shrinking market for the crop that had ruled the county for more than a century. The government that had bought potatoes to feed its soldiers during the war—as much as 90 percent of the local harvest—now bought them merely to prop up their price, and was about to stop. Too many potatoes were being grown (acreage and production efficiency had soared to match the war's demand), too few were being eaten (the average American consumed 102 pounds a year now, down from 200 pounds in 1900), and farmers were turning instead to soybeans and other crops. By the mid-1950s, Monmouth County was growing fewer potatoes than it had since the late 1830s, just before the wave of famine-fleeing Irish arrived. The egg market was in similar turmoil. Too many urban refugees had pursued their chicken-farm idyll, and their coops—some the handiwork of Lopatin Construction—were overrun with eggs they couldn't sell. Busloads of chicken farmers were traveling to Washington, seeking a federal cushion against collapsing prices. In fruit growing, though, the long and deep investment required discouraged dabblers, and kept supply more in line with demand.

More migrants trickled into the orchard over the next few weeks, their arrival as predictable as the ripening of the peaches they came to pick. The Denise camp was easy to find—just follow East Main Street out to the giant cartoon of Mickey Mouse that was waving from the side of a two-story wooden building. It was an old candy store that had once stood on what was now the navy's nearby weapons depot; Walter's father had bought it, moved it and converted it to housing when the site was being cleared. Behind the tall building stood some smaller huts and a long, low cinderblock barracks like a roadside motel. Each morning the men donned hats against the sun and filed out among the peaches. Draping baskets around their necks, they climbed the slender ladders that leaned against the trees. The women worked mostly in the barn behind Walter's house; it had been converted into a packinghouse, where the peaches were sorted into bins by size, and fed through a machine that brushed and vacuumed off the excess fuzz. Buyers called at the packinghouse all through the day, offering prices that pitted the strength of Walter's resolve against the fragility of his fruit.

"See that lot of fifty baskets? I'll give you a quarter apiece."

"It costs more than that to grow them."

"They're not worth more than that."

"Well, if you don't like it, go somewhere else."

Apples could keep for months after picking, but peaches were lucky to last a week, and selling them required a poker player's instinctive mixture of calm and bluster. Buyers sniffed and squeezed and hefted, while Walter raised and called and folded. During apple season, his father could sit at a desk and, with a single phone call, sell a thousand bushels, which could be loaded at leisure into a boxcar at the railroad siding on Throckmorton Street. To sell a thousand bushels in a day during peach season, Walter might haggle with fifty buyers or more, all of them trying to outguess him, and then help them hurriedly load the baskets onto their dusty old pickups. Peddlers and roadstand owners usually came on weekends. Small groceries restocked during the week. The orchard's own trucks made regular deliveries to the warehouses of distributors and the larger food chains.

"Put four hundred on this one," Walter said one morning, patting the side of a truck. The other drivers were out, and the peaches couldn't wait. "I'll have to take it up to Acme myself."

Driving north toward Elizabeth, Walter eased onto the New Jersey Turnpike, the six-lane concrete channel that had been cut across the state several years earlier, smoothing and shortening his delivery routes. Stacked in the back were the baskets filled with his favorite peach variety, Sunhighs—dark red on top fading to orange beneath, tapering to a point at the bottom that gave them almost a heart shape. (A close second were the Blakes, bright yellow and named for his old Rutgers professor.) He backed up to the warehouse and dropped his tailgate as the loading dock foreman approached.

"You have a card?" the foreman asked him with a scowl. "If you want to get unloaded you've got to have a card."

Walter knew what kind of card he meant, a union card, and he stiffened at the challenge. Unions had assumed a powerful role in shaping the American workplace in the last decade, and represented more than a third of all workers now, trying to secure for them better wages, benefits and conditions. In the first years after the war—when there suddenly seemed to be so much more money around, and everyone thought they deserved a bigger share of it—the battles were especially bitter, with strikes that shut down whole industries for weeks at a time: meatpacking, railroads, steel mills, auto plants, coal mines. In 1946, the worst year so far in America for labor relations, 4.6 million workers went out on 4,985 work stoppages. Things had eased since then, but Walter's opinions hadn't changed much. A union might be right for a larger manufacturing company—for General Motors, say, maybe even for the rug mill—but it was all wrong for a family operation like the orchard. His relations with his small year-round workforce were based on loyalty and longevity, not contract; the migrants were only around for a few months; and he wasn't going to let any outsider dictate to him who could or couldn't drive his peaches to market, and when.

"I grew this fruit, I packed it and now I'm delivering it," he said firmly. "I don't need a card."

The peaches waited, untouched, between them. "I've got to inspect this fruit—put it here," the foreman finally grumbled, pointing to an empty pallet.

Walter lifted one basket off and set it before him. "All right, give me another," the foreman said after squeezing a few peaches, barely feigning an interest in their quality.

Walter moved another basket, and another, and another, one at a time, working in silent defiance, a dozen, two dozen, three dozen. He had held his ground against union bullies before, and he wouldn't yield now. Delivering a truckload of apples once to an Argentina-bound freighter at the Manhattan docks, he had waited a full twenty-four hours to be unloaded, locked in overnight with nothing to eat but his own cargo, because he wouldn't pay a bribe. The longer and slower he worked now, the larger an obstacle he became, blocking the flow of the loading dock like one of the pesky beavers who dammed the orchard's streams. The foreman soon had no option but surrender, and he called some men over.

"Go ahead and unload him," he ordered as Walter stood aside. "We've got a stubborn farmer here."

• • •

Riding east out of town in the gray light before dawn on a Saturday in October, Jake Errickson noticed through the passenger window of the pickup truck that the trees near the road in the Denise orchard—all Codlings, Twenty Ounces and other varieties that were green, a color less tempting to passing pilferers—had already been harvested. He yawned and rubbed the sleep from his eyes, still bleary after working until midnight at the rug mill the night before. His next-door neighbor was driving, and squeezed between them was another mill hand. Rattling around in the back were several bows and quivers full of the arrows they hoped to harvest some deer with.

Five miles past the orchard, they turned off onto one of the yellow gravel lanes that branched off the main roads and crisscrossed the countryside between settlements. The land was wide and open, a meadow for the horses raised by the farmer who had granted Jake and his friends permission to hunt. They parked where the gravel gave out and walked the rest of the way in, toward the dense wall of woods and the six-foot chain-link fence that marked the border of the Earle Naval Weapons Depot. Each man had built his own crude perch up in a tree, and they wished each other luck as they split up. Jake's was a board laid across a Y about ten feet up, overlooking a hole in the fence. The deer would slip out at night to filch the horses' hay and then retreat back inside, where they, like the shells and bombs and bullets, were protected from intruders by armed marines. Trespassing to hunt at Earle brought a stiff fine, and as Jake sat watching on his stand, a patrol jeep cruised by on the perimeter road just inside the fence.

The morning air chilled Jake as he waited in silence, keeping him alert after a long week of late nights at work. He had been promoted to foreman in the broad-jacquard department, where the looms ran round-the-clock and shifts rotated from month to month, days, evenings, nights, a schedule that had made him miss some of Wayne's Little League games last season, but that freed him for mornings of hunting. His office was on the third floor of the newer section of the mill, which had been expanded by another 105,000 square feet to accommodate more of the larger looms that wove the wider carpet the market was demanding. A short walk away in one direction was the shipping department, where his father worked along the conveyor that wrapped and sewed the logs of carpet in burlap. Thirty yards the other way was his sister, Georgianna, the plant nurse, presiding over a first-aid and examining room more placid and orderly than the Pacific field hospitals where she had served during the war. Two floors below, Dot worked in the Axminster department, where lower-quality carpet was woven on the only looms the mill trusted women with. Across the bridge in Jake's old department, a single new piece of equipment had been installed amid the venerable narrow jacquard looms—a tufting machine that, instead of weaving the threads together into a whole, simply punched them through a burlap back, which was then sealed with latex.

"They can pump that stuff out like rain," Jake had said when he saw the tufting machine in action for the first time. As fast as the new technology was, though, he, like most of his colleagues, considered it little more than a curiosity, because the carpet that came out of it made the Axminsters look like imported Persians.

The raise that accompanied the promotion had finally allowed Jake and Dot to buy their first car and move out of the apartment on East Main Street. For eight hundred dollars they bought a piece of land on the edge of town, a block from Bill Lopatin, and for eight thousand dollars—one thousand dollars down, the rest from a 4 percent veterans' mortgage—they hired a weaver who moonlighted as a contractor to build a neat one-story house on it. Jake stopped by often to check up and pitch in. Before the dirt was pushed back, he painted tar on the concrete-block foundation, sealing it against leaks. The house was near enough to hear the cheers from the high school football field, where Jake often spent autumn Saturdays in the company of three or four thousand other fans, more than had ever watched a Sunday baseball game on the other side of town.

Television had taken hold of the nation at the start of the decade—"a new force unloosed in the land," a member of the Federal Communications Commission had said—introducing Americans to Lucille Ball, Howdy Doody and Elvis Presley, and dramatically altering the daily rituals, the social fabric and even the landscape of towns like Freehold. The Liberty Theater was only the most obvious local casualty—converted into a bowling alley after declining attendance forced it to close. The Strand was struggling, too. The Gulistans had also faded: The team had aged past its prime, and local baseball fans began to stay home and watch the major league games now beamed directly into their living rooms. The Colonials, though, still managed to draw large crowds to their football games, with several unbeaten seasons and back-to-back Shore Conference titles. The star of the first championship team was a senior halfback named Danny Lewis, Buddy's nephew, who put together the kind of year his uncle had dreamed of himself before the war interrupted. Danny's 120 points, a conference scoring record, had earned him a scholarship to the University of Wisconsin, where he was rushing his way onto the pro scouts' draft lists.

Behind Jake's house, the backyard ran unmarked into woods and fields that stretched unbroken for half a mile to the lake where he liked to fish. During hunting season, he could walk out his door with a gun and spend a morning chasing rabbits and squirrels, pheasant and grouse. His neighbor was a hunter, too, with a bale of hay and a bull's-eye target set up for bow-and-arrow shooting. Jake practiced enough in the yard to try it in the field, where bow hunters—whose deer season started earlier— got a head start on the shotgunners.

Earlier in the week, Jake and his partners had only stayed out for a couple of hours, but with no work looming later today, they had agreed to hunt until lunch. Motionless in his perch, Jake tuned himself to the rhythm of the woods, alert to any disturbance that would betray the presence of a deer. He listened for a snapping twig or a rustle of leaves as he had once listened for Japanese transmissions from the jungles of New Guinea; looking for a blur of sun and shadow, an unexpected movement, as he had, more recently, looked for uninvited visitors in the sky from the roof of the rug mill as a volunteer ground observer. After the war ended, America had found a new enemy, with a new shape—at once more elusive and more pervasive than the Axis powers Jake had fought. The enemy was Communism now, and it might attack from any angle—from Korea, China, the Soviet Union, Southeast Asia, from within America itself, if Senator Joseph McCarthy was to be believed, perhaps even from someplace that no one had yet imagined. Jake had been standing an observation shift on the roof on a July night a few years earlier, near the end of the Korean War. Anything, he was told, might be out there. And then, in the northeast distance, a bright light appeared, joined a few moments later by a second light, and the pair of them hovered back and forth, back and forth, for ten minutes, in a manner distinctly unlike an airplane.

"That's no Russian bomber," his spotting partner said.

There had been widespread reports of flying saucer sightings all over America lately—maybe this was another one. Their instructions were to report anything suspicious to the air force, which had said it would dis-

patch fighter jets to investigate, and if necessary, shoot down, any unidentified flying objects.

"No, they definitely weren't stars," Jake told the officer at McGuire Air
Force Base at Fort Dix who took his telephone report, and who asked him
a long series of questions. "It was like somebody suspended big lights
from the sky."

Jake and his partner resumed their skywatch, but no other mysteri-
ous lights—and no air force planes—appeared that night. The *Transcript*
put their story on the front page, and even took them back up to the roof
for a photograph. Other people were seeing things in the sky, too, but that
was it for Jake. He continued his shifts at the mill post, but he never spotted anything else that made him wonder the way that pair of lights had.

His hand resting lightly on his bow now, Jake sat all through the
morning in a trance of concentration, waiting for the deer he knew were
around somewhere. He had shot at one a few days ago, but all he found
afterward was a bloody arrow. In the mill two days later, another hunter
reported coming upon a bloated carcass not far from the tree stand—the
one that got away, Jake thought. As noon neared, his stomach growled
and his attention drifted toward home, until he caught in the corner of
his eye a brush of tawny fur near the gap in the Earle fence.

Jake notched a razor-tipped arrow on the string, and without drawing back, slowly lifted his bow and sighted along the shaft. He had five
other arrows in his quiver, but he knew he would only get one shot. The
deer was fifty feet off, a spike buck, alone, stepping lightly toward the
meadow. Jake fixed his aim on the upper chest of the deer, the heart and
lungs he needed to hit for a clean kill, tracking its approach with the tip of
his arrow. At forty feet, at thirty feet, the deer still hadn't looked up, but
Jake felt on the edge of being unmasked. He was looking at his best shot,
he decided. He had reached the instant that all the long hours pointed to.
When the deer was twenty-five feet away, Jake pulled back on the string,
slow and steady, feeling the pressure as if lifting a heavy weight. He inhaled
and held, then let go, and the breath of the released arrow split the air.

He believed his aim was true, but he knew that wasn't always enough:
A shotgun shell could blast through intervening branches or defy a gust
of wind, but an arrow was easily deflected. The deer started when the arrow hit, then dashed forward awkwardly, its forelegs crumpling before it
had gone twenty yards. Jake slung his bow over his shoulder and climbed
down, hailing his companions. He had killed deer before, but never so

silently, or expertly. They gutted it, lashed it to the ladder rack of the pickup and discussed how to divide up the meat. As Jake helped hang the deer from a beam in his neighbor's garage, he heard the fire trucks wailing and a brass band blaring a block away on Broadway.

"They must have won again," he said.

He knew the commotion was for the football team's victory—the Colonials' parade was marching downtown—but for a moment it was easy to believe it was for his.

The Freehold police station was squeezed into a couple of rooms on the second floor of the yellow-brick firehouse, at the top of a long, narrow stairway in the back, and as Stu Bunton descended to walk his beat one afternoon, his holster bounced against his hip, heavy with more firepower than he had ever carried against the Japanese in the Pacific. In the navy, he had rarely even seen a gun, but as a patrolman he wore one daily. He saw that Main Street was, as usual, parked tight with cars, and he felt for his ticket book as he passed the bus station. No matter how many cars he cited, the merchants would give him an argument—too many, and he was harassing their customers; too few, and he was blocking access to their stores. Crossing Throckmorton Street he glanced up by habit at the red lightbulb on the corner utility pole, the signal system that tethered him to headquarters. Because the department had no portable radios, the only way for the station to reach an officer walking a downtown beat was to flick a switch at headquarters that turned on one of the two red lamps—the other was in front of the courthouse—and hope he noticed. The light was off now, but if Stu saw it go on, he would duck into the nearest store and call in.

After six years of waiting, several seasons of political wrangling and a second round of testing, which he topped as he had the first, Stu had finally become the police officer he had wanted to be since he was a boy. Because the radio room wouldn't give him a leave of absence—and because he wanted to make sure he had a job to return to if he failed his probationary period—he spent his first six months working almost every hour he wasn't sleeping: eleven P.M. to seven A.M., five nights a week as a dispatcher, nine-thirty A.M. to five-thirty P.M., six days a week as a cop. When he was hired onto the force permanently, his wage was $1.12 an hour, considerably less than he had made at the radio room. He inquired then about the new houses going up on Firemen's Field by the racetrack,

$10,999 apiece, but he wasn't earning enough for his interest to be taken seriously.

Some of his friends were skeptical about his new career. "What do you want to be a cop for?" asked one who had seen him in uniform recently.

"I'm doing what I want to do," Stu said. What he was thinking was, It's a hell of a lot better than what you're doing, working in the rug mill, but he held his tongue. "Are you?"

At the railroad track, Stu walked across a square of pavement paler than its surroundings, like a patch of wall from which a picture has been removed. Trains were sparser in town now—passenger service to New York halted entirely, freight traffic diminishing—and the watchmen's shacks that had guarded all the grade crossings had been dismantled. Now that almost everybody had a car—more than three-quarters of all American families had at least one—nobody seemed to need the train anymore. People drove where they wanted to go, and new roads were opening all the time; President Eisenhower had committed billions of dollars to building the Interstate Highway System. Stu's beat offered evidence of other changes, too. Across the street was the bowling alley that has once been the Liberty. Chain stores had shouldered onto Main Street (Newberry's, Grant's), and large groceries had replaced the coal yard and the lumber yard on Broad Street (Grand Union, A&P). The Norkus brothers had moved their food market to a new building, with a wide parking lot, on the edge of town out on Highway 33. When Stu passed the courthouse, he couldn't stop to see his old radio-room colleagues, who had moved out to new quarters next to their broadcast tower on Briar Hill.

Making his rounds, Stu looked in at the scene of two recent, brazen robberies that had seemed to confirm the town's wisdom in expanding its police force—the Prudential Insurance office, where a holdup man, his hand in his pocket as if brandishing a gun, had made off with $2,500 in a late-model green sedan; and Slattery's Esso Station, whose owner was waylaid by a car full of thugs at closing time, blackjacked across the mouth and relieved of the day's receipts. Two of the three gas-station robbers had been captured—Stu had stood guard duty outside the hospital room where they were being held—but the insurance money was still missing. At the Strand Stu tugged on the glass doors to make sure they were locked, as they would remain until the evening show. To earn a few extra dollars, he sometimes worked uniformed details at the theater dur-

ing weekend matinees, his official presence meant to discourage the kids
from getting too wild when Elvis Presley danced across the screen. He
stood similar duty at high-school football games. He worked the A&P,
too, on Friday nights, watching for shoplifters; occasionally, he was even
pressed into service as a pallbearer for the new funeral director in town,
Jimmy Higgins.

After leaving his job in Hightstown, Jimmy had opened a funeral
home of his own in a town that didn't have one—the wealthy enclave of
Rumson, near Sandy Hook—but his fiancee, Angela, made clear her wish
to stay in Freehold. He sold it two years later and, for $19,000, bought a
solid old white house on Center Street, behind the post office and a block
from the mill, with a wide porch and a deep backyard for parking. He
opened for business the month they were married. The wakes were
downstairs, home was upstairs. Angela taught math at the high school,
and on the days between funerals—he did nineteen his first year—Jimmy
worked in the clerical pool at Fort Monmouth, where Joseph McCarthy's
hunt for Communists had finally sputtered out. ("He has little or no respect for the law, the constitution or the president, much less human dignity," declared an anti-McCarthy editorial in the reliably Republican
Transcript. "Not a single Communist was found at Fort Monmouth,
though there was noise enough created to round up a band of saboteurs.") When Jimmy was at his government job, the funeral home calls
bounced to the answering service run by Bill Lopatin's wife, who then
called to tell him who needed him where.

As the daylight faded, Stu returned to the station and joined his partner, Gene Urbelis, in a patrol car. The department's shifts rotated
monthly, like the mill's, but were broken into odd segments—noon to
eight P.M., eight P.M. to four A.M., four A.M. to noon—that put Stu out of
sync with the rest of the town, and with his own young family. He had resigned from the Masons because he was missing too many meetings, and
his wife, Ginny, had become accustomed to keeping the house—and their
two young boys, just eighteen months apart and not yet in school—quiet
during the days when he was sleeping. She was tall, like him, but a few
years younger; they had met on the beach at Manasquan one summer
day, when he spotted her talking to a friend of his. They were married the
year before he joined the force, and had finally saved enough to buy the
house by the racetrack, on the same street where Buddy Lewis had recently been looking.

Buddy was working as a custodian in the county courthouse now, and he needed a bigger home for his growing family. The coat factory had paid a higher hourly wage, but he left when he could no longer depend on getting steady work there. On a long layoff before one recent Christmas, he had worked briefly for Bill Lopatin, and was strapped enough for gift money that he sold the carton of cigarettes he received as a holiday bonus. Bill offered to train him as a carpenter, but Buddy, with two young daughters, couldn't afford an apprenticeship, and chose instead the stability and benefits of a county job that would, he hoped, allow him to trade a rent check for a mortgage payment. He and Ruth had squeezed into several different apartments along Throckmorton Street, most recently in the home of the woman who ran the migrant center at the Colored School. Another tenant there was the man from the state who showed movies out at the migrant camps, and who sometimes set up the projector in the backyard and invited Buddy to a private screening.

The houses by the racetrack looked to Buddy as if they would fit his family well, but in the real estate office the agent kept stammering excuses about why they wouldn't. "Why don't you just tell him the truth?" the impatient secretary suggested after listening with mounting frustration.

"It's not me, you understand," the real estate agent finally explained to Buddy, who finally understood: There were still lines he couldn't cross. "If I sold to you, a lot of people would be mad."

When Stu's house was being built he had often patrolled past to check on its progress, and he steered the cruiser in its direction again this evening. Behind the lighted drapes, he knew, Ginny was busy with their boys, who would probably be asleep by the time he got home. He looped around through the West End of town, past the foundry and the coat factories and the old cannery and into the Peach Orchard section, where the police had recently raided another ramshackle house that was selling liquor and women. Easing up Throckmorton Street toward headquarters, he noticed in the gap between two houses a smoky blue-gray light flickering beneath the backyard trees, the same light he knew from inside the Strand.

The fresh gash that had been carved into the marshy earth along the western border of the Denise orchard was slowly filling with water from the feeding stream, and it sucked Walter in up to his hips as he climbed down through the muck. The hole was meant to become another irrigation pond, shared by the orchard and the neighboring farm, and contained by a concrete dam due to be poured this morning. Walter sloshed along the base of the wall-like wooden forms that had been staked into the mud, checking for gaps the slurry might leak through. He climbed back out when he heard the gears grinding on the mixer truck as it downshifted and turned off the road into the meadow. A log drive had been laid across the soggy ground to keep the heavy truck from sinking, but as it crept nearer it began to list like a ship in a storm. Walter watched more in anger than surprise as the truck slowly teetered over onto its right side.

"How many yards do you have in there?" Walter snapped when he reached the driver. The more yards of concrete, he knew, the heavier it would be, and the likelier to do just what it had done.

"Seven," the driver said.

"I told you not to come down here with any more than three."

Before the concrete could harden, a wheelbarrow brigade was organized to carry it the quarter mile from where it was beached to where it belonged—shovel, push, dump, shovel, push, dump, until it had been emptied into the dam. A cable was attached to the mixer, and a bulldozer tugged it upright. The first truck was barely gone when a second arrived and started down the log road at a familiar, disquieting angle. Walter tried to wave the truck back, but it was already rolling onto its side, the left this time, like a sick cow.

"How many yards do you have?" Walter asked the second driver, though he could already guess the answer.

"Seven."

"All right, now you're going to do what I tell you," Walter ordered as firmly as if he were still a lieutenant.

The wheelbarrows and the bulldozer were pressed into service again, but the trucks that followed, finally carrying the lighter loads that Walter had specified, crossed the meadow without tipping. The concrete hardened, the forms were removed and the water began pooling behind the new dam, proving again what Walter had learned many times over in the orchard—that the land bent to his will more easily than people did.

Before the war, Walter had passed up a chance to study engineering at the Stevens Institute of Technology, a decision that, on days when he was stuck in the mud of the orchard, he sometimes regretted. His mind was inclined toward science and mechanics, and he was happiest when tackling problems that yielded to rational solutions: What new peach varieties should they try planting this year? Why was the sorter dropping so many seventy-two counts in the sixty-four count bin? Was there enough time before harvest for another round of sulfur spray? Some of his best days were spent in his workshop, zipped into coveralls, coaxing a balky pump or a sputtering tractor back to life. But many other problems were beyond his powers—frost and drought, codling moths and peach scab, hard-headed concrete-mixer drivers and, above all else, unreliable migrant pickers—and as the seasons wore on, the aggravations wore on him.

"You've got a screen missing here," the state labor inspector said one day, scribbling on a clipboard as he toured the Mickey Mouse camp.

Walter had replaced the window screen that was missing at the inspector's last visit, but it was gone again, torn out by tenants who preferred an unobstructed egress for tossing out their waste.

"Why don't you come after I've gotten it fixed?" Walter asked in frustration. "You blame us. You've got to start blaming the people who do it."

The worst part of being a farmer, Walter had long since learned, was that he had to be a landlord, too. Because the crop demanded a larger workforce than the town itself could supply, the orchard, like every other large local farm, had to hire, and briefly house, crews of traveling pickers. The Denises could accommodate about fifty workers at a time. (The other hundred they employed at the peak of the harvest were borrowed from local potato farms.) Some farmers worried more than others about how their workers lived. When a field representative from the state's migrant labor division visited the Freehold Rotary Club, he showed photos of the Mickey Mouse camp, citing it as a model of decent housing. Walter's mother watched over the orchard's regular migrants with a maternal eye, and when they were sick or injured she took them to doctors that she herself, as a Christian Scientist, didn't believe in a need for.

Walter's house stood just across the road from the migrant camp, but a much wider gulf separated his life from theirs. The migrants were mostly blacks from the South, and though he had worked with them since boyhood, he was no nearer to understanding them. He grew older with each harvest, more deeply rooted in his own family, but the seasons seemed never to change them. He and Marilyn had three children now— a daughter had followed their two sons—and the orchard was a paradise for them: the dirt lanes and shadowy barns for exploring, the ponds for swimming in summer and skating in the winter. Walter especially loved to watch his daughter squealing as she rode in an empty crate in the packinghouse, whipping around the turn on the roller line like at an amusement park.

Among the farmworkers, new children appeared regularly, too, but they multiplied mostly without benefit of wedlock, and while some attended the Migrant School on Court Street, many others did not, and remained confined, like their parents, by illiteracy. Walter banked money for some of the migrants in savings accounts, but card games and barroom binges emptied the pay envelopes of many others. A few attended the Bible schools and religious programs offered by the local churches, but whatever private creed the others followed was none he recognized. Walter never drank himself, and he warned them against it, but Saturday nights were inevitably fueled by liquor. He defused violence when it flared in the camp, but was powerless against explosions elsewhere: In two successive autumns, two of his workers were charged with murder— a man who didn't live at the camp stabbed a fellow picker, puncturing his lung, in a quarrel over a bottle of whiskey outside a bar on Highway 33; and a woman who did live there stabbed her boyfriend in the groin and upper leg during a Saturday night argument at a house in the Peach Orchard section of town. And the improvements Walter made to the living quarters were often greeted by seeming indifference: When he replaced the outhouses with flush toilets, he found a pair of blue jeans stuffed in one, as if by a tenant who, unaccustomed to such conveniences, seemed to think it might double as a washing machine.

Until the war, and for the first years after, migrants had been regarded locally with a sort of bemused disinterest. "Our colored friends from the south," the *Transcript* wrote in an editorial, were "a picturesque lot" whose clothes were "loud enough to make the eyes pop out of a potato," and who were possessed with "the gift of song and a gay disposition." The local blacks, protective of whatever status they had managed to earn for themselves, mixed uneasily with the unschooled visitors. Buddy Lewis cringed when he saw migrants walk barefoot down Throckmorton Street, or heard them shout at the screen at the movies, warning the cowboys against the Indians.

But over the next decade—as the schools were desegregated locally, and the civil rights movement was born nationally—concern mounted for the plight of what the *Transcript* now called the "pathetic migrants." The camps on some of the larger farms had evolved into year-round settlements—"rural slums . . . that are like a cancer," thundered an outraged ed-

itorial, "focal points for immorality, crime, poor health conditions and social problems . . . that wring from unfortunates even what little they have."

Of the 250 migrant camps in the county, only a handful ranked
among the most grievous offenders, but their sins sparked a wide outcry.
"There should be two indictments here," argued the court-ordered lawyer
for a migrant convicted in a fatal stabbing after a gambling dispute at a
potato camp. "The second should be against the feudal system which ex-
ploits migrant laborers and breeds these incidents." In another case, a migrant was acquitted of wounding his common-law wife with a shotgun
blast at a notorious camp with the cruelly ironic name of Prosperity
Street. The real blame, the jury was told and apparently believed, lay with
the society that had permitted such "deplorable conditions."

The newspapers published harsh photos of squalid hovels and sad-
eyed children, compiled grim lists of camp deaths (by accident, by fire, by
violence), and told the story of a boy whose face was scarred and whose
arm hung limp after being gnawed by rats. A grand jury was impaneled to
investigate. Most farmers, it found, provided "clean and well-supervised
facilities," but a "small percentage" of others so thoroughly ignored health
and safety codes—open cesspits, mounds of garbage, swarms of vermin,
dirty water, rickety tarpaper shacks—that their camps were "virtual hell
holes."

"Stabled animals are better off," the grand jury declared in a scathing
presentment to the Superior Court that called for the strict enforcement
of building and sanitary codes, for the condemnation of camps beyond
rehabilitation, and for a continued investigation by the county prosecutor, who was directed to seek indictments if conditions didn't improve.
After the judge who heard the grand jury's findings seemed to deflect
some blame to the migrants themselves—especially the recent influx
from Puerto Rico, an island he called "the filthiest place I've ever seen"—
he was dismissed by the governor for "intemperate conduct."

In the wake of the grand jury, inspectors appeared more often at the
Denise orchard, but they rarely found any violations to cite. The migrants
gradually drifted back south as each variety of apple was exhausted, leaving the camp mostly vacant by Thanksgiving, when the last of the Winesaps were finally harvested. The dwellings weren't designed for cold
weather, and Walter would have preferred them empty in the off-season,
but a handful remained occupied by migrants who reasoned that even
sporadic winter work at the orchard was better than whatever they might

have gone home to in the Carolinas. They moved apples out of the cold-storage warehouse, packed them into crates in the drafty packinghouse, and pruned deadwood from the trees the next crop would grow on.

In the middle of an afternoon in the week before Christmas one year, Walter was in the packinghouse, preparing an order for shipment, and blowing on his hands occasionally to keep warm. Kerosene space heaters, the same kind the camp dwellings relied on, chugged and sighed and tried to drive the chill from the tall, yawning space, creating pockets of hearthlike comfort separated by corridors of hollow cold. Walter started and turned when someone came crashing in from outside. The messenger was frantic, his breath fogging as he shouted the worst news Walter could imagine hearing.

"There's a fire in the camp!"

Walter gunned his pickup down the slope and across the road to the cluster of migrant dwellings. A plume of smoke rose from a wood-frame cabin behind the Mickey Mouse building.

"There's a little girl in there!" a woman screamed as Walter dashed out.

The woman had been minding five children—four of her own, all under the age of five, and a thirteen-month old girl whose mother was in the hospital after delivering another baby. The girl's father was at work somewhere in the orchard. The five children were left alone in the cabin while the woman visited a neighbor, less than fifty feet away. When her oldest child burst in, crying about a fire, she dashed back out. Her own four children got out safely, but the other girl was trapped inside.

"She's on the bed, she's on the bed," she screamed.

Walter ducked his head and shielded his face with his arm as he approached the burning cabin. He swung open the front door and found its frame outlined in flames. The rooms inside had vanished behind a shroud of smoke so thick it seemed solid. He went in low, crawling beneath the gray pall, groping blindly toward a bedpost he hoped to grasp and drag out, but smoke filled his lungs until he felt as if he were tunneling through earth. He backed out and watched helplessly as flames broke through the roof. The fire trucks were barreling in off the road behind him—their sirens finally drowning out the crackle of burning wood, the sobs of the woman and her children—but he knew they would be too late. The flames hissed out into steam under the spray of the hoses, the smoke whitening as it lifted, revealing the charred, wet wood. Several firemen with air packs rushed inside, but the lifeless child they carried out was beyond anyone's help. The woman wailed, the children cried, and Walter offered the only thing he had—his prayers.

The cabin smoldered in the cold like one of the ruined houses in Frauenberg or Bettviller or any of the other occupied villages the 324th had blasted the Germans from. Walter suspected a space heater of sparking the fire—upended perhaps, or set too near something flammable—but he stood mute and powerless before whatever larger forces had placed the child there and taken her life. He hadn't been able to save her as he had once saved a wounded soldier, and the loss brought him low, leaving him to face the darkest, saddest Christmas since the one he spent huddled in a foxhole overlooking the Blies River. He had been armed there, though, with weapons and a cause, but where exactly was the enemy here, he wondered, and what was he meant to fight with?

Before starting the long climb up to the police department's home atop the firehouse, Buddy Lewis paused and stood alone at the bottom of the narrow stairway, still unsure if the job he had been promised was really waiting for him at the top. He was ready to become a police officer, but he wasn't sure the police were ready for him. He had walked over from the courthouse on his morning break, hoping to find out when he was supposed to start. Police hiring was governed by civil service now, and Buddy's combined score on the written and physical tests had placed him first among more than two dozen candidates for the department's two latest openings. The mayor and council had approved his appointment, the chief had taken him to Charlie Miller's haberdashery to be measured for a uniform, but he had heard nothing since. He wanted to know when he should give notice to the county, when he was due at the state police academy for training, when he would be sworn in as the first black police officer in the town's history.

A few years earlier the town had hired a black man, the strapping Joe Baskerville, as a special part-time officer, but he functioned more as a glorified bouncer for Ollwerther's on Throckmorton Street, the only bar in town where blacks could routinely drink. His main duty was to stand outside on Friday and Saturday nights and break up drunken brawls. He was strong and reliable, but he had no training and no radio. If he needed help from headquarters he had to duck into Kehs' market next door to use the phone. Buddy, on the other hand, would be a full-fledged member of the department, riding in the front seat of the cruiser as a partner to white officers who were more accustomed to blacks riding in the back.

For Buddy, becoming a police officer had never been the kind of single-minded dream it was for Stu Bunton, but when the test was announced he recognized the size of the opportunity it offered, and he asked a friend who was a math teacher to help him study. At thirty-five, already at the upper limit of eligibility for a job whose starting salary was no more than he was already making, he was drawn instead by the less tangible benefits—the chance for advancement, the respect, the service he could offer his town. News of the appointment had elated his large extended family, especially his older brother, Guggy, the Gulistans' old center fielder, who had been a constable for many years, serving papers when needed in the black neighborhoods, and who only wished he were young enough to apply himself. The town's black citizens had already begun calling Buddy at home with questions and problems, so relieved were they to finally have what they perceived as an ally in a place that had often seemed stacked with adversaries.

"You're our Jackie Robinson," more than one well-wisher told him.

Some of the town's whites stopped to congratulate him, too, but others offered blunter opinions. "You showed them how smart you are, isn't that enough?" asked one man, who thought that passing the test was one thing, but that actually putting on a uniform was quite another. "What else do you want?"

From the department itself Buddy felt a distinct chill. One officer, who had played on the football team a few years before him, had extended a welcome, but the others were loud in their silence. The police arrested a lot more blacks than whites, it seemed to them, a number swollen by the migrants, and they were skeptical about having one on their side. Stu had especially bitter memories of his sister's rape in the railroad yard while he was serving in the Pacific, too far away to do anything but seethe: The black man who was the chief suspect was never arrested, for lack of evidence, and was dead by the time Stu joined the force. Veterans mostly, the white officers hadn't served beside blacks in the war, and they weren't enthusiastic about serving beside them now. They all knew, and had even cheered for, Danny Lewis—an All-American at Wisconsin and now a fullback with the Detroit Lions, rated as one of the five fastest men in the National Football League—but that didn't mean they wanted to share a squad car with his uncle.

At the top of the stairs, Buddy opened the door into the muffled clatter of the small offices that housed the department. Stu sat at a typewriter, recording summonses and judgments: Because he had learned to type in high school, the navy had made him a radioman, and now the police chief had made him clerk to the municipal court, an extra unpaid assignment that consumed a small portion of each workday. The chief greeted Buddy cordially, but was evasive about a starting date, and just about everything else related to the pending job.

"What about the police academy?" Buddy asked.

"I don't know yet, but you don't really need that before you start," the chief demurred.

"Is the uniform ready?"

"I don't think so, but you could start in your street clothes."

"I don't know if I should be out there without any training or any uniform," Buddy ventured, but the chief assured him he had nothing to worry about.

"It's shift work, you know—a lot of nights," the chief added, as if that might dissuade him.

Buddy left with no more information than he had arrived with, his steps echoing down the stairs as the door closed behind him. The police station was small enough that the other officers couldn't help but overhear Buddy's conversation with the chief, and when he was gone, Stu heard another sound—somebody clapped, and the slow muted applause spread through the room. It looked as if Buddy might be retreating, just as most of the department had hoped he would.

Buddy's job at the courthouse was to supervise the prisoners who worked as custodians, and when he returned from the police station, he shepherded his crew, a ragged-looking bunch wearing whatever they had been arrested in and exuding a faint scent of the lice spray their bunks were treated with, up to the second floor. They were all minor miscreants, serving a month or two for being drunk and disorderly or failing to pay child support, and he treated them with the same respect he had accorded the German POWs in Belgium. There was nothing evil in them, in his view, they were just men who had taken a bad turn. As he watched them sweep, he tried to figure out what he should do about the police job.

The courthouse had moved a few years earlier—two blocks off Main Street to a rise overlooking the triangular, green park punctuated by the Battle Monument, leaving the old building to serve as the county's Hall of

Records—and from a window, Buddy could see the front portico of Box-wood Hall, the grand, white-columned house that was its neighbor. When he was a boy his mother had taken in laundry for the wealthy owners of the house, and sent him to deliver it. Always go to the front door, she told him, not the back, a lesson that rooted early and deeply in him. In the first year of the war, some high school boys were enlisted to help out at a farm short of hands, and a teacher put Buddy in charge of the group.

"I don't know why they have a nigger as leader," one boy wondered loud enough for Buddy to hear.

The other boys braced for a fight as Buddy walked toward him. "You go home tonight and look up that word in the dictionary, and you see if it applies to me," he said firmly, deflating him without a punch. "And then don't ever say it to me again."

Black citizens in all parts of America had begun to take a similar stand in the years since the war. In Montgomery, Alabama, a seamstress named Rosa Parks had refused to move to the back of the bus one day, sparking a year-long citywide bus boycott that brought to national prominence a young minister who was serving at his first church, Rev-erend Martin Luther King, Jr. The United States Supreme Court, in the *Brown v. Board of Education of Topeka* case, had struck down as unconsti-tutional the "separate but equal" doctrine that had allowed public schools to remain segregated—a decision that a leading black newspaper called a "second emancipation proclamation," but that also unleashed a wave of school integration battles. President Eisenhower had to send the para-troopers of the 101st Airborne Division to Little Rock, Arkansas, where they fixed their bayonets to their rifles and escorted black students past the jeering mobs to formerly all-white Central High School.

In Freehold—where the schools had integrated without incident soon after the war—the challenges were less dramatic. The minister of Buddy's church organized local protests against racial atrocities in the South, and more benign neglect here at home. The owner of a downtown restaurant accused town officials of "persecuting" her with excessive in-spections because she dared to seat black customers on a street where their trade had previously been unwelcome. "If colored people are good enough to plow your fields and fight in the army, then they are good enough to eat in a restaurant on your Main Street," she angrily told the council. Black students walked out in protest from a high-school assem-bly when the singing of "Old Black Joe" ended with mocking comments from some whites. The town's lone black lawyer—or the nearest to one anyway, since he had never passed the bar—was a perennial thorn at council meetings, rising in his white shirt and skinny tie to complain about the lack of gutters and sewers in the Peach Orchard, the lack of a black officer on the police force.

Buddy had always stood up for himself before, but he wasn't quite sure what was standing against him now. The more he turned it over in his mind, the more complex it became, a dilemma that confused and frustrated him more than any simple racial insult he had endured. He knew that many of the white officers just didn't trust him—that they worried what would happen if, when partnered with him, they were confronted by a man with a gun in a Throckmorton Street alley—but he didn't really trust them either. Just as they balked at putting their lives in his hands, so did he at putting his in theirs.

He felt more alone in his decision than any other he had ever faced. Nobody whose advice he normally might have sought could see the issues clearly enough to help. His family and friends were blinded by their pride and excitement at his ascension. The mayor and council could assure him of their public support, but they couldn't tell him much about the private mood of the police department itself. Joe Baskerville's insight was limited by his own narrow and peripheral role as a special-duty officer: His main contact with the white cops was when they arrived to make arrests in the wake of a fight. Buddy could think of only one person who was both informed and neutral, who knew both him and the police—Fred Quinn, the former mayor, who had grown up with his mother and been a staunch family ally ever since. "Don't worry Sadie, I'll take care of it," he would tell Mrs. Lewis if she called with a problem, and he always did.

"Do you think I'm doing the right thing?" Buddy asked when he went to Quinn's house and laid out his concerns.

"Bud, do you want to be happy?" Quinn asked him back.

"Of course I do."

"Then leave them alone. If they don't want you, they're just going to make your life miserable there."

When he looked at himself, and the police, through Quinn's eyes, the whole picture snapped into sharp focus. Buddy finally realized that, for all their surface differences, he and the police were alike in one critical way: They were steadfast and prickly of temperament, and not likely to yield to anything they perceived as an assault on who they were or what they believed. If the police were going to push, and Buddy was not going to bend, then somebody was going to wind up in trouble sometime. He thanked Quinn, and, his mind clearing and his burden lifting, began composing his resignation on the way out the door.

"Why the hell are you doing this?" his brother Guggy exploded when he learned of the decision. "Who made you do it?"

"Nobody made me do anything," Buddy answered, and he gave him the same answer he gave anybody else who asked. "I just found out I'm no Jackie Robinson."

"I can't accept this," the chief said when Buddy had climbed the stairs again, this time bearing a letter of resignation. "Everybody will think I had something to do with it."

"I'll take full responsibility," Buddy assured him. "I'm not making any accusations against you."

"Well, let's go down and see the mayor," the chief suggested.

They walked together in silence down the long stairway. The mayor, Bart Callahan, was also an undertaker, and his funeral home stood two doors down from the firehouse. His face took on the grim cast of one of his mourners when he heard the news. He was ready for an integrated police department, and he believed the town was, too, and he viewed the resignation as a large step backward. If not Buddy, went his unspoken question—if not the scion of one of the most respected black families in town, the top scorer on the exam, the one unmistakably qualified black candidate in sight—then who?

"You'll be secure in the job, Buddy," Callahan told him. "Nobody can take it away once you're in."

But it wasn't the mayor who would be riding in the patrol car at night, worrying about his partner's loyalty as his partner worried about his, and Buddy stood his ground, offering no other reason than that he just didn't want to anymore. It had taken him long enough to figure out himself, and he didn't expect he could explain it to them.

"No, I've made up my mind about this," he said firmly, and he walked back to the courthouse alone.

11.

"Half the Town's on Fire"

As the cards came around the table, Jake Errickson picked his up one by one, fanning them out near his chest to inspect the hand he had been dealt. The game was five-card draw poker, nothing wild, with a quarter ante. Smoke from the cigarette in the ashtray beside him curled up into the blue haze that overhung the dim social hall of the Lithuanian Club, where the rug mill foremen were gathered for their monthly stag evening together. Jake quietly grouped and ordered his cards into the most promising pattern, studying what he had and calculating what he needed, a process that involved instinct as much as arithmetic. The clutch of hearts kept jumping out at him, the ace, the king and the ten, presenting possibilities that were forbiddingly remote, but too tantalizing to pass up. He had played enough poker in his life to know not to draw to an inside straight, but he hoped he might pick up a flush, or maybe a royal pair, and he held the hearts tightly.

"I'll take two," he said when the dealer turned to him, and he tossed down his discards.

The evening had started with the roast beef dinner the foremen had cooked themselves—Jake, as usual, pitched in with the mashed potatoes—proceeded through a round of singing with Harry Grasberger at the piano, and then dispersed among the card tables. The conversation wandered almost everywhere except into the mill where they had spent the day, and were due again in the morning. The Foremen's Club was a social group, a reprieve from work, not an extension of it. More than a century of rug-making experience was clustered in Jake's game—the other players were Percy Lewis, the superintendent of broad jacquard, and his immediate boss; Harold McCormack, the industrial relations director; Art Tain from quality control and his brother, Charlie, from time study; and Dick Dorian from the spinning plant in Roselle Park—but all the attention focused now on the cards they had each drawn to finish their hands.

"I'm out," Percy Lewis said, laying his cards down and pushing away from the table, but everyone else fingered their chips contemplatively.

Jake blinked hard and then widened his eyes as he stared at his hand, struggling to cap the gusher that was welling up inside. He had drawn exactly the cards he would have in a dream, the jack and the queen of hearts, and his first impulse was to turn them over with a triumphant flourish, to share the sheer improbable joy of his luck with the rest of the table. He had never seen anything like it in a lifetime of poker, a royal straight flush, a hand that looked as if it had been lifted whole from a fresh, unshuffled deck, and he gazed at it with the same slack-jawed adoration he would have accorded any other object of such unexpected radiance. He slid the jack and queen into clear view, reassuring himself that neither was a phantom diamond masquerading as a heart.

"I'm in for two," Harold McCormack said, tossing in a pair of dollar bills.

The whisper and jingle of money accumulating in the center of the table stirred Jake from his aesthetic reverie. What he was holding, he realized now, was as valuable as it was beautiful. Though no one else knew it yet, the pot was already his—not even four aces could beat a royal straight flush—and the only question left was how high it would mount.

"I'll see you, and three better," Jake said, counting five singles from his own pile.

The four other players looked from their cards to the pot and back again, weighing the cost of staying in the game, and all decided to make the investment. Jake felt a jab at his shoulder, an elbow of acknowledgment from Percy Lewis, who, back from the bathroom, had peeked at the golden hand.

"I'll see, and two better," McCormack said.

Jake was delighted that someone other than himself had a hand strong enough to keep raising the stakes. The other players thought harder about the latest price, but nobody dropped out, and the cash multiplied. Jake made his face as blank as he could, and tried to squeak the pot up one more time.

"And two better," Jake said.

From all around the table came one more contribution from players who had climbed too high to bail out now, until McCormack, all of his money having migrated from his seat to the pot, finally said, "Call."

"Four nines," McCormack said, laying down a hand he couldn't imagine anyone beating.

The other players set down the cards they had hoped might be enough to win themselves—a flush, two pairs, three of a kind—until Jake silenced all pretenders to the throne.

"Look at this," he said, finally able to show the rare gift he had barely been able to keep to himself.

"Sonofabitch!" McCormack cried, his face reddening as he picked up the leftover cards and flung them across the room.

Jake swept in the cash and counted it—forty-five dollars, by far the most he had ever won—and signaled to Sid Jackson, his ride home, that he was ready to leave.

"Hey, it's only ten o'clock," one of the losers grumbled halfheartedly. The games sometimes stretched as late as eleven. "Don't we get a chance to win it back?"

"Sid and his father are waiting for me," Jake pleaded, an excuse that was genuine but also superfluous. A royal straight flush was such an exotic creature that most of the players privileged enough to glimpse it understood instinctively that it should be left to retire unchallenged. "They have to get home."

At work the next morning, Jake made his foreman's rounds through a mill that needed a lucky break itself—something just as grand and transforming as the hand he had been dealt last night. He was relieved to hear the clatter of the looms again after a recent twelve-day silence—imposed by a wildcat strike that started in the department where Dot was a weaver—but he knew the sound wasn't as loud as it had been a year or two earlier, and he wondered when the volume would reach that reassuring level again. As a manager, he had crossed the picket line each morning, while Dot, a union member, stayed home, where conversations were confined to other topics each evening. What sparked the walkout was a small and simple dispute over the promotion of two Axminster setters, but what lurked beneath it, what made it spread so quickly through the one thousand members of Local 26 of the Textile Workers Union of America, what made it just the latest eruption of the growing mistrust between the mill and its workers, was the larger and more complex problem of the company's economic health. In the years since the initial burst of postwar prosperity, the mill's fortunes had been rising and falling like the heddles that lifted the threads into the patterned rugs on the jacquard looms, a new and disquieting rhythm dictated by forces far beyond Freehold's control.

Jake's rounds took him through the most recent addition to the mill, the five stories that were tacked onto its northern end in 1950 in an attempt to better supply a changing market. The looms he passed were gargantuan—nine, twelve, fifteen, even eighteen feet wide, the carpet spilling out of them broad enough to cover floors as fully as consumers now demanded. Decorative tastes had shifted away from patterned area rugs to solid-colored wall-to-wall carpet, and the mill had tried to shift with them. Karagheusian's biggest, most visible job lately was not a richly figured deco tableau like the one Radio City Music Hall had once ordered, but a plain gray salt-and-pepper design with a textured loop pile—five miles of it, nine feet wide, for the forty-five-story, stainless-steel Socony-Mobil Building at Lexington Avenue and Forty-second Street in New York. Oriental patterns had fallen far enough from favor that the company was preparing to close its shrunken import division.

Crossing the Center Street bridge into the old section of the mill, Jake pushed through the doors of the corner lunchroom—the only place where smoking was permitted—and lit up a cigarette. The company's president had gathered Jake and all the other foremen here two years earlier to outline an even larger problem the mill faced, something more troubling and harder to address than a mere shift in carpet fashions—a flood of foreign carpet, manufactured so cheaply in overseas mills that American companies were losing market share at an alarming rate. Blame rested largely, as a worried editorial in the *Transcript* put it, with "excessive handouts by the Federal government to war-stricken countries." In its zeal to rebuild the nations that had crumbled into the rubble of Europe, America was helping to provide raw materials to shattered industries, and then easing trade by lowering its own tariff barriers. The tariff on imported carpet had plunged from 60 percent to 25 percent since the war, and Congress considered dropping it further still, perhaps as low as 10 percent. A delegation of company and union officials, including Jake's poker partner Harold McCormack, traveled to Washington to lobby against the reduction.

"Every yard of carpet imported into the United States means the loss

of one hour of American labor," Karagheusian president Steele Winterer
had told the foremen.

Winterer's charts had starkly illustrated a troubling gap: Rug workers
in Germany, Japan, Italy, Belgium and England earned as little as a quarter of their American counterparts' wages. Compounding the import onslaught was a separate domestic challenge—stiffening competition from
cheap carpets made on tufting machines, a technology that had arisen in
the Southern bedspread industry but that was now transforming the carpet business more radically than any innovation since the introduction of
the power loom more than a century earlier. Karagheusian itself had, in
1952, bought a plant in Albany, Georgia—where wages, in the absence of
a union, fell somewhere between England and Freehold—and was tufting
carpet from cotton, instead of weaving it from wool. Suspicions spread
about Freehold's future, but were regularly dispelled by confident company pronouncements.

"Pay no attention to any rumors you've heard about future operations," Winterer had told the foremen. "We have no other interest but a
continued efficient and improved operation here."

Jake had always accepted the company's statements as sincere, and its
intentions as honorable. Loyalty was an inherited trait in him. His grandfather, a farmer, had also delivered mail along the Smithburg route, until
he finally keeled over dead in the wagon one day; the horse brought him
home. His father had worked for thirty years at the Farmers' Exchange on
Throckmorton Street, until the Friday evening when he was told that the
business was closing, and he needn't bother to come in on Monday; he
had wrapped rugs in the mill's shipping department ever since. But Jake's
hopeful belief in the mill's future was built on what he considered a stur-
dier foundation than his own inborn habits of trust—the sheer weight of
the factory itself, and the imprint it had left on the town over more than
half a century.

Jake stubbed out his cigarette in the lunchroom and continued on
his errand to the main office in the old section of the mill, passing age-
burnished looms in the narrow-jacquard department that had been
bolted into the same places on the floor since their ocean voyage from
Kidderminster. The mill was still issuing regular paychecks to the couple
of dozen employees with more than fifty years of service who reported to
work each day. (Alf Draper, once the oldest of them all, had finally retired
home to England at eighty-four, but the strained postwar economy there

soon convinced him to return to Freehold.) Only a handful of places in all
of America—Amsterdam, Auburn and Yonkers in New York, Framing-
ham and Worcester in Massachusetts, Bloomsburg, Carlisle and Philadelphia in Pennsylvania—could match the rugmaking expertise clustered in
Freehold, and as Jake moved among weavers and looms so deeply rooted
here, he couldn't imagine that any of it could ever leave. On his way back
to broad jacquard, though, he glanced warily at the lone tufting machine
in the mill, a curiosity when it was first installed, but now something
nearer an enemy with whom an uncertain truce prevailed.

All through the winter, Jake spent more hours than he would have
liked juggling schedules at his foreman's desk, trying to fairly distribute
too little work among too many workers. Business had declined 30 percent since the president's warning visit to the lunchroom, and the payroll
was down to just over half the postwar peak of seventeen hundred. The
union had relented without a fight when the company broke its contract
and asked for a pay cut. Weavers with as much as fifteen years experience
were laid off, and many of the rest were sharing three-day workweeks. In
January, the semiannual carpet markets yielded a decent crop of dealer
orders for Karagheusian, but demand for the cheaper tufted cotton and
rayon from Georgia was threatening the more costly woven wool from
Freehold. The gloom of February was broken briefly by a camera crew
from CBS television, taping a segment for the Sunday afternoon show,
Let's Take a Trip. In March, Jake started a month of overnights, the shift
that, even in flush times, wrung the most from his body and his family.

In the deepest hours of the night, the whole mill belonged to Jake, the
senior manager on the shift, and his duties included patrolling its dark
and brooding bulk for fire hazards and other troubles. He usually made
two rounds, one soon after midnight and the other just before dawn,
starting in the oldest section, by the Central Railroad station, and finishing in the newest, overlooking the house where he grew up and his parents still lived. At five-thirty one morning in the middle of a bleary
March, he walked alone through the narrow-jacquard department, where
the tufting machine sat as silent and alone as the old looms surrounding
it. Through the tall grids of windows, he saw a weak, gray light rising outside. Maybe 150 people were at work now, almost all of them at the big
looms in his own department, broad jacquard. Jake poked his head into
the cigarette-break haze of the lunchroom and continued across the
bridge and up to the fifth-floor velvet department, where solid-colored

carpet was woven on looms stripped of the intricate jacquard mecha-
nisms that patterned rugs required. He walked to the windows and admired the lofty view—the morning slowly ascending through the town
that lapped the mill on all sides, asleep still beneath the spiny canopy of
winter-stripped trees. But then he noticed something out of place: an unfamiliar pair of flatbed trucks parked in the lot below. The boxy screened
elevator took him down to investigate.

"What are you here for?" Jake asked the driver of the first truck, who
had rolled down his window.

"We've got orders to pick up some looms to take to North Carolina,"
the driver said.

Jake's initial impulse was to regard the truckers as thieves whom the
authorities should be summoned to remove, until he realized, with sadness and shock, that it was in fact the authorities themselves who had already done the summoning.

"Nobody told me anything about that," a stunned Jake managed to
say. "There won't be anybody here who can help you until eight—that's
when the millwrights come in."

"Is it all right for us to stay parked here?" the driver asked.

"Why don't you move over by the railroad track before the lot starts
to fill," Jake instructed before returning upstairs with the news no one
wanted to hear.

"Well, we knew that was coming," one of the weavers said resignedly.

A formal announcement came later in the day: Karagheusian was
transferring its entire velvet-weaving operation to a sprawling new plant
it had bought in rural North Carolina from a bankrupt rayon manufacturer—240,000 square feet on 140 acres, far more room than Freehold
could offer to a department that was expanding to meet growing con-
sumer demand for plain wall-to-wall carpets. The move was expected to
take almost a year, and cost one hundred local jobs.

"The company has no intention of transferring any other operations
out of the present mill," Karagheusian's president assured the union, and
the town.

Making his rounds through the somber velvet department that night,
Jake was halted by an unfamiliar absence, the empty spot from which several small looms had already been removed—disassembled, lowered onto
the trucks and dispatched south. The floor they had stood upon was dark
and mottled, as if by a shadow that had failed to follow. He walked back

and forth in a space he had never crossed before, measuring the vacancy the way a tongue probes the hole left by a lost tooth.

Working alone in his shop on a quiet spring evening, Bill Lopatin slid a slender, whippy strip of cove molding incrementally along his miter saw, stopping every 6 inches to cut it at a ninety-degree angle. When he had a dozen short pencil lengths of the gently curved wood, he carried them over to a large plywood box that sat like a sarcophagus in the middle of the concrete floor, beside a stack of bookshelf-sized pine boards he had cut earlier. He held a board vertically along one of the box's corner edges, hammered it lightly into place with finish nails, then crowned it with a piece of molding. Stepping back to check before nailing the next in, he was pleased to see that the crisp and narrow shadow line cast by his simple wooden trim made it a fair likeness of the Doric pilasters on the solemn monument in the photograph he was working from—the Tomb of the Unknown Soldier in Arlington National Cemetery, a shrine he had first visited on his senior-class trip in high school. His version was smaller, though, ten feet long by five feet wide by five feet high, its dimensions dictated by the size of the flatbed truck it would ride upon in the upcoming Memorial Day parade.

After years of delays, the remains of unidentified servicemen killed in both the Second World War and Korea were scheduled for interment in Arlington on Memorial Day, and Post 4374 of the Veterans of Foreign Wars planned to commemorate the occasion with a float in the local parade. Bill, a charter member, had volunteered his carpentry skills. When his wooden replica was finished, it would be painted the same pure white as the marble original, and the engraved inscription would be carefully hand-lettered on: HERE RESTS IN HONORED GLORY AN AMERICAN SOLDIER KNOWN BUT TO GOD. Board by board, pilaster by pilaster, he ornamented his way around the box, as the dusk breeze through the window stirred up the scent of sawdust.

The workshop sat in the rear shadow of a four-story buff-brick building on Main Street, a proper home finally for Lopatin Construction after decades of makeshift quarters in Bill's basement, his father's garage and the backs of their respective trucks. They had built the low, L-shaped concrete-block structure as an addition to the tall front building, and then moved in themselves after the original tenant, a tinsmith, moved out. Bill was running the business now—his father had finally retired, at seventy-nine—and work had continued to flow steadily through the shop in recent years. Residential jobs still occupied most of his time, but he had stretched out lately with some larger commercial projects, too—a two-story redbrick furniture store on Throckmorton Street; a small factory of steel and concrete near the old hobo jungle by the railroad tracks; and several ambitious renovations of Main Street storefronts. He had proven especially adept at helping merchants expand and modernize their quarters in the old and cramped downtown buildings.

Straightening up after affixing the last pilaster, Bill felt a familiar twinge in his back, a persistent souvenir from the war. He had first injured it in the rough landing after his flak-plagued thirteenth bombing mission, and it had flared up periodically in the years since, most recently when he bent over to pick up a piece of wood while working alone on a storage closet in a client's basement. Frozen double in pain, he managed to crawl up the stairs, into his truck for an awkward drive home, then into his bed, where he had to spend a week before he could stand up straight again. He allowed himself a moment now to admire the wooden tomb, because he knew he wouldn't see it in the parade. He and Selma usually planned their annual vacation around their wedding anniversary—June 6, also the anniversary of D-Day—and they expected to be gone by Memorial Day, starting a driving tour through New England.

On the warm and clear Friday morning of the parade, while Bill was heading for Vermont and President Eisenhower was paying respects at the solemn rite in Arlington, Walter Denise brought his family into town from the orchard. Despite all his decorations, Walter never marched himself, preferring to stand privately with his memories on the sidewalk and watch. The parade was the largest the town had yet staged: sixty units, a thousand marchers and one Nike antiaircraft missile—disarmed, local officials were assured—from the arsenal that had been deployed around America's coastal cities to deflect any bomber attack the Soviets might attempt. (Just a week earlier, eight live Nikes had exploded accidentally when a new trigger device was being installed in one at a base in Middletown, near Sandy Hook, killing six soldiers and four civilian workers.) The long, finned, spearlike missile sailed safely up Main Street, followed by the VFW float. The crowds fell into respectful silence as Bill's tomb passed, an army sergeant from Fort Monmouth standing rigid sentinel in dress uniform beside it. At the ceremonies at the racetrack at parade's end, the VFW's entry won first prize as "most original and appropriate" float, and was invited to appear in another parade in Atlantic City. Bill's onetime political sponsor, Clifton Barkalow, a state assemblyman now, struggled to make himself heard over the gleeful noise of out-of-school children on a free and sunny holiday.

"I hope these youngsters with us will never have to go through the sad experience of war," he said in a tone that mixed fatherly annoyance with hope.

The Memorial Day ceremonies marked the unofficial start of another summer—an emancipated idyll for the children so giddy with anticipation, but for Walter the season of his hardest labor. His orchard was warming and growing and demanding attention. The strawberries occupied him for the next two weeks, and the peaches elbowed their way forward soon after. The clingstones came first, valued less for their flavor—the Albertas trucked up from Georgia and the Carolinas tasted better—than for the simple heartening fact of their arrival. As pallid and fleshy as winter-softened bodies, they were nonetheless the first fresh local peaches anyone had eaten in ten months. The Jersey Reds, the first freestone variety, arrived by the end of July, but the stars of the crop—the Triogems, Sunhighs, Golden Easts and Blakes, the peaches with the sublime taste and texture that everything else was either preparation for or imitation of—wouldn't peak until August.

The different varieties of peaches were planted in rows that ripened sequentially, and the migrants moved methodically from one to the next during the harvest weeks, steadily filling their baskets. By the second week of August, halfway through the Triogems, the pickers were melting under a sun that felt as if it had wandered north with them from Georgia. A pall of heat and humidity had settled heavily—and, it was starting to seem, permanently—over New Jersey. While the pickers sweated, the orchard baked, and Walter worried. The longer the muggy weather held, he knew, the more likely it was to upend the natural cycle of his staggered plantings. He borrowed some extra hands from the potato farms to help rush through the Triogems, and he watched the other varieties for signs of premature ripening. But the days remained dense and feverish, and the Sunhighs and the Golden Easts and the Blakes soon began gasping and panting, pleading to be picked. Once a peach started to turn, there was nothing Walter could do to stop it.

"We've got to get these in," he said as he inspected the reddening Sunhighs one morning, and returned to his office in the packinghouse to recruit some reinforcements. "As many as you can spare," he told all the other farmers he called.

On the first morning of the assault, the first tree in each row was mounted by two men with ladders, while Walter reconnoitered the opposite end of the peach grove, fifty or sixty trees away, measuring whether they might reach it in time. The odds, he saw, were long. Forty acres of peaches had ripened in a single week, fully two-thirds of his annual crop, far more than he had ever tried to harvest at once before. Fanned out across the orchard's full breadth, the wave of pickers advanced like a cresting flood, each pair at a pace of five or six trees daily, moving as determinedly as the infantry regiment Walter had once led across the dark fields of Bettviller. The enemy they were chasing here, though, was retreating rapidly beyond their grasp. In the quiet moments between the rustle of branches, they heard the unmistakable sound of defeat—the soft thud of overripe peaches falling to the ground ahead. Each day they found fewer peaches to pick, and more to step around. By the end of the eighth day, when they finally reached the end of each row, most of the crop had fallen. The fruit of a year's labor lay strewn across the ground as haphazardly and worthlessly as glass shards after a car crash. Drops might fetch fifty cents a bushel for canning, but not a thousand bushels at once. He sent the borrowed migrants back to the potato fields, and called the Sisters of Charity in Elizabeth to give away what he knew he couldn't sell.

"We've got a lot of peaches down here if you want them," he said, transforming his loss into their gain.

After the last of the velvet looms had migrated south, the snow began to fall in Freehold, and it fell all through the winter of 1958, more than in any single winter since the year of the first big rug-mill strike in the cold depths of the Depression. The soiled, frozen sheet that lay grayly over everything almost without pause from December to March gave the town the dour look of a faded New England mill village. On the last morning of the bleak season, Jake Errickson awoke to a slow, dull rain that he tried to regard less as a remnant of what was ending than as a harbinger of what was beginning. The ground was finally clear, the snow melted and tallied and safely relegated to the record books, and hopes for the green promise of spring seemed reasonable. But as he made his morning foreman's rounds through the mill, he saw through the wide grid of windows that the rain was turning into what he thought he had seen the last of—snow, heavy and wet, bending the tree limbs, bowing the power lines, falling and falling and falling until the lights flickered out, the looms clattered into silence, and Jake and all the other workers filed down the stairs and out into the storm. When the snow finally stopped, the town was shivering in the dark, and another fourteen and a half inches were on the ground. The winter's new total was three times the norm, and just shy of Jake's own height.

The mill didn't open again until late the next afternoon, the first day of spring, but a chill lingered all through the warming season, a cold and persistent fear that it would close again, for more than a day and for reasons beyond the weather. The rugs made in Freehold were as elegant and durable as ever, but the industry they were competing in had changed so utterly in just a few years that men who had devoted their lives to it were left scratching their heads in amazement and frustration. Tufting had finally overtaken weaving this year, accounting now for three-fifths of all domestic carpet production, most of it from Southern companies that hadn't even existed a decade earlier. A tufting machine cost about the same as a loom, around fifty thousand dollars, but it made carpet five times as fast, and with cheaper, less-skilled labor. The quality was cheaper, too, but buyers didn't seem to mind, as long as it stretched from wall to wall in their new living rooms. The arithmetic was merciless, and the old factories in the rug enclaves of the North were bleeding.

Karagheusian ads still appeared regularly in *Life* and *Good Housekeeping* and *House Beautiful,* featuring such glamorous endorsers as Elizabeth Taylor and Christian Dior, but demand had stalled for woven wool carpets from Freehold. Orders slumped in April, a spring-decorating month when they should have picked up, and a small layoff was announced. "The layoffs are only permanent so long as the situation is the way it is," Harold McCormack explained to the union, but how long the situation would last, no one could say.

Jake persisted in his belief that, no matter how much tufted carpet spilled out of the South, the world would always need a good sixteen-dollars-a-square-yard, 125-knot-per-square-inch, richly figured wool rug, and that the Karagheusians had poured too much into their Freehold facility—five stories and 750,000 square feet now, two long full blocks of brick and steel, where half a century ago had stood only a modest, defunct shirt factory—to ever forsake it. Some of his coworkers were more skeptical, and looked for work elsewhere—at the Nescafé coffee plant, the Brockway glass bottle factory that had just opened, or any other employer who seemed to offer the kind of stable future the rug mill had once promised. Just look at what happened in Yonkers, they said, where the venerable Alexander Smith rug mill, the city's largest employer, had shut down after a strike and moved south. Almost half of the 2,400 workers who lost their jobs had more than twenty-five years of service. The pattern was well established in the textile industry, and showed no sign of reversing—manufacturers abandoning their hulking old factories in the unionized Northeast and following the new interstates south to sprawling new plants in places where organized labor had no foothold. In July Karagheusian tried cutting prices by as much as 5 percent, and announced another round of layoffs, this time among supervisors and foremen. By August, just seven hundred people were rattling around the mill, 10 percent fewer than had started the year, and down from almost one thousand before the velvet department's departure.

"We're not moving out," the mill manager said emphatically, squelching a rumor that the rest of the Freehold operation would follow the velvet department to North Carolina, and the buildings would be sold to the American Can Company. "It's absolutely untrue."

Jake survived the foremen's layoff and sweated through the rest of the summer, both from the stagnant heat that the breeze through the mill's windows only faintly stirred, and from worry about the future. He knew he couldn't control what happened outside the mill, so he tried to concentrate instead on what happened inside, making sure that the decline in the rugs' market wasn't reflected by a corresponding decline in quality. As he watched closely for snags, thin copper wires were woven—as a ground against static electricity—into the lightweight Moresque carpet for Boeing's new 707 jetliners, one of the high-profile customers Karagheusian still served. More than nine thousand square yards from Freehold had just been laid in the staterooms, dining rooms, language rooms, theaters, libraries and social lounges of two new ocean liners, the *Brasil* and the *Argentina* of the Moore-McCormack Lines, a deep-pile gold diamond pattern that cushioned the feet of passengers cruising the South American coast. And after radio commentator Lowell Thomas deplored on air the sorry state of the official red carpet the city of New Orleans rolled out to greet visiting dignitaries ("ragged around the edges, and threadbare down the middle"), Karagheusian wove a new forty-foot length and presented it as a gift to the mayor.

Since the demise of the Gulistans, Jake had rarely spent a Sunday af-

ternoon at the Lincoln Field baseball diamond, but some of the old players had kept the games going, for themselves more than for the few spectators who turned up—a ritual suffused with the same nostalgic longing
for a better past that he often felt himself as he circuited the shrinking
mill. When Dave Cashion had organized an old-timers game the previous
summer, it attracted more players than fans, and netted just twenty-four
dollars. After sliding safely into home in a game this summer, Cashion lay
on his back across the plate for a full minute, not injured, just spent from
his trip around the bases, a feeling shared by many others in the sagging
town.

Orders remained flat through the autumn and into the winter, not
rising, but not falling either, and Jake allowed himself to hope that the
bottom had been reached. As it pared its workforce, the mill also shed
some production capacity, and he was trying to get used to the new,
leaner scale. The warehouse and research plant at the old Brakeley cannery complex was closed—the county bought the property to use as a rehabilitation center for the jail—and its operations transferred to the
original section of the mill, which was partly emptied when most of the
manufacturing was consolidated into the newer section. The Axminster
looms were dualized, configured so a single weaver could run two at once.
The changes were meant to boost efficiency and cut costs, and the union,
the company said, was cooperating admirably and responsibly so far.

Not long before the lunch whistle blew on a Monday in February,
Jake and the other foremen in the jacquard departments were dispatched
to deliver a message to the workers they supervised: The company treasurer was coming down from New York the next day for a meeting at
which their presence was requested.

"What's it all about?" a union shop steward asked him.

"They didn't tell us," Jake said. "But we're all supposed to go."

As word of the meeting spread from loom to loom, concern mounted
about what it meant. Jake expected another chart-filled economics lecture, like the tariff talks a few years earlier, but the union officials took a
less benign view. Negotiations would be starting soon for a new two-year
contract, and the company, they suspected, was trying to soften the
ground for concessions, to plead hardship loudly enough that the workers would agree to give back the gains in wages and benefits they had won.
An executive board meeting of Local 26 was hastily called, representatives
of the international union consulted, and a strategy hatched.

"We want the international there," the local president told the mill manager.

The manager declined the request. "This is a family affair," he said.

By midnight flyers had been printed and were being distributed to workers arriving for the late shift. DAMN THE UNION, the headline proclaimed. "This seems to be the attitude of the A&M Karagheusian Company."

The meeting, the union argued, was not only ill advised but was actually illegal, a sly attempt by the company to negotiate directly with its employees, and circumvent the union's role as the legally recognized bargaining agent.

"THIS MEETING IS IN VIOLATION OF THE NATIONAL LABOR RELATIONS ACT! THIS IS CLEARLY AN ATTEMPT TO BREAK THE UNION! . . . You cannot be forced to attend this captive audience meeting. So don't attend! BOYCOTT THE MEETING!"

The next afternoon, Jake left his glassed-in office and walked toward the lunchroom along a row of looms that rattled on without interruption, the shuttles clacking back and forth like loud clocks determined not to wind down. Some of the weavers looked up from their work as he passed, but none made a move to follow.

"You going?" he asked one weaver.

"What are they going to tell me?" the weaver answered. "They've been crying poverty around here for a long time now. They're making money—they just don't want to pay us anything."

Jake looked over his shoulder as he started across the Center Street bridge, and saw no one behind him but other foremen and supervisors. The lunchroom waited forlornly for more guests, offering him as wide a choice of seats as it would have on a cigarette break. The treasurer, Walter Corno, stood at the front and let the start time tick past, watching the doors for any latecomers who might have changed their minds.

"Well, I guess that's everybody," Corno finally said, surveying an audience much sparser than he had expected—a couple of dozen managers, and just nine, out of two hundred, workers. "I am here today because our company has problems that require solution."

The problems he outlined were familiar to all—the sudden and unforeseen rise of the tufting industry, the competition from imports, the failure of the Tariff Commission to grant any relief. He acknowledged the loyalty of the workers, and the company's "obligations" to Freehold.

"Tradition is a wonderful thing—it's nice to reflect on the past," Corno said. "However, when reflection on the past blinds us to the realities of the present and of the future, the time has come to break with tradition in the interest of protecting our operation here and your jobs. We trust that you will not let tradition stand in the way of the things that must be done."

But exactly what those things were, and how they must be done, he spoke about more obliquely—"cost structures" and "reshuffling," not wage cuts and layoffs. "You all know that the company with the lowest prices generally gets the customer's orders," he said, and alluded to, without specifically enumerating, the advantages the Southern firms had in the battle for carpet buyers. "Believe me, if we are to survive in Freehold we must win that fight."

What the treasurer was implying was as clear as what he was saying, and Jake shifted uncomfortably in his seat as he sensed the presentation nearing its end. "We would like to assure you that we are trying to stay in Freehold, but what will drive us out are things that we cannot control," Corno concluded. "Gentlemen, that is my story. We have the desire and the willingness to do something about it. Do you have the same desire?"

The board of education met one Monday evening a month in the library of the newest school in town—the Intermediate School, built to handle the crop of baby-boom children now surging into their teens—and as Jimmy Higgins took his seat at the long head table, he looked out into the small audience and saw a face that had become all too familiar recently, the tool-and-die maker from West George Street who didn't want his two young daughters praying in their classrooms. Waiting at each board member's place was the latest document in the case, a petition of appeal to the state commissioner of education.

". . . forcible imposition of religious doctrine, . . ." Jimmy read as he scanned the appeal before the gavel. ". . . open proselytizing on behalf of the Christian religions . . . a clear and present danger to the welfare of their children . . ."

Jimmy had been appointed to fill a vacancy on the board three years earlier, and then won the seat on his own in the next election, driving friends and family to the polls to assure enough votes in a contest that usually hinged more on civic popularity than educational ideology. He viewed the board not as a gateway to higher office, nor as a chance to shape his children's education—he planned to send his two young boys to St. Rose of Lima, the Catholic grammar school—but as a way to serve publicly the community that was providing his private livelihood. At the age of forty, he was finally the full-time funeral director he had been trying to become since before the war. His opportunity had arrived with the death of an aged competitor, Richard Van Sant of South Street, one of the town's three other undertakers. Jimmy not only absorbed the extra business, he also bid on, and won, the contract Van Sant had held to bury the patients from the nearby state mental hospital. For ninety-six dollars apiece, he provided a cloth-covered casket, a dignified funeral in the hospital chapel, usually attended only by himself and a clergyman, and burial in a local cemetery—not the unmarked hillside plot across the road where hundreds of earlier patients lay beneath small, identical stone markers that carried no names, only numbers. He jumped from thirty or forty funerals a year to almost eighty, and left his part-time job at Fort Monmouth. Because the funeral trade in Freehold was not, as it was in many larger towns, split along ethnic or denominational lines, Jimmy buried the dead of every kind, and moved easily among races and religions—from the black churches of the Peach Orchard to the white Protestant strongholds of Main Street, from the synagogue to his own Catholic parish. He heard God invoked so often and in so many ways during his workdays that he was surprised at the school board meetings to hear such spirited opposition to what he regarded as a universal, nonsectarian practice.

In classrooms all over America, the school day had traditionally begun with a ritual that, in honoring both God and country, was meant to impress upon the students the weight of all that watched over them—the pledge of allegiance, a patriotic song, a prayer. In Freehold it was called "morning exercises," and it culminated with the reading of a Bible passage selected by the teacher, and the recitation of the Lord's Prayer. The practice had rarely been questioned, at least not out loud, until now. But America had changed since the war: It had left behind its previous isolationism, and grown more deeply engaged with the wider world; and, though still overwhelmingly Christian, it had begun to take grater notice of the widening range of faiths within its own borders. From the excesses of McCarthyism—which Jimmy had witnessed firsthand through his job at Fort Monmouth—had arisen a heightened awareness of the value of private belief and individual conscience. The changing climate meant that parents who were troubled by the prayers their children said in school began to feel bold enough to speak up, and complaints were trickling in to many other school boards like Freehold's. Cases in New York, Pennsylvania and Maryland were moving through the state courts toward the federal courts, raising constitutional questions about the separation of church and state that it seemed the Supreme Court itself would ultimately have to answer.

The issue had first come before Jimmy as soon as he joined the board. In response to the complaints of the same parent who was before him tonight, he had voted in favor of a unanimous resolution declaring that schoolchildren were not required to join in the saying of grace before the morning milk break, but could sit in respectful silence instead. Any further steps, though, seemed limited not only by the board's own beliefs, but by the state. New Jersey law not only permitted the Bible readings, it required them: "At least five verses taken from that portion of the Holy Bible known as the Old Testament shall be read, or cause to be read, without comment, in each public school classroom, in the presence of the pupils therein," instructed N.J.S.A. 18:14-77.

Over the next two years, Jimmy had heard arguments several more times from the aggrieved parent—about grace again, about the daily Bible verses, about the Lord's Prayer, the saying of which the state law specifically permitted if local officials so decreed, as Freehold's had. "[W]e do not urge this upon you lightly, but only upon the most serious constitutional considerations," the legal director of the American Civil Liberties Union wrote to the board upon taking up the case, urging that the prayer be dropped. "We believe that the principles which underlie the First Amendment can be most fully realized only if government scrupulously declines to intrude itself in any way in matters of religion."

After the school board meeting was gaveled open now, Jimmy read the petition more closely and saw that the debate had returned to where it started, to the words the students said with bowed heads and folded hands before their snack: "O give thanks unto the Lord; for He is good; for His mercy endureth forever." Because grace was not explicitly mentioned in the state law, it was, in the complainants' view, the practice most vulnerable to legal challenge. But the grace said in Freehold was the first verse of Psalm 136, and thus perfectly compatible, the board believed, with the state mandate. News of the latest appeal had circulated in the previous week, luring some vocal board supporters to the school library, including the president of the synagogue and the commander of the Jewish War Veterans post. (The rabbi had initially offered some muted opposition to the prayers, but then retreated into silence.) After the petition was read into the record, a letter was presented from the secretary of the American Legion auxiliary.

"Regardless of one's faith or belief, our country, the good old U.S.A., was founded and settled by folks worshipping God," it offered. "If more teaching from the Bible were given to children in their youth perhaps there would not be so many drunks and crimes today."

The school superintendent agreed. "My feeling is that what we are doing follows the will of the community and a deeper sense of moral obligation and conscience," he said. "That public schools should be Godless is a queer perversion of the concept of religious freedom."

The tool-and-die maker sat quietly with his wife, adding nothing to what the petition had already said. Jimmy and the other board members were similarly reticent, understanding as they did that the issue had now moved beyond their reach, and would ultimately be decided someplace other than the library of the Intermediate School. They directed the board attorney to prepare a response to the petition for the hearing the state education commissioner would convene, and they moved on to the next item on the agenda.

For the next six months, Jimmy and the other board members spent their meetings discussing budget numbers and teacher hires, not prayers, but the citizens he met in his daily rounds—while greeting mourners at a wake, or walking to the diner for coffee in his familiar black suit—often had an opinion to offer about the largest pending matter. "What harm can it do?" most of them wondered, and Jimmy tended to agree. He thought often of midnight mass on Christmas Eve in Tilloloy, looking up at the moon through the shell-blasted roof of an old barn packed tight with shocked and saddened soldiers, listening to the mumbled Latin of a deeply sectarian ritual, but hearing, all of them together, Catholics, Protestants and Jews alike, a wider, more comforting message about death and loss, sacrifice and eternity. Public prayer was, to him, unifying, not dividing.

Every so often, though, somebody suggested what Jimmy himself suspected: "They're going to win this, you know."

On a Wednesday morning in August, more than one hundred people squeezed into a red-carpeted courtroom in the Hall of Records that

Buddy Lewis's jailed custodians had readied for the public hearing. Presiding from the bench was the assistant state commissioner of education. The petitioner and his lawyers sat at one table, the school board's lawyer at the other. The board members sat in the jury box—observers only, like the commissioner, with no power to render any judgment. Busy with a funeral, Jimmy was missing. For the next five hours, expert witnesses from both sides took the stand, as the board and the petitioner listened in silence.

"It has a ritual characteristic, with the closing of eyes, the bowing of heads and the folding of hands," a Unitarian minister from Princeton testified, describing how grace was said, and why it constituted what he considered an inappropriate "religious exercise." "It simulates postures of worship, it quotes theology and sectarian theology and imposes religion on all present."

In addition to grace, the petition also challenged the singing of carols in school during the Christmas season—"Away in a Manger," "O, Come All Ye Faithful" and the hymn the men of the 391st Bombardment Group had sung together in the winter of the Battle of the Bulge, "Silent Night." The board members had the clear support of the audience, teachers and parents mostly, but as they sat in the jury box through the accumulating hours of testimony, they could sense their case slipping away. To be debating the issue at all at this level—to be questioning in such reasoned and measured tones what they had previously considered a practice beyond question—was already, they knew, a kind of defeat. No decision would be rendered for months, but they sensed among themselves, and told Jimmy later, that something had started here that couldn't be stopped: An older idea of America, a shared belief in the primacy of the common good, was passing; and rising in its place was a newer vision of public life, built around the sanctity of individual rights and personal freedom. What had allowed America to unite so fiercely in the face of war was being supplanted as a defining national principle now by what it had fought to defend.

As the hearing neared its end, the board's closing witness found his logic spent, and deployed emotion instead. "This would be a catastrophe for the country," the chairman of Columbia University's religion department pleaded, defending a belief, a custom, a whole way of life that had always been, but that was bound for the same fate now—he could see it, they all could see it—as the body Jimmy Higgins had buried today. "I think American education is in great peril of succumbing to requests by minority groups. We must remember that there are majority rights as well as minority rights."

When Jake Errickson reported to work on a raw November morning that spoke coldly of the winter ahead—fifty-five years after the first looms arrived in Freehold from Kidderminster, nineteen months after the meeting the union boycotted, and exactly one week after another South Pacific veteran of his own generation had been elected president of the United States—he saw from the sad and stunned face of Percy Lewis that it was finally over. Lewis had not been able to contain his excitement when he peered over Jake's shoulder in the poker game and spied the royal straight flush, and he couldn't mask his disappointment now.

"It doesn't look good, Jake," Lewis told him. "You better go look for a job."

Meetings were scheduled later in the day with the union and the borough council to announce the move the mill had vowed as recently as a year ago never to make: The broadloom department, home to Jake and Percy and 150 other workers, was following the velvet department to North Carolina. Two fifteen-foot looms were already being disassembled for the trip, and the rest would leave as the last orders were finished. In the contract negotiations that followed the disputed meeting, the union had accepted a modest increase in wages and benefits, an average of thirteen cents an hour, but the competition from tufting and imports was so overwhelming that even a large giveback probably couldn't have saved their jobs.

Unfavorable business conditions, the plant manager explained in his brief and bloodless statement, had "forced the company to seek the most economical means of producing carpet." And what was painfully obvious now—in an industry so radically and rapidly reinventing itself, jettisoning its bulky old brick shrines and the craftsmen who kept them humming— was that the most economical means were someplace other than they had always been before. "The inefficiency of the multistory layout of the Freehold plant has made it necessary to move to a modern single-story operation." Karagheusian was planning to start over again, far from where it had started in the first place. As a company, it was exhibiting the same mobility, the same willingness to leave behind the old and set off in quest of the new, the same urge to reinvent itself, that had infected many individual Americans, who were also packing up and moving to the south and the west.

The company told the four hundred workers remaining in departments other than broadloom—Axminster, narrow jacquard, dyeing, finishing, research, design and custom tufting, the one small corner of the mill still running round-the-clock—that their jobs were staying, but the union told them to get out while they could. Nobody believed the mill's promises any more, and as Jake walked the somber floors, he heard a sad and bitter chorus of betrayal.

"We stuck with them through thick and thin," one of the weavers said, trying to comprehend the loss. "We worked for fifteen dollars a month during the Depression, and now they're throwing us out."

"I worked in this damn job for thirty-five years and this is how they treat me."

"Where can a man sixty years old get a job?"

"They think we should be willing to work for a buck an hour."

"We've got families to take care of."

Jake was forty-two years old, and like many of his colleagues, had never drawn a paycheck from any employer other than A.&M. Karagheusian or the United States Army. He had a son in high school, a daughter in grammar school, and an expertise in an industry that was dying around him. He was eighteen months shy of qualifying for the company's Quarter Century Club and the accompanying gold service pin engraved with the winged hourglass, and he had no idea what to do next.

Freehold itself seemed to mirror his gloom as the mill emptied and the days shortened. Main Street's merchants were feeling squeezed, and the Strand had cut back to a three-day week. Many of the gracious trees whose gray, leafless limbs overarched the winter streets would not bloom again in the spring, victims of the virulent plague of Dutch elm disease that was fraying the town's ancient shade canopy. The dead elm extracted from Broad Street recently, one hundred feet high and four feet thick, had been planted on the eve of the Civil War by the owner of the abandoned iron foundry, the ruined shell of which the borough council had finally ordered razed. The high school football team had sunk similarly low, its former glory as firmly a part of the past now as Karagheusian's own. Two weeks after the mill's announcement, the Colonials had lost their Thanksgiving game to Neptune, 45–12, bringing to a merciful end the first winless season in school history.

Each week, a loom or two or three would be taken apart and removed from the broad-jacquard department, and the thin winter light slanting in through the windows would pool like a rising tide in the wide empty spaces left behind. A few looms took the route Jake had taken at the start of the war: onto a ship, through the canal, and across the Pacific to New Zealand, trailed by a handful of weavers willing, as the first Kidderminster migrants were, to swap their country for their trade. Most of the rest went to North Carolina.

"There goes 268," Jake would say, watching the dismembered form of a machine whose habits he knew as well as his own lowered onto a waiting truck. And then the next week, sighing again, "There goes 272."

On a Friday morning in the middle of February, three months after the broadloom announcement, union officials from Local 26 were summoned to the company's Fifth Avenue headquarters to hear the final verdict: Karagheusian would make no more rugs in Freehold. The Axminster and narrow-jacquard departments would simply shut down; orders had dipped so low that a transfer south was pointless. The building would be sold—to another manufacturing concern, all hoped—and the seventy-five jobs that remained (in dyeing, design, research and, of course, custom tufting) would retreat like squatters to a corner of the old wing. Employees with between two and ten years service would receive one week's severance pay; those with more—whether eleven or fifty-one, the longest current tenure—would receive two. The news reached Jake and the other foremen in Freehold just before the week's closing whistle.

"Losing the Karagheusian plant is like losing an old friend," the *Transcript* said in a mournful front-page editorial. "The rambling, gaunt Jackson Street plant will be remembered with a good deal of emotion for what it has been for us over an eventful fifty-six years—The Mill."

The union took a less sentimental tone: "a virtual double-cross," the director of the international called it, blaming the company for "the destruction of a community and the handling of its people as if they were used machinery to be tossed on the scrap pile."

What happened, he wondered—aloud and in anger and along with everyone else both in the mill and out—to the company that once cared enough about its employees to sponsor baseball teams and subsidize the town's first ambulance squad? "The management today is interested in dollars, not human beings," he said. "If this is the American free enterprise system of the 1960s, then big business should hang its head in shame."

The final shutdown was set for June 30, but Jake's department would be gone before spring. So few looms remained, and so much space had opened between them, that the foreman's rounds he still made, his long shadow trailing across the dusty, vacant floors, began to resemble the treks from one listening station to another in the hills of New Guinea. As the mill's future shrank, its size seemed actually to grow, the cavernous interior, gradually stripped of machinery, ballooning into an echoey void that illustrated precisely and alarmingly just how large a hole the town now needed to fill. Even in its diminished last years, the mill was the biggest factory in the county, annually paying out $2 million in wages and $100,000 in local property taxes, a loss too great to absorb without pain.

"It's like a ghost town in here," Jake said one day near the end.

"What the hell are they going to do with this big building?" somebody else wondered.

By the middle of March, only a dozen looms, and a handful of workers, were left in the broad jacquard department. Dot's job in Axminster was gone, too; one of the last rugs to come out of her department was patterned with three-foot-tall *Mayflowers* in full sail, for the Provincetown Inn in Massachusetts. At ten in the morning on Wednesday the fifteenth, Percy Lewis handed Jake two paychecks, one for himself and one for a colleague who had skipped the final workday.

"Francis didn't make it in," Lewis said. "Could you take his check out to him?"

Jake made his delivery and was home an hour before lunch, and more than two decades before he had counted on. He had stayed at the mill right to the end, just as he had planned when he first walked through the door in 1937, the same week the *Hindenburg* exploded, but he had always assumed that his own end, the natural close of his career at a decent retirement age, would precede the company's. He looked around the house his mill salary had bought and wondered how he would continue paying for it, where he would find new life insurance to replace the canceled company policy, what would happen to the money he and Dot had been putting aside for a trip back to Australia, and the family she hadn't seen since she left sixteen years ago. Two weeks' severance was still coming, plus the money that had been deducted for his pension plan—without any interest, though, or the matching contributions the company was supposed to have made—but no new job awaited him anywhere yet. He hadn't heard anything from the new 3M factory in town, where he had applied, and he had turned down offers to follow the looms to New Zealand and North Carolina.

Jake opened a beer from the refrigerator and retreated to the dim, comforting sanctuary of his basement workshop, with its shelves of paints and oils and solvents, its rows of tools and drawers of hardware, its reassuring air of offering anything a man might need to fix whatever was broken. Pressed up against one wall was the old loom-fixer's bench he had reclaimed from the mill's discard pile, so heavy and bulky and stubborn that three friends had to help him wrestle it down the stairs and into place. Lying on it was a torpedo-shaped shuttle he had kept as a memento. He set his beer down and ran his hand over the bench, its smooth and seasoned surface speckled with ancient grease spots. It yielded not even a quiver under his touch, built as it was in the sturdy manner of things never meant to be moved. The purpose it had served for half a century was ended now, but it remained an immovable fixture in Jake's life, as permanent a part of the house as the foundation itself.

The fire whistle blew at 1:47 on a Saturday afternoon in April of 1962, the first spring after the mill closed, and its coded signal—two blasts, then one, then another two—called all volunteers within hearing to the heart of downtown. Something was burning inside the neon sign at the Freehold Pizzeria on East Main Street, sending out a plume of white smoke like a snuffed candle. The fire trucks rushed past the Strand, sirens clearing the traffic, and the children standing in line for the matinee turned away from the "Playing Tonight" posters they had been eyeing: *The Four Horsemen of the Apocalypse* and *The Innocents*. Curious shoppers and clerks drifted out to the sidewalk from the neighboring shoe store and haberdashery. The call seemed routine, though, a simple electrical malfunction that would only briefly disturb the day's rhythms. The merchants resumed their transactions, the children filed into the theater for *tom thumb*.

A few of the most curious pedestrians stopped to watch as two ladders were laid against the storefront—PIZZA SLICES 15¢, the darkened neon announced—and a pair of firemen climbed up with axes. Whatever was burning in there, they had to stop it fast, because the town couldn't afford to lose any more than it already had. After the rug mill closed, several stores had followed, and many others were slumping. Just as Freehold's fortunes had risen with the mill, so, too, had they fallen with it. The slide down from the peak of those first flush postwar years had been slow and steady, and left the town as low and uncertain as it had been since the depths of the Depression, when the locked-out weavers stood in a soup line just about where the firemen's ladders were standing now.

When the firemen pried off the board above the sign, they were startled by the flames that licked out at them—a fire burning with an unexpected violence, and a dangerous invisibility, in a confined space with uncertain boundaries. Several other firemen dragged a hose up the stairs to the second-floor apartment and drowned some flames that had seeped through the wall, but heat was rising around them like an oven. A hidden fire was loose inside the building's frame. They couldn't see it but they could certainly feel it, and they were forced to retreat, making sure the other apartments were empty as they left. It looked as if it might prove just as hard to pinpoint and contain, and just as potentially destructive, as the elusive forces that had caused the mill's demise.

"This is bigger than it looks," one of the firemen said.

"We'll have to get at it from up on the roof," said another.

Walter Denise had parked his car in the lot behind the stores across the street and was walking with his family to the Strand when he spotted the fire trucks, the tangle of hoses, the figures scrambling atop the buildings. Some of the old roofs were tin, and the firemen had trouble breaking through. Each hole they managed to make, though, and many others they didn't, released a trail of smoke. Walter's children pulled him toward the theater—they didn't want to miss any more of the cartoons that preceded the main attraction—but he stopped them in front of the Acme market, one of the chain stores that had been squeezing aside the small groceries. The wind was blowing to the west, he saw, and the smoke was creeping up the block in the same direction his children wanted to go. No flames were visible yet, but he knew how fast a fire could move, he remembered all too vividly how one had outraced his best efforts in the orchard's migrant camp, and he hurried across Main Street, leaving the children with his wife.

"You've got to get them out of here," he told the manager, who, behind the box-office window, was unaware of the fire's progress. The barest hint of smoke was gathering near the ceiling, faint as cobwebs. "Leave the film running and make an announcement. Tell them to exit quietly and to meet their parents on Court Street."

Two police officers came in on Walter's heels to formally order what he had already advised, and the manager set off down the aisles with one usher, sending the other up to the balcony, gently herding the two hundred children out the rear door. Walter returned to his own children and watched the flames blow out the windows of the apartment above the pizzeria, and shoot through the roof of the shoe repair shop next door. The smoke was blackening now, billowing up into a dense cloud tall enough to be seen from every corner of town, marking the site for the stream of spectators who, hearing the whistle blow again and again, could no longer ignore the growing sense of calamity.

Walter spotted a woman running frantically toward the Strand. "My children, my children!" she screamed.

He intercepted her with happier news than he had been able to deliver at the migrant-camp fire. "Don't worry, they're safe," he said. "They've all been evacuated to Court Street."

Bill Lopatin was working on a job estimate in his basement office—checking the plans spread across his drafting table, calculating how many two-by-eights he would need—when the insistent alarm of the auxiliary whistle, mounted on the barn behind the high school across the street, finally drew him outside. He followed the smoke downtown, coming up on the fire from behind Main Street, and spotted his foreman, a volunteer fireman, up on the roof. Bill had worked in the buildings that were burning and he knew that although they looked like individual structures, and in fact had separate foundations, they were attached in a way that would allow a fire that started inside one wall to travel, quick and hidden, to another. They were as closely linked to each other as the town had been to the mill, and if one went, then they all would go. Watching the fire bear down on the Strand, he remembered with a jolt what was stored inside the warren of professional offices in the two stories above its street-front lobby: All of the records from the synagogue—including minutes of meetings of the Hebrew Benefit Society and the Workmen's Circle, which Bill's father had long served as secretary—were in the law offices of Arthur Goldberg, who was working on its fiftieth-anniversary history.

"Can I get in there to get something?" Bill asked a fireman at the perimeter, but it was too late.

On the other side of Main Street, Jimmy Higgins had walked over from the funeral home and was watching from in front of the library as the firemen backed down the ladders from the roofs. The heat they had felt in their boots was a sign that what they were standing on was melting beneath them. Some climbed to the roofs of the neighboring buildings to keep fighting from above, while others sprayed their hoses up from the sidewalk. With no ladder truck of their own, they waited for the nearest one to arrive, from Neptune. On the other side of the Strand, the owner of the auto parts store carried out the shotgun shells he stocked for hunters. The swelling crowd kept looking up into a sky that was gray beyond the smoke, wishing aloud for a return of the morning's rains, but all that came was more wind, fanning the flames westward.

"It's like a chimney," someone standing beside Jimmy said. "All those drop ceilings and hollow walls, the fire just shoots right through there."

The water pressure dipped so low that the sewer grates were covered with canvas to catch the runoff to be pumped in again, and the tanker truck kept racing out to the pond and back, filling up and emptying out. Jake noticed the tanker as he was slipping into town the back way after working some overtime at the new job he had finally found, at an RCA plant out near Trenton, but he thought it was just a drill until he walked into his kitchen and saw Dot.

"What are you doing here?" she asked. "Half the town's on fire."

She drove him down to the diner, as near as she could get, and he hurried up to Conway's Bar, where the truck from the volunteer fire company he belonged to, Engine No. 1, was parked.

"It's running like crazy," one of the other firemen told Jake as he put on his boots and coat and helmet. "We can't keep up with it."

He followed the hose up a stairway in the building that stood between the Strand and the Hall of Records and found Gene Coyne at the top landing, spraying through the broken-out window at the theater's roof. They held the hose together, trying to keep the fire from marching any farther up Main Street. Downtown Freehold had almost burned down once before—almost a century ago, when a fire that started in the newspaper office ate through a dry goods store, a sewing machine agency, a law office, a dental office, the grandest house in town and finally the courthouse itself—but it had been stopped right here, where Jake was standing now, and the block was rebuilt. If they could stop it here again, could it be rebuilt again?

More than two hundred volunteer firemen from Freehold and a dozen surrounding companies had responded to the call now, and a parade's worth of trucks were parked up and down Main Street. Stepping carefully through the maze of fat, snaking hoses, Stu Bunton stood at the intersection of Main and South, in front of the Hall of Records, diverting traffic around the scene. He had been off-duty, at home with his wife and sons, when he was summoned downtown. Buddy Lewis had been called in from home, too, by his boss at the courthouse: He was needed at the jail behind the Strand to help evacuate the prisoners from cells in which smoke was beginning to collect. He stood watch in the dining room over minor offenders while the guards handcuffed the more serious criminals. Stu and the other officers cleared Court Street for a half dozen school buses and a caravan of state police cars, which disgorged thirty-two troopers carrying riot guns, submachine guns and revolvers.

"All right, we're just going for a little ride," Buddy told his charges, herding them into the buses.

The entire population of the jail—eighty-two men and six women— traveled two blocks up Court Street to the new courthouse. The troopers locked the twenty-three maximum-security prisoners in the basement detention cells. Buddy stayed with the others on the parked buses, trying to keep the mood as light and routine as one of the work details he supervised.

Up on the landing, Jake watched the flames sidling nearer across the roof, barely blinking under the stream from the hose. He had never felt so vulnerable in his years as a fireman, and couldn't help but think of the coat-factory blaze of his boyhood, when thirteen volunteers were burned by a gasoline explosion, and three young men, two of them brothers, were killed, the only fatalities in the department's history. He was sweating now, and began to suspect the cause was more than his own exertion.

"It's getting hot in here," he told Gene over the rush of the hose, and then stepped back and looked down. In the gaps between the stair treads, he saw an orange glow surging like a furnace. "We've got to get the hell out of here."

Backing quickly down the stairs, shielded by their spouting hose, they escaped ahead of the danger and stood on the sidewalk, shooting water up at the perch they had just been standing on, and watching with a mixture of relief and dread as the flames that might have killed them ate away at it. Half the block was on fire now, every building between the dry cleaner's and the Hall of Records, whose lawn was heaped with boxes of shoes, clothes, papers, auto parts and whatever else the frantic merchants had managed to salvage. Flames moved like taunting faces from one upper-story window to the next. Gas company crews jackhammered through the street to cut off the buried lines. The aerial truck finally arrived, and a fireman was strapped to the ladder and lifted high above, spraying down water like the rain that still wouldn't fall.

The fire had spread so deeply and rapidly within the buildings that all the volunteers could hope to do now was contain it within its natural boundaries, and keep it from leaping across the moatlike alleys at either end. Firemen stood with their hoses atop the adjacent roofs like border guards, determined to let no intruders through. The buildings' interiors collapsed first, leaving the hollow facades to look out over the street like an abandoned movie set. Standing intact with an improbable endurance amid all the destruction was the pizzeria storefront, and the neon sign that started it all.

Almost four hours after the first fizzing, unseen spark—after nine stores, eight apartments and five offices had disintegrated, after the last facades, even the pizzeria, had tumbled in upon themselves, after the fire's appetite was finally sated and it seemed disinclined to cross the alleys to devour anything more—a truce was declared. Jake and the other firemen stayed all through the evening, pouring water on a pile of charred, smoldering wreckage that occasionally flared up, but showed no sign of resuming its earlier fury. The prisoners returned to their cells, and the few Saturday night moviegoers who hadn't heard the news, and had driven into town for the early show, returned home to their televisions when they saw that the Strand was gone. A few hundred spectators were still around to cheer when a crane arrived at midnight to knock down the last teetering walls.

Jake went home at two-thirty to sleep for a few hours before reporting back for fire watch duty at dawn, sitting in the truck, hose at the ready, scanning for stray, persistent flames. As terrible as the fire itself had looked, the aftermath—the black scar in the heart of downtown, glistening and oozing in the pale, contemplative light of a Sunday morning—looked even worse. Injuries had been light, six firemen treated for smoke inhalation, cuts and bruises, but the toll was heavy, $750,000 in damage. A hole had opened in Main Street, two blocks from the hole the mill had just left, and it looked like everyone's darkest vision of the future. A steady stream of spectators filed past all through the day, like mourners at a wake. They had never seen such ruin in Freehold before, and for comparisons had to call up the worst they had seen elsewhere. Jake looked at smoking remains and saw the burned and blasted beach at Buna. Stu saw the kamikaze's flaming crash. Bill saw the cratered hedgerow country of Normandy, Jimmy the shells of villages around Tilloloy. Buddy saw the battered riverside at Wesel, Walter the rubble of Frauenberg. Those places, though, had belonged to other people. This place belonged to them.

12.

"Here Lieth ye Body of . . ."

The street unfurled wide and empty through the largest piece of open land left within the town limits, bordered on either side by a sunbaked field that had been shorn of its last crop of wheat the previous autumn. Freshly poured concrete imposed a ghostly, tentative form upon the raw space—sidewalks, curbs, gutters, driveway aprons unattached to any driveways. A lonesome signpost gave it all a name that was still more an idea than an address, BROOKWOOD DRIVE. Bill Lopatin and his partners had christened the street after the brook that ran alongside it, and the trees it backed up to. It had never occurred to them to follow the custom of other developers and name it after themselves. Buried securely beneath the unblemished blacktop were water lines, sewer lines and gas lines, the intestinal network necessary to transform Charlie Hall's wheatfield into a neighborhood called Colonial Park, which at the moment existed only on the site plan the borough council had recently approved, and in the most ambitious, optimistic precincts of Bill's head. At the far end of a two-block stretch whose length was magnified by its vacancy, a single house frame was rising, the first of what he expected would ultimately total forty-nine.

Bill and his partners had paid for everything on the street—including the squat brick hut housing a lift station to pump the sewage through the pipes up the hill to the nearest main—and as he drove slowly along it in his pickup, he hoped it would pay them back. He was fifty-three now, and staring at the biggest fiscal risk of his career. Lopatin Construction had always been a custom builder, rarely breaking ground before a signed contract was in hand. Bill planned to build the houses in Colonial Park one at a time, too, according to each buyer's tastes and needs, but if the buyers didn't come, he would be stuck with the street he had already built first. Charlie Hall's contribution to the newly formed corporation was the nineteen acres of land. Bill, his brother and his father got the bank loan that financed the site work. The first house was a four-bedroom split-level with a half-brick facade, a wide bow window in the living room, sliding glass doors and a sundeck in the rear. Three, four, maybe five more houses each year—that was all Bill asked, enough to fill both the land and the years to his retirement.

The exterior siding was going up on the rear of the house, one-by-twelve vertical redwood boards, and after Bill checked on his crew's progress, he drove to his Main Street shop, passing through a town that was, like him, entering new, and unfamiliar, territory. Two summers after the Strand fire, a new three-story office building had risen beside the courthouse, but the rest of the ruined site remained a gaping empty lot. Enough other storefronts were vacant that "urban renewal" had entered the vocabulary of the borough council, which was considering proposals to bulldoze the old to make way for something else—exactly what, though, no one was quite sure. Rumors rose occasionally about a big company interested in the cavernous rug mill building—RCA, where Jake Errickson was working, was the latest—but for now only a few small manufacturers, and the last handful of Karagheusian employees, were rattling around inside. When another company dropped the vaguest of hints about leasing the property, more than a thousand job applications poured in. The movie theater had been rebuilt, but it was no longer called the Strand, and it had migrated from Main Street to the highway, just a blank brick cube now, surrounded by acres of asphalt at the new shopping center on Route 9, too far and inconvenient for anyone to walk to.

The new roads that had opened up the nation in the years since the war—smoothing the delivery routes for Walter Denise's peaches, offering a swifter retreat to the southbound rug mill—had also drawn Freehold more firmly into the orbit of the city that had always loomed just beyond its reach, New York. When passenger trains were still running, a few dozen local residents had made the two-hour trip to work each day, but for everyone else, the city was a destination of occasion, not routine. The money spent and banked in Freehold was mostly made in Freehold by people who lived in Freehold. Seen from the congested precincts to the north, the town beckoned like a pastoral idyll, the capital of a lush swath of broad fields and sturdy farmsteads that might as well have been in Iowa. But the distance shrank with the opening of the New Jersey Turnpike and the Garden State Parkway, and the expansion and extension of the state highways, and urban refugees spotted an inviting escape route. Over the previous decade, 1.5 million people had left New York City for the suburbs, and the same exodus was underway from other cities all over America. A vast, swelling tide of tract houses was filling in the open spaces of the northern part of the state, and it began washing ever farther south, until it was finally lapping at the edge of Freehold, almost sixty miles from Times Square.

When the first of the new developments opened locally, two hundred houses on an old potato field near the shopping center on the highway, Bill went out to inspect the competition, only to find that there was none. Every house was cut from one of just two designs—a split-level or a two-story contemporary—and was built with an indifference to detail he would never have permitted on a job that had his name on it. Walls and doors were flimsy, lines off-plumb, windows poorly hung, yards ungraded. If he built a house like one of these, he thought, no one would ask him to build another. But people were buying them—people, he could only surmise, who had lived in apartments so long, and were so eager for a house of their own, that they didn't know or care what a good one looked like.

Bill expected that most of the buyers at Colonial Park would not be transplants, but locals, who did know what a good house looked like, and who knew that he could be counted upon to build one. Late in the afternoon, he returned to Brookwood Drive to find the rear of the house fully sided, sealed off from the yard that stretched back to the woods behind. In front of the house, and in a orderly line all the way down the street, stood the oak saplings he hoped to watch grow to shade height over the years, planted not in the narrow median strip beside the curb, like most of the rest of the town's trees, but in the front yards, where their roots would have room to spread without displacing the concrete sidewalk blocks from below. On his way home for supper, Bill looked at the lot a prospective buyer was coming to discuss tonight, the largest of all he had laid out, on the corner of the short side street that looped off Brookwood. They would sit together, he and the customer, in the basement office of his house, paging through all his design books, searching for the right style, picking the best combination of features, imagining the brightest future, and when they were done, he hoped, he would take a red pencil in hand and color in another blank space, the second, in the map of Colonial Park tacked over his drawing board, which would leave forty-seven more to go.

The new developers were working at a more rapid, and less personal, pace. The buyers kept snatching up the new houses, though, and the developers kept building. As Bill watched the supply and the demand feed off each other, both sides apparently heedless to the standards of craftsmanship he had spent his career upholding, he was struck by the same vaguely uneasy feeling that had troubled Jimmy Higgins during the school prayer debate—a sense that the old world he knew, his world, was fading, elbowed aside by something new that he neither quite understood nor approved of. The rules were changing: Public displays of belief were suspect; homes were no longer permanent. Bill had learned from his father that the proper way to build a house was as if you expected to live in it yourself until you died. But if people moved around so much now, who would be around long enough to see how well you built it? His own journeys to Freehold—to get here in the first place as an immigrant boy from Russia, and to get back after seventy-two missions in the war—had been so hard that he couldn't imagine leaving again. Other Lopatins, though— nieces and nephews and cousins—had begun drifting away. His daughter Lynn had graduated from college, married and gone, too.

Bill had felt a similar sense of dislocation a few months earlier on his annual anniversary vacation with Selma. Overcoming her fear of flying, they traveled overseas together for the first time, a three-week tour of Europe that started in England. Bill hadn't been back since the war, and he was eager to see his old base. They took a train from London out to the rolling, green Essex fields from which the Marauders of the 322nd Bombardment Group had flown off on missions over the occupied Continent. Bill wasn't sure what he expected to find exactly, just some sight or sound or smell that would speak to him in some way of the waist-gunner he had once been, the danger and fear and tedium he had once endured, and the lost airmen who last touched earth alive on this patch of southeast England. All he found, though, was ruin and emptiness. The land had reclaimed the runways, and every building but one, the teetering shell of a hangar, was gone. His war had vanished. The only evidence here of his service was in his own memory, and to keep it intact there, to protect the past from the present, he quickly returned with Selma to London and left

England sooner than planned. They continued on to Denmark, Holland and France, places he had seen before only from above, through the haze of flak blossoms and the smoke of exploded bombs—places of which he had nothing he feared forgetting.

The last corner of the old farm that remained untouched—that hadn't yet been flattened and dug and paved and planted with houses—was the tiny family burial ground at the crest of a hill, five weathered tombstones still standing straight in the shade of a single oak. Bulldozers had gnawed away the surrounding earth, leaving a lonesome grassy tussock. A raw, new neighborhood of 120 split-levels and colonials spilled down the slopes, reaching almost all the way to the treeline along the stream that bordered the neighboring Denise orchard. As a gravedigger sank a shovel into dirt last disturbed more than two centuries earlier, Jimmy Higgins knelt and ran his fingers across the chiseled inscription on one of the gray stones.

HERE LIETH YE BODY OF SAMUEL FORMAN WHO DIED YE 13TH DAY OF OCTOBER 1740 IN YE 78TH YEAR OF HIS AGE, it read.

"You can read that clear as anything," Jimmy said. "It could have gone up yesterday."

Some of the stones had disappeared over the years, and the records were spotty, but at least a dozen members, and maybe more, of the Forman and Wikoff families were buried in the plot, where they now lay in the way of the last half-acre lot in a housing development called Burlington Heights. After 250 years of cultivation, the farm had been sold several years earlier, and the fate of the cemetery—in which the last body was interred when New Jersey was still a colony—was entrusted to the Chancery Division of the Superior Court. Genealogies were traced, descendants notified, and permission finally granted to move the graves. A licensed funeral director was ordered to be present.

"I don't think we're going to find anything," Jimmy said as he stood up and surveyed the site, pocked with groundhog holes and laced with roots. "Maybe a piece of old shoe leather, that's all."

The gravedigger dug deeper and deeper at the first stone and, finding nothing but dirt, moved to the next, and the next, and then anywhere it looked as if a stone might once have stood, but he turned up no evidence at all of the bodies that had been buried there—no bones, no coffin wood, no scraps of clothing, nothing at all that distinguished the graves from the surrounding earth. The first settlers had completely returned to the land they had once tilled. A bulldozer idled nearby, waiting to reduce the knoll to the level of the surrounding lot. Several shovelfuls of earth were collected from each grave—symbolic really, but perhaps containing some molecular remnants of the departed—and loaded with the stones in the back of a truck. In his black Chrysler, Jimmy led the truck away to the cemetery where a new common grave awaited, and the bulldozer moved in to erase what remained.

Jimmy was one of just two undertakers in town now—the third, Bart Callahan, who was also the mayor, had died suddenly of a heart attack at the age of forty-six, barely a year after the death of Richard Van Sant, who had been the fourth—and he was doing close to one hundred funerals a year. He sometimes had two wakes going at once in his downstairs viewing rooms, and he bought from Callahan's widow an extra prayer rail to accommodate the kneeling mourners if both happened to be Catholic. He also bought Callahan's caskets, not that he needed any more, such an easy mark was he for the salesmen who called that he could rarely bring himself to send one away without an order. To accommodate the increased traffic, the basement of the funeral home had been dug out, making new rooms for embalming and casket display. He and Angela and their two boys still lived upstairs.

Jimmy's standing in the community had risen along with his business. He was an inveterate joiner, and active member, of service clubs—Lions, Optimists, Exchange, Rotary. When some local history buffs began a "Let's Bring Molly Home" campaign—Molly Pitcher, the soldier's wife who had brought water to the wounded on the sweltering day of the Battle of Monmouth, and, legend said, taken over the cannon of her fallen husband, was buried in her birthplace of Carlisle, Pennsylvania—Jimmy volunteered to move her remains to a new and honored grave beneath the tall battle monument in front of the courthouse in Freehold. His fellow members elected him president of the board of education, whose duties now included ensuring local compliance with the national ban on prayer in schools. After the earlier hearing, the state had upheld the board's policy, but the Supreme Court, in a later landmark case, had since declared school prayer unconstitutional everywhere, no matter what the Freehold officials might believe.

At Old Tennent Cemetery, a concrete vault waited in a freshly opened grave, beside a wide, new stone engraved with the names of the known dead from the uprooted family plot. Tennent was the oldest active cemetery around, peacefully encircling a small hill crowned by a white-shingled Presbyterian church that had served as a hospital for the Continental Army in the Battle of Monmouth. A dark stain on one of the pews inside was said to be blood from a wounded soldier. George Washington slept beneath a tree here the night after the fighting, awaking to learn that the British had stolen away before he could fight them another day, and some of the battle's casualties lay buried up in the shadow of the church.

Jimmy stood to the side as the dirt from the displaced graves was poured into the vault, and the weathered, old stones then stacked on top before it was sealed and covered over. He opened his small black prayer book to the twenty-third psalm and solemnly read the words he had heard so often he could recite them by heart, the words the schoolchildren could no longer hear, the same words that were once said over these dead at their first resting place:

> The Lord is my shepherd; I shall not want.
> He maketh me to lie down in green pastures: he leadeth me
>   beside the still waters.
> He restoreth my soul: he leadeth me in the paths of righteousness
>   for his name's sake.
> Yea, though I walk through the valley of the shadow of death,
>   I will fear no evil . . .

"Waaaalter!" the voice shouted through the peach trees. "We've got a problem here!"

Walter Denise was bouncing up the dirt lane in his pickup when he heard his name called. Up ahead he saw that the sprayer, and the tractor pulling it, were sitting idle—a clogged nozzle, he guessed. He would just clean it out, he hoped, and then he and the sprayer would both be back on their way.

"Gummed up again?" he asked as he walked toward the worker who was bent over the back of the sprayer.

"No, take a look at this."

Walter bent, too, and saw that the tow bar, the two-inch square piece of metal that hitched the sprayer to the tractor that pulled it, had snapped—rusted, fatigued and brittle after its years traversing the rutted orchard roads.

"We'll have to get this back to the shop," he said, already mentally rummaging through his workbench for the plates he would need to weld the two pieces back into a whole.

Walter was growing weary himself after his own years in the orchard, and uncertain about how many more he wanted to spend in its service. The summer so far was the driest in three decades, and he had been moving irrigation pipes from one row to the next every eight hours without a break for weeks, trying to keep the peaches moist. Everywhere he turned, it seemed, something was demanding his attention—buyers haggling over bushel prices, a faulty piece of equipment in the packinghouse, a truck driver with a flat on the way to a delivery, a tractor in need of a new spark plug, and, most frustratingly and persistently, the migrants. He had been called out again in the middle of one recent night to quell yet another drunken fight in the Mickey Mouse camp. He was forty-three now, the oldest of his three children already a teenager, but he still felt like a hired hand sometimes.

Walter's father, Tunis, was in his seventies, but he continued to run the orchard as he always had, with a strong and solitary grip. He alone knew what the profit or loss was each year, how much was owed on mortgages and crop loans, how much was spent on labor and equipment. He owned the house in the peach orchard where Walter and his family lived, and paid his only son a flat salary, seventy-five dollars a week. A stern clarity of purpose had allowed him to build a thriving orchard from a patchwork of old vegetable fields, and kept him from relinquishing it easily. He occupied a large space not only in his family and his town, but in the wider circles of the state's agricultural community—past president of New Jersey State Horticultural Society, longtime director of the Jersey Fruit Cooperative Association, former vice president of the state Board of Agriculture. The New Jersey Agriculture Society had recently awarded him its highest honor, the Gold Medallion.

In his workshop, Walter slipped into his coveralls, donned his safety glasses and lit his welding torch to mend the sprayer's broken tow bar, the kind of job he had once found pleasure and satisfaction in, but that he now wished he could assign to someone else. Ever since he was a boy, his life had been shaped by a largely silent, but always weighty, expectation—that he, as the latest in a line of Denises who had been farming the local land for almost three centuries, would one day assume his father's place. The orchard was what he had always come back to, what had always been unthinkable not to come back to, from the war, from college, from marriage. Now that the orchard was almost his, though, he wasn't sure he wanted it. The droning rhythm of his work had worn down into ruts, and he had come to feel mired in a life that didn't demand enough of the skills that had allowed him to sail through college in two and a half years. And as he had changed inside, so, too, had the land outside, its face altered and threatened by a shift in the agricultural economy so swift and dramatic that even the most committed local farmers were wary about the future. Roughly one million Americans were leaving their farms each year; farmers accounted for just 7 percent of the nation's population now, down from almost a quarter in 1939.

With the sprayer returned to service, Walter drove into town on an errand, passing the sloping field of houses that had pushed aside the graveyard. Another FOR SALE sign had sprouted by the roadside a few fields closer in, advertising another farm's availability for development. The exodus from the cities to the north had proceeded, as it had elsewhere in America, with a speed and hunger that outstripped all projections, and counties like Monmouth, with wide, green spaces waiting at the ends of new highways, were the raw material for the nation's most profound and vast population shift since the cities themselves had first filled up. Since the war, the county had been losing farmland at a rate of three thousand to four thousand acres a year, nearer the coast at first, and along the route of the Parkway, but now around Freehold, too. The potato fields had dwindled to 5,000 acres, from a peak of 25,000. In just the last ten years, the number of egg-laying chickens had dropped by half, from 3 million to 1.5 million. Demographers were now predicting that over the next twenty years the county's human population would triple, reaching an almost unimaginable 1.1 million.

"There are those of us who shudder at the picture of more than a million people living in Monmouth within the next generation," an editorial in the *Transcript* lamented. "We are witnessing the rape of Monmouth. Daily we see our lovely county ravaged by the bulldozer. Nothing can stem the tide of humanity pouring into Monmouth, seeking homes, green grass, clean air."

As the farms faded, a chorus of grief and anger mourned their passing in a tone that echoed the rug mill's eulogies—the sadness at the loss of something old and familiar and essential magnified by bitter disbelief at such a spectacular squandering of resources. Just as the mill had abandoned a rare asset, a battalion of weavers whose concentration of skill was almost unmatched in America, so, too, had the farmers—land so fertile, a climate so temperate, that the county was routinely referred to as "the Eden of the Garden State." Before widespread irrigation pushed the Midwest ahead a few decades earlier, Monmouth had regularly ranked as one of the nation's most productive agricultural counties, swapping the annual title back and forth with Pennsylvania's Lancaster County. New Jersey's farms still led the nation in cash receipts per acre ($205), but they also topped the list of highest real estate taxes (more than $10 an acre). Economics and sociology were triumphing over agronomy, making the land, whatever its qualities, too valuable to grow anything but houses on, and turning the county into what the *Transcript* feared would become "a dreary, sprawling appendix of the New York metropolitan area." All those new highways, all those new refrigerated trucks, all those bricks of frozen foods in all those gleaming, new supermarkets, meant that great clusters of consumers like New York City no longer needed great swaths of producers just outside their doorsteps. New Jersey, long the kitchen garden of New York, was fast becoming its extra bedroom instead.

The rain finally came late in July, breaking the drought and freeing the local farmers to resume the conversation that had consumed them before it started. Walter heard them everywhere he went, talking about value—not of what was growing on their land, but of the land itself. His uncle and his father's cousin were both bank presidents in town, and the rich land deals they spoke of sparkled like jewels. The farm at the highway junction where the new supermarket sat had sold for two thousand dollars an acre, four times what it might have brought a few years earlier. In every rising increment, every fresh sale, every indication that this was not a real estate bubble but a genuine, unstoppable force of nature, Walter heard a door opening into a new life.

As the migrants moved out of the peaches and into the apples, the decision hardened in his mind: He would ask his father to sell. His burden lifted as his resolve grew, and he maneuvered through the harvest with the light and certain touch of someone passing for a final time through routines he had long since mastered, but had gladly decided to forsake. He told his children first. The orchard had been a paradise to them, with all its trees and ponds and winding lanes, and they were reluctant to leave. If they wanted the orchard, he told them, he would stay and run it, with their help, until their time came to take over. But they had seen the way he had worked, and they declined.

Telling his father would be harder, and he waited until after the last of the Stayman Winesaps were in, the official end of the season—the same deadline that had once determined the date of his wedding. One evening late in November, Walter drove slowly up the orchard's main road, through the dark and leafless apple trees and past the main packinghouse and the cold-storage building, to the low-ceilinged colonial farmhouse he had grown up in, and been expected to return to. He had crept silently through enemy forests on scouting patrols, led men into battle under fire, faced down drunken, flailing migrants in the camp across the road, but rarely had he ever been as nervous as he was now, walking across the driveway toward the warm, yellow lights of his childhood home. His parents' dog, a German shepherd, barked at the unexpected crunch of gravel underfoot.

Walter's grave face, his somber and deliberate manner, wordlessly told his father that the visit was more than casual. "Dad, there's something I need to talk to you about," he began, before finally saying out loud what he had been practicing silently in his mind for months. "I don't want to spend the rest of my life on the farm."

"What do you mean?" his father asked.

"What I mean is, if you get an offer to sell it, take it," he said. "I've had enough. If it takes two or three or four years, fine—I just don't want to be here for the rest of my life."

Tunis Denise tried to hold his stern mask of old-Dutch reserve intact, but the news punctured him so sharply that some air inevitably leaked out. As much as he might have prepared for this moment—which wasn't entirely a surprise, given what he had seen lately of the decline in both the local farm economy and Walter's own enthusiasm—he still felt his heart sinking, realizing in an instant that his life's work would not survive him. He knew his son well enough, though, to understand that this declaration was final, that there would be no talking him out of it.

"What will you do?" he asked.

"I don't know yet," Walter said. "Something that makes better use of my abilities. When one door is closing, another is opening."

Developers quickly came courting. Walter spent the winter in the barns, overhauling the machinery yet one more time, while his father wrangled with suitors, and by early spring the town's planning board was reviewing a sketch plat for 165 house lots in a development called Orchard Hill Estates on 122 acres still thick with apple and peach trees just beginning to bud. Another developer bought much of the remaining land for a similar price, about one thousand dollars an acre, and dubbed it "Colts Glen." When Walter examined the maps of the new streets planned for the land whose individual trees, all twelve thousand of them, he had once cataloged on graph paper, he noticed that some were named for family members of the developers. None were christened "Denise."

As the builders and the bankers navigated through the shoals of paper, securing permits and approvals, mortgages and loans, Walter sent his crews out to nurture the orchard through a final crop. Most of the trees were slated for execution, but through their final months they were tended with the same care that had allowed them to grow over the decades from spindly saplings into sturdy monuments as tall as the houses that would replace them. Each meal this season was their last—the usual round of fungicides and insecticides, washed down by water from the irrigation ponds—and when their fruit was gone, so, too, was their purpose. The migrants drifted away, packing up and heading back south, as each variety reached the end of its harvest, until all that remained were the Winesaps.

Enough other farmers were harvesting their last crops, too, that the anger and resentment the exodus had first sparked was fading now into a sad and weary acceptance of the inevitable. "In a way, it is to weep," a *Transcript* columnist wrote. "But what is a farmer to do when age slows his stride and the longing for ease overtakes him and the developer waves a shaft of greenbacks at him? Why, the only sensible thing is to bow to fate and sell."

With each new field that went fallow, the region's characteristic rural rhythms grew quieter and less distinct. There were still migrant shacks and grange halls and tractors meandering on yellow gravel roads—as well as the occasional arrest for cockfighting, moonshining and deer poaching—but there were also daily commuter buses to Newark and New York, and a new department store in the highway shopping center, the first since Perrine's Big Red Store and Levy's on Main Street closed in the Depression, that carried white vinyl go-go boots and op-art minidresses. When one of the local farm-equipment dealers closed up and moved out, a biochemical company moved in, and the fireflies that children captured on grassy summer evenings suddenly acquired a value, fifty cents per hundred: Their taillights contained luciferase, an essential ingredient for one of the purified enzymes the company prepared.

The Denise's cold-storage warehouse was laden with apples all through the winter, and the remaining workers in the packinghouse filled and dispatched crates whenever an order came in. As the delivery trucks were parceling out the last harvest, the bulldozers were busy ensuring that no new crop would arrive—knocking down trees and carving new streets and generally mangling what had been so carefully cultivated for so many years. Walter's father couldn't watch. He retreated with his wife to a retirement house near the ocean, and began planning trips to distant places. When the apples were finally exhausted, the auctioneer came again—the first auction had followed the peach season—and the local farmers who were still in business gathered to pick over the equipment Walter was glad to no longer be caring for: conveyors, sorters, forklifts, tractors, irrigation pumps and sprayers, including one with a welded tow bar.

Walter wasn't much given to sentiment but he did keep one large memento, the cast-iron field bell that had once called the help in, and he tried to negotiate a deal with the developer to remain in his rambling old, turreted farmhouse, and keep the barns out back. His father had already sold it, though, all of a piece with the other land, and the developer, wary of too much rustic charm lurking amid the split-levels, wanted an extortionate price for its return. Walter passed on a chance at one of the model homes in the new development, and bought instead the house in town—around the corner from both the high school and Bill Lopatin, and on ground the British had camped on the night before the Battle of Monmouth—that his aunt was leaving after the death of his uncle, the bank president. Driving past the orchard one day after moving, he saw that his old home and his barns had, without warning or ceremony, been obliterated, leveled as flat as the bulldozed migrant camp.

Walter's new neighbor across the street was an old friend, the courtly Mac Clark, the county agricultural agent for more than three decades whose recent retirement had coincided with the orchard's own. "My one regret—the thing I've hated most to see—is that this area, endowed by nature with nearly perfect soil and climate for the growth of many farm products, couldn't have remained as it once was instead of succumbing to the urban sprawl," Clark had told the *Transcript* upon his departure. "I hate to see the land being taken over and the loss of open space. We are destroying our environment."

Walter's own view of the future wasn't quite so dark. He had applied for jobs as a school administrator—he had spent some time on the board of education, and he knew how to handle people and money—but his only offer was too low and too far away, and he was still searching for work when he bumped into a friend, the real estate agent Bud Lamson, on Main Street one day.

"How about working for me?" Lamson suggested when he heard of Walter's availability.

The logic of it was so inescapable that Walter wondered why he hadn't thought of it earlier. He had spent his life on the land, and understood better than most people how to measure its value. His new job put him in a jacket and a tie and an office, but it allowed him to continue roaming outside, without an orchard constantly tapping his shoulder for attention, and to circulate among people who didn't tax his nerves the way the migrants had. He was still working the earth, as Denises had for centuries, only now he was selling it instead of tilling it. When his rounds took him back to the orchard, he tried to see something recognizable through the web of curving streets that had been imposed upon it, but the view was blurring. Hundreds of families, none of them known to him, lived there now, and the surviving trees that had charmed them at first were fast becoming a nuisance, scraggly and untrimmed, and dropping fungus-infected, insect-bored fruit that rotted in piles on the ground.

His shovel scraping against the sidewalk, Jimmy Higgins was bent over and swiping at the snow when he looked up to see a young man in uniform walking toward him along the uncleared portion of the path. A war was on, he knew, but soldiers were scarce in town, their comings and goings unrecorded by the front page of the local paper, as his own had been. As the figure approached, Jimmy recognized the uniform as belonging to the marines, and the face as one of his neighbors from the next block.

"What are you doing home, Bart?" Jimmy asked, pausing to lean on his shovel.

"I'm on leave before they send me overseas," Bart Haynes said.

The last time Jimmy saw him, Bart was a scrawny high-school kid with an unruly mop of hair running up Center Street to the duplex where his family lived in the shadow of the mill, right next door to Goldstein's corner grocery and across the street from the pool room and Caiazzo's music store. The other half of the house was occupied by Tex Vinyard, a factory worker who moonlighted as manager and godfather to a rock-and-roll band called The Castiles. Bart was the band's drummer. The lead guitarist was an even skinnier and gawkier kid a year younger, Bruce Springsteen, whose cousin—Frankie Bruno, the only son of the last man from Freehold killed in the war—had first taught him to play. The Castiles practiced in Vinyard's dining room, and, wearing black vests and pointy Beatles boots, swaggered through the local circuit of teen clubs and high-school dances for thirty-five dollars a night. Bruce was a quick-silver guitarist, but a rough singer; his regular spotlight moment was a cover of The Who's "My Generation." "Hope I die before I get old," he would wail. But by the time the band all piled into Vinyard's 1961 Mercury on a rainy Sunday afternoon and drove to a fifty-dollar-an-hour strip-mall studio to record their first single ("Baby I," backed with "That's What You Get," both cowritten by Bruce and George Theiss, the rhythm guitarist and lead singer), they had a new drummer. Bart had quit school and enlisted in the marines just a month before.

Bart was only eighteen, and even in uniform, he still looked to Jimmy like the quiet, diligent neighborhood boy who had once done odd jobs around the funeral home—cutting grass, trimming bushes, painting. But an unfamiliar heaviness seemed to have settled upon him, and when he spoke, Jimmy heard in his voice the weight of the world.

"I'm saying goodbye to everybody," Bart said in a way that made clear he didn't mean temporarily. "I won't come back alive."

"Don't talk like that," Jimmy said.

"No, the next time you see me you'll be burying me," Bart said as he walked off toward Main Street.

The casual fatalism of the young marine haunted Jimmy long after the sidewalk was cleared of snow, so different was it from the wary confidence he had carried with him into his own war. But his journey as a soldier had started on a bus on Court Street packed with other local young men, seen off by a crowd of family and friends and Legionnaires, bound for a war that was understood and accepted and supported as much as any war could be. Two out of every three American men between the ages of eighteen and thirty-four had worn a uniform then; only one-third of draft-age men (itself a smaller pool, with the draft cutoff at twenty-six) served now, and only 10 percent actually went to Vietnam. The young men who left for the war left alone, like Bart, and they came back alone to a town that often didn't even know they had gone. Like most veterans of his war, Jimmy assumed that if the government was sending men into battle now, then there was a good reason for it. Exactly what the reason was, though, wasn't as unmistakably clear as the reason behind Leyte and Bastogne.

"The U.S. policies and actions in Vietnam are vitally necessary deterrents to Communist expansion and as part of America's security," the keynote speaker at the last Memorial Day parade, the national commander of the Jewish War Veterans, had declared, just before a fighter jet from McGuire Air Force Base swooped over the town. "We must back our boys. We must continue to press for peace—but peace with honor and peace with justice. But if fight we must, then fight we will and we will not shirk from our patriotic responsibilities as proud Americans. . . . Communist aggression must be stopped here and now. It is a serious threat to our American way of life."

The mayor and council had unanimously passed a similarly strong endorsement recently. "The United States Government follows the sound policy of putting out a fire down the street before it reaches our homes," the resolution said. "America is strong today and, in order to keep her strong, we must stand up for what we believe to be right against any Communist aggression whether it be on our soil or on foreign soil. We fully support the president and our armed forces, we do not condone demonstrations that tend to weaken our policies and demoralize our fighting men in the eyes of foreign countries, we do not condone young men tearing up their draft cards. We are Americans, we believe in America and we are ready and willing to defend America."

Vietnam was the latest battle in a war that had begun even before Jimmy's had ended—when the Soviet Union started annexing the broken nations of Eastern Europe as it rolled through on the way to Berlin. The enemy now wasn't a single nation, but an ideology, Communism, that many nations had embraced, and the fight was against anyone who was trying to spread it, whether in Moscow, China, Hanoi or America itself. The new war surfaced periodically in Freehold, but never with the same sustained force as the old one. Two white crosses were added to the memorial at Elks Point, casualties from Korea. Jake Errickson had scanned the sky for enemies from the observation post atop the mill, and Stu Bunton halted traffic when the town froze for one of its regular air-raid drills. If real bombs ever did fall on New Jersey, and disabled the state civil-defense control center in Trenton, Freehold High School was its designated stand-in; the old Brakeley cannery would be pressed into service as an emergency hospital. Jimmy and the board of education approved the use of the schools' basements as public fallout shelters. To encourage citizens to build shelters of their own, a concrete-block model went up on the front lawn of the Hall of Records, large enough for six people, complete with stores of water and canned food and a chemical toilet.

But an ideology—no matter how repellent it might be, or how many innocents may have died in its service—was never as galvanizing an enemy as the evil conquerors who had once bombed Pearl Harbor and blitzkrieged Europe, and Freehold, like most of America, enlisted in this new war more from duty than passion. There were no bond drives, no ration tickets, no honor rolls downtown, no housewives saving bacon grease for bullets, no high-school boys rushing to the recruiting stations. Jimmy had worked at Fort Monmouth when Joseph McCarthy was sniffing for Communists there, but like most of his colleagues, he never believed that anything threatening the nation's security would ever turn up. Bill Lopatin was prepared to build bomb shelters if anyone ever asked, but the rest of the town must have shared his skepticism about their value, because no one ever did. Walter Denise was relieved that his oldest son was bound for college, shielded from the draft at least temporarily by a student deferment. Vietnam, too distant to worry about daily, had sent home no casualties yet.

Jimmy did have a veteran to bury, though, soon after Bart's visit—a marine with a Purple Heart, wounded on Guam, but killed here at home in the winter of 1967, when his car skidded on an icy patch on Highway 9 and slammed into a telephone pole. The veterans of Jimmy's war hadn't reached the age of dying yet, and the wake packed the funeral home, the mourners' breath fogging in the March cold as they waited outside to get in. On the morning of the funeral, he led the procession out the driveway in his black Chrysler, the line of cars behind him long enough that Stu Bunton stood at Elks Point stopping traffic so it could proceed uninterrupted onto Main Street.

The flag-draped casket was carried into St. Rose of Lima, Jimmy's own church. His two sons were in the adjacent school the parish had built on the old military-school grounds, but neither was old enough yet to be excused for altar-boy duty this morning. The funeral mass had taken on a different form lately—not even the millennial traditions of the Catholic church, it seemed, were immune to the forces of change all around—and though he preferred it, he was still getting used to it. The priest faced the congregation, not the altar, and spoke in English, not Latin—liturgical reforms unleashed by the Second Vatican Council. At the cemetery, though, the same one where Major Peter Vredenburgh and the other heroes of the Civil War were buried, the ritual was touchingly intact—the flag folded into a tight triangle for the widow, taps from a bugler, a marine honor guard firing a rifle salute.

As Jimmy left the cemetery and drove back down Main Street toward the funeral home, the somberness of the day seemed mirrored by the forlorn face of the downtown—such a pale echo now of the boisterous, prosperous place that had once welcomed him, and the marine he just buried, home from the war. In the years since the mill left, the exodus from the business district had continued unchecked, hastened by the shift of the local economy's weight to the surrounding highways. Several more fires had followed after the Strand block burned, punching more holes in the streetscape. Window displays tried to mask some of the vacant stores—paintings from the local art society, patriotic assemblages from the Americanism department of the Women's Club. "In its deep and abiding faith in the ultimate triumph of freedom, America still holds the key to the future of mankind," read a placard quoting from J. Edgar Hoover's book *A Study of Communism.* In another hung a stark, bold-faced poster with a darker message.

URBAN RENEWAL COULD TAKE YOUR HOME AWAY, it warned.

Downtown Freehold had slid low enough that the earlier musings about urban renewal and revitalization had hardened into a radical plan to bulldoze half of it and start over again. America's urban landscapes—even such small ones as Freehold's—had been battered by merciless new economic and social forces in the years since the war, and the solutions that had arisen were equally merciless. In many places it seemed simplest to just erase the last century—to tear down vacant stores to make way for shopping centers, and tenements to make way for apartment blocks. The federal government—which had opened a new agency, Housing and Urban Development, to tackle these problems—was flush with cash to help cities and towns remake themselves, and Freehold had been allotted almost $2 million for a proposal that would alter its face more dramatically than all the past fires combined had. More than fifty old buildings would come down and an enclosed shopping mall would go up, fronting a pedestrian plaza with trees, benches, fountains and kiosks. Two blocks of

South Street would vanish, with traffic rerouted around a widened Throckmorton Street. Retail space would quintuple, in an effort to resurrect the bustling shopping nights of earlier decades by luring downtown all the people who lived in the new houses on the old farms, and who would otherwise stick to the highway strip malls. Steinbach's, the grand department store from Asbury Park, was said to be interested. Opinions about the plan were sharp and deeply divided. Jimmy, chairman of the Citizens Advisory Committee for Community Improvement, was an emphatic supporter. His business was downtown, and although it was thriving—a funeral home wasn't subject to the same economic forces as a shoe store—he didn't want to watch the streets around him wither.

"It is the future of Freehold that is at stake—a future which may either erase the borough from the map of progress or increase its standards in tune with the times in which we live," the *Transcript* editorialized.

Two days after the funeral, Jimmy boarded a small airplane with six other community leaders for one of his rare days away from Freehold. Because death kept no schedule, and bereaved families expected to find him when they needed him, he rarely strayed too far from town, and habitually informed local waiters and movie ushers of his whereabouts, but his devotion to the cause of urban renewal took him on a brief excursion to Norfolk, Virginia, which had already, on a much larger scale, done what Freehold was contemplating. In Norfolk, in the company of Freehold's mayor, a few councilmen, the borough's engineer and its attorney, he toured the shiny, landscaped mall that had risen from the bulldozed remains of what the Virginia hosts called a "seamy honky-tonk district." He returned to Freehold that evening—despite a fuel gauge on the plane that worried him by dipping perilously close to empty—even more convinced of what he already believed.

A referendum on urban renewal was scheduled for June, and as the weather warmed through the spring, so did the rhetoric from doomsayers on both sides of the issue. Lined up firmly behind it was the vast bulk of the civic establishment—the mayor and a majority of the council, the chamber of commerce, the Downtown Merchants Association, the board of education, the Jaycees, the clergy, the doctors, the lawyers, the bankers and, most loudly and stridently, the newspaper. Against the plan stood a looser coalition of merchants whose businesses would have to make way for it; fiscal conservatives wary of the ultimate local tax bill; traditionalists generally averse to such sweeping, irreversible measures; and homeowners in a white neighborhood who feared the relocation to an adjacent garden apartment complex of the seventy tenants, mostly Puerto Rican or black, who would be displaced.

"The town has cancer and urban renewal is the only cure for it," said a salesman from a downtown men's shop at one of the crowded public meetings.

"Urban renewal takes from the needy and gives to the greedy," protested a window sign, one in a series from a printer whose building was slated for demolition, and who, wounded on the beach at Normandy, was unlikely to back down from the fight.

"What future is my child to have here if nothing is done?" a lawyer wondered at another meeting.

"To build new stores for the merchants with money that should go to our boys in Vietnam is immoral," another poster argued.

On the morning of Monday, June 19, 1967, Jimmy walked out the back door of the funeral parlor, crossed the public parking lot that would be expanded to accommodate the new mall's shoppers, slipped along the same alley he had once hurried through to watch the Strand block burn, climbed down the steps to the basement of the redbrick public library on Main Street—one of the seventeen hundred that Andrew Carnegie had sprinkled philanthropically across the nation more than half a century earlier—and checked the "yes" box beside the single question on the ballot: "Should the Borough of Freehold go forward with the Urban Renewal Project in its Downtown Business Area?" By the end of the day, 1,969 of his fellow citizens had joined him at the polls, at the firehouse and the synagogue and the Intermediate School and the first-aid squad and the Hall of Records and the YMCA, not quite half of the town's registered voters in all, much fewer than had turned out when Dwight Eisenhower and Bill Lopatin shared the ballot. A total of 878 of them voted "yes." 1,091 voted "no." Though the referendum was not legally binding, the mayor and council pledged to "abide by the mandate of the people," and voted the plan dead.

"Small men in a small town," sniped the headline of a *Transcript* editorial mourning the defeat.

"What now?" the newspaper asked. "What is to happen to Freehold's rapidly spreading blight, turning our once proud business district into a slum area? Where will the county seat of Monmouth, and one of the nation's historic cradles, go from here? To oblivion, where many have placed it already, or will there be, despite its temporary moral and economic defeat, enough will left to salvage whatever can be salvaged?"

A minister from the Presbyterian church was more succinct. "Nobody won and everybody lost," he observed. "That's the story of Freehold's attempt at progress, isn't it?"

In the weeks after the urban renewal defeat, news from another front seeped through town—a soldier from Freehold, Army Chief Warrant Officer Walter Wrobleski, had been reported missing in action in Vietnam—and Jimmy wondered about Bart, whose farewell still echoed eerily in his memory. At the end of October, two marines drove past the funeral home and stopped in front of the Haynes house on the next block. Bart's sister, Connie, came to the door in the same pink nightgown she had been wearing in a dream two nights earlier, a dream in which her brother had died, and when she saw them she knew what they had come to tell her. On Sunday, October 22, the day after the first big march on the Pentagon had ended in tear gas and cracked heads and the arrest of hundreds of antiwar protesters, Barton E. Haynes, lance corporal and former drummer of the Castiles, was killed by mortar fire in Quang Tri Province, near South Vietnam's border with the North. He was nineteen years old. The Castiles' lead singer, George Theiss, had also dreamed of him before his death: Bart was calling on the phone, saying, "I'm all right, I'm all right." Connie heard her father scream in the night at the loss of his only son.

Bart's body was accompanied home from Vietnam by a soldier from Freehold who had known him, and was received at Higgins Memorial Home on Mischief Night, the evening before Halloween when kids just a few years younger ventured out with soap and toilet paper and mild maliciousness. The news was reported not on the front page of the *Transcript*, as all the battle deaths of Jimmy's war had been, but inside, with the rest of the obituaries. At the wake, two marines in full-dress uniform flanked the casket, rifles at parade rest, eyes staring stonily beyond the crowd that had come to pay respects to the latest of the eighteen thousand Americans who had died so far in Vietnam, and the first from their own town. Jimmy watched the slow, somber line of mourners and wondered if he had ever really been that young himself when he served.

The small troop of soldiers marched up Main Street to the respectful applause of the sidewalk crowds, stopping every block or so to unshoulder their rifles, sprinkle black powder from their small leather satchels down the barrels, and aim up into leafy June oaks. They wore buckskin and linen, knee breeches and vests, buckle boots and tricorner hats, the irregular uniforms of the rebellious colonists who had won America's freedom from England. Behind them trailed fife bands, drum-and-bugle corps, women in long dresses and bonnets, local politicians adorned with ruffled bibs like their colonial predecessors, and a line of floats depicting the era when Freehold was a fervent Patriot stronghold in the nation's most unambiguously glorious and triumphant war. The parade was the closing act of Colonial Week in 1968, a celebration that officially marked both the 275th birthday of the town and the 190th anniversary of the Battle of Monmouth, but that also offered, in the face of a more uncertain contemporary conflict, a safe and indirect forum for demonstrating loyalty to America's founding ideals. As the riflemen fired their blank charges, the crowd flinched, the children squealed, and the parade resumed its march toward the racetrack.

Stu Bunton was stationed outside the track, the same duty he pulled most years for the July Fourth fireworks displays, keeping the traffic from disturbing the flow of marchers and spectators across the street and inside. An announcer heralded the arrival of each unit on the dirt oval, interrupting the narration with news bulletins from the Battle of Monmouth, reporting on its progress as if it were even now underway just a few fields over: General Lee's advance force snaps at the tail of the British; Cornwallis chases them back across town; a furious Washington gallops up on his white charger and relieves Lee; Lafayette and Wayne regroup on the high ground; Greene's cannons block a British advance; Molly Pitcher hauls water to the wilting soldiers; the British vanish in the night, too far ahead for pursuit. Trilling curlicues of fife music drifted over the crowd from one of the bands—"Yankee Doodle" first, then "The World Turned Upside Down," the tune that tradition said the British played as Cornwallis surrendered at Yorktown, three years after Monmouth, ending the war for America's existence.

When the parade had finally tailed out, the hats and bonnets removed from sweaty, matted heads, the calendar returned to the present century, Stu went home for supper before he was due to report, still in uniform, for one of the private security details he worked to supplement his police salary. He was a sergeant now—he had hung a chin-up bar in his basement to prepare for the fitness portion of the test—but the rank added only three hundred dollars a year to his pay, and it still kept him on a rotating shift schedule. In sixteen years on the force, he had yet to call in sick, and leave his partner to work alone. The chief would be retiring soon, and if Stu were promoted to lieutenant then, as seemed likely now, he would finally lose the midnight shift, and rotate only through days and evenings. He would also become an obvious candidate for chief himself one day, but he wasn't sure he wanted to go that far. The world was changing fast, and when things went wrong, when old values and standards were crumbling, when the young and the lawless seemed to run wild, when politicians needed to shift blame away from themselves, the police chief was an easy scapegoat, a role Stu was reluctant to assume.

"This is no longer a sleepy little town," a councilman had declared recently, accusing the police of behaving as if it were, and complaining of slow response times, of "gang activity," of streets that residents were afraid to walk at night.

Yes, the numbers were up, the chief acknowledged—nationally, crime rates had been rising steadily since the end of the war, and locally the police had handled a record number of complaints and investigations in the previous year, 7,289, almost 1,000 more than the year before—but the problem, and whatever solutions there might be, lay beyond his jurisdiction. In defending himself and his department, he turned to a higher source for support, quoting from the FBI *Law Enforcement Bulletin*.

"The small town is no longer the typical American way of life," declared the report the chief cited. "Today's society is increasingly mobile, urban, impersonal, anonymous; it is no longer capable of enforcing its moral and behavioral codes simply by force of community opinion. . . . Today thousands of Americans live in fear. . . . Crime is our nation's number one internal problem."

All through the previous summer, on the hot and angry streets of Detroit and Milwaukee and Houston and Atlanta and scores of other cities where race riots erupted, Americans had shot at each other the way they had once fired at foreign enemies from Germany and Japan. Blacks had made significant gains since the Montgomery bus boycott—culminating in the Civil Rights Act of 1964 and the Voting Rights Act of 1965—but frustrations rose when it became clear that laws can't always change beliefs, or provide better jobs and housing. Protests broke out, and sometimes ended with armored tanks rolling through black neighborhoods like the occupying army in Normandy. When a cab driver was seen being dragged from his car by police in Newark—the largest city in New Jersey, and the source of many of the urban emigrants now decamping to the new suburbs in the fields of Monmouth—rumors spread of his beating, even his death, and rock-throwing crowds soon gathered around the fourth precinct station house. Fires blazed and looters smashed store windows, making off with whatever they could carry, sparing only those marked "soul brother" to indicate black ownership. The governor finally sent in five hundred state troopers and three thousand National Guardsmen. After five days the toll was $10 million in property damage and twenty-three people dead—one white police officer, one white firefighter, and twenty-one black civilians, including two children, six women and a seventy-three-year-old man. Racial unrest spilled over into Jersey City, Elizabeth, New Brunswick and, most violently, Plainfield, the small city of Jimmy Higgins's apprenticeship, where a white cop was beaten to death by a gang of young black men.

"The ethical collapse of the civil rights movement," the *Transcript* called the riots in an editorial. "By actions such as those in Newark and Plainfield, the Negro cause may not only lose respect in the eyes of the average well-meaning citizen, but the civil rights movement may lose in weeks what it had gained in the last decade under diligent and enlightened leadership. White guilt may be replaced by defensive anger."

Their concern was echoed in other quarters. "Here we are fighting over in Vietnam, fighting to keep the country free," a soldier wrote home from overseas. "But what's the country doing to be free? Killing our leaders, having race riots, destroying millions of dollars worth of property, having sit-ins, love-ins, draft card burnings. What's the United States turning into?"

No rocks were thrown in anger in Freehold—except for the usual teen vandalism of the wide and tempting grid of windows in the rug mill—and no shots were fired in retaliation by the police, but a few months earlier Stu had been sent by the department to a special course in riot control at the New Jersey Police Academy. Newark had been such a violent shock to the state's equilibrium that the governor, determined to forestall any further surprises, ordered the state police to prepare the local police for the battles that might be coming their way. "Operation Combine" was designed "to help municipalities cope with problems covering prevention and control of civil disturbances," and every day for two weeks, Stu drove to the academy in Sea Girt for a tutorial in societal breakdown. He learned what happened in Newark and the other cities,

how order was restored and at what cost, what worked and what didn't—
the ill-trained guardsmen firing wildly at elusive snipers, the three different radio frequencies (one each for the guard, the state police and the
Newark police) that prevented proper communication, the way rumor
was mistaken for fact. Tear gas was the weapon of preference, he was told,
but if they fired at you, then you fired at them. He studied the charts an
intelligence officer presented, prepared with the same elaborate care
Jimmy Higgins had once taken before mission briefings for the 391st
Bombardment Group—organizational trees of the Black Panthers, the
United Afro-American Association, the Students for a Democratic Society and any other group, large or small, the state considered a potential
threat to civic order. They were the new enemy, he learned, not invading
from another nation, but tunneling away within his own.

At his security detail that night, though, at the Hullabaloo dance club
on Broad Street, Stu expected an assault only on his ears. Over the years,
he had spent many off-duty hours moonlighting as a guard, standing in
uniform in places where the presence of a police officer would help in-
hibit misbehavior—football games, the supermarket, the old Strand,
CYO dances, the gate to the barns at the racetrack. Inside the track, he
stood by the fifty-dollar window. His latest venue was the new teen hang-
out that had taken over the vacant Grand Union, one of the many that
had opened across the country in conjunction with the *Hullabaloo* television series.

"The Hullabaloo scene is a step forward in providing good, supervised entertainment for our teenagers," the mayor had said when granting the license. "We wish you all the luck in the world."

Hullabaloo had debuted with a flourish a few months earlier with an
appearance by Screaming Lord Sutch, the eccentric British rock singer
and candidate for Parliament from his own National Teenagers' Party,
who stepped out of a Rolls-Royce in full, top-hatted, Carnaby Street mod
splendor. The club served no alcohol, but every Friday and Saturday night
its small stage featured acts of major local and minor national note: the
Psychedelic Excursion, Circus Maximus, the Fantastic Fanatics, the Can-
terbury Fair, Upward Movement, the Junction Blues Band, the Sidewalk
Theory, Mother's Little Helpers, the Younger Society, the Generations,
King James and his Court, the Spontaneous Love Combustion, the Flowers of Youth, the Words of Luv, Last Judgment and, of course, the Castiles.
Like the modest kiddie parks that had flourished briefly nearby a decade

earlier—Space City, Storyland Village, Cowboy City—Hullabaloo catered to the demographic bulge created by Stu and all the other returning veterans. The babies born in the years after the war were coming of age, and like the young of every other generation, they believed that whatever they thought and did had never been thought or done before by anyone anywhere at any time. The world was America's, their fathers had seen to that, and now America, they believed, was theirs.

When Stu was their age he, too, had wanted more than it seemed Freehold could offer. He, like them, had listened to music that held little appeal to his elders. But he had grown up in the Depression, and it had straitened his expectations. They had grown up in flusher times, with more opportunity, more freedom, and their expectations were stratospheric. They had an especially acute case of the idealism that always infects the young. Anything was possible, they believed; America could be whatever they wished it to be. The war had taught Stu otherwise, of course, had made him want only to return to the Freehold he had once so eagerly wished to escape. But what, he wondered, would do the same for them? What would make them appreciate what they already had?

More local boys were going to Vietnam than speaking out against it—Jake Errickson's son had just become, to much local acclaim, Freehold's first-ever graduate of the Naval Academy, and was headed to flight school in Pensacola—but on Main Street a record store had opened that sold black-light posters, rolling papers and other head-shop paraphernalia. Teenagers were occasionally led up the stairs to the police station above the firehouse, arrested for smoking marijuana. At a recent council meeting, a high-school sophomore had appeared as the self-appointed representative of what he called the International Commission for the Introduction of Flamboyance to Freehold. A be-in was what the town needed, he argued, and he offered a sunny, beatific vision of artists displaying their canvases, poets declaiming their verse, folksingers strolling under the trees.

"For one day, Freehold would be raised above the humdrum of daily life and would become a culturally stimulating and very much alive town," he said, as the councilmen smiled indulgently and promised to think about it.

The Hullabaloo was a larger, commercial version of a teen club that had opened the previous year in space provided by the Episcopal church on Throckmorton Street. More than 250 high-school students paid two dollars apiece to become members of the Left Foot, and Phelps Dodge, the electronics manufacturer in the next town where Jake was working now as a purchasing agent, donated fifty large cable reels that were converted to tables. An old parachute was draped from the ceiling, and the walls were painted a dark, cavelike brown. Entertainment was coordinated by Tex Vinyard, manager of the Castiles, who shared the bill on opening night with a band called Purpul Dyneste.

"It is vital to the life of a locale that new ideas and the creative energies of young people are not stifled—to do so is to contribute to a line in the epitaph of a community," the *Transcript* wrote in support of the Left Foot.

The Castiles were on the marquee again as Stu pulled into the packed parking lot of the Hullabaloo the night of the colonial parade. Another band was playing, too, the 8th Majority, but the crowd had come to see the Castiles, who had grown popular enough locally to test their appeal in a bigger arena, and had ventured, briefly and inconclusively, up to some bookings in Greenwich Village. Bruce Springsteen had blossomed from the silent guitarist who first appeared at the house next door to Bart Haynes, and his ambition and abilities were beginning to outstrip his bandmates'. He was hearing and writing and playing things that they couldn't, and he had begun to frequent the clubs of Asbury Park, the proving ground for the area's best musicians. The band stood at a decisive juncture—they would either move up to the next level, and the larger venues there, or they would break up—and their fervent following wanted to embrace them again before they were out of reach.

The room was dim and cavernous and throbbing, the space once covered with grocery aisles swarming now with kids just a bit older than Stu's own. Go-go dancers gyrated in cages beside the stage. Whenever Stu checked the bathroom, smoke billowed out as if from a fire—cigarettes, not marijuana.

"Why doesn't he get a haircut?" Stu asked half in jest, shouting over the din to his partner, Gene Urbelis, as they stood in the back.

Bruce's long wavy hair was parted in the middle, and dropped across his face like window curtains when he bent over a guitar solo. Something about the sound he was making, Stu could see, was piercing the audience in a way no one else had, and they screamed their gratitude.

"He's a good kid," Gene said. He had married Bruce's Aunt Edie, who had been widowed by Okinawa. "I try to slip him a few bucks once in a while."

"They love him, don't they?" Stu said.

Stu tried to hear what they heard in it, but he couldn't. There was no melody, no harmony, nothing that moved him or touched him or lodged inside him like the songs that had once floated through his bedside Philco from *Make-Believe Ballroom* in the years before the war; or that he had heard at the big-band concerts he went to in Asbury Park, before it was invaded by rock-and-roll; or that he and Ginny had danced to when the Johnny Desider Orchestra played at the PBA ball at the racetrack a few weeks earlier. The kids shouted and whistled and shook and swayed, and he listened and listened before he finally stopped, because all it was, as far as he could tell, was just so much noise.

13.

"Attempted Murder"

The borough council chamber shared the upstairs of the yellow-brick firehouse with the police department and the municipal offices, and on a Monday night in April of 1969 it was overflowing with citizens who wanted to be heard. Council meetings were usually as staid and predictable as the Doric columns that held up the building's pediment and peeked now through the tall windows behind the rostrum, but tonight's was edging toward chaos. Whenever someone rose to speak, hand-lettered picket signs bobbed up from the crowd like exclamation points. What the town had feared seemed finally to be here: The racial unrest that had troubled America in recent years—that had sparked the riots in Newark and Detroit and so many other cities—had now, officially and unmistakably, reached Freehold.

WE KNOW THIS IS A RACIST TOWN . . . MR. FIRE COMMISSIONER TAKE A
    STAND.
DON'T DISGRACE OUR COMMUNITY BY SUPPORTING A SEGREGATED FIRE
    DEPARTMENT.
WITHHOLD THE $5,000 FROM THE FIRST AID SQUAD.
DOOMED . . . DOOMED THE RACIST WAY IN THIS TOWN.

"We have all read the pickets," the exasperated mayor finally said, banging his gavel and ordering them lowered. "You are in front of the mayor and council of the Borough of Freehold and I require respect."

Respect was what everyone in the room required; the debate was over how it should be paid. The immediate question tonight focused on the

volunteer fire department and first-aid squad—why were they still exclu-
sively white?—but the larger issues behind it, the tensions and resent-
ments and suspicions, had been simmering for years. The council was, as
it had always been, entirely white, while many of the voices rising in the
audience were from blacks, who comprised maybe a fifth of the town's
population, but held none of its power. Like other black citizens who had
been standing up to protest all over America, they wanted some action
now—some acknowledgment that their grievances were genuine, that
somebody would try to answer them, that they wouldn't have to wait forever to see things change.

"You need to recognize the growing discontent in the black community, to create better community conditions," said a spokesman for a
restive new group called the Concerned Citizens. "We want freedom now."

The latest debate had been ignited the previous summer when a white
college student home on vacation protested—loudly, openly and for the
first time ever—the fire department's membership policies. For almost a
century, the town's firemen had comprised a kind of civic elite, racing out
from their homes and workplaces whenever the whistle blew, marching
proudly up Main Street in their brass-buttoned blue tunics in the Memorial Day parade, bringing their sons and grandsons into the line behind
them. When a fireman died, long black mourning drapes hung from the
firehouse columns, and his place was filled from the bulging waiting list.
Entrance was by election, and the dissenting vote of a single member, a
blackball, could keep an applicant out. No blacks had ever served, or even,
as far as anyone could remember, applied. "De facto segregation," the student called it, an opinion that cost him both the rear window of his car,
shattered by a firecracker as it sat in his driveway in the middle of the
night, and his upcoming summer job as assistant director of the YMCA
camp; the Y's executive director resigned in protest over the firing.

"Could you explain why anyone who is considered qualified by accepted standards must also be voted upon before he can prove his performance?" someone in the audience asked. An amendment to the fire
department's selection policy had been offered at tonight's meeting—a
concession that would, it was hoped, cut short an investigation by the
state's Division of Civil Rights—but applicants would still have to pass a
members' vote, a simple majority in an open ballot now. The presump-
tion among the protestors was that no black applicant would survive such
a vote.

"Because," answered the councilman who was the fire commissioner.
"Because of what?'

"Because I think it's fair. We live in a democracy, although some
people try to disrupt it, and in a democracy you vote."

"But that's a volunteer company—do you vote in any volunteer company?"

"I haven't been voted upon in the U.S. Army, for which I volunteered," the president of the Concerned Citizens interjected.

"You want to know with whom you are in line when you fight fires,"
another councilman retorted. "I know the army doesn't vote, but sometimes you wish they had."

Tonight's debate was the most public evidence yet of the local black
community's unwillingness to remain a silent minority any longer. Freehold's black residents had been raising their voices sporadically and ten-
tatively over the last twenty years, ever since Ferdinand Fenderson first
stood alone before the borough council in his white shirt and narrow tie
to complain about rough policemen and sewage runoff on Avenue A. By
the mid-1960s, a group called the Neighborhood Council was lobbying
quietly for better housing and job opportunities, and successfully
protesting a billboard the John Birch Society sponsored in the heart of
the black neighborhood: SUPPORT YOUR LOCAL POLICE, it urged before it
was removed, staring directly and tauntingly across Throckmorton Street
at the black Elks Club. The mayor appointed Buddy Lewis's nephew
Danny, retired now from the NFL, to head an interracial recreation committee that organized a downtown block dance and other youth activities. A black woman was elected to the school board, the first black official
in the town's history, and the police department finally had a black officer, almost a decade after Buddy had balked. And Danny Lewis had just
filed to run in the Democratic primary for a borough council seat.

But after the riot summers, and the assassination of Martin Luther
King, Jr., the patient tactics of the past began to feel like surrender. The
Concerned Citizens who were here tonight had formed to speak with a
louder voice—for a youth center, a Job Corps program, stricter code enforcement of substandard housing, more voter registration, as well as the
desegregation of the fire department and first-aid squads. To much of
Freehold's white population, and the council that was representing them,
there was little incentive to change the way things had always been:

Change was potentially hazardous, and needed to be incremental. To the town's blacks, though, there was nothing but incentive: Change was progress, and needed to be swift and decisive.

The big clock with the Roman-numeral face ticked deeper into the evening, and any chance of agreement seemed to recede with the hours. Each side was speaking past the other, flailing at issues that had roiled the nation, that were beyond the ability of any one town to resolve. The council felt both besieged and frustrated: How could it be expected to undo centuries of discrimination in a night, a year, a decade even? The Concerned Citizens were frustrated, too: If they couldn't get answers from the council, then where else were they supposed to turn?

The debate was still circling inconclusively when, a few minutes before ten, the room was jolted by a blast from the fire whistle in the cupola perched on the roof above. Two-two-four bleated the coded signal—Avenue C and Court Street, in the Peach Orchard, near the old Colored School. Some in the audience went to the windows as the fire engines raced out of the garage bays below, and the red lights flashed through the darkness.

"False alarm," someone announced when the trucks were spotted rumbling back five minutes later, but then the whistle blew again: Two-three-four, Throckmorton and West Main, just around the corner.

The sirens rose back into a scream as the trucks sped past again, stopping in front of the YMCA, where four Molotov cocktails were burning. While everybody up here in the council chambers was debating—fighting with words, harsh sometimes, but still just words—somebody down on the street was speaking a rougher language. Three of the crude incendiaries—pint whiskey bottles filled with kerosene, paper wicks stuffed down their necks—stood where they had been planted, on a first-floor roof, directly under a second-floor window. The fourth had slid to the ground and started a small trash fire. The flames were quickly doused, just as the council meeting adjourned, its own heat finally dissipated, too.

"The fact that two elderly persons reside there," the fire chief said, referring to the caretaker couple who occupied a third-floor apartment, "makes the charge arson."

Words were turning to action, and the stakes were rising. The impulse behind the attack was apparently the same as the shattered windshield last summer—whites lashing out at those unwelcome forces demanding unwanted changes—but the circumstances were graver: a diversionary false alarm, an inhabited target, an apparently genuine attempt at destruction. If this kept up, somebody was going to get hurt.

"If one had been left, we might consider it just a threat—but not four," the police chief said. "As far as I'm concerned, it was attempted murder."

Stu Bunton was a lieutenant now and he spent less time in a patrol car than at his desk at the top of the long stairway up to the second floor of the firehouse, a perch that, like the radio room on the bridge of the *Santa Fe,* offered a wide and penetrating view of the surrounding disorder. The promotion had finally removed the overnight shift from his life—he switched between days and evenings with the department's other lieutenant—but it gave him more responsibility for keeping the town's peace. He supervised the officers on his shift, deploying them to the spots where the social fabric was frayed the thinnest. Crime was still rising, boosted by a recent flurry of drug arrests and downtown muggings; the chief told the merchants' association that, while narcotics were new in town, "they came in very strong." What was more difficult to police against, though, what was more troubling in its way than thieves from the outside invading by night, was the unrest boiling up from within—the epithets, the fights, the finger-pointing and name-calling, the seething mistrust, the silence and noise when blacks and whites intersected, the sound of a town turning against itself. He couldn't fight that the way he had once fought the Japanese.

The police, like the council, had little power against the larger social and cultural forces that had been unleashed. All they could do was try to keep the peace, and find out who left the Molotov cocktails. The state police lab had found a fingerprint on one of the bottles, but there were no suspects to match it with, and no new leads in a case that had raised the temperature of an already overheated spring. Memorial Day was approaching, and with it a new problem for the police: A splinter group from the Concerned Citizens wanted to stage its own march—"a black protest parade objecting to the racist type attitudes of the Establishment," a spokesman said.

The Memorial Day parade was the ceremonial center of Freehold's civic life, the ritual through which it most clearly defined itself as a community, and as a part of America. All through the century since the Civil

War, it had brought the town together in times of uncertainty and victory, sadness and joy. Blacks and whites had always marched together—not always side-by-side as Buddy and the other soldiers had in that first parade after the war, but always in the same line. To split the parade would be to split the town. The proposed protest march would include twenty-seven black organizations from Newark, Paterson and other cities to the north, and would gather in the Peach Orchard and proceed up Throckmorton Street to Main Street, where, if the mayor and council approved, it would join the main parade; if they didn't, it would instead defiantly cross Main Street, loop around toward the mill, and the other substantial black neighborhood in town, and end with a rally in front of the Hall of Records. Either way, it was a direct assault on everything Freehold believed about itself.

The news about the parade spiraled into rumors that kept the phone lines busy at police headquarters—the kinds of things Stu had heard about at "Operation Combine," but had found hard to imagine in his own town. The Black Panthers were coming. The National Guard would be mobilized. Black leaders had been offered money and a spot in the fire department to cancel the march. Whites were stockpiling firebombs and taking target practice at the rifle range. Bands of black youths were roaming the streets.

"Information Received from my Informant who was Present at Meeting Held by our Local Hippies and the Black Panthers Organization," announced an investigation report that reached Stu's desk from one of the patrolmen.

The meeting, according to the unnamed informant, was held at the black Masonic Temple on Avenue A, and was attended by twenty-five "local hippies" and four Black Panthers. "Subject of meeting was to have a riot in Freehold," the report claimed. The riot was scheduled for Memorial Day.

"The Panthers stated to the Hippies: 'We will start the riot, you (the Hippies) just fall in line.' Other statements made:

1. 'We will burn Freehold May 30, 1969.'
2. 'Freehold is old anyhow.'
3. 'We will bring machine guns and other weapons.'
4. 'It is about time we have a new Freehold anyhow.'"

A week later another report came in from another patrolman's informant. "Stated that a group of hippies and young colored people were recruiting for a burn down Freehold day. It seems that while the parade is going on various groups of hippies and young colored are going to go behind the stores in downtown Freehold and start a series of fires and watch downtown Freehold burn to the ground. They are therefore trying to get as large a group as possible to make sure there are enough fires going so that the fire department can not handle them all at once."

The adult leaders of the parade group tried to defuse the fears about their motives and their plans, and to distance themselves from whatever their younger allies might be blustering about. "We're hoping the city of Freehold will realize this is a peaceful endeavor," their spokesman said, "and that if there is any validity to the rumors going around about violence, we assure you, the public, that this violence will come from the white community, especially the bigots, the racists and the emotionally insecure people of our fine community."

As rumors spread and fears grew, as the term "powder keg" crept into more conversations, pressure mounted to cancel the parade entirely. "I won't call off the parade," the mayor declared. "I don't want a segregated parade. I feel there should be one parade in which all residents of the borough and surrounding communities—black and white alike—can participate. . . . I sincerely hope that the parade for our dead heroes will be dignified and that no unfortunate incidents occur. If anything happens because of flared-up emotions, it would be the innocent bystander who would suffer."

The parade group called a public meeting for six P.M. on Monday, May 21, the evening of the last council meeting before Memorial Day, to announce their final plans. As the black leaders and several dozen supporters filed into the council chamber, the *Apollo 10* mission was racing away from the Earth toward the dark side of the Moon, where the lunar module would make a practice descent to within ten miles of the Sea of Tranquillity, the target for the upcoming landing in July. Out in space, America was making a breathtaking leap into the future, but down here on its streets it was still plodding through the unfinished business of the past.

The police chief joined the meeting. Stu Bunton was at his desk at the other end of the floor. A spokesman for the parade group stood to read from a statement. A decision had been made, and the audience leaned forward in their seats to hear it: Was the protest march on or off?

"We are nonviolent, peace-loving black men and women," the spokesman said. "We are calling off the parade effort because of rumors started by the sick minds in this community."

Stu was relieved when the news filtered back—however peaceful its intent, it would have been up to him and his colleagues to keep the black march from fulfilling the rumors—but the crowd groaned its disappointment. "Don't give in," somebody said. "We want our parade."

"This is not a capitulation by any means, but an attempt to save lives," the spokesman argued. "Black people would be both blamed and hurt."

"Stay home on Memorial Day, because your presence on the street could cost you your life," added another leader, Norma Randolph, Buddy Lewis's niece, and Danny's sister. "Each of us who discussed the parade received up to fifteen threats a day—threats of violent reprisals, not only against us but against our children as well."

The black leaders noted some progress—the first-aid squad had agreed to a meeting, although the fire department still had not—but much more, they said, remained unacknowledged, unaddressed, undone. "There are people of goodwill among the blacks as well as among the whites— people who wish to continue living together as neighbors," Danny Lewis said, sounding less angry than sad. "It is unfortunate that the borough must witness such tension, but perhaps it will serve some purpose and make a few people understand what's really going on in our lives."

Another group member struck a harsher note. "Unless attitudes change, the town will be destroyed," he said. "Unless there is a definite and positive change, we'll be picking ourselves up from the rubble of revolution."

"That's right, tell him about it, brother," a teenager in the crowd erupted. "We're going to have our parade."

"If the racist and bigoted attitude of the official 'establishment' persists," he continued, "they will have to blame themselves for destroying their community."

"Preach, brother, preach. They ain't seen black power yet—but they'll see it."

The speaker seemed slightly unnerved by the emotions his words were unleashing. "People, this is not a circus, this is real," he said to the smoldering teens, and then turned to the cluster of white officials. "You think now you have nothing to fear? You have more to fear. We must look for another way to vent our anger."

He singled out the police chief next. "I want to leave you with this parting remark. This is your time to revamp. I will never capitulate again—if this town has to burn down."

The councilman who served as police commissioner drew his own line in the sand. "I wish it to be understood," he said firmly, "that any residents—black or white—disturbing the peace or inciting riots will be arrested and answer for their actions to the fullest extent of the law."

The meeting had nowhere left to go, had only opened yet another gap between the sides, had reached no neutral ground where blacks and whites could talk to, and not beyond, each other, but before it broke up and spilled out into a warm, cloudy night that was threatening rain, a teenage girl rose and shouted in frustration. "We just can't stand the way people are treating us here anymore," she cried, voicing the simplest, strongest grievance of all, the one that lurked beneath all the others. "Stop treating people like dogs."

At the bottom of the long stairway, the black leaders went one way, the white officials another, and the black teenagers surged over to the bus station next door, where a crowd of their peers had collected. News of the canceled march sparked a shrill chorus of indignation. Their cause had been slighted again, betrayed even, and they yelled at no one in particular, just the world at large. A diesel-belching bus heaved off for New York with a handful of passengers, and a car full of white teenagers sped past in its wake.

"Go home, niggers," the white kids yelled as they zipped away.

For the last three nights, white teens and blacks had been jabbing at each other, glancing verbal battles and scattered real ones, and when Stu saw the bus-station group gathering itself into a fist now, he quickly dispatched some patrolmen to break it up. The teens dispersed through town with the news, its meaning and their anger multiplying with each telling. Calls began to trickle in to police headquarters, reporting new groups of black teens gathering, and carloads of whites cruising tauntingly. As evening deepened into night, the police tried to keep the groups small and the cars moving, while the mayor and council convened in chambers for their scheduled meeting.

"We all have to work out the racial and social problems which exist in our community," the mayor said. "If we shall not do it now, we shall suffer not only loss of property and perhaps lives, but also a loss of decency and integrity."

At the bus station, a blue Pontiac Catalina rolled to a stop, and one of the white teenagers inside reached down for something as several black teens approached. "White boy, what are you doing with a tire iron?" one of them said. "Get the fuck out of here."

The Catalina screeched away, chased all the way out to Route 9 by a car full of black kids. More reports filtered in about similar running car battles between blacks and whites, rocks and insults flying back and forth as they careened through the streets. At 8:27, a call came in from South Street—a pair of plate-glass windows at the Two Vets Pool Hall had been smashed, and a rowdy gang of black teenagers was lingering outside. With no witnesses to identify the vandal, and no wish to inflame passions any further, the police simply moved them along. Another gang assembled at the bus station, and it, too, was soon dispersed.

At 8:48, the worried mother of a white teenager called the police. "My son is driving into town," she said nervously. "There's going to be trouble."

The black teens didn't challenge the police who chased them away, but they didn't go home either. By nine-thirty, two large groups had massed in the black neighborhood behind the mill—one on the railroad overpass, the other at the corner by the old union hall. The carloads of white teens kept circling, too, bristling with epithets and crude threats. News of movements and sightings and clashes reached Stu at headquarters the way reports of Japanese ship positions had once flowed into the radio room of the *Santa Fe*. A windshield was shattered by one baseball bat, a car door dented by another. Sometime after ten, the blacks began marching toward Main Street, a grim enactment of the parade they had been denied.

The Catalina had returned to town by then, but when its driver saw the police stopping other cars, he headed back out South Street toward the highway. Glancing in his rear-view mirror, he noticed a new, green Oldsmobile 442 filled with six black kids tailing close behind with only its parking lights on. Harsh words were exchanged, and a bottle flew out of the Olds. The Catalina sped out Route 9 again and ducked into a liquor store parking lot until the Olds had passed by and turned back toward Freehold.

Armed with the shotgun they had picked up at home after the first time they were chased from town, fortified by the two six-packs of beer from the Blue Moon Inn they had drunk, bent on exacting some kind of retribution for the disrespect they believed they had been shown, the three white teenagers drove back to town behind the Oldsmobile that thought it had gotten rid of them. The Olds was stopped at a red light at the corner of South Street and Route 33 when the Catalina suddenly pulled up beside it. The shotgun barrel poked out from the side window. In the backseat of the Olds, one of the three black teens leaned forward while another leaned backward to see what was happening. And then—in the most irrational, overwrought single gesture of the whole irrational, overwrought night, the most irrevocable outburst of the inarticulate rage fueling both sides of the battle—the sixteen-year-old brother of the Catalina's seventeen-year-old driver pulled the trigger. The shotgun pellets blasted through the side window of the Olds, lead and glass slashing into the two black teens who hadn't imagined that someone would actually shoot at them, while missing the third, who had, and had ducked. The Catalina vanished. The driver of the Olds raced to the most logical place he could think of to find help—the police station.

"They've been shot, call an ambulance!" shouted someone in the group that was milling outside.

The heads of the two wounded teens were red and glistening, and when the car door was opened, blood dripped onto the pavement and splattered the shirts of the people who came to their aid.

"It's Dean Lewis," somebody noticed—nephew to Buddy, cousin to Danny, and the son of Donald, one of the six Lewis brothers who had served in the war.

The ambulance screamed up Main Street from the first-aid squad—still all white, but beginning, even before tonight, to show less resistance to the idea of admitting a black member—and the two injured teens were loaded in for the ride to the hospital.

"They're killing our kids!" shouted a middle-aged black man, and several teens ran down Main Street toward the group that had been marching in from behind the mill.

"My God, that's it," a patrolman said, as glass shattered in the distance, and a burglar alarm sounded its hollow, pleading clang.

"Let's go downtown and see what's going on," Guggy Lewis said when he stopped by his brother Buddy's apartment on Throckmorton Street not long after the shooting. "There's all kinds of trouble down there."

Buddy hadn't heard yet, no one in the extended Lewis clan had, that Dean had been shot. All he knew was what everybody in town knew—from the sirens and whistles, from the shouts from passing cars, from the nuggets of news and rumor that passed along a chain of phone calls from

worried house to worried house, from the gathering sense of portent—
that something was going wrong, and his first impulse was to try to fix it.
He and Guggy walked up the empty sidewalks toward Main Street, past
the A&P, the hardware store, the black tavern, the furniture store, the dry
cleaner, the gas station, all intact and silent and dark, as if hoping to sleep
through whatever storm was coming.

Buddy had attended a couple of the early meetings of the Concerned
Citizens, but he stopped when he felt the group sliding toward an ac-
tivism he didn't share. His niece and nephew were of a different generation, and they spoke a language of confrontation he was not fluent in
himself. A quarter of a century earlier, when he was a young soldier chaf-
ing at the indignities forced upon him by a segregated army, he would
have been at the front lines of any protest, shouting slogans of defiance.
He had grown into a different person now, though, and had come to believe that anger led nowhere but violence, and violence led nowhere but
trouble. He was a vested member of the community, the building foreman of the courthouse and the Hall of Records, the father of four children, a pillar of the Bethel AME church, and while he knew things were
wrong, he believed there were solutions short of anarchy.

"Is it true the Black Panthers are coming to Freehold?" a white Jaycee
he knew had asked him excitedly on the street one day recently.

Buddy looked at him in puzzlement and hurt. "My God, I live here,
too," he said, insulted at being lumped with the loudest of the protesters.
"You think I would uphold someone coming into this town to destroy it?
Don't you think we care as much about Freehold as you do?"

Buddy and his brother passed the spare and elegant white shingles of
St. Peter's and turned onto Main Street, where they felt shards of glass
crunch under their feet like gravel. The first broken window they saw was
at Wynn's Jewelers, where the burglar alarm was still ringing. The line of
earrings on display was interrupted by several gaps, like the holes left by
extracted teeth. The Lopatin Agency—the insurance and real estate business run by Bill's brother, Sol—was untouched, as was Porkey's Luncheonette, but Ben's Shoes had been hit, and Al's Bootery, too.

"What a mess," Buddy said as they kept walking, looking for the next
broken windows, and the kids who had broken them.

The foot patrols trundled down the steep stairs in full riot gear—helmets
with visors, shotguns, tear gas canisters, gas masks—and as Stu watched

them go, he couldn't help but think that it was all a bit absurd. The police were dressed as if for battle, but exactly who, he wondered, had declared a war? He, like most of the department's senior officers, knew what combat looked like, and it didn't look anything like what was happening now on the streets outside. An argument had escalated tragically into a shooting, windows were splintering and display cases being raided, civic order was collapsing, but what he saw behind all the trouble, what he believed essential to keep in perspective as he and his colleagues considered how to stop it, was not some hardened enemy bent on conquest and ruin, not a mustachioed kamikaze pilot blazing toward a ship, but just a bunch of teenagers—frustrated, angry, violent even, but teenagers nonetheless. This was Freehold, after all, not the Battle of the Philippine Sea.

"Remember, they're just kids breaking windows," he said.

Two main groups of black kids seemed to be at large, maybe 150 of them altogether, merging and splitting amoeba-like as they swelled and washed through the downtown streets. They had left in their wake the glass trail Buddy followed along Main Street, and then turned up South, gathering strength. Five fifths of Four Roses were gone from the liquor display window of Freehold Pharmacy, and five stuffed animals from the toy window. At the appliance store, looters dashed off with radios, vacuum cleaners, can openers, phonographs, pressure cookers, hair dryers. Most of the windows that were broken, though, were broken just because they were there, not because they opened onto anything of value or interest—the children's clothing store, the women's dress shop, the beauty salon, two barber shops, a real estate agency, the luncheonette, the cobbler, the printer, the upholsterer. One of the drugstore's stuffed animals lay sprawled amid the glass shards across the street at Pinky's Tot 'n' Teen. At the sweet shop, a tide of gumballs spilled across the floor from two upended vending machines.

The gangs had formed so quickly and moved so decisively after the shooting that the police—vastly outnumbered, even with the entire twenty-one-man department on duty, and wary of sparking a counterattack they couldn't control—had little choice at first but to exercise the restraint that was Stu's natural impulse. Patrol cars hovered on the periphery like a fence line, waiting for the reinforcements who had been called—from the state police, the county sheriff's department, neighboring towns. A witness had claimed that one window was broken by a garbage can, another by a sledgehammer, but no one in the crowd appeared armed with anything more lethal, and no one made a move toward any policeman. The local officers in riot gear arrived as the mob was withdrawing from the business district, veering off South Street and clustering on Mechanic. One of the most potent rumors that had circulated among local blacks lately was that the police were eager for an excuse to start shooting, but no guns were fired now, just a few tear gas canisters that scattered the crowd.

By eleven, half an hour after the bloody Olds had screeched up to the firehouse, the reinforcements, fifty in all, were pulling into town, but the front line they were to be deployed against had collapsed. The kids melted back into their neighborhoods, or straggled in groups too small to be threatening, as the helmeted officers fanned out through the streets. Buddy and Guggy ran across several boys they recognized, and delivered the calming message they had set out with.

"Why don't you go on home," Buddy told them. "You've got sticks and stones. They've got guns. It doesn't make any sense."

The mayor declared a state of emergency, ordering everyone inside until dawn, and the town made it through the rest of the night without losing anything more than it already had. Forty-six windows at twenty-eight different businesses were broken, and several thousand dollars worth of goods were missing. Four people were treated for tear gas exposure, and one boy's ankle was cut, but no one else was shot. Stu finally went home at five A.M., twenty hours after he had reported for work the morning before. He was back at his desk again by eight, helping to plot a strategy for preventing another eruption when the sun went down again.

By the middle of Tuesday morning, as Jimmy Higgins was leading a funeral cortege past the boarded-up storefronts of Mechanic Street, the peace meetings—between black leaders and whites, police and politicians—had already convened. In facing its civil unrest, a town like Freehold had an advantage over a city like Newark: proximity. The police and the teens who had met on the street last night had not met as strangers. They knew each other's faces, names, families, and they also knew that, however strained and tenuous their connection might be, the cost of breaking it would be high. One side was not simply a bloodless symbol to the other, a cartoon villain on whom it would have been easy to vent rage. They were fighting for the same town, for different visions of it to be sure, but a town they had always shared, and when they found themselves pitted against each other, armed and tensed and staring into the confusion of a confrontation for which no rules of engagement had been written, some protective instinct made them hesitate before doing anything that would destroy that town, stopping the kids from throwing rocks at the cops, and the cops from shooting at the kids.

The civic leaders who met through the day in the council chamber were similarly bound, and were concerned less with fixing blame for the night before than with keeping peace through the night ahead. The police wanted the black kids to stay home. The black leaders wanted the police to refrain from showing "excessive force," and to keep the state troopers at a distance. And both sides wanted a quick arrest of whoever shot the two black teens in the green Olds, a crime that would only fester into rumors and conspiracies and vengeance the longer it went unsolved.

Just a few minutes before nine P.M.—when the blast of the curfew whistle would instantly make lawbreakers of anyone who was abroad in town, whether by car or on foot—news came that a white teen had been arrested in the shooting, and was on his way to the county jail in the company of a Freehold police detective. The boy's action had triggered the worst of the black anger, and his arrest now seemed to defuse it. The council chamber was given over to state troopers and the county sheriff's officers, who waited quietly to see if they would be needed. Several false alarms were sounded, sending Jake Errickson and the other firemen racing in vain through the ghostly streets, and some disturbing weapons, a rifle with a scope and three Molotov cocktails, were ditched from a car on a chase up Elm Street, but no one came downtown to break any windows. Stu went home at midnight. By Friday night, two more white teenagers had been arrested in the shooting, Dean Lewis had lost his right eye (his father had lost an eye, too, in an accident while serving with the Army Air Corps during the war), the parade had been canceled altogether, and Stu had worked fifty-three hours of overtime in five days, but the curfew had eased, the police had begun patrolling without their riot gear, and nobody—neither black nor white, nor the town itself—had died.

On the morning of Memorial Day, a small troop of veterans gathered at Elks Point, where they listened to a prayer and laid a wreath before the stark, white markers that bore the names of the town's war dead, a number that, since Bart Haynes's funeral, had grown by two more. Shoulders back, chests out, they saluted as the flag was raised and the bugler played. But as taps faded out, the last note echoed into an unsettling silence. For the first time since Dolly the gray mare began leading the Union soldiers out to Major Vredenburgh's grave, no one marched up Main Street in honor of those who had died. The veterans looked around now, instinctively waiting for what was supposed to happen next, but when nothing did, they turned and walked sadly away.

All through the summer after the parade was canceled, the town teetered on the edge of disorder, wondering if it would ever be peaceful enough again to have another. A wary truce held for the first weeks after the shooting, bolstered by some signals that the grievances of the black protesters had been heard—federal money for a summer jobs program; promises of a low-income housing project; a youth center in the vacant Hullabaloo Club, shuttered not long after Bruce Springsteen had moved on. But then Buddy Lewis's sister and her husband, driving past a sub shop on South Street, saw the owner hitting a black man in the doorway, and temperatures rose again.

The news reached the Concerned Citizens, who convened a meeting. The owner explained himself—the man, a familiar headache in the shop, was drunk, he said, had ordered two subs, then changed his mind about hot peppers on one and decided he didn't want the other, had sworn when asked to leave and thrown the first punch when hastened out—but the group was troubled by his "arrogant attitude" and voted "to take some action to show him he should not treat his customers this way." Sign-toting pickets marched back and forth in front of the shop, words grew hotter, and when a young black girl yelled "You old dirty Italian" at one patron, he raced to his car for a hatchet, threatening mayhem. He was disarmed before he could swing it, but the stomping, flailing brawl he sparked ended with nine men arrested.

"Ain't gonna let nobody turn me around, turn me around, turn me around; ain't gonna let nobody turn me around," the pickets sang when they resumed their protest at the sub shop, under the watchful eye of Stu and several other police officers. "I'm gonna keep on a' walkin', keep on a' talkin', marchin' up to Freedom Land."

The pickets continued through the weeks between the fight and the court hearing, but the police hovered constantly in the background—boring duty, in Stu's view, but necessary for keeping the two sides from crashing into each other again. The courtroom was packed when the nine defendants finally appeared, and loud with competing versions of who said what, who hit whom, and what it all meant.

"I seriously doubt that the purpose of the picketing was to further human brotherhood," the magistrate said after hearing testimony and before passing sentence. "It brings to mind the Plainfield incident in which a police officer was kicked to death."

He sentenced three of the nine to jail time—ninety days for one black man, sixty days for another, and fifteen days for the white man with the ax—a decision that only reinforced among the indignant blacks in the audience, and in those who heard the news later as it seeped through town, the prevailing belief that the official version of justice was dangerously estranged from their own. There were two sets of laws, many blacks suspected—one for them, and another for the whites.

"They succeeded in what they wanted to do—to take our black leaders, but they're not going to do it!" Buddy Lewis's niece shouted as the court adjourned.

"We are moving back in time in Freehold instead of forward," said Danny Lewis, who had lost his bid for a council seat in the primary election a few weeks earlier. He had campaigned as a peacemaker—he praised the police as "one of the best departments in the state . . . fair, impartial, humane"—but his rhetoric sharpened now. "Mississippi-styled hearings," he called the proceedings.

"The black man shared in the bloodshed and hardship and helped make this country as great as it is today, and he will have his equal share of the rights guaranteed to him in the Constitution," he said. "We've got to do something. That's all there is to it. Black people are shocked and dismayed with this country. We know we're going to have to stick together to work this thing out. I hope it can be solved peacefully."

The Concerned Citizens hatched another picket plan, this time for the law offices and the home of the magistrate, but there were young and angry people in town who couldn't wait to register their protest, who thought that words were insufficient. Just past eleven on the night of the sentencing, the Molotov cocktails started to fly—at the old Colored School; at the Intermediate School; at the high school's agricultural building, across the street from Bill Lopatin's house; at the Hillpot farm store; at a warehouse by the railroad tracks. Jake Errickson and the other firemen, roused from their beds on a work night, raced from one fire to the next. Only one got away from them—the potato brokers' office that occupied the old Central Railroad station beside the mill, where a burning, gas-filled bottle had smashed through a window and ignited the interior, gutting it. At the power company substation on Throckmorton Street, the police later found two more incendiaries and a length of wire—apparently meant to connect with a live line and short-circuit the town's main electrical supply—that had been tossed over the high chain-link fence. The sabotage attempt the evidence implied seemed so weighty and alarming, so far beyond the bounds of the usual mischief, that two officers were assigned to personally carry the devices to FBI headquarters in Washington for testing.

For the next five nights, watchmen from the fire department cruised slowly in their cars on a circuit of the town's most vulnerable spots. As Freehold crouched into this defensive and unfamiliar position, something within it changed. A spasm of broken windows, a brawl on a picket line—the violence there had been limited and focused; had grown naturally, if not legitimately in everyone's view, from the genuine grievances of long-standing neighbors; had attempted, however crudely, to make some larger point about racial injustice. The fires, though, were just reckless destruction, and the town wasn't about to let itself burn, not for anyone's cause, no matter how worthy. Everybody knew what had happened in Newark; nobody wanted that to happen here.

But then the fires stopped. The defensive line had hardened, and the protests had pulled back. There were no negotiations, no concessions, no peace treaties; it seemed instead as if everyone came to realize at the same moment, just as they had on the night Dean Lewis was shot, that the cost of going any further was simply too high. If Freehold were lost, then who would win? Rumors did soon spread of some other discontent brewing in town, but it surfaced in a new, less threatening guise—a loosely organized group of young people, mostly white, who had watched the marches on the Pentagon, the protests at Berkeley and Columbia and all the other campuses, and, most recently, the vast and hopeful gathering at Woodstock, and thought that Freehold needed some shaking up, too.

They called themselves the Street People. Their hair was long and their jeans were ripped, and they spoke in the earnest but fuzzy platitudes of youthful idealists who rejected the values and conventions of their parents and regarded the police, all public officials really, as a repressive occupying force. Most of them were transplants from the new housing developments in the outlying districts, with only the shallowest ties to, and understanding of, the town they had appropriated for their stage. They came to Freehold to raise their voices not because, like the angry blacks, they had something specific to ask of the local government, but because it was a natural forum for public displays—the place where, for almost three centuries, the county's roads led and its power resided.

"Long Hairs will demo again tonight," the police chief scrawled on a notepad to himself barely two weeks after the night of the fires, jotting down an informant's report. "Blacks involved—threatening to burn."

The Street People tried to make common cause with the local blacks, with little success. A crowd of about seventy-five, almost entirely white, gathered in front of the Hall of Records that evening, ostensibly to protest the alleged mistreatment of a teenager arrested by the state police but with no apparent plan of action beyond milling noisily and occasionally chanting, "All power to the people."

"This is a disorderly assembly," a police officer declared through a bullhorn, and ordered them to disperse. When they didn't, the police started arresting them, slapping on handcuffs and marching them back through the alley to the county jail.

Buddy Lewis had been called to the scene by a nervous night custodian, arriving before the first policeman, and he watched with satisfaction now from the Doric-columned porch of the Hall of Records, relieved that the protesters were being herded away before they could damage the building it was his job to care for. The small public square at his feet—where the newly signed Declaration of Independence was once read aloud to local patriots, where Civil War soldiers were dispatched on their journey south with rousing speeches and brass bands and solemn prayers, where the veterans of his own war were welcomed gratefully home—deserved more respect, he believed, than it was being shown tonight. The institutions in his life, from the army to the local government, hadn't always worked for him, but he trusted in them anyway. He was saddened each Memorial Day by the giddy summer mood of the parade crowds, the ease with which the day's real meaning was masked, and he was saddened tonight by the civic contempt he was witnessing. Whenever he met any black kids who were entangled with the street people, his advice was always the same.

"You know what these white kids are going to do?" he would ask. "They're going to cut their hair and clean themselves up and go back home to their mamas and daddies, and leave you hanging high and dry. You guys are going to be marked in this town."

Restoring order to the town, Buddy knew, was not the job of the police alone, but of the town itself. A place as old and settled as Freehold, its population so thickly and intricately interwoven with families as deeply rooted as Buddy's own, was held together by unspoken bonds of history and custom, duty and respect—bonds whose strength was being tested now as never before. For the town to survive, enough people would have to stand in its defense—whether, like Buddy, by clearly voicing their disapproval of those who would undermine it; or, like Stu and the other cops, by physically blocking those who would harm it; or, like most everybody else, by simply staying put and refusing to flee, the way whole neighborhoods in Newark had.

"Social change is not going to come about through lawlessness," the mayor said, explaining the firm hand the police used against the protesters.

Buddy's advice to the restless black youths presumed that his fellow citizens shared his civic commitment, that the town would emerge from the turbulence sufficiently intact to remember who had caused it, and by year's end his faith had been rewarded. No significant uprisings followed the street people's night at the Hall of Records, and in the fall elections, local power passed to a new mayor and council who had vowed an even harder line against disorder. A haphazardly organized independent party had offered an all-black slate of write-in candidates—with Danny Lewis for council and Guggy for mayor—but few voters took the trouble on Election Day. The new mayor appointed Danny to the town's planning board.

And so on the morning of Memorial Day in 1970, a year after the parade was canceled, the town was ready to try again, and the pastor from Bethel AME church, the Lewis family's church, stood amid the veterans beneath the flagpole at Elks Point. All the heads around him bowed in silent prayer as he offered a benediction for the men whose names were inscribed on the markers. The air was unseasonably cool, leaning more toward the spring that was passing than the summer that was nearing. When taps was sounded, Guggy Lewis held a sharp salute with his white-gloved hand against the shiny brim of his white marines cap. Ballplaying had kept his body in fighting trim, and he still fit easily into the dress blues he had earned as a drill sergeant during the war. As the service ended, he turned and walked a short way up Broadway, where the units that would lead the parade were forming up—the 389th Army Band from Fort Monmouth, a platoon of troops and a color guard from Fort Dix, American Legion Post 54, VFW Post 4374, JWV Post 359, the mayor and council, the reigning Miss New Jersey, and the winners of the safety essay and parade theme contests. He climbed into a low convertible sports car and positioned himself on the rear shelf, pulling his cuffs taut and tugging his tunic straight. Signs that hung on both of the car's doors announced that it was carrying the parade's grand marshal.

Buddy marched behind with the black Elks, whose float featured an array of flags and servicemen in uniform. The Legion post entered a similarly patriotic float—a black sailor and a white soldier standing together behind a row of white grave markers: THEY DIED SIDE BY SIDE IN WAR SO WE COULD LIVE SIDE BY SIDE IN PEACE, declared the banner strung along it, a message that, in its ardent wish to bridge the racial divide that had doomed the last parade, conveniently forgot the military segregation the six Lewis brothers had endured.

"Buddy, you stick around and see if we won anything," the other Elks said when the parade ended at the racetrack, eager as they were to get to the barbecue at the lodge. Buddy came back with the trophy for the "Best Appearing Lodge."

But the summer weather ushered in by the parade lured the Street People back out for another round of battles over whose values should prevail in town. After the shootings at Kent State and the invasion of Cambodia, they had protested quietly and peacefully at a rally in Veterans Park that no one had tried to stop, even though their stance was at odds with many of their elders, especially the World War II veterans who, like Buddy, believed that, since the government had once had a good reason for sending an earlier generation overseas to war, it must now have another good reason for sending a younger generation to Vietnam. It wasn't until the Street People publicly demonstrated their contempt for something deeper than a transient political issue that they truly became the enemy.

"Get up and salute the flag!" a burly marine veteran yelled at a crowded borough council meeting. "I fought for it! Get up or I'll knock your blocks off!"

The long-haired cluster of young dissenters, a group even whiter now than it had been at the Hall of Records the previous summer, had come to the meeting to voice their opinions—against a new ordinance that limited their ability to assemble in public, and for a commune they hoped to build at the town-owned lake where Buddy had swum as a boy—but they remained defiantly seated when the rest of the room rose to recite the Pledge of Allegiance.

"If they can't show respect for their flag, they don't belong in this country," the marine said.

The Street People planned a rally for the courthouse parking lot the next Sunday afternoon, and among their unexpected guests were some angry legionnaires, eager to share a contrasting viewpoint, and ninety unfamiliar policemen, decked out in helmets and shields—riot officers from the special tactical unit that had been assembled from the county's individual police departments. Stu Bunton and the rest of the local police were there, too, along with a detachment of county sheriff's officers. The 175 protesters just barely outnumbered the officials assigned to keep them in line. Buddy Lewis had also been summoned to the scene, in case the courthouse was needed to process a mass arrest. Speeches were made and insults exchanged—"pig town," the rally's leader called Freehold—but the confrontation never escalated beyond scattered shoves and chest bumpings. The protesters then marched down Court Street to borough hall behind a Yippie banner and a black flag with a marijuana leaf over-laying a red star.

"Down with the fascist state," they chanted, but the only arrests were the two teenagers caught with paint on their hands later that evening af-ter scrawling graffiti on the base of the Battle of Monmouth monument: "Power to the People," they had written, and "Feet of the Pig."

They tried again two Sundays later, the day of another parade, the one the town had lately inaugurated to celebrate the Battle of Mon-mouth. Early that morning, Buddy was awakened at home by a call from his boss. "We need you to let some people into the Hall of Records," he was told.

The buildings he passed on his way downtown were draped with red-white-and-blue bunting for the occasion. On a similarly sunny Sunday exactly 192 years earlier, General Charles Lee had followed the same route on the morning of the battle, and found the entire British army waiting for him. Buddy found several dozen officers from the county's tactical police team, outfitted again with helmets, shields and billy clubs. They filed silently inside as he opened the rear door, and sat with their backs against the wall along the main corridor that led to the front entrance. The town was taking no chances today.

Buddy stood at the brass double doors, watching the parade units pass by on Main Street on their way to the assembly point. A steam cal-liope rolled past, and a car carrying the town's last surviving veteran of the Spanish-American War. Most of the marchers—with their tricorner hats and knee breeches, their muskets and fifes—were more meticulously outfitted with colonial gear than Lee's own troops, and they made a sharp contrast with the long-haired kids unloading sound equipment on the square out front.

"This is an illegal assembly," the police chief announced. "You need to move out or you'll be arrested."

The Street People continued milling, ignoring the orders. From where they stood, they could see no hint of the tactical police arrayed inside the Hall of Records, but just the upper half of Buddy Lewis, framed by the glass panel as he awaited the signal to unlock the door. The police outside tightened the perimeter around the protesters.

"You are violating a local ordinance," the chief said. "You must disperse or you will be arrested."

No one moved to leave, and the chief spoke into a hand radio, relaying orders to the local officer stationed inside with the tactical unit.

"Put your key in the door," Buddy was told, and he did.

The police outside moved in closer still, the police inside assumed a preparatory crouch, and Buddy held tightly on to the key, ready to swing the door open and then step out of the way. Some of the Street People started to move. Buddy heard the chief's voice crackle over the radio, as the tactical unit tensed expectantly behind him.

"Hold it, hold it," the chief said. "They're taking their stuff down."

Buddy slid his key from the door, and the tactical police eased back against the walls, flipping up the visors on their helmets. The Street People had conceded defeat before the battle could even begin. Some among them drifted down toward Elks Point with a Woodstock flag, where they tried to jump in front of the line of marchers, and were arrested. Several others were arrested for disorderly behavior and scuffling with the police, but most of the rest simply faded into the crowd. The floats and the bands passed without incident, and the front door of the Hall of Records remained locked until Buddy opened it for the start of business the next morning. As at the battle the parade commemorated, the invaders had been driven away, a victory that, though lacking a decisive finality, left the town standing intact, just as the retreating British had.

A week later in Asbury Park—the dowager beach resort whose department stores and theaters still beckoned like Manhattan to those looking for things they couldn't find in Freehold—some rock-throwing by kids on Independence Day soon grew into arson and looting and shooting in the streets. For three days and nights, the small city endured a chaotic and violent race riot of a kind that Freehold, about half its size, had itself managed to avoid a year earlier. Stores were torched and stripped, firemen chased away with a hail of bottles. The trains to New York sped through without stopping, stones rattling against their skins like the shrapnel that once pelted Bill Lopatin's B-26. On the afternoon of the third day, a shouting mob surged across the railroad tracks from the black neighborhood of the West Side, pushing three blocks into downtown before they were turned back by a force of 225 state and local policemen, including several on loan from Freehold, in a storm of tear gas, pepper spray, swinging clubs and shotgun fire that echoed Walter Denise's infantry battles in the villages of France. When order was finally restored, more than 100 people had been arrested, 165 injured—92 of them, ranging in age from fourteen to seventy-five, with gunshot wounds—seven blocks of Springwood Avenue, the heart of the West Side business district, were gutted, and property damage had topped $4 million. The governor arrived by helicopter to tour the destruction, and called on President Nixon to declare the city "a major disaster area."

On Asbury Park's worst night, Freehold flared briefly, too, in what seemed a sympathetic, though half-hearted, attempt to resurrect the capped passions of the previous summer. Crude firebombs scorched a car around the corner from Bill Lopatin's house, sparked a smoky fire in the rear of Jay's Pharmacy, ignited a pile of boards at the lumber yard, smashed through a window at the Court Street school, and landed harmlessly outside a Mechanic Street luncheonette. A window was smashed at Charles' Slacks, and thirteen pairs of men's pants were stolen. The police swarmed through town in riot gear, but whoever had lashed out had slipped back again into the night, and the streets were empty and silent.

"If they try to get away, they are to be shot—wounded or killed, it makes no difference to me," the new mayor said later, issuing an ultimatum against looters. "The only way to stop these people is to drop them."

Stu and the other police officers had no intention of ever shooting anyone for breaking a window, and they regarded the order for what it was—a dramatic public declaration of limits that had already been tacitly set, and implicitly agreed upon by both sides, in the heat of the previous summer, limits that no one expected would ever require such drastic enforcement. Freehold had already passed its toughest test, in a way that Asbury Park and Newark had not. If it didn't burn last summer, the police believed, it wasn't going to burn now. The town had already proven, as Washington's army once had on the same ground, that it could stand firmly against those who would destroy it, whether from within or without.

At the courthouse in the morning, Buddy had to thread his way through hallways narrowed by tables set up to process the scores of rioters arrested in Asbury Park. Their faces were all black, and as he looked at them he realized with a start how easily they might have been his own neighbors. Had events last summer taken a few slightly different turns, Freehold might have erupted on the scale Asbury Park had, a realization that filled Buddy with both regret and relief—regret at what had happened to their community and to so many others, relief that it had not happened to his. At the end of the day, when the halls had emptied, he closed up the courthouse, and then the Hall of Records, too. He turned his key to lock the same door he had stood ready to unlock for the riot police. He shook the door hard to make sure it held. It did, as it had for so many years now, as it would still, he expected, for many more ahead.

14.

"Let's Finish the Job"

After his work day was ended and his supper was eaten, Bill Lopatin often went out again in the evenings—to review blueprints with a customer, to double-check a job site, to attend another meeting of one of the many civic and service groups he belonged to—and in the warm twilight of a Tuesday in August he found himself driving along Main Street away from home once more, his briefcase riding in the passenger seat beside him. The storefronts were dark, the sidewalks empty. A bank had replaced the gracious estate that his zoning board decision once spared—the borough council, in a closed-door session, had later changed the ordinance to permit it—but otherwise Freehold looked much the same as it had since the mill closed. It was faded but, spared the urban renewal bulldozers and the fires of racial unrest, it was still intact.

Once the tall oaks and the fine, old houses gave out, though, Main Street crossed over Route 9, and Bill could see exactly how much some things had in fact changed. The highway flowed past town like a flood-swollen river carrying run-off from the north, its banks silting up with strip malls and tract houses. Many other farmers had, like the Denises, sold their land to developers, and Freehold—which had been variously, over almost three centuries, a village, a county seat, an agricultural center and a factory town—was evolving into a new and unfamiliar role, as an adjunct to New Jersey's suburbanizing economy. Bill passed raw treeless fields now sprouting new homes at a rate that would exceed in a year what he and his father had built in two lifetimes.

Not quite two miles out, just at the border between where the landscape was changing and where it wasn't, he turned into a new asphalt driveway that curved up toward a long, low-slung brick building that rose from an old potato field like an abandoned Cubist fortress. Lights shone in only a handful of the few windows that pierced the stark facade. The tall cornstalks of the neighboring farm swayed and glowed in the evening breeze, tinted red by the sun that was fading behind the treeline to the west. Bill parked and walked happily inside the building that he—and the other volunteers behind the town's most ambitious community project yet—had spent the last decade trying to get built: Freehold's own hospital.

"I want to thank all of you whose diligent efforts have made this possible—our first meeting in our new hospital," the board president said after the roll was called and the meeting brought to order. "It's been a long and difficult road, as you all know, but here we are at last."

Bill had first joined the hospital committee about the same time he broke ground at Colonial Park, and the two projects—acts of faith in a community whose future was clouded by the rug mill's departure—had since proceeded at the same slow but steady pace. The empty lots in his modest subdivision were filling at the rate of three or four new houses each year, and the oaks he had planted in all the front yards were growing thicker and taller. He had just closed on one house a week earlier for a local lawyer—he had measured all the furniture in the buyer's old living room on Broad Street and then laid paper cut-outs across the blueprint to make sure it would all fit in the new one on Dogwood Lane—and he was scheduled to close on another next week, a brick ranch with a bidet in the bathroom, the first he had ever installed, for a European-born couple. He expected a third to be ready within a month or so, just about the same time as the hospital.

Bill and two dozen or so other trustees were sitting around a long table in a windowless room deep inside the west wing of the new hospital, running through the long list of things that still needed to be done before the scheduled opening next month. The 120 patient rooms gaped vacant and dark along the silent corridors that branched off around the conference room. The trustees shuffled through their papers as each of the committee chairmen and chairwomen rose to deliver their reports: $2,340,829.48 had been pledged by local donors, and almost half had been collected; sixteen people were already on the payroll and more were due within a week, including a chief X-ray technician and a chief lab technician; the nurses' stations were almost finished.

"Our biggest problem now is getting the equipment in and the contractors out," one trustee said.

"Some furniture was moved upstairs Saturday with some fine volunteer help from the Lions Club," reported another.

One Sunday a month earlier, rain had fallen all through the afternoon of the hospital's first tentative unveiling, an open house hosted by the trustees and the volunteers, but 2,500 people had driven out and filed through anyway, so eager were they to see the final results of a local campaign that had taken so many people, and so many years, to finally get Freehold something it had needed for so long. Bill was the designated host in the X-ray room. He knew nothing about radiology, but he could tell the visitors plenty about the hospital, and how it had come to be.

For roughly a decade during the Depression, Freehold was served by a small private hospital—twenty beds maintained by Dr. Reynolds in the old Governor Parker mansion—but in all the years before and since, anyone who dropped with a heart attack or wrapped a car around a tree had to pray they could survive at least a twelve-mile trip to the nearest facility that could help them. When Dean Lewis and his backseat mate were shot by the carful of white boys, the ambulance carried them almost all the way to Asbury Park, to Fitkin Hospital in Neptune. In the mid-1950s efforts had begun stirring to secure the town a hospital of its own—a half-million-dollar, twenty-six-bed satellite of Fitkin that would function mainly as a glorified emergency room. The local Jaycees led the fundraising drive for the seed money, organizing a "Night of Stars" benefit show at the 4-H Fair at the racetrack. Ticket sales were alarmingly sluggish, though, and the night's headliner, Joni James, sang her latest release, "There Must Be a Way," to row after row of empty seats. The Jaycees had hoped to raise as much as $10,000 for the hospital, but instead ended up going to the bank to take out a $3,600 loan to pay the rest of what they owed the performers.

In the three years it took the Jaycees to pay off their loan, with barbecues and auctions and other fund-raisers, another plan emerged, for a larger, nonprofit community hospital unaffiliated with Fitkin. The chamber of commerce appointed thirty-seven people—bankers, teachers, merchants, doctors, lawyers and assorted other community leaders, Bill among them—to the Greater Freehold Area Hospital Steering Committee, and staged a charity ball at the racetrack. Hostesses in colonial maid costumes escorted guests to their tables, the Charlie Spivak Band played the theme song, "The Charity Ball Builds a Hospital for All," to the tune of "Yankee Doodle," twenty thousand dollars was collected for the cause and the prospects began to seem more plausible.

Bill and the other volunteers met the second Tuesday of every month, groping their way through the rough early stages of a project to which they initially brought more enthusiasm than expertise. The charity ball had certainly raised more than the "Night of Stars," but they still needed another $2.4 million, and nobody was lining up to hand it over. They incorporated themselves, assessed each other annual dues of fifteen dollars (they didn't want to dip into the donations to cover their own administrative expenses), sought guidance from the state agency that regulated health-care facilities (the response was "somewhere between realism and pessimism," according to the member who reported back to the committee), investigated the possibility of obtaining federal funds (small), accumulated statistics about projected population growth and optimum hospital bed-to-resident ratios, visited other new hospitals for ideas about their own, started scouting possible building sites and kept asking their fellow citizens for money. Nobody was ever going to give them a hospital, they realized; if they wanted one, they would have to do it themselves.

The charity ball became an annual event, the peak of the local social calendar, built around a different theme each year: "Neapolitan Nights," "An Evening in Paris," "A Night of Medieval Pageantry." The governor came one year, and the crowning of the charity ball queen once pushed the Beatles' movie *Help* out of the theater where it was showing. So deep was the town's commitment to the hospital drive that, just five days after the near-riot in 1969, on the curfew-ruled weekend of the canceled Memorial Day parade, fourteen hundred people, among them several of the most vocal black leaders draped in dashikis, filled the racetrack for the "Spanish Fiesta," dancing to flamenco music, drinking wine from goatskin bags under bullfight posters, and raising another $35,000.

After three balls, the board had enough money to buy the thirty-eight-acre Donovan farm for $89,000. A large, gray barn stood near the road, and on its side a hopeful sign was painted: FUTURE HOME OF FREE-HOLD AREA HOSPITAL. A tall thermometer sign went up, too, the red paint rising as the donations mounted. Money flowed toward the hospital in a slow, steady stream from every corner of the community, with a handful of gifts in the ten-thousand-dollar range, but the vast majority in much smaller increments. The kids at the Left Foot, the teen club where the Castiles had played, contributed one hundred dollars, and many local families whose charitable giving had previously been limited to the Sunday collection plate managed to scrape together twenty-five-dollar pledges.

But as the money accumulated, the goal receded—the logistical hurdles rising, the projected costs growing, the target amount at the top of the thermometer mutliplying. The federal funds the board had hoped for fell through, forcing them to try to squeeze another million dollars or so out of the already generous local populace, and the state kept urging them to merge with another community hospital project underway in the northern part of the county. Bill and the other trustees, though, remained committed to their original vision: Freehold's own hospital, built with Freehold's own money. In their view, if not the government's, the need for the hospital was surging with the population, as more and more farms were plowed under for subdivisions. New people—most of them from cities where they never had to worry about how far away the nearest hospital was—were moving into the area anchored by Freehold at the rate of six hundred a month, into houses thrown up so hastily, and often carelessly, by outside developers that complaints of mudslides, cracked foundations and leaky roofs were rampant, and some fast-growing neighboring towns considered instituting a builders' code of ethics, the kind of regulatory mechanism that had never been necessary for Bill and his peers.

The hospital board staged a ceremonial groundbreaking on a cold December afternoon when they were still a couple of million dollars shy. After another round of federal funds passed them by, they launched yet another local campaign to raise what they had been denied. LET'S FINISH THE JOB!" commanded the Day-Glo orange bumper stickers that were plastered on cars all over town. Pledge cards were distributed, phone banks organized, volunteers—almost a thousand of them—mobilized. To convince the Federal Housing Administration to back the $3 million mortgage they would need even after they reached their fund-raising goal, a rally was organized at the Presbyterian church, and hundreds of townspeople, Bill among them, squeezed into the pews, rising in turn to voice their support for the hospital.

When the mortgage was secured, the contracts went out to bid for a project whose total cost had more than doubled from its original estimate, to $5.7 million, and the concrete was soon being poured for the west wall footings. Bill watched the hospital rise only as a trustee, not as a contractor. He had not bid on any portion of the job, and was so intent on not appearing to benefit from his position on the board that when a truck with the name LOPATIN on it was once spotted on the property—working at the old house that was occupied by renters before it had to be razed— Bill made sure the meeting minutes were corrected to note that it was his cousin's, Lopatin Electric, not his own.

That night's meeting ended with an announcement of the dedication ceremonies—on a Sunday afternoon a month hence—and Bill drove home from the hospital past lights that were coming on now in places that had always been dark before. He was approaching sixty-five, and his ideas about what to do when he passed that milestone differed from his late father's. Sam Lopatin had swung a hammer until he was almost eighty, and then later, a widower, moved into the bedroom that Bill had added on to the house for him. Bill planned instead to retire. His daughter had long since married and moved away, and he had no son to follow him into the business as he had followed his father. When the last house in Colonial Park was finished, he hoped to set aside his tools and pick up the college education the Depression had interrupted. This time around, though, with no career to prepare for, he would study not what seemed most practical, as accounting first and then architecture had forty-five years earlier, but what seemed most interesting. History, he had decided, would be his new major.

Another more poignant piece of unfinished business loomed ahead for him, too, and he didn't want to be tied up with work when its demands came due. A few years earlier his wife, Selma, had felt her back and neck stiffening, uncomfortably and persistently enough to send them to a neurologist in Philadelphia. The doctor asked her to write something on a sheet of paper, and when he saw her letters trailing off into a flat line he told her she had Parkinson's disease. Her condition was not immobilizing, and no one could say at what pace it would worsen, but she soon sold the businesses she had built—the answering service, the direct-mail operation that distributed advertising circulars for local stores, the gift and card shop in the shopping plaza where the Hullabaloo dance club had briefly flowered. She was still able to travel, and Bill still had a list of destinations they hadn't gotten to yet on their annual anniversary trips.

On a damp September afternoon, Bill and Selma made a shorter journey together, out to the official dedication of a hospital that still wasn't quite ready yet. A thousand seats had been set out on the wide front lawn, but the threat of rain kept several hundred of them empty. An honor guard of local veterans raised the flag, and a forty-piece band from Fort Monmouth played the national anthem before the low, heavy skies opened, forcing the crowd and the speech makers inside to the hospital basement.

"As I accept this key," the president of the trustees said after the official presentation from the architect, "I am humbly grateful to each of you who have helped make our vision of a desperately needed hospital for this area become a living, breathing reality."

Bill sat among the other trustees, watching the hospital's christening with the same quiet pride and proprietary satisfaction, only in even larger measure now, that he felt at the closing of one of his houses. Of all the civic duties he had fulfilled in his life—from the soup kitchen he and the Young Men's Hebrew Association had set up in the back of a Main Street ice cream parlor during the big rug mill strike in the Depression, to his continuing role as the town's building inspector, a position that paid far less than the time it cost him from his business—the only one that matched this in consequence and size was his service in the war.

"What drives an ordinary citizen to give up so much time and energy to a cause of this nature?" the president continued. "It is a deep commitment to be of service to his fellow man, and to be concerned with the welfare of those around him."

When the ceremonies ended and Bill and the rest of the crowd filed back out into the rain, the hospital was locked up behind them. The opening had been scheduled for the next morning, but some surgical equipment hadn't been delivered yet, and the state health officials still hadn't visited for the final licensing inspection. Not until the following Monday—a week after the dedication, eight years after Bill was first appointed to the board, twelve years after Joni James sang to rows of empty seats at the Jaycees fundraiser—did the new hospital treat its first patients. Seventeen cases arrived in the emergency room through that first day, and four patients stayed overnight. The next day Bill closed on the third and final house of the season at Colonial Park.

The Hudson Street School had been closed just since June, but by September it was already a wreck, its pale yellow bricks smudged and sallow, its windows mostly broken, the shades flapping in the dark gaps like loosened teeth. Weeds pushed up through the cracks in the asphalt playground that lapped all around it like the rising tide. Anyone stopping to peer through the front entry—the tall, white doors and the colonial fanlight opening onto the same yawning staircase that Bill Lopatin had climbed as a nervous ten-year-old on one of his first days in America—saw nothing but shadows and dust.

When it had opened, a full century earlier, the school had been a showplace, the first free public school in the county, a key landmark in the transformation of education from the preserve of the wealthy to the right of all. Its first principal, who went on to become the state commissioner of education, had planted around it a gracious arboretum befitting its status—Norway yews, Australian pines, Circassian walnut, mahogany from Burma, ginkgo from China, and some seventy other varieties of trees and shrubs. The lower grades were downstairs, the upper grades above. As enrollment grew, new additions were grafted on, until the high school finally got its own building on the adjacent block. The school's rear windows overlooked the rug mill, and let in a low, steady, thrumming soundtrack that played beneath the teachers' patter. On days when classes dragged, Jake Errickson had often stared out at the mill and seen the future career he expected while Stu Bunton had seen the job he hoped to avoid.

More recently, though, the school had aged beyond both use and salvage, and the school board members, Jimmy Higgins among them, voted for retirement over renovation. A new school to replace it had opened on the edge of town, behind Walter Denise's house. As the autumn deepened, and the oaks lining Hudson Street lost their cloaking leaves, the old school's battered hulk stood ever more naked and forlorn, peering crookedly at Jimmy each morning when he walked out of his funeral home, just across from the locked front door through which no more children passed. Unlike the other board members, whose relationship with the school had ended with their vote for closure, Jimmy remained on intimate terms with it, as both a neighbor and as a member of the town's planning board, which would help decide its fate. Although nobody seemed to want the building itself, the site was attracting some interest. The state association of civil service workers had proposed an apartment tower, as tall as the neighboring mill, for its retired members, while the town was considering its own senior citizen complex.

Jimmy wasn't particular about who built what there, as long as some-body did something to keep the neighborhood he had planted himself so deeply in from crumbling all around him. As his business had grown, pushing toward two hundred funerals a year, he had been forced to find more room to hold it. He briefly considered following the stream of com-merce out to the surrounding highways—the last downtown grocery store had recently made that trip—but he chose instead to expand where he was. He owned the smaller house next door to the funeral home, where his mother-in-law had been living, and he connected the two with a sprawling new chapel that could accommodate three funerals at once, an investment that countered the pervasive gloom about the local economy.

"An air of depression and forlornness seemed to grip this borough," wrote a *New York Times* correspondent in a moody Christmas Eve dis-patch from the town where he had grown up, but not returned to visit for several decades. He found the changes "mildly shocking"—the vanished stores, the fading farms, the empty street echoing with scratchy carols playing through a loudspeaker in front of the courthouse.

"This once vibrant banking, trading and commercial hub no longer seems to care very much about Christmas or, in the opinion of many here, about anything else," he wrote, striking a dismissive, funereal note that stirred up an indignant, defensive backlash of protest.

Exactly a year after its closing, the school finally fell to the wreckers, reduced in less than a week to mounds of broken brick and splintered wood. Resting in the rubble of what was once the gymnasium was a mas-sive support beam, cut a century ago from a white pine that must have been larger, as those who passed by speculated with wonder, than any left standing in the county now. Jake Errickson was among the stream of spectators who couldn't let the old school go without a final look. Until the rug mill shut down, his whole life had been spent within a small orbit around the school—in the classrooms where his father was among the earliest students, and where he and all his siblings once went; in the rented house a block away where he was raised and his parents lived un-til they died; in the foremen's office that overlooked the schoolyard where his own children played—and it was hard for him to imagine the town without it.

After the mill left, Jake had worked for several years as a purchasing agent at an RCA aerospace plant out near Trenton—long enough to feel a certain pride whenever he looked up into the night sky and imagined the spy satellites his company helped make gazing back down at him, but also long enough to feel that, at twenty miles each way, he was driving too far from home each day. He moved to a similar job in a smaller, closer factory, in the town next to Freehold, that made antennas and other radio equipment. A few other old mill hands had landed there, too, but it was nothing like their old job—no Foremen's Club, no baseball team, no intricate employee genealogy, no company tradition large and old and engaged enough to shape and sustain a community. Although Jake's salary now was roughly equivalent to what he made at the mill, the twenty-four years he had invested in building a career there were lost, and he knew he would never rise as high in his new field as he might have in his old one.

Just a few weeks after the school came down, he and Dot were scheduled to leave on the trip they had long been saving and planning for—a three-week journey to Australia, her first time back, and her first time seeing her mother and father, since she was a young war bride standing on the deck of the *Lurline* three decades earlier, crying as the band played "Waltzing Matilda" and her homeland slipped off into the distance behind her. It was Jake's first time back, too, since he was shipped home, minus an appendix, near the end of the war. In between, though, their son Wayne had gotten at least within the same hemisphere, when the aircraft carrier he was serving on, the USS *Saratoga*, was summoned for a tour of duty in the Vietnam War. After graduating from Annapolis, Wayne had become the backseat radar and weapons man in a two-seat F-4 fighter-bomber. Jake and Dot saw him fly only once, when the carrier was approaching its Virginia port, ending a Mediterranean cruise before heading to the Pacific, and the planes came in ahead of it. His plane's number was 107, and they watched proudly as it glided down from the sky and Wayne vaulted out onto the tarmac with the same confident grace that had once made him a state champion in gymnastics. The *Saratoga* reached the Gulf of Tonkin in April of 1972, just in time to provide more airpower for a stepped-up bombing campaign against targets in North Vietnam. Wayne flew on 155 missions and earned a Distinguished Flying Cross, the same decoration once bestowed on Bill Lopatin, for serving as the lead radar intercept officer on a thirty-eight-plan attack on "a heavily defended petroleum products storage and railroad staging complex" near Hanoi.

Buddy Lewis had spent a recent winter watching his son garner some acclaim, too, but in a much different arena. While his own athletic career had been truncated by the war—leaving him with the memory of his three-touchdown day as a sophomore against Manasquan, and the nagging, unanswered question of what might have been—his son Steven's flourished undisturbed. As a six-foot-five senior center, averaging 19 points and 13 rebounds per game, Steven led the high school basketball team to an 18–5 record, its best in years, and a share of the Shore Conference Division D championship, his father cheering from the bleachers all the way. The Colonials' season finally ended in the Central Jersey Group II quarterfinals, when a late rally, 11 unanswered points in the last four minutes, fell just short. Steven led all scorers that night with 22 points.

After years of renting, Buddy finally owned his own home now, the first black family on a white street a block away from the one he grew up on. He was rising through the supervisory ranks of the county's buildings-and-grounds department, trading his old gray metal rolltop desk—he painted it every year to keep it looking as sharp as it could—in the courthouse basement for an office in a new building outside town. He added a half dozen more facilities to his domain, and some new duties, including a few not in his job description.

"You said something to one of my men you shouldn't have," he told a judge whose chambers he visited on behalf of an offended custodian.

Because Buddy was one of the few black managers in county government, he was often called upon to serve as a de facto discrimination officer, mediating conflicts, both obvious and subtle, between the races. Although nobody was tossing rocks in the streets anymore, he still felt some of the old tensions—when he overheard a prosecutor disparage a defendant as "just another nigger," when his kids came home from high school with tales of scattered insults and fights, when his nephew Danny ran, and lost, in another election for borough council, which remained all white. (Bill Lopatin had helped lure Danny into the race, as a Republican this time, but some party members were less than enthusiastic about a black candidate, just as they had been two decades earlier about a Jew, when Bill himself ran.) The older Buddy got, the more he turned to his religion for a sense of the justice that often seemed elusive here on earth. His church was outgrowing its gray shingled home in the Peach Orchard—some members had asked Bill about digging out a basement level, but he advised them against it—and was eyeing a lot for a new home a few blocks away, on a hill across from the old Colored School, where he and all of his siblings, but none of his children, had gone.

Walter Denise's church was feeling cramped, too—the converted white house on Main Street that had been dedicated just before he left for the war. His late parents were among the founders of the local Christian Science congregation, and he remained among its leaders, making plans for a more proper home. As he had with the cold-storage building back on the orchard, he came up with the design for the new church himself— red brick and a tall, white steeple that would better fit the street's ecclesiastical lineup. His cold-storage building was still standing, solid and empty and overlooking a new highway, but he only glimpsed it occasionally now and from a distance, when he was out driving clients to see houses for sale among the developments that had replaced his verdant rows of fruit trees.

After several years of working for others in the real estate business, Walter had decided to work for himself again, and opened Denise Realty Associates. The office was in a converted Cape on a small rise beside the Route 9 traffic circle, on the southbound side, directly in the path of the steady stream of home seekers flowing down from the north. His business prospered, growing to a dozen brokers, as more and more of his old fellow farmers made the same decision he had and sold their land to developers. He found, though, that the ethics in his new profession weren't as deeply rooted as in his last.

"Half acre?" another broker asked him at a meeting once. "No problem."

Walter was representing a large out-of-state developer who wanted to fill three thousand acres of empty pinelands south of town with houses. They had surveyed the tract from a small airplane, tossed around a price of $3.5 million, and were turning now to the crucial question of zoning. A smaller required lot size would mean more houses, and more money for everyone.

"What do you mean, 'no problem'?" Walter asked. "It's one-acre zoning."

"With a little money here and a little money there we can get whatever we want," the broker said. Before Walter stood up, snapped his briefcase shut and walked out, he heard the suggested price he refused to even consider paying—fifty thousand dollars, half of what he would make from the deal. "You're getting a pretty good commission out of this—it doesn't hurt to spread a little around."

In his own daily rounds, Stu Bunton encountered varieties of illegal behavior not quite so bloodless and genteel as attempted bribery, and the toll was beginning to weigh on him. One of his two sons had followed him into the police department, but he often wondered whether he would make the same decision if he were starting out himself now. When Stu joined the force, the job, in his view, was mostly about helping neighbors and serving the town. Over the years, though, it had come to remind him more and more of his role in the war, enlisting him as a combatant in a constant battle to keep the world from spinning apart. Drugs had raised the volume on everything—theft, violence and all-around disorder—and a policeman's uniform no longer commanded the same respect. One recent Mischief Night, some kids unsatisfied with the usual window-soaping and egg-tossing prankishness had smashed a concrete block through the rear window of a police cruiser.

Stu was a captain now, one of two in the department, ranking below only the chief, the job he was next in line for and still didn't want. He and the other captain had risen through the ranks together, but he had already made clear his intention to stay exactly where he was when the chief retired soon. The police, he knew, were where fingers pointed when things went wrong. He had watched his chief fend off occasional assaults from the mayor and council in the years since the riot—the noise was especially loud after the chief had, in the opinion of some council members, failed to take seriously the order to shoot looters—and he had no interest in taking up the fight himself. Police work was his job, he reasoned, not politics. The department had finally moved out of its cramped longtime home in borough hall, atop the fire trucks and adjacent to the council chambers, but Stu realized the distance was only physical. The new station was in one of the retired schools that hadn't been torn down, in the block adjacent to the one that had, and every day on his way to and from the captain's office there, the first proper office he had ever had, he passed the corner where as a young patrolman he had stopped traffic for the children crossing the street on their way home.

A few months after the police moved into the old Bennett Street school, Jimmy Higgins stood on the site of its vanished counterpart, the old Hudson Street school, quietly admiring what had taken its place—a six-story brick apartment complex for senior citizens. The plan for the retired civil servants' residence had been supplanted by a locally grown nonprofit group, Freehold Senior Citizens Housing Corporation, that secured a $6-million state-financed mortgage to build subsidized elder housing, and in the process shore up a vulnerable edge of downtown. Jimmy was among the group's founding trustees. Construction on Hudson Manor began two years after the school was demolished, and by the time the first tenants moved in two years later, the waiting list had climbed past one hundred.

The dogwood saplings in the lawn of the new building were just coming into bloom on the spring day of the dedication, and the speechmakers were similarly festive and bright, almost giddy at the spectacle of what they had accomplished. Hudson Manor's contribution to the town was both practical and psychological. The 164 neat and sunny apartments were a welcome haven to an aging population, including many veterans and the widows of veterans, and the complex itself represented the largest investment anywhere downtown in the lean years since the mill closed and the Strand block burned. As Jimmy listened to the words of praise and congratulations, and looked at the object of everyone's affections, he felt that his decision not to move his business had been sound, that his faith had been rewarded. The funeral home was still thriving, and the older of his two sons had just joined him in running it. He had reluctantly turned down a chance to run for mayor—his wife worried that partisan politics would erode the goodwill he had earned over the years—but the building before him today was proof of how much he could still do from offstage.

Before the ceremonies ended, a group of residents who called themselves the Hudson Manorettes sang a song they had written to the tune of the "Marine's Hymn" ("From the Halls of Hudson Ma-aa-nor . . ."). The beat was still playing in Jimmy's head as he walked past the new trees, and through the shadows of the tall old ones that survived, on his way across the street to his business, his home.

Sitting alone in the small, hushed library of the county historical museum, shadowed on all sides by tall bookcases heavy with the weight of the past, Bill Lopatin bent closely over the manuscript he was studying, trying to decipher the blurred and faded outlines of words written two centuries earlier. He gently turned the pages with the eraser end of his pencil, as the curator had requested. The only sounds were the ticking of the clock, and the rattle of the windows as they were nudged by the winter wind. The massive copper beeches lining the street outside had lost their leaves, and when Bill looked up from his work he could see clear through the arched uppermost panes to the slender granite column of the Battle of Monmouth monument. He was researching a paper for an undergraduate history seminar, hoping to understand what life was like in Freehold during the Revolution, sifting for clues in the records of a jury that was convened at the old courthouse just nineteen days before the great battle the monument commemorated. As Bill aged, his perspective had lengthened. He wanted to understand better how it all fit together—his own life, his war, his town's history—into the larger story of America.

The paper was tawny with age but still supple, flaking lightly at the edges, mottled by ghostly old water stains. Each of the fifty-one pages started with the same printed phrase: "An Inquisition taken and made at Freehold in the said County of Monmouth the Ninth Day of June in the Year of our Lord One Thousand Seven Hundred and Seventy-eight, by the Oaths or Affirmations of . . . ," followed by a handwritten list of the jurors, "good and lawful Men of the said County," many of whose family names were still prominent locally and familiar to Bill: Mount, Wikoff, Craig, Taylor, Vanderveer. What came next were the names of the accused, and the grave charges against them.

"Clayton Tilton, late of Shrewsbury in the County aforesaid, did . . . on or about the first Day of March One Thousand Seven Hundred and Seventy-seven, join the Army of the King of Great-Britain, against the Form of his Allegiance to this State, and against the Peace of this State, the Government and Dignity of the same."

History, as Bill was learning, was usually more complicated than it first seemed. As a boy, he had been taught about the noble struggle of the Revolution, the aggrieved colonists rising as one to throw off the shackles of British tyranny. The more he read now, though, the more tangled the story grew—a county divided against itself, those who would remain loyal to the king battling those who would not, a violent collision of ideals and self-interest, a guerrilla war of raids and skirmishes, hangings and torchings, theft and confiscation. The defendants in the inquisition Bill was perusing were from families just as prominent as the jurors, but once they were judged guilty of disloyalty to the newly declared nation they were in danger of losing both their lands and their lives.

"We whose Names are hereunto set, and seals affixed, being the Jurors above-named, do, upon the Evidence to us produced, find the Inquisition aforesaid true," Bill read at the bottom of each page, the official and unanimous verdicts, signed by the hands of men who had fought to make

America a nation, as he himself had fought much later to assert the primacy of its ideals in the world.

When Bill was turning sixty-five, he couldn't resist bidding on one last big contract—a restaurant in a Route 9 strip mall—and when he didn't get it, he decided he had been given instead a signal to retire, just as he had planned all along. Before he closed his business, though, he had a special job to finish, on the eighteenth-century house where Walter Denise had grown up, in the hands of new owners now that the orchard was gone. Bill managed to find some white cedar boards to match the original siding, and, using a power planer his colonial counterparts didn't have, put a bead along the bottom edge. He attached the boards with wrought-iron nails and left the heads showing, so the line between what was old and what was new was hardly discernible.

Bill kept a couple of the few lots that remained unbuilt in Colonial Park, sold a couple more to the man who had worked for him for many years, and wrote to get his credits from the two colleges he had attended before the Depression cut short his academic career. He enrolled as a history major at Monmouth College, a liberal arts school in West Long Branch that was built around the grand mansion Woodrow Wilson once used as the summer White House. He took one class, sometimes two, each semester, with young students who could barely imagine the epochal sweep of textbook events—from the Russian Revolution through the Second World War—he had witnessed. His duties at home were beyond their experience, too, as he cared for his ailing wife. Selma's Parkinson's was worsening, and when they returned home from a vacation to Seattle, he suspected they had taken their last trip together.

He concentrated in American history, exploring the questions that had preoccupied him since he was a young immigrant boy, a nickel short of a matinee on rainy Saturday afternoons, reading Lincoln biographies in the library: How did America become what it is, and what did it mean to be one of its citizens? All of his studies kept bringing him around now to the same conclusion his life had already led him to—that for all Americans, everywhere and always, from the local colonists debating independence to Major Vredenburgh and the Fourteenth Regiment marching down Main Street on their way south to face the Confederates, from the soldiers of his own war to the long-haired students whose protests of the last war he never quite understood, America was not so much a settled nation as a sustained act of will. America was not born, it was made, and the struggles to make it were often hard and bloody.

"Monmouth County suffered from the ravages of war more than any other county in New Jersey," Bill wrote when he finished the research for his thirty-page paper, drawing a distinction between the two wars fought on its soil during the Revolution—the big public one, starring Washington and Clinton and their respective armies, and the smaller civil war, between the local Tories and Patriots. "The other war was an amorphous struggle that had no recognizable boundaries, and no organized armies drawn up in definite battle lines . . . This was a war in which quite frequently former friends and neighbors and even near relations were pitted against each other. It was a war which brought forth both the noblest and basest in human nature. It was a war for which the civilian population paid a high price in lives lost and property destroyed."

Freehold was a Patriot stronghold, while Tories dominated the coast, in the protective shadow of the British naval ships anchored off Sandy Hook. Some calculating landowners managed to install members of their families in both camps, hoping to protect their property from confiscation no matter which side ended up winning. Extremists on both sides— the Committee of Retaliation for the Patriots, the Pine Robbers for the Tories—decided for themselves what the laws would be. Farms and homes were burned, goods plundered, women raped, enemies summarily executed, bodies displayed at the courthouse. When the most notorious of the Pine Robbers was killed in an ambush, vengeful Patriots dug up his body, wrapped it in tarred cloth and hung it by chains from a chestnut tree a mile out of town on the road to Colts Neck, where it swayed in the breeze until the birds picked off the flesh, and the bones dropped one by one to the ground.

A few unequivocal heroes shone in Bill's account, and the one he most clearly admired was Nathaniel Scudder. A Princeton graduate and a prominent Freehold physician, Scudder was an ardent and honorable Patriot—a colonel in the Monmouth militia and a delegate to the Continental Congress, where he was among the signers of the Articles of Confederation. Four days before the British surrender at Yorktown in October of 1781, a Loyalist raiding party from Sandy Hook marched to Colts Neck and took six prisoners. Scudder and his regiment rode out from Freehold in pursuit, catching up with them at the Shark River. As he stood on the banks of the river, talking with a fellow officer, a shot from an ambush on the other side struck him in the head. He was the only member of the Continental Congress to die in battle. He was buried at Tennent Church, within sight of Bill's grandfather's farm, where the Lopatin family had first lived after their epic journey to America. Bill found, and quoted in his paper, a letter Scudder had written to a friend not long before his death. ·

"I early entered into this contest," Scudder wrote, "firmly resolved never to retire from such Service, as my country should call me to, until the Liberties of my Country (dearer to me than Fortune or Life) should be firmly established or until necessity should compel me to it."

Bills' paper earned him an A, and after he got his bachelor's degree, he started on his master's. He turned some of his new research skills to a side project, compiling a history of the hospital he had helped build, and that was helping to care for Selma now as her health failed. The long hospital drive had embodied to him more clearly than anything since his Marauder missions over occupied Europe the central lesson of his life, his war and his studies: America does not give, it only offers, and what it becomes for you depends entirely on what you become for it. He collected old meeting minutes, newspaper clippings, letters and other documents; set out with a tape recorder to interview the early and prominent leaders of the community effort; and then found in his copy of de Tocqueville's *Democracy in America* the quote he wanted to use as an epigraph, because it said exactly what he felt.

"As soon as several Americans have conceived a sentiment or an idea that they want to produce before the world, they seek each other out, and when found, they unite," de Tocqueville had written. "Thenceforth they are no longer isolated individuals, but a power conspicuous from the distance whose actions serve as an example; when it speaks, men listen."

15.

So Ordinary, So Special

The line of old soldiers marched along the drive in front of the courthouse, the color guards of one veterans group after another, keeping in step as much as age, memory and lack of practice permitted, turning at the bust of Lincoln and continuing toward the reviewing stand that had been built across the wide entrance to accommodate the day's dignitaries. Some younger, active-duty units followed, their steps surer and sharper, as a high school band played "You're a Grand Old Flag," over and over again. All of the marchers formed ranks flanking the stand, their flags held straight and tall. Looming behind them were the four-story limestone columns holding up the courthouse's Ionic pediment, two of which were draped with banners for the occasion: TO BERLIN 3,979 MILES, read one, and the other, TO TOKYO 6,757 MILES. Spread out before them was the broad, sloping park at the foot of the battle monument, the grass parched after a dry summer and crowded now with hundreds of other veterans and spectators.

"Today we have gathered on this very historic site, a site where the Battle of Monmouth was fought in 1778 so that we as a nation would have our freedom and our democracy," said the top county official who was the event's host, Ted Narozanick, himself a veteran of the war that had ended almost exactly fifty years ago, the anniversary that all had come to celebrate. "After the end of World War Two, our great nation had the opportunity to reshape the world with American values, and the resources and the inspiration to turn the United States into a superpower. Our victory in World War Two allowed us to do all these things."

Thousands of county veterans had signed up to receive a special certificate of appreciation for their service in the war, but neither Stu Bunton nor Jake Errickson were among those who came to collect one. Stu wasn't much for parades or ship reunions or veterans meetings and the like. He also stopped at this same building every afternoon, picking up his wife from her job in the prosecutor's office, and he wasn't eager to come back on a Saturday morning. He was still working himself, too, and he preferred to spend his weekends at home. He had retired as a captain after thirty-one years on the police force, and then spent a year or so building his days around long-neglected chores and trips downtown for the newspaper, a routine that soon left him bored enough to start looking for another job. His career had come full circle now: He was an assistant to the superintendent of the county's youth detention center, right next door to the old radio room, where, as an operator on the night shift, his duties had included overseeing whatever juveniles were being held in the six cells that shared the building. In quiet moments sometimes, he could still summon the face of the Japanese Zero pilot who had dived on his ship.

Jake was just three blocks away, working in the finely groomed yard of the house he didn't like to venture too far from, in the shade of the red maple he had planted outside the bedroom window when he moved in, and that now reached over the roof. His second wife, Millie, was inside making lunch. He and Dot had gotten back to Australia once, but before they could get back again, she died of a stroke, in the country far from her birth where she had chosen—happily, and with no regrets—to make her life after the war. A few years later he married Millie, who had worked with him at his last job, and who had lost her own husband many years earlier. His son Wayne had survived his tour in Vietnam, and retired soon after, settling into a more predictable career as a mechanical engineer that spared his family the frequent moves and long separations of a navy life. Jake himself had retired for good as soon as he could, but he never went down Jackson Street past the vacant mill without thinking of how much more he, and the town, might have done had it not closed. Some nights he still had the same dream that had visited him periodically ever since he was stranded in New Guinea by his appendectomy, waiting endlessly for a ship home: He was trying and trying to get somewhere, but he was stuck, always blocked by some obstacle he couldn't surmount.

Among the veterans who did attend the courthouse ceremony, though, were Bill Lopatin, Buddy Lewis, Jimmy Higgins and Walter Denise. Like Jake, Bill had also lost his wife, twenty years after she was first diagnosed with Parkinson's. He had cared for Selma himself until she needed what only the hospital could give, and when they told him there that she couldn't go back with him, but only to a nursing home, it was the saddest day of his life. In the year after her death, he bought an Eastern Airlines passport ticket and traveled all over America—stopping to see his old flight crew buddies and getting as far west as Hawaii, all the while trying to outrun his grief. Back home, he often found himself in the basement, reading the letters Selma had sent him during the war, until he finally remembered the lesson of his melancholy return trip to an England that had forgotten him: Don't look back. Looking ahead, always ahead—in the opposite direction from sadness, regret and fear—was what had gotten his family to America, what had pulled him through the war, what had built his business and the hospital, what had earned him his bachelor's degree. He burned the letters in the fireplace and started taking classes again, working toward his master's in history. In the bank one day, he met a woman for whom he had built a house soon after the war. She was a widow now, and their brief courtship soon led to marriage, not long before he finished his degree. For his American foreign relations seminar, he wrote a paper that asked in its title, "Was the Use of the Atomic Bomb Justified?" In both of his roles—as a history student examining the official record, and as an airman whose name had once been on a list of B-29 crews headed to the Pacific in 1945 for the final onslaught on Japan—he came to the same conclusion: Yes, it was.

Buddy Lewis stood alone in the crowd of veterans, outside the building he had spent much of his career caring for, still trying to get used to the idea of being a widower. His own loss was so recent and raw—Ruth had died just six weeks earlier, after a long battle with the complications of diabetes—that he couldn't imagine any other woman ever filling even a fragment of the hole left by the wife he had spent forty-six years with. He visited her grave daily, and left her pocketbook hanging from its customary spot on the bedpost. In another two weeks, in another public ceremony that he knew would leave him more emotionally spent than this one, he would have to stand up and speak about her for the first time since her death. The Bethel AME church was celebrating the one-hundredth anniversary of the building that had been its longtime home, and the members planned to march from the old church to the new, right past the old Colored School, meticulously restored now as a memory of a divided time. At the new church, a plaque would be hung and a tree planted in memory of Ruth—the minister's daughter, the congregation's first pianist, and the girl who had cried when Buddy left home for the war.

"She was so ordinary," Buddy planned to say in his tribute, "that she was special."

As Jimmy Higgins stood listening to the procession of speakers—county and state officials, and officers from each branch of the armed forces—he turned around briefly and glanced back down Court Street, toward the spot from which he and most of the town's other veterans had departed for the war. The bus stop had long since moved, and the surrounding streets had changed faces many times over, but the downtown was, despite many fears otherwise, still alive. Most of the old retail establishments were gone—hardware stores, ladies' dress shops, even the post office, which had decamped to a shopping plaza next door to the hospital—and a giant new mall had opened across the highway from the racetrack, and adjacent to the cemetery where Major Vredenburgh and the other heroes of the Civil War were buried. But Main Street abounded now with restaurants, law offices and antique galleries—a different kind of hub for the surrounding towns. Jimmy was nominally retired, but he still lived upstairs at the funeral home, and during many wakes could still be found in his accustomed chair in the vestibule between the chapels, greeting mourners with his signature blend of sympathy and cheer. The veterans of his war had begun dying at a pace that kept his son busy folding government flags into neat triangles to present to widows at graveside services. One recent funeral was for a marine who had suffered a head wound at Guadalcanal, and spent much of the next half century in veterans' hospitals.

"We just buried a man who died in World War Two," Jimmy's son said that day.

Walter Denise was standing near Jimmy, the small bars for his Bronze Stars and Purple Hearts pinned into the lapels of his blue blazer. Like Stu, he was still working, too. He had sold the real estate agency at what turned out to be a crest in the market, and set up shop as an independent appraiser and consultant. His expertise was especially valued in helping to evaluate farmland assessments—determining which of the county's ever-shrinking number of undeveloped private landholdings qualified for agricultural tax breaks. He was also the chaplain of his old infantry regiment, and a stalwart at their reunions, at one of which he met for the first time the family of Earl Vincent, the man he had dragged to safety at Remoncourt. Vincent himself had died before he could make a reunion, but when the regiment met in Missouri, his home state, his children, grandchildren and great grandchildren went in his stead. Walter asked them to stand and be recognized, and he and they and a roomful of old soldiers were inexpressibly moved by the sight—an entire family that might never have existed had he not turned back on the battlefield one night to answer the cries of a wounded comrade; a stark portrait in miniature of all that might never have been had not the regiment, the army, the entire nation, once answered the call to arms.

"We just owe you so much," the colonel from McGuire Air Force Base was saying now as the program neared its end. "Thank you, thank you, thank you."

The Joint Armed Forces Color Guard had come all the way from Washington for the day, and they passed in review with all the stoic precision the old veterans themselves could no longer muster. In the pause after each service's flag was presented, a team of three soldiers, two with shouldered rifles flanking one bearing the American flag, began marching along the front of the courthouse. The only sound was the measured tread of their boots. There was something different about their uniforms, but exactly what didn't become clear until they reached the center and swung slowly around in a high-stepping pivot. When they were facing full forward, the decades collapsed in an instant. They were wearing the olive drab woolens of the Second World War, and they seemed to have emerged, young and strong and alive, from a sepia-tinged photograph that had been lying in an attic ever since. Their faces under their garrison caps were anonymous and expressionless, blank, ghostly masks on which everyone in the crowd could see their own pasts—their husbands, their fathers, themselves.

A moment of silence was called for those who had died in the war, but it was twelve-fifteen on a Saturday afternoon and, by an accident of scheduling, the fire whistle was bleating its regular weekly test. It blew as heads were bowed in reverence, and it blew some more, like an off-key echo from a distant field, as the bugler on the courthouse steps started into taps. The whistle was meant neither to disrupt nor to honor the veterans, but was simply part of the normal respiration of a living town. It was the same sound that had trumpeted the end of the war on V-J Day, that had cleared the streets for air-raid drills during the Cold War, that had summoned the firemen when the Strand block was burning, that had called curfew on the nights of racial unrest, and it didn't give up until the bugler reached his longest, highest note, the great heaving sob of the climactic G. It fell silent then, finally, and left the last notes to echo in peace.

ACKNOWLEDGMENTS

My first and largest debt is to the veterans of Freehold, for the service they rendered to both the nation and our town, and their willingness to share their stories with me. None of the six men in this book asked to be in it, and none would ever claim that what he did made him more worthy of note than any of his peers. There are scores of other veterans in town, and millions more in other communities all over America, whose lives are equally deserving of the kind of attention I have accorded these few. They were chosen, though, not just for the quality of their character, which was abundant in every veteran I met, but for the way their individual stories helped tell the larger story I was after in this book—the story of the war, and of the decades that followed, as it was embodied in the lives of a handful of veterans in one American town. They were chosen because what they did and where they served illustrated the terrible breadth of the war; and because how they lived when they came home illustrated the whole scope of the peace. I will always be grateful to them for what they have given to me.

It saddens me to report that one of the six didn't live to see the book published. Walter Denise died on March 4, 2001, just six weeks after I finished writing. He had read the manuscript, but I would have liked for him to see the final product, and to enjoy whatever fresh attention might have come his way. Like many soldiers who had seen the kind of action he had, Walter was initially reluctant to talk much about his war. He never marched in the Memorial Day parades, preferring to watch from the Main Street lawn of his beloved Christian Science church. Once he started talking, though, and once he saw the full intentions of the book, he became its most ardent champion. His ashes are buried in a family plot with several generations of other Denises, not far from Captain Conover and Major Vredenburgh, the Civil War heroes around whose graves the Memorial Day marchers gathered to hear taps at the end of each year's parade in decades past.

Of the many other veterans who shared their stories with me, I'd like to especially thank Eugene "Bobo" Nowack, Ken Conover, Frank Fedullo, Bill O'Donnell, Marty Urban, John Maziekien, Frank Gibson, Joe Copeland, Tip Randolph, Tom Blanchet, Bill Boyle, Gene Kelsey, Bill Lackett, John Kowalski, Russ Keimig, Jim Carney, Alex Levchuk, Ted Narozanick, Dave

Bulk, Harry Frank, Leland Treat, Joe Callaert, Ernest Taylor, Bill Biddle, Tom Perrine, Phil Martinez, Nick Van Malden, Gene Peterson, Bob Evans, Stanley Benezet and John Bartek.

This book took much longer than my previous ones, and it consequently trails an additional set of debts to those people who kept me working along the way, and kept some wages coming in—to Arlene Schneider for the job she created for me at the *Asbury Park Press;* to Chris Hann at *New Jersey Monthly;* to David Klatell at Columbia University's Graduate School of Journalism.

The most important day in the life of this book came in the spring of 1999 when it won the J. Anthony Lukas Work-in-Progress Award. Endowed in honor of the master of narrative nonfiction—the author of the book that I and many other reporters revere above all others, *Common Ground*— the award provided $45,000 that allowed me to finally finish, and it garnered some attention the book might not have otherwise received. My enduring gratitude, and my wish that the book will honor Tony Lukas's legacy, go to Linda Healey, Marion Lynton, Arthur Gelb, Cynthia Gorney, Tracy Kidder, Tom Goldstein and Evan Cornog. I am also grateful for a $2,000 grant from the New Jersey Historical Commission, and offer my thanks to Mary Murrin from the commission, and to Bill Gillette of Rutgers University for steering me toward it.

I spent a lot of time in libraries and archives, and am grateful for the assistance I found at all of them: the Monmouth County Historical Association; the Freehold Borough Public Library; the Monmouth County Library; Alexander Library at Rutgers University; the Columbia University libraries; the Freehold Township Municipal Building; the U.S. Army Military History Institute in Carlisle, Pennsylvania; the Air Force History Support Office at Bolling Air Force Base in Washington, D.C.; the Modern Military Records Branch of the National Archives, in the Washington National Records Center, Suitland, Maryland; the Navy Historical Center at the Washington Navy Yard. Special thanks are due to Carla Tobias, Lee Ellen Griffith, Megan Springate, Bernadette Rogoff, Barbara Carver-Smith, Patricia Burke and Eileen Thompson at the MCHA; and to David Keough, Yvonne Kincaid, Ted Gilbert, Barry Fowle, Dick Bingham, Kam Patel, Esther Oyster and Samuel Lowenthal.

Among the other people who offered information, materials and other kindnesses were: Carl Beams, David and Cindy Bowman, Ginnie Bunton, Dominick Cerrato, Jack and Kathleen Corcoran, Mark and Elaine Costanzo, Bob Coutts, Gene Coyne, Nancy Daley, Dick Dalik, John Dawes, Marilyn

Denise, Barney and Peggy DiBenedetto, Mike DiBenedetto, Millie Errick-
son, Wayne Errickson, Julie Griffiths, Meghan Griffiths, Greg Higgins,
Nolan Higgins, Jack Horenkamp, Jane and Chuck Hutchins, Liz Hutchins,
Connie Jiminez, George Kelder, Catherine Kennedy, Hank Lefkowich,
Kathy Lockwood, Joan Lopatin, Patricia Mackey, Ed Matthews, Hans and
Susan Muhler, Tracy Reason, Al Rogers, Sam Sagotsky, Lynn and Lee Seidler,
Laurie Seidler-Quinciny, John Smothers, Carl Steinberg, Grace Sverapa,
George Theiss, Arthur Thieme, Harry Thompson, Eda Urbelis, Sam Venti,
Doug Vincent, Mary Jane Whalen, Kate Williams and James Wishbow.
Among those who died before they could see the results of their help were
Angela Higgins, Ruth Lewis and Stuart Whalen. Two late local historians—
Ira Tilton and Jeannette Blair—were particularly helpful, as was the work
of Dick Metzgar, longtime reporter for the *News Transcript*. My aunt Mary
Grasberger saved a boxful of valuable material from the rug mill; and my
late uncle Paul Grasberger not only explained his work at the mill in great
depth over the years, but let me watch over his shoulder at the Langhorne
(Pa.) Carpet Company as he worked a loom similar to the ones that had
once woven rugs in Freehold. My aunt and uncle Joe and Jackie Tabacsko
along with my father accompanied me out to Carlisle as research assistants
and prowled the stacks with a list of questions I gave them.

Writing friends who have provided guidance and encouragement include Andrew Miga, Jill Bilzi, Tom Benner, Craig Tomashoff, Steve O'Con-
nell, Joe Sapia, Shannon Mullen and Wally Patrick. I also owe a debt to my
students at Columbia: To teach them, I have to keep learning myself. I am
especially indebted to two colleagues who have enriched my life profes-
sionally and personally: Steve Giegerich; and Sam Freedman, whose book,
The Inheritance, which I read as he was writing it, constituted my own
graduate education in the reporting and writing of historical narrative; and
who lent his sharp and generous eye to these pages.

For turning this idea into a book, I have to thank, as always, my agent,
Reid Boates, and at Viking Penguin, three editors whose insights made the
book better: Pam Dorman, Beena Kamlani and Stephen Morrison. I am
also grateful for the efforts of Francesca Belanger, Noirin Lucas, Sandra
Maffiore and Hilary Redmon.

My family has been especially close to this book, because it is about the
town where we have been settled for six generations. My father's ancestors
were potato-famine immigrants from Ireland who arrived in Freehold just
before the Civil War. My mother's parents, immigrants from Slovakia, arrived in the 1920s, drawn by the new jobs at the rug mill. I was especially

lucky to have known my late grandparents as long as I did, each of whom opened a window for me into a different corner of Freehold's life: Hank Coyne, who was a letter carrier and a longtime volunteer fireman; Michael Tabacsko, a veteran of the First World War who operated the shearing machine in the finishing department at the rug mill; Dorothy Tabacsko, who ran their small farm and worked in a coat factory; and Johanna Coyne, the longtime telephone operator at the county courthouse. I owe my greatest debt to my mother and father, Anne and Budd Coyne, who had the good fortune to be born in Freehold, and the wisdom to stay. Without them, this book, quite literally, would never have been written. It always seemed as if there would be enough time to dedicate a book to them, but my father died before he saw this one. He knew this book was theirs, but I'm sorry he didn't get to hold it in his hands. I am also grateful for my siblings, Brian Coyne and Kate Frank; and Doreen and Reed Feuster. My most enduring thanks goes to my own family, who lived for years with both the joys and consequences of this book—to Laura, Alice and now Richard, too; and to Jane Kaye, without whom I never could have written any books at all.

SOURCES

A Certain War

The information about the lives of these six veterans during the war comes not only from scores of interviews over several years with them and with other participants, but from the records of the units they served in, as well as from secondary sources. Any dialogue, both in this section and in the second section, comes either from the memory of the participants, or from some documentary source.

Stu Bunton and Jake Errickson

USS *Brooklyn*, Box 867
    Serial 008—Action Report of the "Husky" Operation (Sicily) (July 10–14, 1943)
USS *Santa Fe* War Diary, Box 1415/1416
USS *Santa Fe* Action Reports, Box 1403/1404
    Serial 00496—Night Antiaircraft Action (November 14, 1943)
    Serial 00501—Tarawa (November 18–25, 1943)
    Serial 0034—Kwajalein (January 31–February 1, 1944)
    Serial 0035—Truk/Marianas (February 12–26, 1944)
    Serial 0060—Hollandia Landings (April 21, 1944)
    Serial 0196—Marianas (June 28, 1944)
    Serial 0218—Iwo Jima (July 4, 1944)
    Serial 0265—Chi Chi Jima (August 4–5, 1944)
    Serial 0311—Mindanao (September 9, 1944)
    Serial 0328—Dive Bomber, Formosa (October 13–17, 1944)
    Serial 0407—Leyte Gulf (October 22–28, 1944)
    Chronologies, TBS (talk between ships) logs, addressed dispatches, intercepted traffic, maps
USS *Turner* Box 1532
History of USS Santa Fe (CL 60). Ships Data Section, Office of Public Information, Navy Department, 1947.
Unit History, 126th Signal Radio Intelligence Company (February 1941–September 1945)
Operational History of 126th Signal Radio Intelligence Company (February 1941–February 1944)
Record Group 407, SGC-126-0.1 (44579) History of 126th Signal Radio Intelligence Company (July 25–December 24, 1944)

Bank of New South Wales. *Australia for the Visitor.* Sydney: The Bank of New South Wales, 1956.

Bartek, Johnny. *Life Out There: A Story of Faith and Courage.* New York: Charles Scribner's Sons, 1943.

Bellafaire, Judith A. *The Army Nurse Corps.* Washington, D.C.: U.S. Army Center of Military History, 1993.

Bjerre, Jens. *Savage New Guinea.* New York: Hill and Wang, 1964.

Blumenson, Martin. *Sicily: Whose Victory?* New York: Ballantine, 1969.

Coker, Kathy R. *A Concise History of the U.S. Army Signal Corps.* Fort Gordon, Ga.: Office of the Command Historian, U.S. Army Signal Center and Fort Gordon, 1991.

Cutler, Thomas J. *The Battle of Leyte Gulf, 23–26 October 1944.* New York: HarperCollins, 1994.

Fahey, James J. *Pacific War Diary, 1942–45.* Boston: Houghton Mifflin, 1963.

Fox, Matt J. *Displaying Australia and New Guinea.* Australia Story Trust, 1945.

Garland, Albert N. and Howard McGaw Smith. *Sicily and the Surrender of Italy.* Washington, D.C.: Office of the Chief of Military History, Dept. of the Army, 1965.

Gilbert, James L. and John P. Finnegan, eds. *U.S. Army Signals Intelligence in World War II: A Documentary History.* Washington, D.C.: Center for Military History, United States Army, 1993.

Hall, Chester A. *Signal Corps Technical Intelligence: A Brief History, 1940–1948.* United States: Signal Corps Training Center, 1949.

Hall, Rodney. *Australia: Image of a Nation, 1850–1950.* Sydney: Collins, 1983.

Harris, Lelia Gott. *Sunny Australia: A Photographic Picture Book.* Philadelphia: David McKay Company, 1941.

Haskell, Ruth G. *Helmets and Lipstick.* New York: G. P. Putnam's Sons, 1944.

Hersey, John. *Into the Valley.* New York: Knopf, 1943.

Jensen, Oliver. *Carrier War.* New York: Pocket Books, 1945.

Kahn, E.J., Jr. *G.I. Jungle: An American Soldier in Australia and New Guinea.* New York: Simon and Schuster, 1943.

McMahill, Thomas A. Jr., ed. *USS Brooklyn (CL-40): Just a Touch of the Sea, USS Brooklyn 1858–1946 and Some of Her Crew,* 1979.

Manchester, William. *American Caesar: Douglas MacArthur, 1880–1964.* Boston: Little, Brown, 1978.

———. *Goodbye, Darkness: A Memoir of the Pacific War.* Boston: Little, Brown, 1980.

Marshall, Max L., ed. *The Story of the US Army Signal Corps.* New York: Franklin Watts, 1965.

Mayer, Sydney L. *MacArthur.* New York: Ballantine, 1971.

Milner, Samuel. *Victory in Papua.* Washington, D.C.: Office of the Chief of Military History, Dept. of the Army, 1957.

Moore, John Hammond. *Oversexed, Overpaid, and Over Here: Americans in Australia, 1941–1945.* St. Lucia, Brisbane: University of Queensland Press, 1981.

Morison, Samuel E. *History of United States Naval Operations in World War II.* 15
    vols. Boston: Little, Brown, 1947–1962.
    III. *The Rising Sun in the Pacific, 1931–April 1942.*
    IV. *Coral Sea, Midway and Submarine Actions, May 1942–August 1942.*
    V. *The Struggle for Guadalcanal, August 1942–1943.*
    VI. *Breaking the Bismarck's Barrier, 22 July 1942–1 May 1944.*
    VII. *Aleutians, Gilberts and Marshalls, June 1942–April 1944.*
    VIII. *New Guinea and the Marianas, March 1944–August 1944.*
    XII. *Leyte, June 1944–January 1945.*
    XIII. *The Liberation of the Philippines: Luzon, Mindanao, the Visayas, 1944–1945.*
———. *The Two-Ocean War.* Boston: Little, Brown, 1963.
Morton, Louis. *Strategy and Command: The First Two Years.* Washington, D.C.:
    Office of the Chief of Military History, Dept. of the Army, 1962.
Navy Department, Bureau of Naval Personnel. *Chaplain's Manual.* Washington,
    D.C.: The Bureau of Naval Personnel, 1970.
Potts, E. Daniel, and Annette Potts. *Yanks Down Under 1941–45: The American
    Impact on Australia.* New York: Oxford University Press, 1985.
Reynolds, Clark G. *Famous American Admirals.* New York: Van Nostrand Rein-
    hold Company, 1978.
Rickenbacker, Edward V. *Rickenbacker.* Englewood Cliffs, N.J.: Prentice-Hall, 1967.
———. *Seven Came Through: Rickenbacker's Full Story.* Garden City, N.Y.: Dou-
    bleday, Doran and Company, 1943.
Russ, Martin. *Line of Departure: Tarawa.* Garden City, N.Y.: Doubleday, 1976.
Sherrod, Robert. *Tarawa: The Story of a Battle.* New York: Duell, Sloane and
    Pearce, 1944.
Shukert, Elfrieda B. and Barbara S. Scibetta. *The War Brides of World War II,
    1942–1952.* Novato, Calif.: Presidio, 1988.
Smith, Robert Ross. *The Approach to the Philippines.* Washington, D.C.: Office of
    the Chief of Military History, Dept. of the Army, 1953.
———. *Triumph in the Philippines.* Washington, D.C.: Office of the Chief of Mil-
    itary History, Dept. of the Army, 1963.
Smith, S.E., ed. *The United States Navy in World War II.* New York: William Mor-
    row & Co., 1966.
Special Services Section, United States Army. *Displaying New Guinea to the
    Philippines.* The Australia Story Trust, 1945.
Spector, Ronald H. *Eagle Against the Sun: The American War with Japan.* New
    York: Free Press, 1985.
Steinberg, Rafael. *Island Fighting.* Alexandria, Va.: Time-Life Books, 1978.
———. *Return to the Philippines.* Alexandria, Va.: Time-Life Books, 1979.
Terrett, Dulany. *The Signal Corps: The Emergency (To December 1941).* Washing-
    ton, D.C.: Office of the Chief of Military History, Dept. of the Army, 1956.
Thompson, George Raynor and Dixie R. Harris. *The Signal Corps: The Outcome
    (Mid-1943 through 1945).* Washington, D.C.: Office of the Chief of Military
    History, U.S. Army, 1966.
———. Pauline M. Oakes and Dulany Terrett. *The Signal Corps: The Test (De-*

cember 1941 to July 1943). Washington, D.C.: Office of the Chief of Military History, Dept. of the Army, 1957.

Tregaskis, Richard. *Guadalcanal Diary.* New York: Popular Library, 1959.

United States Navy. *The Bluejackets' Manual.* Annapolis, Md.: United States Naval Institute, 1940.

Vader, John. *New Guinea: The Tide Is Stemmed.* New York: Ballantine, 1971.

Voss, Forrest W. and Lewis A. Kremer, eds. *USS Santa Fe Cruise Record: A Pictorial Record of a Light Cruiser During the War Years 1942–1945.* Chicago and Dixon, Ill.: Rogers Printing Company, 1945.

Watson, Mark Skinner. *Chief of Staff: Prewar Plans and Preparations.* Washington, D.C.: Historical Division, Department of the Army, 1950.

Whittaker, James C. *We Thought We Heard the Angels Sing.* New York: E.P. Dutton, 1943.

Zich, Arthur. *The Rising Sun.* Alexandria, Va.: Time-Life Books, 1977.

Walter Denise and Buddy Lewis

In May and June of 1945—after the war in Europe had ended, and while he was waiting in Austria for an expected transfer to the China-Burma-India theater—Walter Denise recounted his war experiences in a forty-nine-page single-spaced typescript that he titled "My Military Career."

324th Infantry Regiment
    Record Group 407
    Entry 427
    Box 10842/10843/10844
    344-INF(324)-0.3
    (monthly narrative reports, daily unit journals, after action reports)
1317th Engineer General Service Regiment (Colored)
    Record Group 407
    Entry 427
    Box 19696
ENRG-1317-1.13 General Orders, 1943–1945
ENRG-1317-0.1 (21234) History, December 15, 1944–March 15, 1945
ENRG-1317-3.7 (26194) Site Maps, March 1945
ENRG-1317-3.17 (26193) Operations Instructions, February–March 1945
ENRG-1317-3.17 Operations Orders, 1945

Combat History of the 324th Infantry Regiment, 44th Infantry Division. Baton Rouge, La.: Army & Navy Pub. Co., 1946.

Combat History, 44th Infantry Division. Atlanta, Ga.: Albert Love Enterprises, 1946.

World War II Survey Collection (U.S. Army Military History Institute)—Response to questionnaire: 1st Lt. Frank Herkness, HHC, 1st Bn, 505th Parachute Infantry Regiment, Eighty-second Airborne Division.

General Benjamin O. Davis, Sr. Papers (inspection reports).

Clarence D. Molyneaux papers, 1153rd Engineers Combat Group.

Allen, Peter. *One More River: The Rhine Crossings of 1945*. New York: Charles Scribner's Sons, 1980.

Ambrose, Stephen. *Band of Brothers: E Company, 506th Regiment, 101st Airborne from Normandy to Hitler's Eagle's Nest*. New York: Simon & Schuster, 1992.

———. *Citizen Soldiers*. New York: Simon & Schuster, 1997.

Beck, Alfred M., and Abe Bortz, Charles W. Lynch, Lida Mayo and Ralph F. Weld. *The Corps of Engineers: The War Against Germany*. Washington, D.C.: Center of Military History, U.S. Army, 1985.

Blumenson, Martin. *Breakout and Pursuit*. Washington, D.C.: Office of the Chief of Military History, Dept. of the Army, 1961.

Bowman, Waldo G. *American Military Engineering in Europe from Normandy to the Rhine*. New York: McGraw-Hill, 1945.

———. "D-Day on the Rhine." *Engineering News Record*, May 3, 1945.

Christian Science Publishing Society. *The Story of Christian Science Wartime Activities*. Boston: The Christian Science Publishing Society, 1947.

Clarke, Jeffrey J. and Robert Ross Smith. *Riviera to the Rhine*. Washington, D.C.: Center of Military History, United States Army, 1993.

Cole, Hugh M. *The Lorraine Campaign*. Washington, D.C.: Center of Military History, U.S. Army, 1993.

Coll, Blanche D., and Jean E. Keith and Herbert H. Rosenthal. *The Corps of Engineers: Troops and Equipment*. Washington, D.C.: Office of the Chief of Military History, Dept. of the Army, 1958.

Colley, David. "Operation Northwind: 'Greatest Defensive Battle.' " *VFW Magazine*, January 1995.

Dalfiume, Richard M. *Desegregation of the U.S. Armed Forces: Fighting on Two Fronts, 1939–1953*. Columbia, Mo.: University of Missouri Press, 1969.

Davis, Franklin M., Jr. *Across the Rhine*. Alexandria, Va.: Time-Life Books, 1980.

Essential Facts About the Army Specialized Training Program. Washington, D.C.: U.S. Government Printing Office, 1943.

Fine, Lenore and Jesse A. Remington. *The Corps of Engineers: Construction in the United States*. Washington, D.C.: Office of the Chief of Military History, U.S. Army, 1972.

Johnson, Jesse J., ed. *A Pictorial History of Black Soldiers in the United States (1619–1969) in Peace and War*. Hampton, Va.: Hampton Institute, 1970.

Keefer, Louis E. *Scholars in Foxholes: The Story of the Army Specialized Training Program in World War II*. Jefferson, N.C.: McFarland & Co., 1988.

Lee, Ulysses. *The Employment of Negro Troops*. Washington, D.C.: Office of the Chief of Military History, United States Army, 1966.

Leinbaugh, Harold P. and John D. Campbell, *The Men of Company K: The Autobiography of a World War II Rifle Company*. New York: William Morrow, 1985.

MacDonald, Charles B. *The Last Offensive*. Washington, D.C.: Office of the Chief of Military History, United States Army, 1973.

———. *The Siegfried Line Campaign*. Washington, D.C.: Office of the Chief of Military History, Dept. of the Army, 1963.

MacGregor, Morris J. *Integration of the Armed Forces, 1940–1965.* Washington, D.C.: Center of Military History, U.S. Army, 1981.

Miller, Donald. *An Album of Black Americans in the Armed Forces.* New York: Watts, 1969.

Motley, Mary Penick. *The Invisible Soldier: The Experience of the Black Soldier, World War II.* Detroit: Wayne State University Press, 1975.

Nalty, Bernard C. *Strength for the Fight: A History of Black Americans in the Military.* New York: Free Press, 1986.

Osur, Alan M. *Blacks in the Army Air Force During World War II: The Problem of Race Relations.* Washington, D.C.: Office of Air Force History, 1976.

Perret, Geoffrey. *There's a War to Be Won: The United States Army in World War II.* New York: Random House, 1991.

Potter, Lou. *Liberators: Fighting on Two Fronts in World War II.* New York: Harcourt Brace Jovanovich, 1992.

Ruppenthal, Roland G. *Logistical Support of the Armies, Volume 1: May 1941– September 1944.* Washington, D.C.: Office of the Chief of Military History, Dept. of the Army, 1953.

———. *Logistical Support of the Armies, Volume II: September 1944–May 1945.* Washington, D.C.: Office of the Chief of Military History, Dept. of the Army, 1959.

Smith, Graham. *When Jim Crow Met John Bull: Black American Soldiers in World War II Britain.* New York: St. Martin's Press, 1987.

Tillim, Sidney. *A History, Company A, 252nd Engineer Combat Battalion, July 23, 1943–July 23, 1945.* Privately printed, 1945.

Timothy, Patrick Henry. *The Rhine Crossing: Twelfth Army Group Engineer Operations.* Fort Belvoir, Va., 1946.

United States Army Training Center, Infantry, Fort Dix, New Jersey. *The History of Fort Dix, New Jersey, 1917–1967.* Fort Dix, N.J., 1967.

Whiting, Charles. *The Other Battle of the Bulge: Operation Northwind.* Chelsea, Md.: Scarborough House, 1990.

Bill Lopatin and Jimmy Higgins

322nd Bombardment Group
391st Bombardment Group
394th Bombardment Group

BO 241
BO 243
BO 245
BO 427
BO 428
BO 447
AO 617
AO 645

Group Histories and Operations Records: war diaries, monthly reports, mission summaries, crew interrogations, air battle narratives, action reports, encounter reports, field orders, logs of mission activities, awards, weather reports.

Bailey, Ronald H. *The Air War in Europe.* Alexandria, Va.: Time-Life Books, 1979.

Bavousett, Glenn B. *World War II Aircraft in Combat.* New York: Arco, 1976.

Bentley, James. *The Gateway to France: Flanders, Artois and Picardy.* New York: Viking, 1991.

Birdsall, Steve. *B-26 Marauder in Action.* Carrollton, Tex.: Squadron/Signal Publications, 1984.

Bowyer, Michael J.F. *Action Stations: Wartime Military Airfields of East Anglia, 1939–1945.* Cambridge: Patrick Stephens, 1979.

Boyne, Walter J. *Clash of Wings: Air Power in World War II.* New York: Simon & Schuster, 1994.

Brown, Kenneth T. *Marauder Man: World War II in the Crucial but Little Known B-26 Marauder.* Pacifica, Calif.: Pacifica Military History, 2001.

Childers, Thomas. *Wings of Morning: The Story of the Last American Bomber Shot Down Over Germany in World War II.* Reading, Mass.: Addison-Wesley, 1995.

Condensed Analysis of the Ninth Air Force in the European Theater of Operations. Washington, D.C.: Headquarters, Army Air Forces, Office of Assistant Chief of Air Staff, 1946.

Craven, Wesley Frank and James Lea Cate. *The Army Air Forces in World War II.* 7 vols. Chicago: University of Chicago Press, 1948–1958.

   I. *Plans and Early Operations, January 1939 to August 1942.*

   II. *Europe: Torch to Pointblank, August 1942 to December 1943.*

   III. *Europe: Argument to V-E Day, January 1944 to May 1945.*

   VI. *Men and Planes.*

Eperon, Barbara. *Normandy, Picardy and Pas De Calais.* Lincolnwood, Ill.: Passport Books, 1997.

Francis, Devon. *Flak Bait: The Story of the Men Who Flew the Martin Marauders.* New York: Duell, Sloan & Pearce, 1948.

Freeman, Roger A. *B-26 Marauder at War.* New York: Scribner, 1978.

———. *UK Airfields of the Ninth Then and Now.* London: Battle of Britain Prints International, 1994.

Gebelin, Francois. *The Chateaux of France.* New York: G.P. Putnam's Sons, 1964.

Havener, J.K. *The Martin B-26 Marauder.* Blue Ridge Summit, Pa.: TAB Books, 1988.

Hoyt, Edwin P. *The Airmen: The Story of American Fliers in World War II.* New York: McGraw-Hill, 1990.

Jablonski, Edward. *Airwar.* 2 vols. Garden City, N.Y.: Doubleday, 1971.

———. *America in the Air War.* Alexandria, Va.: Time-Life Books, 1982.

Maurer, Maurer, ed. *Air Force Combat Units of World War II.* USAF Historical Division, Air University, Department of the Air Force, 1961.

Leuthner, Stuart and Oliver Jensen. *High Honor: Recollections by Men and Women of World War II Aviation.* Washington, D.C.: Smithsonian Institution Press, 1989.

Moench, John. *Marauder Men: An Account of the Martin B-26 Marauder.* Long-
    wood, Fla.: Maia Enterprises, 1989.

Northern France and the Paris Region. Michelin Guides, 1997

Perret, Geoffrey. *Winged Victory: The Army Air Forces in World War II.* New York:
    Random House, 1993.

Rust, Kenn C. *The 9th Air Force in World War II.* Fallbrook, Calif.: Aero Publish-
    ers, Inc., 1970.

Stiles, Bert. *Serenade to the Big Bird.* New York: W.W. Norton & Co., 1947.

Ziegler, J. Guy. *Bridge Busters: The Story of the 394th Bomb Group.* New York:
    Ganis & Harris Publishing Co., 1949.

Other Works

Ambrose, Stephen. *D-day, June 6, 1944: The Climactic Battle of World War II.* New
    York: Simon & Schuster, 1994.

———. *The Victors: Eisenhower and His Boys: The Men of World War II.* New
    York: Simon & Schuster, 1998.

Bailey, Ronald H. *The Home Front: U.S.A.* Alexandria, Va.: Time-Life Books, 1978.

Baldwin, Hanson W. *Battles Lost and Won: Great Campaigns of World War II.* New
    York: Harper & Row, 1966.

Blum, John Morton. *V Was for Victory: Politics and American Culture During
    World War II.* New York: Harcourt Brace Jovanovich, 1976.

Blumenson, Martin. *Liberation.* Alexandria, Va.: Time-Life Books, 1978.

Botting, Douglas. *The Second Front.* Alexandria, Va.: Time-Life Books, 1978.

Brinkley, David. *Washington Goes to War.* New York: Alfred A. Knopf, 1988.

Buchanan, A. Russell, *The United States and World War II.* 2 vols. New York:
    Harper & Row, 1964.

Calvocoressi, Peter and Guy Wint. *Total War: The Story of World War II.* New
    York: Pantheon, 1972.

Chambers, John Whiteclay II. *The Oxford Companion to American Military His-
    tory.* Oxford: Oxford University Press, 1999.

Churchill, Winston S. *The Second World War.* 6 vols. Boston: Houghton Mifflin,
    1948–1953.

Cole, Hugh M. *The Ardennes: Battle of the Bulge.* Washington, D.C.: Office of the
    Chief of Military History, Dept. of the Army, 1965.

Costello, John. *Virtue Under Fire: How World War II Changed Our Social and Sex-
    ual Attitudes.* Boston: Little, Brown, 1985.

Dear, I.C.B., ed. *The Oxford Companion to World War II.* Oxford: Oxford Univer-
    sity Press, 1995.

Diggins, John Patrick. *The Proud Decades: America in War and Peace, 1941–1960.*
    New York: W.W. Norton and Co., 1988.

Eisenhower, Dwight D. *Crusade in Europe.* Garden City, N.Y.: Doubleday, 1948.

Eisenhower, John S. D. *The Bitter Woods: The Battle of the Bulge.* New York: G.P.
    Putnam's Sons, 1969.

———. *Yanks: The Epic Story of the American Army in World War I.* New York:
    The Free Press, 2001.

Ethell, Jeffrey, ed. *There Once Was a War: The Collected Color Photography of World War II.* New York: Viking Studio, 1995.

Fairchild, Byron and Jonathan Grossman. *The Army and Industrial Manpower.* Washington, D.C.: Office of the Chief of Military History, Dept. of the Army, 1959.

Fussell, Paul, ed. *The Norton Book of Modern War.* New York: W.W. Norton & Co., 1991.

———. *Wartime: Understanding and Behavior in the Second World War.* New York: Oxford University Press, 1989.

Gannon, Michael. *Operation Drumbeat.* New York: Harper & Row, 1990.

Goolrick, William K. and Ogden Tanner. *The Battle of the Bulge.* Alexandria, Va.: Time-Life Books, 1979.

Gregory, Ross. *America 1941: A Nation at the Crossroads.* New York: Free Press, 1989.

Harrison, Gordon A. *Cross-Channel Attack.* Washington, D.C.: Center of Military History, 1984.

Havighurst, Robert, ed. *The American Veteran Back Home: A Study of Veteran Adjustment.* New York: Longmans, Green, 1951.

Hickam, Homer H., Jr. *Torpedo Junction: U-Boat War off America's East Coast, 1942.* New York: Dell, 1991.

Hoyt, Edwin. *The GI's War: The Story of American Soldiers in Europe in World War II.* New York: McGraw-Hill, 1988.

———. *U-Boats Offshore: When Hitler Struck America.* New York: Stein and Day, 1978.

Hynes, Samuel. *The Soldier's Tale: Bearing Witness to Modern War.* New York: Penguin, 1997.

Jones, James. *WWII.* New York: Grosset & Dunlap, 1975.

Keegan, John. *The First World War.* New York: Knopf, 1999.

———. *The Second World War.* New York: Penguin, 1989.

———. *Six Armies in Normandy: From D-Day to the Liberation of Paris.* New York: Penguin, 1983.

Kendall, Park. *Gone with the Draft.* New York: Grosset & Dunlap, 1941.

Kennedy, David M. *Freedom from Fear: The American People in Depression and War, 1929–1945.* New York: Oxford University Press, 1999.

Kennett, Lee. *G.I.: The American Soldier in World War II.* New York: Charles Scribner's Sons, 1987.

Klingaman, William. *1941: Our Lives in a World on the Edge.* New York: Harper & Row, 1998.

Lariar, Lawrence. *The Army Fun Book.* New York: Crown, 1943.

Liddell Hart, B.H. *History of the Second World War.* New York: G.P. Putnam's Sons, 1970.

Liebling, A.J. *The Road Back to Paris.* Garden City, N.Y.: Doubleday, Doran and Co., 1944.

Lingeman, Richard R. *Don't You Know There's a War On?: The American Home Front 1941–1945.* New York: G. P. Putnam's Sons, 1970.

Longmate, Norman. *The G.I.'s: The Americans in Britain, 1942–1945*. New York: Scribner, 1975.

Lord, Walter. *Day of Infamy*. New York: Bantam, 1971.

MacDonald, Charles B. *The Mighty Endeavor: American Armed Forces in the European Theater in World War II*. New York: Oxford University Press, 1969.

———. *A Time for Trumpets*. New York: William Morrow, 1985.

Mauldin, Bill. *Up Front*. New York: Henry Holt & Co., 1945.

———. *Back Home*. New York: William Sloane Associates, 1947.

———. *The Brass Ring*. New York: W.W. Norton & Co., 1971.

The New Yorker Book of War Pieces. New York: Schocken, 1988.

Nichols, David. *Ernie's War: The Best of Ernie Pyle's World War II Dispatches*. New York: Touchstone, 1987.

The 100 Best True Stories of World War II. New York: Wm. H. Wise, 1945.

O'Neill, William L. *A Democracy at War: America's Fight at Home and Abroad in World War II*. New York: The Free Press, 1993.

Patton, George S., Jr. *War as I Knew It*. New York: Bantam, 1980.

Petak, Joseph. *Never Plan Tomorrow*. Fullerton, Calif.: Aquataur, 1991.

Pictorial History of the Second World War. 10 vols. New York: Wm. H. Wise, 1944–1949.

Pitt, Barrie. *The Battle of the Atlantic*. Alexandria, Va.: Time-Life Books, 1977.

Pogue, Forrest C. *The Supreme Command*. Washington, D.C.: Office of the Chief of Military History, Dept. of the Army, 1954.

Pronzini, Bill and Martin H. Greenberg, eds. *A Treasury of World War II Stories*. New York: Bonanza Books, 1985.

Pyle, Ernie. *Brave Men*. New York: Henry Holt and Company, 1944.

———. *Here Is Your War*. New York: Arno Press, 1979.

Reporting World War II. 2 vols. New York: Library of America, 1995.

Reynolds, Clark G. *America at War: 1941–1945 The Home Front*. New York: Gallery Books, 1990.

Reynolds, David. *Rich Relations: The American Occupation of Britain, 1942–1945*. New York: Random House, 1995.

Richler, Mordecai, ed. *Writers on World War II: An Anthology*. New York: Alfred A. Knopf, 1991.

Rooney, Andy. *My War*. New York: Times Books, 1995.

Ryan, Cornelius. *The Longest Day*. New York: Fawcett Popular Library, 1959.

Salmaggi, Cesare and Alfredo Pallavisini. *2194 Days of War: An Illustrated Chronology of the Second World War*. New York: Barnes & Noble, 1993.

Simons, Gerald. *Victory in Europe*. Alexandria, Va.: Time-Life Books, 1982.

Smith, R. Elberton. *The Army and Economic Mobilization*. Washington, D.C.: Office of the Chief of Military History, Dept. of the Army, 1959.

Stanton, Shelby L. *Order of Battle, U.S. Army, World War II*. Novato, Calif.: Presidio, 1984.

Steinbeck, John. *Once There Was a War*. New York: Viking Press, 1958.

Sulzberger, C.L. *The American Heritage Picture History of World War II*. New York: American Heritage/Bonanza Books, 1966.

Tapert, Annette, ed. *Lines of Battles: Letters from American Servicemen, 1941–
    1945.* New York: Pocket Books. 1989.

Taylor, Theodore. *Fire on the Beaches.* New York: W.W. Norton & Co., 1958.

Terkel, Studs. *"The Good War": An Oral History of World War Two.* New York:
    Pantheon, 1984.

Toland, John. *Battle: The Story of the Bulge.* New York: Random House, 1959.

The Wall Chart of World War II. Greenwich, Conn.: Brompton Books Corpora-
    tion, 1991.

Walton, Francis. *Miracle of World War II: How American Industry Made Victory
    Possible.* New York: Macmillan, 1956.

The War Against Germany: Europe and Adjacent Areas. Washington, D.C.: Office
    of the Chief of Military History, Dept. of the Army, 1951.

The War Against Germany and Italy: Mediterranean and Adjacent Areas. Washing-
    ton, D.C.: Office of the Chief of Military History, Dept. of the Army, 1951.

The War Against Japan. Washington, D.C.: Office of the Chief of Military History,
    Dept. of the Army, 1952.

Williams, Mary H. *Chronology: 1941–1945.* Washington, D.C.: Office of the Chief
    of Military History, Dept. of the Army, 1960.

The Asbury Park Press
The Freehold Transcript
Life magazine
Yank magazine
Freehold High School yearbook

An Uncertain Peace

For the second half of the story—once everybody was back home, discharged
from military units that kept exhaustive records—I relied upon as my main
source the *Freehold Transcript,* an exemplary weekly that covered the town and its
environs with the kind of sharp attention that was once the signature of local
journalism in America. I read every issue of the *Transcript* from 1940 to the present, compiling a detailed chronology of the town's life into which I was then able
to set the lives of the six men. For the largest events, I also used the *Asbury Park
Press,* the local daily that covered Freehold most closely.

When the rug mill left Freehold, its records mostly went with it, and later
vanished with the company itself. Of what remained, some ended up at the Monmouth County Historical Association, in Collection 51: A.&M. Karagheusian,
Inc. Collection. Most useful were the monthly issues of the illustrated company
newspaper, the *Karagheusian News,* and the weekly mimeographed *Management
Newsletter.* Also useful were:

"Address by Mr. Charles Karagheusian given at Dedication Ceremonies of Ab-
    erdeen Division, Aberdeen, N.C." (November 9, 1957).

Brickett, C.J. *Plain and Fancy Weaving.* Scranton, Pa.: International Textbook
    Company, n.d.

Brinton, R.S. *Carpets.* London: Sir Isaac Pitman & Sons, 1939.

Carpeting by Karagheusian in the American Scene of Today. New York: A.&M. Karagheusian, Inc., 1941.

Contract Agreement Between A.&M. Karagheusian, Inc. and Textile Workers Union of America, 1957.

Crankshaw, W.P. *Weaving.* London: Sir Isaac Pitman & Sons, 1935.

Dumville, J. and S. Kershaw. *The Worsted Industry.* London: Sir Isaac Pitman.

Ewing, John S. and Nancy P. Norton. *Broadlooms and Businessmen: A History of the Bigelow-Sanford Carpet Company.* Cambridge, Mass.: Harvard University Press, 1955.

Grasberger, Henry F. *Jacquard Wilton Rug and Carpet Manufacture.* (unpublished manuscript, 1940).

Greenwood, Henry. *Handbook of Weaving and Manufacturing.* London: Sir Isaac Pitman & Sons, 1926.

Herrin, Dean. "The Makers of Gulistan: A.&M. Karagheusian's Rug Mill in Freehold, New Jersey 1904–1965." (unpublished manuscript, 1987).

"History of A.&M. Karagheusian." Notes from talk presented by Mr. Charles Karagheusian to Freehold Mill foremen on April 9, 1947.

Jarman, Rufus. "What Do You Know About Rugs?" *Saturday Evening Post,* October 25, 1947.

Kershaw, S. *Wool: From Material to the Finished Product.* London: Sir Isaac Pitman & Son, 1937.

Patton, Randall L. *Carpet Capital: The Rise of a New South Industry.* Athens, Ga.: The University of Georgia Press, 1999.

Reynolds, William A. *Innovation in the United States Carpet Industry, 1947–1963.* Ph.D. dissertation, political science, Columbia University, 1967.

Sanders, Gold V. "What Makes a Rug Good?" *Popular Science* (Feb. 1946).

"Setting the Tempo in Fine Gulistan Carpet." New York: A.&M. Karagheusian, Inc., 1959.

The Story of Rugs and Carpets. Amsterdam, N.Y.: Mohawk Carpet Mills, Inc.

Textile Workers Union of America, Local 26—Constitution and Bylaws.

Woven Floor Covering: Retail Sales Manual. Amsterdam, N.Y.: Mohawk Carpet Mills, Inc., 1946.

For the chapter on the racial unrest in town in 1969 and 1970, I am grateful to Freehold Borough Police Chief Mike Beierschmitt and retired Lieutenant Kenneth Mount for unearthing the department's files from the time—a thick trove that included internal memos, incident reports, the department's own investigative reports, the state police investigative reports, damage reports, intelligence reports, complaints logged by both the fire department and the police, correspondence, overtime schedules, mayoral proclamations, and the chief's own handwritten log of events.

Bill Lopatin, with his master's degree in history, had also held on to some valuable documents—the records from his construction business, including the blueprints for the houses he built; and the records from the long effort to build a community hospital. The hospital records included more than a decade's worth of meeting minutes, financial statements, treasurer's reports, controller's reports, administrator's reports, charity ball programs, correspondence and notes, and the transcripts of the taped interviews Bill himself conducted when he was compiling a history for the board of trustees.

At the Monmouth County Historical Association, I used materials from these collections:

Collection 1: Peter Vredenburgh (1837–1864) Papers 1856–1868.
Collection 33: Enoch L. and Samuel C. Cowart Papers 1780–1795, 1803–ca. 1942.
Collection 72: Battle of Monmouth Collection 1776–1997.
Collection 75: Freehold Military Academy Collection.
Collection 140: Freehold Institute Collection 1848–1891.
Collection 144: New Jersey Military Academy (Freehold, N.J.) Collection 1908.
Collection 155: Monmouth County (N.J.) Collection (Courts—Grand Jury Inquisition 1778)
Collection 184: Merchants Association of Freehold, N.J. Minutes Dec. 29, 1903–Dec. 9, 1908.

Other Works

Allen, Frederick Lewis. *The Big Change: America Transforms Itself, 1900–1950.* New York: Bantam, 1965.
Atlas of the American Revolution. Chicago: Rand McNally, 1974.
Axelrad, Jacob. *Philip Freneau: Champion of Democracy.* Austin, Tex.: University of Texas Press, 1967.
Barone, Joseph. *Our Country: The Shaping of America from Roosevelt to Reagan.* New York: Free Press, 1990.
Baseball Encyclopedia. New York: Macmillan, 1993.
Beck, Henry Charlton. *The Jersey Midlands.* New Brunswick, N.J.: Rutgers University Press, 1939, 1962.
———, ed. *A New Jersey Reader.* New Brunswick, N.J.: Rutgers University Press, 1961.
———. *The Roads of Home: Lanes and Legends of New Jersey.* New Brunswick, N.J.: Rutgers University Press, 1956, 1983.
Beekman, George C. *Early Dutch Settlers of Monmouth County, New Jersey.* Freehold, N.J.: Moreau Brothers, 1901 (reprint 1974).
Beers, F. *Atlas of Monmouth County, New Jersey, from Recent and Actual Surveys and Records.* New York: Beers, Comstock, and Cline, 1873.
Bennett, Michael J. *When Dreams Came True: The GI Bill and the Making of Modern America.* Washington, D.C.: Brassey's, 1996.
Bibliography Committee of the New Jersey Library Association. *New Jersey and the Negro: A Bibliography, 1715–1966.* Trenton, N.J.: New Jersey Library Association, 1967.
Bishop, Gordon. *Gems of New Jersey.* Englewood Cliffs, N.J.: Prentice Hall, 1985.

Blair, Jeannette. *Freehold Township: The First 300 Years.* Freehold Township Committee, 1993.

Boorstin, Daniel. *The Americans: the Democratic Experience.* New York: Vintage, 1974.

Borough of Freehold Historical Book. 1968.

Branch, Taylor. *Parting the Waters: America in the King Years, 1954–63.* New York: Simon & Schuster, 1988.

———. *Pillar of Fire: America in the King Years, 1963–65.* New York: Simon & Schuster, 1998.

Brandes, Joseph. *Immigrants to Freedom: Jewish Communities in Rural New Jersey Since 1882.* Philadelphia: University of Pennsylvania Press, 1971.

Brooks, John. *The Great Leap.* New York: Harper & Row, 1966.

Bruce Springsteen: The Rolling Stone Files. New York: Hyperion, 1996.

Bureau of Industrial Statistics of New Jersey. *The Industrial Directory of New Jersey.* Trenton, N.J., 1915.

Carroll, Peter N. *It Seemed Like Nothing Happened: The Tragedy and Promise of America in the 1970s.* New York: Henry Holt & Co., 1982.

Class of 1924, Freehold High School. *Guide to Historic Freehold, N.J. and Vicinity.* Asbury Park, N.J.: Schuyler Press, 1923.

Coakley, Leo J. *Jersey Troopers: A Fifty Year History of the New Jersey State Police.* New Brunswick, N.J.: Rutgers University Press, 1971.

Cole, Bernard, and Harry Groth and William Miles. "A Description of the Contributions Made by the Citizens of Freehold, New Jersey and the Surrounding Communities During the War Between the States." (unpublished manuscript, May 1961).

Cooley, Henry Scofield. *A Study of Slavery in New Jersey.* Baltimore: Johns Hopkins University Press, 1896.

Cross, Charles T. *Backstreets.* New York: Harmony Books, 1989.

Cunningham, John T. *Garden State: The Story of Agriculture in New Jersey.* New Brunswick, N.J.: Rutgers University Press, 1955.

———. *Made in New Jersey: The Industrial Story of a State.* New Brunswick, N.J.: Rutgers University Press, 1954.

———. *New Jersey: America's Main Road.* Garden City, N.Y.: Doubleday, 1976.

———. *This Is New Jersey.* New Brunswick, N.J.: Rutgers University Press, 1978.

Dickstein, Morris. *Gates of Eden: American Culture in the Sixties.* New York: Basic Books, 1977.

Ehrenhalt, Alan. *The Lost City: Discovering the Forgotten Virtues of Community in the Chicago of the 1950s.* New York: Basic Books, 1995.

Ehrenreich, Barbara. *Fear of Falling: The Inner Life of the Middle Class.* New York: Pantheon Books, 1989.

Ellis, Franklin. *History of Monmouth County, New Jersey.* Philadelphia: R.T. Peck & Co., 1885 (reprint 1974).

Emerson, Gloria. *Winners and Losers: Battles, Retreats, Gains, Losses, and Ruins from the Vietnam War.* New York: Penguin, 1985.

Engelhardt, Tom. *The End of Victory Culture: Cold War America and the Disillusioning of a Generation*. New York: Basic Books, 1995.

Etzioni, Amitai. *The Spirit of Community: Rights, Responsibilities, and the Communitarian Agenda*. New York: Crown, 1993.

Federal Writers' Project of the Works Progress Administration for the State of New Jersey. *Stories of New Jersey: Its Significant Places, People and Activities*. New York: M. Barrows & Company, 1938.

———. *The WPA Guide to 1930s New Jersey*. New Brunswick, N.J.: Rutgers University Press, 1986 (originally published 1939).

Fishman, Robert. *Bourgeois Utopias: The Rise and Fall of Suburbia*. New York: Basic Books, 1987.

Fleming, Thomas. *New Jersey: A History*. New York: W.W. Norton & Co., 1984.

Fraser, Caroline. *God's Perfect Child: Living and Dying in the Christian Science Church*. New York: Henry Holt, 1999.

Freneau, Philip. *Poems of Freneau*. New York: Hafner Publishing Co., 1960.

———. *The Prose of Philip Freneau*. New Brunswick, N.J.: The Scarecrow Press, 1955.

Garlick, Rev. Bernard McKean. *A History of St. Peter's Church, Freehold, New Jersey*. Privately published, 1967.

Garrow, David J. *Bearing the Cross: Martin Luther King, Jr., and the Southern Christian Leadership Conference*. New York: Vintage, 1988.

Gelernter, David. *1939: The Lost World of the Fair*. New York: The Free Press, 1995.

Gillespie, Angus Kress and Michael Aaron Rockland. *Looking for America on the New Jersey Turnpike*. New Brunswick, N.J.: Rutgers University Press, 1989.

Gillette, William. *Jersey Blue: Civil War Politics in New Jersey, 1854–1865*. New Brunswick, N.J.: Rutgers University Press, 1995.

Gitlin, Todd. *The Sixties: Years of Hope, Days of Rage*. New York: Bantam, 1987.

Goldman, Eric F. *The Crucial Decade—and After: America, 1945–1960*. New York: Vintage, 1960.

Goulden, Joseph C. *The Best Years: 1945–1950*. New York: Atheneum, 1976.

Greenfield, Jeff. *No Peace, No Place: Excavations Along the Generational Fault*. New York: Doubleday, 1973.

Griffin, William L. *150 Years of Ministry, 1838–1988: The First Presbyterian Church of Freehold, New Jersey*. Privately published, 1989.

Griffith, Lee Ellen. *Images of America: Freehold*. Dover, N.H.: Arcadia, 1996.

———. *Images of America: Freehold, Volume II*. Dover, N.H.: Arcadia, 1999.

Halberstam, David. *The Fifties*. New York: Villard, 1993.

Hart, Jeffrey. *When the Going Was Good: American Life in the Fifties*. New York: Crown, 1982.

Higgins, Angela N. *St. Rose of Lima Centennial*. Freehold, N.J.: St. Rose of Lima Parish, 1971.

Higgins, J. Nolan. *We Trust in Providence: A History of the Freehold Fire Department*. Privately published, 1997.

Hillburn, Robert. *Springsteen*. New York: Rolling Stone Press, 1985.

Hodges, Graham. *Slavery and Freedom in the Rural North: African Americans in*

Monmouth County, New Jersey, 1665–1865. Madison, Wis.: Madison House, 1997.

Hodgson, Godfrey. *America in Our Time.* New York: Vintage, 1976.

Holmes, Frank R., ed. *History of Monmouth County, New Jersey, 1664–1920.* 3 vols. New York: Lewis Historical Publishing Company, 1922.

Hornor, William S. *This Old Monmouth of Ours.* Freehold, N.J.: Moreau Brothers, 1932 (reprint 1974).

Humphries, Patrick and Chris Hunt. *Springsteen: Blinded by the Light.* New York: Henry Holt & Co., 1985.

Jackson, Kenneth. *Crabgrass Frontier: The Suburbanization of the United States.* New York: Oxford University Press, 1985.

Jackson, William L. *New Jerseyans in the Civil War.* New Brunswick, N.J.: Rutgers University Press, 2000.

Johnson, Haynes. *Sleepwalking Through History: America in the Reagan Years.* New York: W.W. Norton & Co., 1991.

———. *Divided We Fall: Gambling with History in the Nineties.* New York: W.W. Norton & Co., 1994.

Jones, Landon Y. *Great Expectations: America and the Baby Boom Generation.* New York: Ballantine, 1981.

Karnow, Stanley. *Vietnam: A History.* New York: Penguin, 1984.

Katz, Donald. *Home Fires: An Intimate Portrait of One Middle-Class Family in Postwar America.* New York: HarperCollins, 1992.

Keats, John. *The Crack in the Picture Window.* Boston: Houghton Mifflin, 1957.

Klinkenborg, Verlyn. *The Last Fine Time.* New York: Knopf, 1991.

Krampf, Melvin C. *To Monmouth—from M.C.K (With Love Yet).* Freehold, N.J.: Ben Alpern Publisher, 1972.

Kunstler, James Howard. *The Geography of Nowhere: The Rise and Decline of America's Man-Made Landscape.* New York: Simon & Schuster, 1993.

Leary, Lewis. *That Rascal Freneau.* New York: Octagon Books, 1964.

Lehrack, Otto J. *No Shining Armor: The Marines at War in Vietnam: An Oral History.* Lawrence, Kans.: University Press of Kansas, 1992.

Lingeman, Richard. *Small Town America: A Narrative History, 1620–The Present.* New York: G.P. Putnam's Sons, 1980.

Lopatin, William. "Monmouth County Tories and Whigs During the American Revolution." Research paper for American history seminar, Monmouth College, 1981.

———. "Was the Use of the Atomic Bomb Justified?" Research paper for American foreign relations, Monmouth College, 1989.

McElvaine, Robert S. *The Great Depression.* New York: Times Books, 1984.

McKay, Lenora Walker. *Blacks of Monmouth County.* Monmouth County Business and Professional Women's Council, 1976.

———. *Mama and Papa (Blacks of Monmouth County, vol. 2).* Privately published, 1984.

McPherson, James M. *Battle Cry of Freedom: The Civil War Era.* New York: Ballantine, 1988.

McPherson, Myra. *Long Time Passing: Vietnam and the Haunted Generation.* Garden City, N.Y.: Doubleday, 1984.

Manchester, William. *The Glory and the Dream: A Narrative History of America, 1932–1972.* Boston: Little, Brown, 1974.

Marsh, Dave. *Born to Run: The Bruce Springsteen Story.* Garden City, N.Y.: Doubleday, 1979.

———. *Glory Days: Bruce Springsteen in the 1980s.* New York: Pantheon, 1987.

Martin, David. *Camp Vredenburg in the Civil War.* Hightstown, N.J.: Longstreet, 1993.

———. *Monocacy Regiment: A Commemorative History of the 14th New Jersey Infantry in the Civil War, 1862–1865.* Hightstown, N.J.: Longstreet, 1987.

May, Elaine Tyler. *Homeward Bound: American Families in the Cold War Era.* New York: Basic Books, 1988.

Miller, Douglas T. and Marion Nowak. *The Fifties: The Way We Really Were.* Garden City, N.Y.: Doubleday, 1977.

"Monmouth County Courthouse—Courthouse Dedication Edition." *The Advocate.* Monmouth Bar Association, 1955.

Monmouth County Planning Board. "Freehold Borough: Urban Communities Study Series." Nov. 1981.

———. "Study of Population and Housing, Western Monmouth Region." March 1964.

Morford, T.C. *Fifty Years Ago: A Brief History of the 29th Regiment, New Jersey Volunteers in the Civil War.* Hightstown, N.J.: Longstreet House, 1990 (originally published 1912).

Morison, Samuel Eliot. *The Oxford History of the American People.* New York: Oxford University Press, 1965.

Murray, David. *History of Education in New Jersey.* Washington, D.C.: Government Printing Office, 1899.

New Jersey, Adjutant-General's Office. *Official Register of the Officers and Men of New Jersey in the Revolutionary War.* Trenton, N.J.: Wm. T. Nicholson and Co., 1872.

———. *Record of Officers and Men of New Jersey in the Civil War 1861–1865.* Trenton, N.J.: John L. Murphy, 1876. 2 volumes.

Olsen, Bernard A., ed. *Upon the Tented Field.* Red Bank, N.J.: Historic Projects, 1993.

O'Neill, William L. *American High: The Years of Confidence, 1945–1966.* New York: Free Press, 1986.

———. *Coming Apart: An Informal History of America in the 1960's.* Chicago: Quadrangle Books, 1971.

"The Pacer." Freehold Optimist Club newsletter.

Patterson, James T. *Grand Expectations: The United States, 1945–1974.* New York: Oxford University Press, 1996.

Polks' Freehold City Directories—from 1937 to 1972, incomplete.

Report of the National Advisory Commission on Civil Disorders. New York: E.P. Dutton & Co., 1968.

Rovere, Richard H. *Senator Joe McCarthy.* Cleveland: World Publishing, 1960.

Salter, Edwin. *A History of Monmouth and Ocean Counties.* Bayonne, N.J.: E. Gardner & Son, 1890.

——— and George C. Beekman. *Old Times in Old Monmouth.* Freehold, N.J.: James S. Yard, 1887.

Sanborn Fire Insurance maps for Freehold: 1885, 1889, 1895, 1901, 1909, 1916, 1923 and 1949.

Schmidt, Hubert G. *Agriculture in New Jersey: A Three Hundred Year History.* New Brunswick, N.J.: Rutgers University Press, 1973.

Sim, Mary B. *Commercial Canning in New Jersey: History and Early Development.* Trenton, N.J.: New Jersey Agricultural Society, 1951.

Smith, Page. *A New Age Now Begins.* 2 vols. New York: McGraw-Hill, 1976.

Smith, Samuel Stelle. *The Battle of Monmouth.* Monmouth Beach, N.J.: Philip Freneau Press, 1964.

Stryker, William. *The Battle of Monmouth.* Princeton, N.J.: Princeton University Press, 1927.

Tocqueville, Alexis de. *Democracy in America.* Garden City, N.Y.: Anchor Books, 1969.

Truscott, Martin. "Monmouth County Census Trends, 1970–1980." Freehold N.J.: Monmouth County Planning Board, 1984.

Van Benthuysen, Robert F., and Audrey Kent Wilson. *Monmouth County: A Pictorial History.* Norfolk, Va.: Donning Company Publishers, 1983.

Viorst, Milton. *Fire in the Streets: America in the 1960's.* New York: Touchstone, 1981.

Walling, Richard S. and students from the East Brunswick campus of the Middlesex County Vo-Tech High School. *The African American Experience in Western Monmouth County, New Jersey: Two Historic Black Communities in Manalapan/Millstone & Freehold Townships.* Friends of Monmouth Battlefield, February 1996.

Wilbur, Lillian Lauler. *The Early Schools of Freehold and Vicinity.* Asbury Park, N.J.: Schuyler Press, 1969.

Wills, Gary. *Reagan's America.* New York: Penguin Books, 1988.

Wolverton, Chester. *Wolverton's Atlas of Monmouth County.* New York, 1889.

Woodward, Carl. R. *The Development of Agriculture in New Jersey, 1640–1880.* New Brunswick, N.J.: New Jersey Agricultural Experiment Station, 1932.

Yard, James S. *Memorial of Joel Parker.* Freehold, N.J.: Monmouth Democrat, 1889.

INDEX